T0361158

THE SOFTWOOD LUMBER WAR

Politics, Economics, and the Long U.S.–Canada Trade Dispute

DAOWEI ZHANG

RFF PRESS

RESOURCES FOR THE FUTURE

New York • London

First published by Earthscan in the UK and USA in 2007

For a full list of publications please contact:
Earthscan
2 Park Square, Milton Park, Abingdon, Oxon OX14 4RN
711 Third Avenue, New York, NY 10017

Earthscan is an imprint of the Taylor & Francis Group, an informa business

Notices
Practitioners and researchers must always rely on their own experience and knowledge in evaluating and using any information, methods, compounds, or experiments described herein. In using such information or methods they should be mindful of their own safety and the safety of others, including parties for whom they have a professional responsibility.

Product or corporate names may be trademarks or registered trademarks, and are used only for identification and explanation without intent to infringe.

Library of Congress Cataloging-in-Publication Data

Zhang, Daowei.
  The softwood lumber war : politics, economics, and the long U.S.-Canada trade dispute / Daowei Zhang.
    p. cm.
  Includes bibliographical references and index.
  ISBN 978-1-933115-55-9 (hbk. : alk. paper) -- ISBN 978-1-933115-56-6 (pbk. : alk. paper) 1. Softwood industry--United States. 2. Softwood industry--Canada. 3. Protectionism--United States. 4. United States--Foreign economic relations--Canada. 5. Canada--Foreign economic relations--United States. I. Title.
  HD9756.Z53 2007
  382'.41498--dc22   2007022198

This book was typeset by Peter Lindeman. It was copyedited by Sally Atwater. The cover was designed by Maggie Powell. Cover photo courtesy of B.C. Forest Information. The cover photo of cedar logs was taken on Baker Inlet on the North Coast of British Columbia.

ISBN 978-1-933115-55- 9 (hbk)   ISBN 978-1-933115-56-6 (pbk)

About Resources for the Future *and* RFF Press

RESOURCES FOR THE FUTURE (RFF) improves environmental and natural resource policymaking worldwide through independent social science research of the highest caliber. Founded in 1952, RFF pioneered the application of economics as a tool for developing more effective policy about the use and conservation of natural resources. Its scholars continue to employ social science methods to analyze critical issues concerning pollution control, energy policy, land and water use, hazardous waste, climate change, biodiversity, and the environmental challenges of developing countries.

RFF PRESS supports the mission of RFF by publishing book-length works that present a broad range of approaches to the study of natural resources and the environment. Its authors and editors include RFF staff, researchers from the larger academic and policy communities, and journalists. Audiences for publications by RFF Press include all of the participants in the policymaking process—scholars, the media, advocacy groups, NGOs, professionals in business and government, and the public.

To my parents

Contents

Figures and Tables

Tables

List of Abbreviations

bbf	billion board feet
FTA	U.S.–Canada Free Trade Agreement
GATT	General Agreement on Tariffs and Trade
GDP	gross domestic product
ICC	Interstate Commerce Commission
ITC	U.S. International Trade Commission
mbf	thousand board feet
MLA	member of the legislative assembly
mmbf	million board feet
MOU	Memorandum of Understanding (signed in 1986)
NAFTA	North American Free Trade Agreement
PPI	producer price index
USTR	U.S. trade representative
WTO	World Trade Organization

Foreword

When I moved to Canada in 1990 to become the dean of the Faculty of Forestry at the University of British Columbia, my fine Yale University colleague, Robin Winks, sent me off with some good advice. He gave me a copy of Seymour Martin Lipset's book *Continental Divide* and commented that any American moving to Canada should be very careful about assuming the countries were similar ("two countries separated by a common language," I think he said). Lipset argues that the American Revolution founded not one country but two, which despite their common roots have developed along somewhat different lines. Those favoring "peace, prosperity and good government" moved north to British North America, which became Canada, and those favoring "life, liberty and the pursuit of happiness" stayed south of "the line."

Nowhere is the divergence greater than in the western part of the continent. U.S. policy moved public land quickly into private ownership, individual and corporate. It was almost an afterthought to retain public ownership of the mountainous forest land remaining after railroads and homesteaders had selected the best parcels. In contrast, the western provincial governments of Canada kept land, especially high-quality forest land, in public ownership. Canada used timber as a wooden magnet to attract capital investment in manufacturing facilities as a means of securing economic prosperity for towns in rural Canada. Timber was allocated via administrative processes, unlike the situation in the United States, where markets generally prevailed. The Canadian lumber industry has prospered under these policies and now supplies roughly one-third of U.S. consumption.

Those structural differences in forest ownership and timber supply promoted misunderstandings. Parties on both sides of the border have used incomplete or erroneous characterizations of the other's system for their own political and economic ends—most prominently in the case of softwood lumber trade, with the United States imposing its first tariffs in the late 1700s.

Of course, the longevity of the modern softwood lumber dispute has its roots in causes far more powerful than simple cultural misunderstanding. Concentrated economic interests can use political processes to further those interests to the detriment of the larger public good. So it is with softwood lumber producers in the United States. They have effectively used U.S. trade legislation to impose restrictions on Canadian lumber imports into the United States. These restrictions have been implemented through a variety of mechanisms—tariffs, quotas, tariff-mediated quotas, and export fees in Canada. The economic effects are more or less the same, with reduced imports from Canada increasing lumber prices in the United States. U.S. producers and most Canadian ones benefit from higher lumber prices in the United States, to the detriment of U.S. consumers. Forest owners—provincial governments to the north, corporate and individual private landowners to the south—also benefit indirectly because higher lumber prices generally translate into higher prices for standing timber.

The fact that lumber trade restrictions take money from U.S. consumers and give it to Canadians has not been lost on Canadian interests—what better than a U.S.-initiated policy that benefits Canada? Throughout the three decades of the most recent round of disputes, the Canadian federal government, provincial governments, and forest products industry have squabbled over who should reap the benefits of trade restrictions.

This cheerful (for some) view of the softwood lumber dispute depends on a static analysis of markets. Thoughtful participants have come to understand that few of the major factors involved in this dispute remain unchanged, particularly over periods measured in decades. In Canada, the various trade agreements have thwarted the very reforms that U.S. interests are nominally seeking—market-based allocation of timber; tenure reforms to create more private and private-like forest land; free trade in logs. Restrictions on the import of Canadian lumber into the United States have created an opening for non-Canadian imports—especially from Latin America and Europe—that come into the States without the impediment of duties. Because lumber demand is quite inelastic in the short run, this surge in non-Canadian imports quickly reduces prices from the levels that they would otherwise attain and offsets much of the advantage U.S. lumber producers gain from restrictions on Canadian imports.

Political ideology in the United States celebrates free trade in instances where subsidies do not distort comparative advantage. As a result of this core political foundation, the persistence of the softwood lumber dispute is surprising. Repeated rulings by trade panels of the North American Free Trade Agreement and World Trade Organization reject the U.S. charges of Canadian subsidy and injurious practice. The one remaining exception is the restriction on log exports from coastal British Columbia, and even this policy appears to be open for reconsideration by Canadian participants. Is now the time to think the unthinkable and do the undoable—create free trade in lumber and logs in North America?

The puzzle is why two countries as closely tied as the United States and Canada have not been able to find a sustainable, mutually acceptable approach to reaching this conclusion. Zhang provides the analytical framework for understanding the puzzle, and, therefore, perhaps for resolving it. His balanced, even-handed analysis draws on history, law, politics, economics, and institutional setting to provide a remarkably comprehensive treatment of one of the longest standing trade disputes in the world. Not only is his book the definitive account of this trade dispute, but it also casts useful light on the larger questions of U.S.–Canada trade and globalization itself.

CLARK S. BINKLEY
Cambridge, Massachusetts

Clark S. Binkley is the former dean of the Faculty of Forestry at the University of British Columbia. He currently is the managing director of International Forestry Investment Advisors, LLC, a private firm that provides timberland investment advisory services. He serves on the board of directors of West Fraser Timber, the second-largest softwood lumber manufacturer in North America, with operations in Canada and the United States, as well as on the board of directors of TimberWest Forests, the largest private forest landowner in Canada. He is a citizen of both the United States and Canada.

Preface

As a forester interested in economics and policy matters, I have followed for nearly 20 years the perennial dispute between the United States and Canada over softwood lumber trade. The dispute, the largest and longest running between the two otherwise friendly countries, has frustrated politicians and business leaders on both sides of the border and has earned the nickname "The Softwood Lumber War." This book is about the political economy of the softwood lumber trade dispute, which has been a constant struggle among U.S. lumber producers, U.S. consumers, and Canadian producers in the last two and a half decades.

The early 1980s was a difficult time for U.S. lumber producers. They experienced an economic recession and the collapse of softwood lumber prices as the result of a change in macroeconomic policy (restrictive monetary supply) in October 1979. Some Pacific Northwest producers had previously submitted high bid prices on public timber that they could not afford to pay in the new economic environment. Concurrently, they saw their domestic market share increasingly taken away by Canadian producers. At this juncture, some of the Pacific Northwest producers requested (and obtained in 1984) federal relief from their timber purchase contracts signed several years previously and sought government restrictions on Canadian lumber imports, alleging that Canadian lumber was subsidized.

Despite initial failure, U.S. producers continued to apply political pressure and eventually secured a 15 percent export tax on Canadian lumber under the 1986 Memorandum of Understanding between the two countries. As a result, Canadian producers' costs were increased, their U.S. market share declined, and lumber prices rose in the United States. The successful negotiation in October 1987 and implementation in January 1989 of the U.S.–Canada Free Trade Agreement gave Canadian lumber producers a chance to fight back by withdrawing from the memorandum of understanding. A long series of controversial trade battles followed against the background of periodic short-ages of timber supply in the United States, changing international lumber markets, overcapacity in lumber manufacturing, and the establishment of the North American Free Trade Agreement and the World Trade Organization. It is this story—how a rather large trade dispute was prolonged by politics, eco-nomics, legal structures (technical details as well as broader principles involved in U.S. and international trade laws), and institutional arrangements—that I tell here. Furthermore, I identify issues that have contributed to the longevity of the dispute and explore how they might be used more universally in the realm of natural resource management and international trade.

Over the past 18 years, I have studied the Canadian forest tenure system in which the alleged subsidy is rooted. I have also written refereed articles directly or indirectly related to the softwood lumber dispute. These articles have been cited by opposing sides of the dispute in support of their arguments. For exam-ple, U.S. consumer groups cited my study on the welfare costs of the 1996 U.S.–Canada Softwood Lumber Agreement to the United States as a whole and to U.S. lumber consumers in particular. The same study was quoted by the Coalition for Fair Lumber Imports, the primary U.S. industry group lobbying for restricting Canadian lumber imports, in its submission to the U.S. Interna-tional Trade Commission, for a different purpose. My paper questioning log export restrictions in British Columbia was cited by the coalition as a back-ground paper. The fact that my work has been used by opposing sides buttresses my effort here: to examine and analyze the dispute from an analytical, politi-cal, and economic perspective. By documenting various episodes in the war, I hope to use the interplay of politics and economics to explain its longevity, to provide an understanding of why various trade dispute settlement mechanisms have not been able to settle the dispute, to offer some insights on possible solu-tions to the dispute, and to inform a better understanding of international trade, globalization, and resource management.

Any success I may have achieved is shared with others. Auburn University provided me with a half-year of sabbatical leave that allowed me to do largely uninterrupted research on the subject. U.S. Forest Service George Andrew For-est Products Laboratory provided me an office in 2005. Dr. Clark S. Binkley, who graciously wrote the foreword for this book, supported my study on for-est tenure and this project in all stages. Many industry insiders and lawyers have given their time for my interviews and insights on the subject. The National Research Initiatives of the Cooperative State Research, Education, and Extension Service, USDA (Grant 99-35400-7741) provided financial support for my earlier research on the subject.

I would also like to express my appreciation to the following people for their collective and individual assistance: to Rao Nagubadi and Yanshu Li for research assistance and reading of the first draft of this book, to Lisa Jones of Ronald Reagan Presidential Library and Ken Hildebrand, George Brandak, and Katherine Kalsbeek of the Irving K. Barber Learning Center of the University of British Columbia Library for help in locating certain historical materials, and to Peter H. Pearse, Roger Sedjo, William F. Hyde, Peter N. Duinker, Larry Teeter, Robert B. Rummer, Ben Cashore, and Len Levin for their encouragement. Special thanks are due to John Allan, M. Jean Anderson, A. Mike Apsey, David Borins, Michael S. Carliner, Frank A. Dottori, Elliot J. Feldman, Carl Grenier, James Holbein, Gary N. Horlick, Gilbert B. Kaplan, Marston J. (Gus) Kuehne, John C. (Jake) Kerr, William (Bill) Lange, Lois McNabb, Susan E. Petniunas, Robert S. Plecas, John Ragosta, John Reilly, Faryar Shirzad, Bruce Smart, Ira S. Shapiro, Mike Stone, James R. Terpstra, Doug Waddell, and Don Wright for their insights and perspectives. A few of these insiders saw the relevant chapters of this book in their penultimate forms and provided further comments, but none of them completely agreed with my perspective, nor did they endorse these chapters. Ross W. Gorte, Warren A. Flick, David N. Laband, John Schelhas, Don Whiteley, and two anonymous referees and Grace Hill and Sally Atwater of Resources for the Future Press provided invaluable comments.

Finally, I would like to acknowledge my appreciation for my family. My parents, Qingxian Zhang and Jiao You, to whom this book is dedicated, are illiterate farmers in China. They sent three of their four children to college and one through high school. Their inspiration and encouragement to me are invaluable. My wife, Zilun Fan, has supported my effort throughout this project, and our children, Rei and Dan, have missed some playing time with me.

DAOWEI ZHANG

1

A War between Friends

With the implementation of the 2006 U.S.–Canada Softwood Lumber Agreement on October 12, 2006, the quarter-century-long softwood lumber trade dispute between the two countries officially takes a pause. Aside from leaving in the United States some 19 percent of the US$5.4 billion duty deposits that Canadian producers said should have been returned to them, this agreement sets up managed trade of softwood lumber between the two countries for the next seven to nine years; Canadian lumber exports will be taxed on an increasing scale as lumber prices fall. If previous lumber trade agreements, signed in 1986 and 1996, serve as a guide, however, the Softwood Lumber Agreement of 2006 will not end the trade dispute. At best, it is a short-term mechanism that does little to resolve continuing trade frictions.

This book is about the political economy of the softwood lumber trade dispute between the United States and Canada. The modern version of the dispute has been going on for nearly 25 years, and no long-term, durable solution has been found. Since the value of softwood lumber trade currently exceeds US$7 billion annually, this disagreement easily ranks as the largest trade dispute between the two countries in the modern era, and its longevity has defied many seasoned observers. Some insiders call the dispute a softwood lumber "war." Others who have studied it predict that the dispute could persist for another decade or more. How to break the deadlock? Is there a durable and long-lasting solution that is politically feasible in both countries?

The United States and Canada have usually enjoyed good diplomatic, political, and economic relationships, and the forest industry in the two countries has been somewhat integrated through cross-border investment and ownership of forest land and forest products manufacturing facilities. Certainly the softwood lumber dispute has, at times, had the attention and intervention of the highest elected officials—presidents, senators, and members of the House of Representatives in the United States, and prime ministers, members of Parliament, and provincial premiers in Canada—as well as industry leaders and corporate executives in both countries. Yet none of them have been able to break the deadlock and find a long-lasting solution. Moreover, as we will see, the Softwood Lumber Agreement of 2006 does not end the dispute, even though it took more than five years to negotiate. What are the lessons from the conflict and its duration? Is this lumber dispute a rare example of official discord between the two countries? To the extent that it is exceptional, why is it exceptional?

A trade dispute of such size and longevity is interesting in its own right, and so is the search for an economic, political, and legal explanation. That search may provide insights into the strange coexistence between cooperation and liberalization—political, diplomatic, and economic integration under the U.S.–Canada Free Trade Agreement (FTA) and the North American Free Trade Agreement (NAFTA)—and discord, exemplified by softwood lumber and other trade disputes. A compelling explanation for Canada's desire to have an administratively set pricing system for its timber resources and American producers' ability to curtail Canadian softwood lumber imports may give clues about why the lumber dispute is an exception in U.S.–Canada relations and ways to secure a lasting solution.

Moreover, insights generated from the lumber dispute may help solve other current and future disputes between the two countries over trade in, for example, corn, sugar, potassium, and certain steel products. The softwood lumber trade dispute has run its course, mostly under FTA, NAFTA, and the World Trade Organization (WTO). Why have the trade dispute mechanisms under these binational and multinational arrangements not been able to solve the problem? Can these mechanisms be strengthened to deal with large trade disputes such as softwood lumber?

Finally, many developing countries that have liberalized their economies in recent decades and are relatively small economic powers may face daunting protectionism when they try to sell their products to the United States, Canada, Japan, the European Union, or other developed countries. A better understanding of the U.S.–Canada softwood lumber trade dispute may help these countries deal more effectively with market access and potential protectionism in the United States and elsewhere. To the extent that the lumber dispute has something to do with the disparate economic and political power between Canada and the United States, the experience of Canada, as a developed nation, can be instructive for developing nations.

The remainder of this chapter provides a brief history of the softwood lumber trade dispute, highlights six puzzles related to the dispute, and presents the objectives and organization of this book.

A Brief History

The central issues of the modern softwood lumber trade dispute have been whether Canadian lumber is subsidized, mainly through provincial stumpage systems, and if it is, whether the U.S. lumber industry is injured or threatened with injury. When these two questions are answered affirmatively by the U.S. Department of Commerce (the actual investigation is carried out by the department's International Trade Administration) and the U.S. International Trade Commission, respectively, a countervailing duty is applied to offset the subsidy. Four phases of the dispute can be distinguished.

The first phase, "Lumber I," officially began on October 7, 1982, when the U.S. Coalition for Fair Canadian Lumber Imports, on behalf of some 350 U.S. lumber producers, filed a petition to the Department of Commerce alleging that certain softwood lumber products from Canada were subsidized by the Canadian government and especially by provincial governments, which own most forest lands in Canada and sell timber harvesting rights through "below-market" stumpage fees. The coalition therefore requested imposition of a countervailing duty against Canadian softwood lumber imports. After investigation, Commerce determined that the alleged below-market stumpage fees were neither provided to any specific industry or group of industries nor offered at preferential rates. The department concluded that the stumpage programs did not qualify for a countervailing duty and that other Canadian programs that were indeed subsidies provided only a *de minimis* (less than 0.5 percent) benefit to Canadian lumber producers (DOC [Department of Commerce] 1983). This marked the end of Lumber I.

In May 1986, in a different political climate in Washington, D.C., and after the Department of Commerce indicated that it had reinterpreted the subsidy protocol for government programs such as Canadian stumpage, a renamed Coalition for Fair Lumber Imports petitioned to reverse the finding in Lumber I. In October 1986, Commerce issued a preliminary determination that Canadian softwood lumber benefited from government subsidies, and the U.S. International Trade Commission preliminarily found injuries to domestic lumber producers. As a result, a 15 percent countervailing duty was immediately placed on Canadian softwood lumber bound for the United States, contingent on a final determination to be made by December 30, 1986 (DOC 1986b).

However, the final determination was averted, and the countervailing duty was never implemented. Instead, the United States and Canada signed a memorandum of understanding (MOU) that transferred collection of the proposed countervailing duty by the United States to the collection of an export tax by Canada. The memorandum allowed provincial governments to increase their stumpage fees in lieu of the full export tax. The policy, applied as either an export tax or a stumpage fee adjustment, was designed to increase the costs of Canadian lumber and reduce any Canadian competitive advantage arising from the alleged subsidy (Wear and Lee 1993). The MOU did not have a termination date, although either country could withdraw from it by giving the other country one month's notice. The period during which the MOU was created and honored is referred to as Lumber II.

On September 4, 1991, the Canadian government notified the U.S. government that it would withdraw from the MOU one month later, as it had honored and would continue to honor all its commitments. The U.S. government immediately self-initiated a countervailing duty investigation and imposed an interim duty for much of 1992 and 1993, arguing that without the memorandum, there was no mechanism to verify promises by the Canadian government. Canada challenged the U.S. decision under the FTA dispute settlement mechanism, which resulted in free trade of softwood lumber in 1994 and 1995. In April 1996, the two countries signed the Softwood Lumber Agreement, which was a tariff-rate quota system restricting Canadian lumber imports to the United States. The quota system was later found to have the same impact on lumber prices as an 11.6 percent export tax. This period is referred to as Lumber III.

After the expiration of the 1996 agreement on March 31, 2001, the Coalition for Fair Lumber Imports requested another countervailing duty investigation; this marked the beginning of Lumber IV. An antidumping component was added to the investigation. In May 2002, the United States imposed an average 18.79 percent countervailing duty and an average 8.43 percent antidumping duty, or 27.22 percent in total on Canadian lumber imports; company-specific duty rates were assessed and then modified annually under the Department of Commerce's annual administrative review. Canada challenged the U.S. decision at WTO and NAFTA. Canada won several major legal cases in both international bodies, especially under NAFTA, while the United States had some success at WTO. In particular, a NAFTA panel ruled in October 2004 that Canadian lumber imports did not threaten to injure the U.S. lumber industry. The United States challenged that panel's decision at a NAFTA Extraordinary Challenge Committee, which affirmed the panel's decision in August 2005. In March 2006, another NAFTA panel ruled that Canadian lumber was not subsidized. The United States had not complied with the NAFTA rulings, arguing that NAFTA panel decisions were only prospective and that its domestic trade laws were consistent with the WTO rules.

In the meantime, several rounds of negotiations between the governments of the two countries and industry failed to generate an agreement, either a short-term deal or a long-term solution, for five years. The breakthrough occurred in April 2006, after heads of state from the two countries made a political commitment to strike a deal; the Softwood Lumber Agreement of 2006 was signed on September 12, 2006, and implemented one month later.

Six Puzzles

In recent years, the United States and Canada have signed bilateral and multilateral free trade agreements such as FTA and NAFTA. They are also major supporters of the General Agreement on Tariffs and Trade (GATT) and WTO. Trade between these two countries in general has become freer. Many tariff and

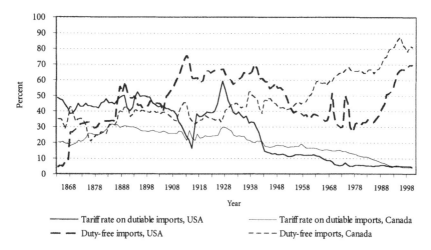

FIGURE 1-1. Tariff Rate on Dutiable Imports and Share of Duty-Free Imports in the United States and Canada, 1868–2005

Note: Data for Canada prior to 1988 were from Statistics Canada (2003). Except for 1997, data for Canada used in this graph between 1988 and 2005 were not available and had to be estimated. According to Foreign Affairs and International Trade Canada (1999), Canada's tariff rates on dutiable imports declined from 11.28 percent to 5.03 percent from 1987 to 1997. The tariff rates on dutiable imports and percentage of duty-free imports between 1988 and 1996 were subsequently estimated using an interpolation (linear average) method. For the years between 1998 and 2005, Statistics Canada (2007) shows the average tariff rate on total imports was 0.81. Because the tariff rate on dutiable imports was five times that on total imports in 1997, multiplying 0.81 by 5 produces an approximate tariff rate on dutiable imports for 2005. Using the tariff rates on dutiable imports for 1997 and 2005, the tariff rates on dutiable imports for Canada between 1998 and 2004 were interpolated using the linear average method.
Sources: Statistics Canada (2003); U.S. Bureau of Census (1975); ITC (2006a).

nontariff barriers have been reduced or eliminated. In 2005, both countries admitted some 70 percent of total imports duty free. The U.S. general tariff rate, measured as the share of tariffs on all dutiable goods, has declined steadily in the past century. The overall tariff rate was about 5 percent in recent years, less than a tenth of the peak reached in 1933 that resulted from the infamous Smoot-Hawley tariff. Canadian tariff rates also trended downward (Figure 1-1).

Tariff reductions and eliminations have led to a dramatic increase in international trade in recent decades. In 2005, the value of U.S. and Canada bilateral transactions in goods, services, and income payments reached US$613 billion, roughly tripled from 1988 (Figure 1-2).

Those tariff reductions did not apply to Canadian softwood lumber. U.S. tariffs, Canadian export taxes, or other restrictive measures have been put on Canadian lumber for most of the past 20 years and now extend into the future (Table 1-1).

This is our first puzzle: increasingly free trade for most goods and services but not for softwood lumber. In fact, lumber trade was free (or freer) for

FIGURE 1-2. Total Value of Trade and Income Payments between the United States and Canada, 1980–2005

* Includes income payments.
Source: U.S. Bureau of Economic Analysis (2006).

decades before the end of 1986, when the memorandum of understanding put a 15 percent export tax on most Canadian lumber. Why is softwood lumber different from other goods and services traded between the two countries? What did Canadians do wrong with softwood lumber? If the Canadians did nothing wrong, were the Americans making mistakes by imposing tariffs or other restrictive measures on Canadian lumber imports?

TABLE 1-1. U.S. Trade Restriction Measures on Canadian Softwood Lumber Imports

Duration	Restriction measure	Magnitude
1/1/1987–10/3/1991	MOU	15% export tax or stumpage adjustment
10/4/1991–2/19/1992	Section 301[a]	Lumber from Ontario, Alberta, Manitoba, and Saskatchewan, 15%; lumber from Québec, 6.2% before November 1, 1991, and 3.1% afterward
3/12/1992–5/27/1992	Interim CVD[a]	14.48%
5/28/1992–8/3/1994	CVD[a]	6.51%
4/1/1996–3/31/2005	SLA 1996	Tariff-rate quota
5/19/2001–5/21/2002	CVD and AD[b]	19.31–31.89%
5/22/2002–4/31/2003	CVD and AD[b]	CVD, 16.37%; AD, 3.78%
5/1/2003–10/12/2006	CVD and AD[b]	CVD, 8.70%; AD, 2.11%
10/13/2006– (for 7 to 9 years)	SLA 2006	Export tax range from 0% to 15%, or export charge (0%–5%) plus volume control

Note: MOU = Memorandum of Understanding; CVD = countervailing duty; SLA = Softwood Lumber Agreement; AD = antidumping duty.
a. Bonds or duties were returned to Canada as a result of WTO or FTA panel rulings or Commerce determination.
b. These rates were determined by Commerce's retrospective annual administrative reviews. The actual duty rates charged for a particular year before the annual administrative reviews were conducted were quite different from these rates. Also, under SLA 2006, some 81 percent of these duties were returned to Canadian producers.

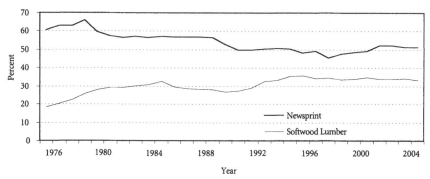

FIGURE 1-3. Share of Canadian Newsprint and Softwood Lumber in U.S. Consumption, 1975–2005

Sources: AF&PA (2006), NAHB (2006).

Our second puzzle is the contrast between forest products: free trade for most forest products but not for softwood lumber, even though they all come from timber. Ostensibly, the initial investigation of subsidy and the subsequent imposition of countervailing duties on softwood lumber were triggered by an increase in the Canadian share of the U.S. lumber market, especially between 1975 and 1982. However, Canadian newsprint has a much larger share of the U.S. market than Canadian softwood lumber. The share of Canadian softwood lumber in the U.S. market has been around one-third in the last decade, while the share of Canadian newsprint has been largely more than 50 percent (Figure 1-3).

One may argue that newsprint and softwood lumber are different in that their supply and demand are not driven by the same forces and that wood constitutes a bigger share in the production cost of softwood lumber than in that of newsprint. However, both lumber and newsprint are made of wood, and wood was the largest component of newsprint production cost in the 1920s, and it is the second largest now. Softwood lumber is made of sawlogs (large logs), and newsprint is made of pulpwood (small logs) and chips that are a residue from lumber production. If the Canadian stumpage system gives subsidies to softwood lumber producers, it should provide them simultaneously to newsprint producers as well. Why was there no complaint about Canadian newsprint imports?

In fact, the United States and Canada fought a series of battles over newsprint tariffs around the turn of the 20th century, and the result has been free trade in newsprint since 1911. Even though these two disputes are some 80 years apart, some lessons may be learned by investigating the importance of political, economic, and institutional factors in determining the outcome of the trade conflicts in forest products between the two countries.

Further, the fact that newsprint is a value-added product yet both it and softwood lumber are imported into the United States in a similar magnitude in value only heightens the contrast between these two trade disputes—since in theory, the United States should impose higher tariffs on newsprint than on softwood lumber. Instead, the United States has let Canadian newsprint come to the country duty free since 1911 but imposed tariffs, export taxes, or tariff-rate quotas on Canadian softwood lumber. This cannot be explained by the difference in the raw material (wood) cost of these products.

How could the two countries be at relative peace in the newsprint trade for so long? What are the similarities and differences between trade in these two products, and what forces have brought about such different outcomes?

Our third puzzle is why both countries, in the course of the lumber trade dispute, were willing to give up trade arrangements that were clearly in their favor from an economic point of view. From an economic perspective, free trade benefits both economies as a whole, but some constraints on trade flows, including export taxes and quotas, appear to increase social welfare in Canada and decrease welfare in the United States. Yet the U.S. government resisted free trade, and the Canadian government objected to export constraints on its lumber exports. Perhaps the distribution of incomes associated with free trade and trade constraints has something to do with this paradox. More importantly, international politics, institutional factors, and the imbalance of political power among players in both countries may help explain why each country has accepted trade arrangements that are inferior or detrimental to its macroeconomy but favor a particular group—for example, lumber producers.

Our fourth puzzle is why politicians and corporate executives in both countries could not find a durable solution for the softwood lumber trade dispute. The two countries have historically had good diplomatic, political, military, and general economic relationships. With few exceptions, the personal relationships between the heads of states of the two countries have been close. The forests in western Canada and in the U.S. Pacific Northwest are similar; so are the forests in New England and the Great Lakes States and in eastern Canada. Corporate ownership of the forest products industry is somewhat integrated across the two countries, and many firms are members of the same industry associations, such as the American Forest and Paper Association. Politicians and corporate executives are heavily involved in the lumber trade dispute. Are there any inherent, institutional obstacles in either country that prohibit them from finding a long-term solution? Have forest products corporations in both countries given too much control of this matter to their trade lawyers?

Along with trade liberalization in the United States, the application for administered protection by U.S. companies under antidumping duty laws has increased in recent years. According to Department of Commerce statistics, the annual number of investigations initiated on antidumping duty allegations rose from an average of 30 cases from 1980 to 1984 to an average of 48 cases between 1999 and 2003 (Figure 1-4). Similarly, the number of antidumping duty orders issued increased from 4.7 per year to 22.8 per year over the same period. However, the use of countervailing duties declined (Figure 1-5). More specifically, Commerce initiated an average of 27.2 countervailing duty investigations and issued 9.4 such orders per year between 1980 and 1984. By 1999–2003, the num-

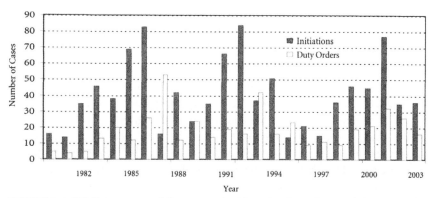

FIGURE 1-4. U.S. Department of Commerce Antidumping Duty Case Activity, 1980–2003

Source: http://ia.ita.doc.gov/stats/iastats1.html.

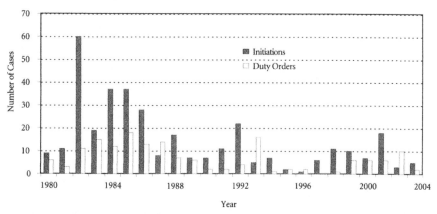

FIGURE 1-5. U.S. Department of Commerce Countervailing Duty Case Activity, 1980–2003

Source: http://ia.ita.doc.gov/stats/iastats1.html.

ber of investigations fell to 8.6 and the number of orders dropped to 5.2 annually. Yet in the softwood lumber case, the allegations of subsidy and demands for countervailing duties have persisted for more than 25 years. Here is our fifth puzzle. Have the American lumber producers been crying foul even though there is no lumber subsidy in Canada? Or have Canadian provincial governments, heavily influenced by their own lumber producers, failed to make real changes to their stumpage systems? Or is there some of both?

Finally, the softwood lumber trade dispute has taken place as trade dispute settlement mechanisms under FTA, NAFTA, and WTO have been implemented. Why have these mechanisms not worked effectively to resolve the softwood lumber trade dispute? What can be done to improve dispute settlement mechanisms?

What explains these paradoxical developments? What are the causes of the softwood lumber dispute? How did it start? Why has the dispute lasted so long?

How long will it continue? Are there any long-term and durable solutions? What does the lumber dispute teach us about U.S.–Canada relations, international trade, and natural resource management?

I hypothesize that interest group politics in both countries has a lot to do with these paradoxical developments and might explain the cause, persistence, and intractability of the softwood lumber dispute. Lumber (and other forest products) companies in both countries are rent seeking, and U.S. consumers are welfare maximizing. All three groups have used political means and taken advantage of the legal and institutional settings in the two countries to advance their interests. They have sometimes succeeded in overriding other national interests when they have enough political clout. The dispute settlement mechanisms under FTA, NAFTA, and WTO have some weaknesses and have ultimately failed in solving the softwood lumber dispute when the two governments, driven by interest group politics, are looking for an easy way out.

Given the economic significance of the softwood lumber trade dispute and the truckloads of documents generated from all parties involved, it is surprising to find that, in fact, there has been little comprehensive analysis of the dispute. Percy and Yoder (1987) and Uhler (1991) are somewhat dated, and their views are perceived to be limited to the Canadian side. Other published academic studies focus on individual aspects of the dispute. For example, Adams et al. (1986) write about the currency exchange rate and the Canadian softwood lumber share in the U.S. market. Wear and Lee (1993), Zhang (2001, 2006), van Kooten (2002), Kinnucan and Zhang (2004), Yin and Baek (2004), Devadoss et al. (2005), and Stennes and Wilson (2005) discuss the economic impacts of the memorandum of understanding and the Softwood Lumber Agreement of 1996. Zhang and Sun (2001) focus on softwood lumber price volatility. Cashore (1998) reviews the policy and institutional differences in both countries that contribute to the longevity of the lumber dispute. Anderson and Cairns (1988), Kalt (1988), and Zhang and Laband (2005) focus on three events and the politics of the softwood lumber dispute.

This book, in contrast, attempts a comprehensive historical, political, legal, and economic analysis that weaves together these separate streams of scholarly literature, while filling in the gaps to develop a rich, compelling tapestry. Further and more importantly, it presents an interest group politics framework for solving the puzzles surrounding the softwood lumber and other trade disputes between the two countries and looks into related trade dispute settlement mechanisms that extend far beyond technical softwood lumber issues and have broad legal, economic, and political implications.

Objectives

This book addresses the politics and economics of the softwood lumber dispute by integrating the most relevant work from multiple disciplines. Using the softwood lumber dispute as the primary case, along with U.S.–Canada trade disputes in newsprint, shakes and shingles, and other forest products, I illustrate and explain the political economy of forest products trade between the two countries. More specifically, the objectives of this book are as follows:

- integrate relevant works in economics, law, and political science to provide a better understanding of the softwood lumber and other forest trade conflicts between the two countries;
- place these disputes in a broader framework examining U.S.–Canada trade relations, economic developments, and the comparative advantages in resource endowments in these two countries;
- explain the longevity of the softwood lumber trade dispute;
- detail the history of the dispute and bring readers up to date on the developments that led to the Softwood Lumber Agreement of 2006;
- examine past and current trade agreements on softwood lumber, including their economic and political impacts, in both qualitative and quantitative terms, and the operation of the Softwood Lumber Agreement of 2006;
- identify potential long-term solutions to the lumber dispute as well as lessons for resource management regimes and international trade;
- provide insight on WTO and NAFTA dispute settlement mechanisms; and
- to inform a broader understanding of international trade.

In short, I intend to tell a story about the softwood lumber dispute by looking into the causes, players, processes, and outcomes as well as analyses at various stages. The story is multifaceted. At the end of the book, I suggest possible solutions based on past forest products trade conflicts, the history of the softwood lumber dispute, and the current legal and institutional frameworks in both countries. Finally, I offer some insights and inference on international trade and resource management.

Plan of the Book

The next chapter provides a literature review of the theory of economic regulation and political processes in each country, develops an analytical framework and research method, and describes historical aspects of forest resource development in the United States and Canada that sowed the seeds for the modern softwood lumber dispute. Chapters 3 and 4 review details of the first two rounds of the softwood lumber dispute—Lumber I and II—which led to the signing of the memorandum of understanding. The economic arguments and political maneuvering on both sides of the border are documented, as are the economic impacts of the memorandum.

Chapter 5 focuses on the dynamics that led to Canada's withdrawal from the MOU, a decision that ignited Lumber III. Chapter 6 is devoted to Lumber III and covers the FTA process that included two binational panels and an extraordinary challenge. Chapter 7 documents the process and factors influencing the outcome of the 1995–1996 government-to-government consultation that ended with the Softwood Lumber Agreement of 1996. The logic and economic impact of the agreement, consumer group actions, and trade frictions during the term of the agreement are presented.

Chapter 8 discusses the litigation track of Lumber IV, covering various determinations by U.S. investigating authorities and numerous rulings by NAFTA, WTO, and the U.S. courts. Chapter 9 focuses on the negotiation track of Lumber IV. It documents the attempts to settle the dispute, describes the Softwood Lumber Agreement of 2006, explains who wins and who loses, and speculates on the operations of the Softwood Lumber Agreement of 2006.

Chapter 10 is a comparison of the political economy of the softwood lumber dispute and the newsprint tariff battle. The last chapter explains the causes and longevity of the softwood lumber dispute from an economic, political, legal, and institutional perspective. It also presents potential long-term solutions and speculates on where the two countries go from here. Finally, it provides a summary of lessons learned from the softwood lumber dispute that may have implications for international trade and resource management.

2

Theory of Economic Policy Formation

Tariffs, tariff-rate quotas, or any other measures that are used to manage trade are forms of government regulation over economic activities. Public ownership of forest resources, private forest practice laws, and restrictions on log exports also are forms of government regulation. All of these controls have broad economic, political, and social implications. How do economic regulations arise and evolve? Do they advance the stated government objectives, such as maximizing social welfare?

Models of Policymaking

Several models of political–economic interaction in policy formation have been set forth in an effort to understand the existence and persistence of government economic regulations. Perhaps the most widely used justification for government regulations is negative externalities, which are a consequence of market failure. An externality exists when the producers of a good do not internalize the full benefits or costs of production, which means that others in society share the benefits or bear the costs. Timber harvesting, for example, may have negative impacts on water quality and wildlife habitats, but forest products companies do not count these negative impacts as part of their production costs.

Government regulations may have social and environmental objectives, such as job creation, community stability, and environmental protection, that are often used to justify intervention in forest management and forest products manufacturing. Regulators may, for example, seek to prevent mill closures, which could hurt local employment and economies, or reduce industrial pollution, which has a negative effect on the environment and human health.

Similarly, protection of domestic industry and employment is often the stated goal of restricting foreign goods and services.

Underlying effective government regulations on economic activities is the notion of government as a benevolent guardian, hampered perhaps only by innocent ignorance as it searches for best policies. In general, this public interest theory of economic regulations assumes that government decisions are based on the public interest of maximizing social welfare, public health, and social order.

A contrary view is the interest group theory, which assumes that government decisions are based on the availability of government-produced scarcity rents and the ability of legislators and government officials to maximize the value they receive for producing these rents (Stigler 1971; Peltzman 1976; Becker 1983; Zusman 1976). Rents are broadly defined to cover economic, political, or other personal gains.

Stigler (1971) and Peltzman (1976, 1984) were among the first group of economists who posit full rationality and self-interest for all policy participants, including elected officials, bureaucrats, and private individuals and firms. They argue that all policy participants use the political process to seek wealth transfers and political and economic rents. In this model, policy analysis by economists alone would serve little useful purpose, since information on the size and distribution of economic impacts caused by regulations alone would not change the behavior of any participant.

For example, after analyzing the economic inefficiency of the Interstate Commerce Commission (ICC, which regulates the trucking industry) regulations, Stigler (1971, 18) states, "The only way to get a different ICC would be to change the political support for the Commission, and reward Commissioners on the basis unrelated to their services to the carriers." In other words, if the public wants to have different regulations, change ICC: Change the incentive structure of ICC commissioners by making it independent of politics and decoupling the remuneration of commissioners from their regulatory policies.

A variant of the Stigler–Peltzman approach appears in Becker (1983), who assumes that political interest groups form in their own self-interest and that politicians rationally choose policies in response to the competing pressures these groups can exert. With competition among groups and the assumption that anything that benefits one group must either be financed directly through a tax or indirectly by costing another group (including deadweight losses), Becker (1983) concludes that resources are allocated through the political process to maximize the benefits (which are negative for the losing group) each group expects to receive.

Olson (1965, 1982) provides insights on how interest groups emerge, evolve, and function. He starts with the "logic of collective action," in which "free-rider" problems prevent the effective collusion of a large number of small losers or gainers. He then provides various hypotheses as to which pressure groups will emerge, which groups will be more effective, and the characteristics of an industry that can organize itself and get its interests effectively represented. These characteristics often include both geographic and market concentration.

In essence, Olson's model posits that economically inefficient outcomes arise because of free-rider problems. It is rational for individuals not to join groups interested in consumer welfare, defined broadly, because the benefits to them are independent of their own activities. That is, the cost of getting these individuals organized (the transaction cost) is prohibitively high. On the other hand, industrial firms, which may be few, could be well organized if they are concentrated geographically or in the products they make. When such firms focus on a single issue or issues that could bring them large benefits by imposing a small per-person cost on a large number of consumers, their interest group can successfully lobby elected officials and bureaucrats. Thus, issue-specific political participation is effectively precluded for large groups of small potential gainers or losers to represent their interests because high transaction costs prohibit them from becoming well organized.

This type of collective action problem has long been recognized by political economists. Pareto (1927) writes, "A protectionist measure provides large benefits to a small number of people, and causes a very great number of consumers a slight loss. This circumstance makes it easier to put a protection measure in practice." Schattschneider (1935) puts it succinctly, "Benefits are concentrated while costs are dispersed."

Those models are the subject of the public choice school, which attempts to use economics to understand politics and political processes (how government works and makes decisions). There are markets in politics, just as there are for ordinary goods and services. Interest groups arise to represent certain economic interests. They "demand" certain actions from public policymakers. In return, they help political candidates who share their views get elected to public offices. They are the demanders of economic regulations.

The suppliers of these regulations are politicians who, upon assessing the benefits and costs of responding to the demand from various interest groups (or lack thereof), make decisions based on their self-interest. These politicians can be viewed as brokers because the real suppliers of regulations are the individuals and groups that do not find it worthwhile to get politically organized and resist having their wealth taken away. The interaction between suppliers and demanders of economic regulations creates a political market in the form of lobbying pressure, political action, legislation, and administrative actions that generally involve some kind of wealth transfer.

A critical question is, given that interest groups explicitly want something from elected officials or policymakers, why do these officials or policymakers listen to them? In other words, most lobbyists are paid advocates of special interests; why should politicians believe anything they say? A possible explanation is that politicians need lobbyists' support and money to finance their election and reelection campaigns, and bureaucrats need constituent support to carry out their missions. Interest groups can be better fundraisers than politicians themselves, or at least can become politicians' allies in fundraising and getting voters' attention.

Once in office, legislators may engage in "logrolling." Such vote trading by legislators is usually done to gain sufficient support for a particular piece of legislation that benefits their electoral districts. Logrolling, which results in the redistribution of income toward certain regions and industries, generally does not lead to a more productive economy. Rather, it leads to unnecessary and costly public works projects and legislation that protects an inefficient domestic industry.

Supposedly, the U.S. president has a much broader constituency than individual members of Congress and would have less interest in favoring particular regions or industries. However, his powers to deal with trade are delegated through trade legislation by Congress, which under the U.S. Constitution has jurisdiction over trade and commerce. Congress therefore can greatly influence the executive branch's trade policy, and U.S. trade remedies can be best understood by keeping clearly in mind the cooperation and tension between Congress and the executive branch over trade power. The president needs to act for the general good without offending specific congressional coalitions. On trade matters, this means that sometimes he must exercise his discretion for reasons not entirely related to the merits of a specific trade dispute or remedies (Percy and Yoder 1987). Often there is give-and-take between the executive branch and Congress in trade and other policy matters.

If collective action problems, protectionism, interest group politics, and logrolling are prevalent in American trade politics, how is it that trade tariffs have come down in the past century? On the surface it appears that the benevolent government argument has prevailed. However, Gilligan (1997) argues that it is not because the public interest theory has somehow prevailed in American politics, but because reciprocity of trade treaties has led to the establishment of exporter interest groups and delegation by Congress to the president in trade negotiation. He notes,

> After Congress delegated to the President, the President negotiated reciprocal trade treaties with other countries in which American trade barriers were reduced in return for greater access by American exporters overseas. As usual protected interests lobbied Congress heavily to maintain their protection and end the reciprocal trade agreements program. However, now exporters had a stronger incentive to lobby in favor of the program than they would have had to lobby for unilateral liberalization. The reciprocal trade agreements mitigated the collective action problems of pro-liberalization groups that are inherent in the political economy of trade policy by concentrating the benefits of liberalization on particular exporters. As a result, the amount of lobby for liberalization increased. (Gilligan 1997, 8)

Furthermore, Gilligan (1997, *10*) points out, "The increase in exporter lobbying explains the progressive shift in Congressional preferences toward free trade, and Congressional willingness to allow such deep reductions of American trade barriers."

A variation on the interest group theory is the "bootleggers and Baptists" paradigm. According to Yandle (1989), "Baptists" are those who promote a public or private interest by attaching it to other issues that have broad public support (such as resource conservation and environment protection), whereas "bootleggers" are those who support the same interest without attaching it to any public issue. Despite their different motives, by working together, Baptists and bootleggers can sometimes secure an economic regulation that would otherwise be unobtainable if they worked alone.

Both public interest and interest group theories have empirical support. Sometimes economically efficient choices may coincide with choices in the interest of one or more groups, and economic and political influences have to be disentangled. Accordingly, a hybrid theory that allows for the influence of both interest groups and economic efficiency has been proposed (Joskow 1972; Noll 1989). These theories have been tested in the utility industry (Nelson 1982), oil industry (Becker 1983), transportation (Teske et al. 1994), agriculture (Gardner 1983, 1987; Bullock 1992; Rausser and Foster 1990), and the Endangered Species Act (Mehmood and Zhang 2001). Further, whereas the Stigler–Peltzman–Becker model of regulation emphasizes legislators' self-interest in determining their behavior, ideology has gained much prominence in some empirical studies (Hird 1993; Zhang and Laband 2005).

This is not to imply that lobbying by interest groups is "bad" or that they always win at the expense of the public interest. First, the proliferation of political interest groups is perhaps a natural and largely benign consequence of economic development. These groups formed spontaneously whenever shared interests were threatened or could be enhanced by political action (Truman 1951). Second, interest groups are protected by the U.S. Constitution. To maintain the freedoms specified in the First Amendment of the U.S. Constitution— to speak, publish, assemble, and "petition the Government for redress of grievances"—a political system must tolerate factions even though they may be, as James Madison (1787) wrote in his *Federalist No. 10*, opposed to the public good. Interest groups, lobbyists, and other political and civic organizations are in effect licensed by the U.S. Constitution and cannot be suppressed without subverting the very purpose of popular government. They can be regarded as essential and valuable participants in the democratic politics of a modern society. Without their participation, policy would be made in far greater ignorance of what citizens actually wanted from their government. Finally, the fragmentation of authority—institutional and social pluralism—would prevent any single interest group from dominating, and diversity would foster a wide variety of competing interests that would use this institutional machinery to thwart one another's selfish designs (Kernell and Jacobson 2000).

But it is undeniable that the groups most visibly active in politics often do not, by any stretch of the imagination, form a balanced cross section of economic and social interests. Some interests may be vastly overrepresented, and others, underrepresented. As Schattschneider (1960, *34–35*) points out, "The flaw in the pluralist heaven is that the heavenly chorus sings with a strong upper-class accent." The readiest explanation for this bias is that organizational resources—money, information, access to authority, skill, and bargaining power—are distributed unequally across interest groups.

A subtler but more cogent explanation for the observed bias in group representation lies in the way the incentive for collective action and the barriers to organization vary across different types of groups (Olson 1965). As noted earlier, some groups—which may be small and concentrated geographically or by industry and whose per-member interests (or prospective benefits or costs) are high—can better solve the free-rider problem.

Political Systems in the United States and Canada

Both the United States and Canada are modern democracies that blend delegation with majority rule. However, the forms of delegation and constraints on majority rule are different. The United States has a presidential system, and delegation is reflected in the fact that voters directly elect the president through the Electoral College system and Congress, which consists of the House of Representatives and the Senate. The apportionment of the 435 members of the House is based on state population, but each of the 50 states sends two senators to the Senate. This bicameral Congress is designed to protect the interests of states with small populations. The separation of powers embedded in the U.S. Constitution ensures deliberate checks and balances among the executive, legislative, and judicial branches and within an individual branch. In addition, there are elaborate rules and institutional arrangements designed to constrain majority rule in the operation of Congress.

The checks and balances are apparent in trade policy. On the one hand, Congress has the constitutional power to "regulate commerce with foreign nations and among several states and with Indian tribes." This "commerce" clause, plus the power "to lay and collect taxes, duties, imports, and excises, to pay the debts and provide for the common defense and general welfare of the United States," provides leverage for Congress to influence foreign policy, including international trade policy. On the other hand, the president is responsible for negotiating with other nations and has access to State Department expertise. This power structure ensures that the president, who is likely to seek the overall welfare of the nation and may therefore prefer free trade, will be checked by Congress, whose members are responsive to constituents who may demand protection from foreign imports. In short, the president, even if he wants to promote free trade, will not get free trade legislation without congressional consent.

In contrast, Canada has a parliamentary system, where a popularly elected legislature has a great deal of authority, including election of a team of executives called the cabinet, one of whom serves as the prime minister (or premier at the provincial level). This system promotes majority rule in the sense that the political party or a coalition of parties that controls the legislature also controls the executive branch and the ordinary operation of the government.

In theory, the parliamentary system may have weaker checks and balances than the presidential system, making it easy for a prime minister who has a free trade or managed trade agenda to implement it through executive and legislative actions. Nonetheless, in forest products trade, this seemingly easy task for the prime minister of Canada is complicated by provincial forest land ownership, as specified in the Canadian Constitution. Provincial governments have a lot to say about trade measures that influence their ability to manage their forests and forest lands. Further, province-based forest products companies, with different resource endowments and productivities, might pressure their respective provincial governments to take different positions with respect to forest products trade matters. Thus there are more players and interest groups with diverse goals with respect to softwood lumber trade in Canada than in the United States. Whether the Canadian government can make a deal with the United States with respect to forest products trade depends on its ability to build a critical level of support from individual provinces and major producers.

Forest Land Ownership in the United States and Canada

The two countries have different systems of forest land ownership. Of the 747 million acres (302 million hectares) of forest land in the United States, about 57.6 percent is owned by private entities. The federal government owns 33 percent of the total (78 percent of the public forest lands); the states own about 8 percent of the total, and county, municipality, and tribal governments own the rest (Smith et al. 2004).

About 67 percent of all forest land (some 200 million hectares) in the United States is classified as timberland—forest land capable of producing in excess of 20 cubic feet per acre (1.43 m^3 per hectare) per year and not legally withdrawn from timber production. More timberland (71 percent) is held privately than publicly. In 2001, nonindustrial private forests—owned by landowners who do not have any forest products manufacturing facility—made up 58 percent of U.S. timberland and accounted for 59 percent of timber harvests. Industrial forests accounted for 13 percent of U.S. timberland and nearly 30 percent of timber harvests. Public forests made up 29 percent of the U.S. timberland base but merely 11 percent of timber harvests in 2001, compared with 23.4 percent in 1970 (Smith et al. 2004).

Canada has approximately 418 million hectares of forest land. More than two-thirds of it (71 percent) is owned by provincial governments, 23 percent by the federal government, and a mere 5 percent by private entities. Of its 245 million hectares of timber-productive forest land—defined as forest land that is capable of producing a merchantable stand within a reasonable length of time— 80 percent is owned by provincial governments, 11 percent by the federal government, and 9 percent by private entities (Canadian Forest Service 2004).

Although the definitions of *timberland* in the United States and *timber-productive forest land* in Canada are not exactly the same, private ownership of productive forest lands is dominant in the United States, and provincial ownership is dominant in Canada. With a few exceptions, the forest products industry depends on private timber in the United States and on public timber in Canada.

Scott (forthcoming) provides an economic explanation of the divergent 19th-century "decisions" of the U.S. Congress and the Canadian provinces about the property interests assigned to loggers and lumbermen. Both the U.S. federal and the Canadian provincial governments may well have wished to sell forest land directly for an appropriate price. However, the U.S. government could not have mounted a system of classification robust enough to stand up to political complaints and business avoidance. Accordingly, it did nothing and let the agriculture-based Homestead Act rule the "distribution" of public forest land. Thus loggers and lumbermen were forced to acquire forest land indirectly and to own it. On the other hand, Canadian provincial governments forced loggers and lumbermen to acquire timber licenses. Why? Again, classification would have been a problem, and in any case, licensing lands could produce a greater stream of revenues than granting outright ownership.

Scott (forthcoming) further explains why the Canadian provinces made forest tenure arrangements instead of privatizing their forest land in the 20th century. He attributes the decision to multiple uses, sustained forest yields, and most importantly, provincial governments' appetites for revenue and investment. In the two centuries of evolution in forest users' property rights, there was no evidence that either the U.S. federal government or the Canadian provinces did not want to maximize economic rents from timber and forest land.

Mature timber is often sold on the stump in both countries. The price for standing timber is called stumpage, or stumpage price in the United States and stumpage fee in Canada. When forests are owned by private parties, the owners sell their timber to the highest bidder through bidding or negotiation. Thus market-based systems are likely to prevail when private ownership of forest land is dominant. Even if private owners do not sell their timber because they have other objectives, such as hunting or recreation, or if they sell it but do not maximize their profits for whatever reason, their actions would be viewed as acceptable even by the proponents of a market-based stumpage system.

When forests are owned by governments, stumpage fees can be set in various ways. The U.S. Forest Service, which manages most federal forest lands, has a bidding system in which timber is appraised using a deterministic formula to set a minimum price and then sold to the highest bidder. In some cases, there is little or no competition, and by default, the administered, not market-driven, minimum price becomes the final sale price. Further, the Forest Service is responsible for all forest management activities and road building. In Canada, harvesting rights to provincial forests are granted to private forest industry firms though long-term or short-term leases or tenures, and the holders of long-term tenures are now obliged to assume most forest management activities and road building. The stumpage fees they pay for public timber, however, are set administratively, which may or may not be adjusted as quickly as market prices. It is thus possible that these administratively set prices are not reflective of market conditions.

Since provincial governments have other objectives in managing their forest resources, such as environmental protection, employment, economic development, and community stability, and are subject to the influence of interest groups, such as the forest products industry, they may, in theory, set a lower-than-market price for public timber. If so, that could constitute a subsidy to the tenure holders, most of whom are lumber producers.

Can a government have nontimber management objectives and, at its discretion, have an administratively determined stumpage system in return for securing tenure holders' assistance in advancing the nontimber objectives? Percy and Yoder (1987) argue that the discretion exercised by Canadian provincial governments is a sovereign right of ownership. In other words, it is the owners' prerogative to request that the resource users meet certain government guidelines and regulations. Just as private landowners can set the conditions under which their timber can be harvested or refuse to sell their timber to certain bidders, a government has similar rights to regulate timber users and charge administratively set stumpage fees. However, others may hold the view that if the government's action goes too far and injures an industry in another country, the sovereign right is subjected to international trade law and domestic laws of the importing country. One lawyer for the U.S. lumber industry puts it this way, "As resource owners, Canadian provincial governments can subsidize however they want, as long as it does not injure the U.S. industry" (Ragosta 2003).

Subsidy or no subsidy is a critical issue in the U.S.–Canada softwood lumber trade dispute, discussed in detail in later chapters. But for now, it is sufficient to say that the 10 Canadian provinces use various formulas to set their stumpage prices. Provincial ownership of forest land gives provincial governments a stake in federal trade policy that affects their stumpage fees and forest resource management activities. So the prime minister of Canada has to negotiate with provincial premiers when dealing with forest products trade issues with implications for provincial stumpage formulas or forest management regulations. The prime minister of Canada does not have an easier task in forest products trade matters than the president of the United States after all. Even if both heads of state want to settle the softwood lumber dispute, they have to go through the Congress (in the United States) and provincial governments (in Canada), which, in turn, may be heavily influenced by special interest groups.

Major Players in the Softwood Lumber Trade Dispute

The U.S. Congress and Canadian federal and provincial parliaments respond to constituents' demands. The major constituents in the United States are lumber producers, timber producers, and consumers (homebuilders and homebuyers). Since several large lumber producers own some of the most productive timberland, these two groups are treated as a single U.S. lumber producer group. Because Canadian consumers' interests are weak relative to U.S. consumers and, especially, Canadian lumber producers, Canadian interests in the dispute are dominated by lumber producers, most of whom prefer free trade and open access to the U.S. market. The Canadian producers' interests are close to those of U.S. consumers. Not surprisingly, Canadian producers and their provincial and federal governments have denied any subsidy and often (but not always) fought along with, and occasionally provided financial support to, U.S. consumer groups on their side. Nonetheless, the interests of Canadian producers and U.S. consumers are not always the same. These two groups sometimes do not get along when their interests diverge.

I view most actions taken by various groups involved in the dispute as rational. Consider the U.S. lumber producers as an example. Small sawmill owners would say they are trying to make a living; the large publicly traded firms seek to pay dividends to their investors, as demanded by Wall Street. One way to increase profits is to restrict Canadian lumber imports and thus raise domestic lumber prices. On the other hand, U.S. consumers naturally have sought affordable lumber and oppose any restriction on Canadian lumber imports. They probably do not care whether Canadian lumber is subsidized as long as lumber prices are as low as possible. The inevitable frictions have arrayed the two interests on opposite sides of a long series of controversies in softwood lumber trade with Canada, although the consumer groups have become better organized in the more recent rounds of the dispute.

Both U.S. softwood lumber producers and consumers have tried to influence the U.S. government. Since the producers are led by a small number of large firms and are well organized, they have often overpowered the widely dispersed, less well organized consumers. However, higher lumber prices lead to market substitution (of nonwood products for lumber and of non-North American lumber for North American lumber), which tends to alleviate lumber consumers' pain. Finally, under U.S. trade law, consumers do not have standing in the softwood lumber dispute and cannot participate in the negotiation or legal battles, even though they eventually pay the majority of the costs associated with any tariff or restrictive measures on lumber imports. In Department of Commerce, U.S. International Trade Commission, or court hearings, U.S. consumer groups can only file amicus briefs as "friends of the court." Legally, U.S. consumers are at a disadvantage.

The major players in the dispute, then, are U.S. lumber producers, U.S. consumers, and Canadian producers, with the U.S. and Canadian governments as representatives, middlemen, negotiators, and arbitrators. This is not to say that either U.S. producers or Canadian producers are a homogeneous group. In fact, Canadian lumber producers are sometimes too divided to build a consistent and united front. Nonetheless, Canadian producers have more in common with each other than with the U.S. producers.

Research Methods

The research methods used in this book include a mixture of historical, legal, institutional, analytical, comparative, and economic approaches. Forestry, forest resources, and forest resource ownerships provide background information. The historical and legal approaches review past and current events and laws and regulations to provide a historical account of the dispute—what happened, who did what, what the rules of the game were, and what results ensued. The institutional approach focuses on the institutions, institutional environments, and decisionmaking organizations, including the U.S. and Canadian constitutions, major policymaking branches of the governments and administrative agencies, interest groups in both countries, and international trade dispute settlement mechanisms.

The analytical approach is based on public choice theory. In particular, interest group politics is used to document the rise and fall of major interest groups involved in the dispute, their motivations, and their strategies and tactics in advancing their interests.

The comparative approach involves contrasting the lumber dispute with disputes over other forest products (logs, shakes and shingles, and newsprint) between the two countries in a historical and political economy framework. The economic approach relies on welfare economics and market impact studies: who wins, who loses, and by how much? These results are used in explaining interactions between interest groups and government branches and the political economy of the dispute—why the results are what they are and in which direction the dispute will go.

3

Lumber I

The First Shot, 1982–1983

The late 1970s witnessed an unprecedented, dramatic increase in federal timber contract prices in the U.S. Pacific Northwest (Figure 3-1). A crisis followed in the early 1980s, when timber values fell precipitously, leaving timber buyers holding contracts that obliged them to pay prices roughly five times greater than the then-current value of the timber. The cause of this crisis has been attributed to federal timber sale procedures, macroeconomic policy—in an effort to curb the inflationary spiral developing in the United States, the Federal Reserve Board instituted a restrictive monetary policy in October 1979 that resulted in record-high interest rates, a collapse in the U.S. housing market, and a severe recession—and human judgment errors, primarily speculation by timber buyers on a timber shortage. In the end, Congress enacted a controversial bailout under the Federal Timber Contract Payment Modifications Act of 1984. The cost of the bailout in U.S. Forest Service Region 6 (Washington, Oregon, and Northern California) alone, where 190 firms applied for the bailout, was estimated at US$5 billon (Mattey 1990).

At that time, most of the buyers of federal timber were small and medium-size sawmills, some of which were represented by the Northwest Independent Forest Manufacturers Association (NIFM), based in Tacoma, Washington. In 1981, federal timber buyers and others that used federal resources organized a lobby group called the Western Resource Alliance, whose headquarters was in Eugene, Oregon, and whose primary objective was to lobby for a federal bailout of timber contracts. The alliance worked with NIFM and other organizations, and in 1984, after securing the bailout, it disbanded itself.

Meanwhile, NIFM and others in the Pacific Northwest contemplated asking the U.S. government to restrict softwood lumber imports from Canada. In a meeting in the summer of 1980, the NIFM board of directors discussed the Canadian lumber issue for the first time (Kuehne 2006). Apparently, some NIFM members noticed that whereas they were held accountable for the federal timber contracts (until the 1984 bailout), lumber producers in British

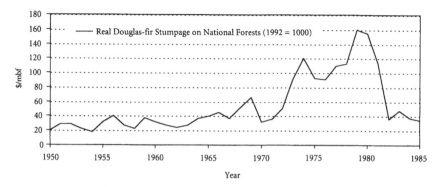

FIGURE 3-1. Real Douglas-fir Stumpage Prices on National Forests in the U.S. Pacific Northwest, 1950–1985

Sources: Ulrich (1990) and Howard (2001).

Columbia, who collectively accounted for nearly 70 percent of Canadian softwood lumber exports to the United States at the time, were able to get a break in stumpage fees from a sympathetic provincial government in the wake of the collapse of U.S. lumber markets. NIFM further noted that the Canadian share of U.S. lumber consumption increased during the recession. Previously, the Canadian share of U.S. lumber consumption fell in a greater proportion (than the U.S. share) when the United States was in a recession, suggesting that Canada was a marginal lumber supplier in U.S. markets. The increasing Canadian share during a U.S. recession threatened the competitive position of the U.S. industry and perhaps signaled that Canada was no longer a marginal player but now a major supplier of softwood lumber to its southern neighbor. NIFM thus began a campaign to attribute the Pacific Northwest lumber industry's problems to Canadian lumber imports.

Marston Johnson (Gus) Kuehne, of Washington State, was the executive vice president of NIFM. With the help of Don Bonker, a Democratic U.S. representative from his state, Kuehne met, on September 5, 1980, an official from the Department of Commerce who explained to him what NIFM ought to do if it wanted to restrict Canadian lumber imports. Kuehne (2006) later said that he had known nothing about countervailing and antidumping duties or other trade restrictive measures before meeting that official.

On October 20, 1980, Kuehne met with Barry Cullen, an assistant lobbyist for the International Paper Company, and discussed his intention of appealing for restrictive measures on Canadian lumber. In previous years, International Paper Company, which had been one of the largest foreign investors in the Canadian forest sector, had felt compelled to sell a Canadian subsidiary, Canadian International Paper Company, citing particular concern over what it viewed as government favoritism given to eastern Canadian mills and provincial government aid given to a Québec Crown corporation, Rexfor, Inc. (Jansen

1984). These two decided to recruit other U.S. producers and establish a coalition. Kuehne was responsible for recruiting small and medium sawmillers and
their associations, and Cullen for large, integrated producers. The first meeting
for the yet-to-be named coalition took place on November 10, 1980, in NIFM
offices. As events progressed, the campaign evolved into the U.S. Coalition for
Fair Canadian Lumber Imports, and Paul Ehinger, executive vice president of
Western Resource Alliance, served as the chairman (Kuehne 2006).

NIFM led a series of loosely organized meetings to explore ways to deal with
the Canadian lumber problem. On August 20, 1981, NIFM released a report
critical of low Canadian stumpage fees and the Canadian softwood lumber
incursion into the U.S. market. The report alleged that government subsidies
to Canadian lumber producers permitted them to undercut U.S. producers,
increasing unemployment in the U.S. Pacific Northwest (Shinn 1987). The
report called upon the government to investigate and suggested, as an outcome, imposition of a tariff on Canadian lumber imports.

Following the release of the NIFM report, the governor of Oregon, Victor
Atiyeh, in early September 1981, asked Oregon's congressional leader, Senator
Robert Packwood (R, ranking member of the Senate Finance Committee and
chair of the Senate Taxation and Debt Management Subcommittee) to "conduct hearings to determine the extent to which Canadian lumber exports to this
country have damaged our own forest products industry" (Atiyeh 1981, 54). In
October, the governor appointed a "timber strategy panel" to inquire into problems facing the lumber industry in Oregon. The panel rendered its report in
November, finding that one of many factors that had contributed to Oregon's
loss of market share was "Canadian subsidies to that nation's forest products
industry." That, combined with a then-favorable exchange rate, gave Canadian
lumber exports "a substantial competitive advantage in the U.S." (Oregon Governor's Timber Strategy Panel 1981, 72).

On November 17, 1981, at Senator Packwood's invitation, Kuehne attended
a hearing organized by Senator William S. Cohen (R, chair of the Governmental Affairs Subcommittee on Oversight of Government Management). The
hearing concerned the impact of Canadian imports (fish and seed potatoes as
well as lumber) on U.S. domestic producers (Kuehne 2006).

One week later, on November 24, in response to Governor Atiyeh's request,
Senator Packwood teamed up with Senator John C. Danforth (R-Missouri)
and organized a joint hearing of the International Trade Subcommittee, which
Danforth chaired, and the Taxation and Debt Management Subcommittee to
discuss forest products industry issues, one of which was increasing Canadian
lumber imports. Four other senators on these two subcommittees, including
Senator Max Baucus (D-Montana), who would play a big role in the lumber
war, made an appearance. Senator Cohen, Governor Atiyeh, and Paul Ehinger
testified, as did representatives of the U.S. trade representative, the Department
of Commerce, NIFM, the Oregon Governor's Timber Strategy Panel, and a few

sawmills from the Northwest and Maine. Senator Packwood offered a resolution to request that the U.S. International Trade Commission (ITC) investigate Canadian lumber imports under Section 332 of the Tariff Act of 1930. Senators Baucus and Cohen as well as several others who testified were critical of Canadian lumber imports and supported this resolution.

Although import restrictions cannot be imposed as a result of such an investigation, it is an avenue for American producer groups to gather evidence at the taxpayers' expense on which to launch a trade complaint later. In fact, the representative of NIFM stated in the joint hearing that the Section 332 investigation "could greatly reduce the expenses we might have in pursuing the filing of a countervailing duty petition" (Westbrook 1981). On December 2, 1981, Senator Packwood, along with Senate Finance Committee Chairman Bob Dole (R-Kansas), John Danforth, and House Ways and Means Committee Chairman Sam Gibbons (D-Florida), formally asked ITC to investigate Canadian lumber imports (Gorte 2001).

On April 19, 1982, the executive summary of the ITC study was released; the full study was released one week later. ITC (1982) found that the increase in Canadian imports resulted from the strength of the U.S. dollar and from low stumpage fees and transportation costs in Canada. However, the principal allegations were refuted: No subsidies were found for Canadian producers, and although Canadian producers had lower stumpage costs than did American producers, log prices were similar on both sides of the border. Thus the difference in stumpage was not considered a Canadian subsidy.

* * *

Those findings mirrored those by a Canadian forest economist and then-associate professor at the University of British Columbia, David Haley, whose article entitled "A regional comparison of stumpage values in British Columbia and the United States Pacific Northwest," was published in the October 1980 issue of the *Forestry Chronicle*, a Canadian professional forestry journal. Haley (1980) found that stumpage in the U.S. Pacific Northwest was considerably higher than in British Columbia and that real stumpage (net of inflationary increases) showed an upward trend in the U.S. Pacific Northwest compared with a slight downward trend for British Columbia between 1963 and 1978. He concluded that the stumpage appraisal methods used in the two regions were similar and that the principal reason for high stumpage value in the U.S. Pacific Northwest was that public forestry agencies encouraged competitive bidding for standing timber, whereas in British Columbia competitive sales of public timber had been virtually eliminated.

Haley (1980) did not infer that low stumpage was a subsidy that gave Canadian lumber producers an advantage over the U.S. producers. But his article provided some ammunition to the U.S. producers in asserting that Canadian producers were subsidized.

Also in 1980, two American forest economists published an article in *Forest Science,* which mentioned Canadian lumber imports. Darius M. Adams and Richard W. Haynes (1980) examined the impact of a 15 percent *ad valorem* duty on Canadian lumber imports and concluded that such a tariff would drastically reduce Canadian lumber exports to the United States. Although they noted that, to their knowledge, no specific tariff had been proposed on Canadian lumber imports, they, too, had taken up a subject of interest to the U.S. industry.

* * *

Canadian producers interpreted the ITC study as a vindication of the Canadian position, but Senator Packwood saw it differently. He said, "This study gives the industry the facts it needs to initiate the review of grievances provided by the law ... I would urge the U.S. industry to study this report very carefully because a case certainly can be made, based on its findings" (*Vancouver Sun* 1982).

On July 14, 1982, six U.S. regional sawmill organizations announced that they would file a petition with the Department of Commerce within 45 days. After a considerable delay, the Coalition for Fair Canadian Lumber Imports filed its petition on October 7, 1982, requesting a countervailing duty of 65 percent on Canadian softwood lumber, shakes and shingles, and fencing. The petition alleged that the Canadian provinces unfairly lowered stumpage prices to ensure that Canadian exports could compete in the U.S. market. The lowered stumpage prices resulted from the provinces' administrative stumpage price determination procedure and conferred an export and domestic subsidy on Canadian lumber production. According to the petition, the value of the stumpage subsidy amounted to US$113.78 per thousand board feet (mbf) of lumber. This, plus the subsidy of US$7.16/mbf in other government programs, created a total subsidy of US$120.94/mbf, or 65 percent. That petition marked the start of the first phase of the softwood lumber "war" in the modern era—known as Lumber I.

The petitioners under the umbrella of the coalition included NIFM, Southern Forest Products Association, Southeastern Lumber Manufacturers Association, International Paper Company, Louisiana-Pacific Corporation, Union Camp, Willamette Industries, and some 350 independent sawmills. Only two companies—Louisiana-Pacific and International Paper—were on the top-10 list of U.S. lumber producers. Like International Paper, Louisiana-Pacific had previously had unfavorable experiences in Canada (with regard to its operation in Salmo, British Columbia) (Jansen 1984). Coalition members accounted for only 20 percent of U.S. lumber production in 1981–1982 (Apsey and Thomas 1997): The majority of U.S. lumber producers were silent or not directly involved. Even the Western Wood Products Association, which represented some 100 mills in the U.S. Pacific Northwest—far more than the 35 mills represented by NIFM—was not part of the coalition.

A Historical Detour

If one looks to the broader category of forest products, this was not the first significant trade dispute between the United States and Canada. Lumber and other forest products were included in the U.S. tariff acts as early as 1794, although a specific rate on lumber made its appearance only in 1872. The 1982 petition was not the first complaint about Canadian lumber imports, either.

The very first large trade dispute over forest products between the two countries, as Reed (1986, 2001) indicates, was actually about land and transportation. In the 1820s and 1830s, disputes over forest lands—control over which affected the profitability of lumber mills—and transportation of logs and lumber along the Aroostook River and the upper St. John River between Maine and New Brunswick threatened the peace between the United States and the British colonies for years.

The cause of those disputes was ambiguities in the description of the boundary between the Maine territory, then administered by Massachusetts, and the colony of New Brunswick. When high lumber demand prompted timber shortages in the early 1830s, loggers from Maine and New Brunswick started to fight for the ownership of timberland in the Aroostook River basin, which flows from the highlands of north-central Maine a distance of 150 miles before joining the St. John River above Fredericton. Maine loggers had no road or river access from Bangor into Aroostook and insisted that they had the right to harvest these logs and bring them down the St. John River. Officials from both Maine and New Brunswick tried to assert control over timber cutting and the collection of timber license fees in the area (Reed 2001).

The dispute was solved under the Ashburton-Webster Treaty of 1842, which drew a boundary line that placed Aroostook timberland within Maine. The British received a strategic winter access route from the ice-free port of St. John north and northwest by way of the Madawaska River and the Temiscouata Portage into Québec City (Reed 2001).

There was still no road access at the time to move logs from the Aroostook area to Maine sawmills, so an ingenious arrangement was adopted. Aroostook logs were granted free entry into New Brunswick via the St. John River and could be sawn in St. John or other New Brunswick locations. The sawn products then could be exported to Great Britain or to the British West Indies under Empire Preference tariffs. In essence, it was an arrangement of free trade of logs for manufacturing of lumber, and manufacturing of lumber for free trade of lumber within British territories: a compromise and, in today's parlance, a win–win solution.

Another large trade dispute in forest products was the 1897–1913 newsprint tariff battle, which had a similar cause as the late-20th-century softwood lumber dispute—and lasted about as long. Chapter 10 covers this dispute.

Lumber trade also figured prominently in an 1853 debate when the U.S. House of Representatives considered the Reciprocity Treaty with "the Canadas." The remark of an Ohio congressman, N.S. Townshend, bears some resemblance to statements heard since 1980 in the softwood lumber debate:

> The British Provinces have almost inexhaustible supplies of pine lumber. This is greatly needed ... But Maine, for which a large share of the best timber is already cut, wants to exclude the lumber of the Canadas, and to force her [Maine's] spruce and inferior pine on the market at high prices. It is asserted that unless competition from the Provinces is prevented, and the absolute monopoly of the trade be secured to Maine, her hardy lumbermen cannot make fair wages, because as they express it "stumpage is so high."
>
> The hardy lumbermen, over whom tears are almost shed, are not benefited in the least, but rather injured by the high duties, and all this humbug of protection is not designed for their benefit but for the benefit of the wealthy few. (Cited in Reed 2001, 50)

In the tariff act of 1872 a duty of $1/mbf was levied on hemlock, "white wood," sycamore, and basswood, and a rate of $2/mbf on pine and other kinds of lumber. These duties caused considerable resentment in Canada, and Ontario retaliated with an export duty of $2/mbf on logs, with serious injury to sawmills in the GreatLakes States, which depended on Canada for their supply (Dana 1956). The tariff acts would be revised several times, and attempts were made to encourage Ontario to abolish its log exports policy. In 1913, the Underwood Tariff Act placed lumber on the free list, where it remained until 1930.

In 1930, a duty of $1/mbf was again assessed on Canadian lumber. This rose to $4/mbf, which was equivalent to a tariff of 24 to 30 percent in 1932, when lumber prices were severely depressed because of the Great Depression (Reed 2001). A 1935 trade negotiation reduced the duty to $1/mbf, but a quantitative limitation on shipments from Canada was imposed. It was not until 1939, with the advent of the Second World War, that the quantitative limitation was eliminated. The duty was temporarily waived from October 1946 to August 1947 by President Truman because of an emergency in U.S. housing construction.

In 1947, the U.S. Tariff Commission (the predecessor of ITC) stated, "From the standpoint of the long term public interest, the United States will face an increasingly important conservation problem as a result of heavy drain on U.S. forests which will be required to support the postwar demand" (cited in Reed 2001, 59).

In 1962, a Pacific Northwest group called Lumbermen's Economic Survival Coalition filed a petition with the U.S. Tariff Commission for relief when the Canadian share of U.S. lumber consumption had risen from 7 percent of volume in 1950 to 15 percent in 1961. Two weeks of hearings were held in October 1962. On February 14, 1963, the Tariff Commission ruled unanimously against the petition, finding that increased imports were caused by a "limited commercial availability of softwood timber in the U.S." (Reed 2001, *60*).

In the ensuing decade, the United States took a leading role in the formation of the General Agreement on Tariffs and Trade (GATT), which set the tone for liberalized trade relations with Canada and the rest of the globe. The new U.S. tariff rates on Canadian lumber were $0.25/mbf on northern white pine and western white spruce, $1/mbf on other spruce, fir, western hemlock, larch, and other pine, and $0.75/mbf on red cedar. As lumber prices rose rapidly, these per-unit tariff rates quickly approached zero in *ad valorem*. On August 15, 1971, a surcharge of $3–$4/mbf (or 3 to 5 percent *ad valorem*) was placed on Canadian lumber imports by the Nixon administration (Widman Management 1982).

The highlight of U.S.–Canada lumber relations was the Kennedy Round of GATT in 1972, when the two countries agreed to duty-free entry of softwood lumber. A North American "common market" in lumber was achieved. In addition, certain U.S. government officials privately sought long-term assurances that Canadian lumber would continue to be freely available, since the United States was running a sizable deficit in consumption, in relation to domestic lumber production, and they feared badly inflated lumber prices if Canadian supplies were reduced or withdrawn. During the same "honeymoon," both countries agreed for the first time to common grading standards, lumber sizes, stress ratings, and span tables, with full commercial recognition of species produced on both sides of the border (Widman Management 1982).

U.S. Trade Remedy Measures

The 1962 petition asked for relief under the "safeguard" clause of U.S. trade law; the 1982 petition asked for countervailing duties. Safeguard relief is based on what is known as the escape clause under Sections 201–04 of the Trade Act of 1974 (19 U.S.C. Sections 2251–2254). If ITC determines that imports have caused or threaten to cause serious injury to a U.S. industry, the president "shall take all appropriate and feasible action," including temporary duties, quotas, and other import restrictions, to give the domestic industry an opportunity to recover its competitiveness (ITC 1998). This protection is available even if the imports are traded fairly. The five-year tariffs on imports of Canadian shakes and shingles in 1986 by President Reagan (see Chapter 4) and year-to-year tariffs on certain steel product imports by President George W. Bush in 2002 are examples of protection under the safeguard clause.

Countervailing duties, on the other hand, are based on findings that imports are subsidized directly or indirectly by a foreign government and that the imports have injured or threatened to injure a U.S. industry. Countervailing relief is authorized under Sections 701 to 709 of the Tariff Act of 1930, as amended (19 U.S.C. Section 1671 et seq.). A countervailing duty (equal to the amount of the net subsidy) is imposed if (1) the Department of Commerce determines that a country (or a person, corporation, association, or other organization in that country) is providing, directly or indirectly, a subsidy for the manufacture, production, or export of merchandise imported into the United States; and (2) ITC determines that a U.S. industry is materially injured or threatened with material injury, or the establishment of a U.S. industry is materially retarded, by those imports.

The procedural timetables of the Department of Commerce and ITC are as follows. After a petition is received, Commerce has 20 days to decide whether it will initiate an inquiry. If Commerce decides to make an inquiry, ITC must begin its injury investigation and render its preliminary finding within 45 days of the date on which the petition is filed. Commerce makes its preliminary findings about the existence of a subsidy within either 85 or 150 days of the date on which the petition is received. If it is an affirmative determination, ITC must resume its injury investigation. Commerce has 75 days after issuing its preliminary finding to render its final determination. If the determination is positive, ITC must make its final injury determination within 45 days. The entire process has a maximum length of 270 days.

Section 1677(5) of the Trade Agreements Act of 1979 defines subsidy as having the same meaning as the term "bounty or grant." It includes any export subsidy and the following domestic subsidies (if provided or required by government action to a *specific* enterprise or industry, or a group of enterprises or industries, whether publicly or privately owned, and whether paid directly or indirectly for the manufacture, production, or export of merchandise): (1) the provision of capital, loans, or loan guarantees on terms inconsistent with commercial considerations; (2) the provision of goods and services at *preferential* rates; (3) the grant of funds or forgiveness of debt to cover operating losses sustained by a specific industry; or (4) the assumption of any costs or expenses of manufacture, production, or distribution.

Thus, proof of subsidy must pass the tests of *specificity* and *preferentiality*. Specificity means that the foreign government program in question must be specific—limited to an enterprise or industry, or a group of enterprises or industries—as opposed to generally available items, such as infrastructure support. Preferentiality means that the benefits conferred to the recipients are substantially higher than for nonrecipients. The degree of preference, if any, would constitute the amount of the subsidy (ITC 1998).

The Coalition for Fair Canadian Lumber Imports also considered, but subsequently did not pursue, an antidumping charge against Canadian lumber imports in 1982. Antidumping relief is authorized in Sections 713–739 of the Tariff Act of 1930, as amended (19 U.S.C. Section 1673 et seq.). Under this provision, Commerce determines whether imports are being sold in the U.S. market at unfairly low prices—lower than in the exporter's home market—and ITC determines whether the dumping has injured a U.S. industry. Positive findings of dumping and injury would lead to the imposition of an antidumping duty on those imports. As we will see, antidumping relief was also considered in 1986 (during Lumber II) but was not pursued until 2001 (during Lumber IV)—partly because of the complexity involved in gathering company-specific data to demonstrate "unfairly low prices."

Finally, the U.S. government considered in Lumber II, and used in Lumber III, Sections 301–302 of the Trade Act of 1974, as amended (19 U.S.C. Section 2411 et seq.). Section 301 is a statutory authority under which the United States may impose trade sanctions against foreign countries that maintain acts, policies, and practices that violate (or deny U.S. rights or benefits under) trade agreements, or are unjustifiable, unreasonable, or discriminatory and burden or restrict U.S. commerce. The U.S. trade representative, upon request or self-initiation, handles Section 301 investigations and decides U.S. trade sanctions, which can include duties or other import restrictions.

Canadian Responses

Although calls for restricting Canadian lumber imports surfaced in previous economic recessions and disappeared afterward, this time the Canadian forest industry considered the threat more serious (Apsey and Thomas 1997). To answer the subsidy allegation and present a united front, the Canadian industry formed the Canadian Softwood Lumber Committee. Because the ITC Section 332 inquiry focused primarily on British Columbia, the president of the Council of Forest Industry of British Columbia, Donald Lanskail, initially led and coordinated the committee and later served as a cochair (along with Adam Zimmerman, president of Noranda Mines Ltd., which owned forest companies across Canada). Its inaugural meeting took place on December 14, 1981, only a few days after ITC initiated its Section 332 inquiry and long before the countervailing duty petition was filed. The objectives of the meeting were to review the issue, lay the groundwork for organizing a Canadian industry response to the ITC investigation, and ensure the cooperation of the federal and provincial governments (Jansen 1984).

The Canadian forest products industry was united throughout Lumber I (Jansen 1984). It realized that although the stumpage subsidy allegations were directed at lumber, shake and shingle, and fence producers, they could seriously harm the entire industry if they were accepted by the Department of Commerce. The harvest of timber for all products is subject to stumpage, and a duty could be applied to these products as well. The value of softwood lumber accounted for less than 25 percent of Canadian forest products exports to the United States in 1981, the year covered by the investigation. Newsprint exports, valued at more than C$3.3 billion, accounted for 40 percent of exports, and wood pulp exports accounted for slightly more than the value of softwood lumber (Jansen 1984).

Maintaining unity was also important when the Department of Commerce made technical calculations to determine the extent of the subsidies, which basically involved dividing the amount of subsidies found by the total production during the time of the investigation. The result would be an average amount of subsidy per unit of production. By persuading Commerce to do a national rather than regional or company-specific determination and ensuring that the production denominator was as large as possible, the average would be minimized.

In August 1982, the Canadian Softwood Lumber Committee retained Arnold and Porter as its legal counsel in Washington, DC. The head of the legal team was Robert Herzstein, a former assistant secretary of Commerce for import administration who had played a prominent role in drafting the 1979 Trade Agreement Act, which covers the countervailing duty law. The legal team had two months to familiarize itself with the forest industry in Canada and the United States before the countervailing duty investigation started in late October 1982 (Jansen 1984).

The committee decided not to ask the Canadian government to interfere with the Department of Commerce and the quasijudicial ITC investigations. Nonetheless, the Canadian federal and provincial governments distributed questionnaires to lumber companies in mid-January 1983 and supplied data concerning all alleged subsidy programs to the Department of Commerce. The Canadian government sent two diplomatic notes to the U.S. government in October and December 1982, stating that Canada believed the subsidy allegations to have neither substance nor merit and that any injury to the domestic U.S. industry must, according to GATT rules, be material and causally linked to imports from Canada. In addition, the provincial ministers responsible for forest management from British Columbia, Ontario, and Québec— accompanied by Canadian Ambassador Allan Gotlieb—visited U.S. Secretary of Commerce Malcolm Baldrige. The visit was intended to convey a united Canadian front and reduce the opportunity for any political interference. The Canadians were assured that the countervailing duty investigation was not going to be influenced by political pressure from within the United States or anywhere else (Jansen 1984).

Satisfied that Commerce would decide the case on its merits, the Canadian Softwood Lumber Committee decided to maintain a low profile and minimize politicizing the issue while keeping government and opposition leaders informed. A low profile was also thought necessary to make the issue nonpartisan and sustain a united front at home and facilitate the continuing neutrality of the 80 percent of the U.S. lumber industry not involved in the case (Jansen 1984).

1983 Determination by Commerce

On March 7, 1983, the Department of Commerce issued a preliminary negative determination. On May 25, 1983, the agency issued a final negative determination, in which it found that no subsidy had been conferred by provincial stumpage programs and that other government programs provided a total net subsidy that was *de minimis* (less than 0.5 percent of the value of production).

Spokespersons for the Canadian industry and governments as well as the U.S. government insisted that this was not a political decision. Secretary Baldrige said, "No other consideration except the law and the facts was involved [in the decision]" (*Vancouver Sun* 1983). Several years later, Gary Horlick, the deputy assistant secretary at Commerce who was responsible for the decision, said, "I can look you or anyone else in the face and tell you that *Lumber I* was not political" (Dezell 1992, *16*). Commerce might not have been pressured politically in Lumber I, but lobbying is a political activity, and the decision had political and economic implications.

In its final determination, the Department of Commerce (DOC 1983) stated that stumpage programs were not an export subsidy because they were not tied to export performance. The programs were widely available for a number of industries, such as the pulp and paper industry and the furniture industry, and thus did not pass the specificity test for a domestic subsidy. In particular,

> ... stumpage programs are not provided to a "specific enterprise or industry or group of enterprises or industries." Rather, they are available within Canada on similar terms regardless of the industry or enterprise of the recipient. The only limitations as to the types of industries that use stumpage reflect the inherent characteristics of this natural resource and the current level of technology.... Any current limitations on the use are not due to activities of the Canadian governments.
>
> Although nominal general availability of a program does not necessarily suffice to avoid its being considered a possible domestic subsidy, the Department further determined that stumpage is used within Canada by several groups of industries ...
>
> Therefore, in view of its general availability without government limitation and its use by wide-ranging and diverse industries, we determine that stumpage is not provided to a "specific group of enterprises or industries." (DOC 1983, *24167*)

Commerce further stated that even if the stumpage programs were specific to the lumber industry, they did not provide goods at preferential rates to the producers of the products under investigation. In doing so, Commerce stuck to its policy "not to use cross-border comparisons ..." and reasoned that "a [cross-border] comparison of Canadian stumpage prices with U.S. prices would be arbitrary and capricious in view of (1) the wide differences between species composition; size, quality and density of timber; terrain and accessibility of the standing timber throughout the United States and Canada; (2) the additional payments which are required in many provinces in Canada, but not generally in the United States ..." (DOC 1983, *24168*)

Further, Commerce (1983, *24182*) stated, "It is not the Department of Commerce's policy to use cross-border comparisons in establishing commercial benchmarks because such *comparisons fail to account for difference in comparative advantage between countries*" (emphasis added).

In other words, Commerce recognized that by attempting to value Canadian timber at U.S. prices, the cross-border comparison method turned the law of comparative advantage into a law of comparative disadvantage. This would surely distort world trade order.

Finally, Commerce stated,

Even if one believes that there is a rational basis for comparing U.S. and Canadian stumpage prices, the record of investigations includes studies showing that once appropriate adjustments are made to take into account the differences in quality, accessibility, as well as additional cash payments and in-kind services, Canadian prices for standing timber do not vary significantly from U.S. prices. Indeed, in some cases the Canadian prices may be higher. Therefore, even if one were to use U.S. prices as a benchmark, there is evidence in the record which establishes that the Canadian governments do not assume costs of production through their stumpage programs. (DOC 1983, *24168*)

The Coalition for Fair Canadian Lumber Imports challenged Commerce's preliminary determination of "no subsidy" at the U.S. Court of International Trade and lost. It did not appeal or seek judicial review for the final determination. This concluded the period called Lumber I.

4

Lumber II

A New Coalition and the Memorandum of Understanding, 1984–1986

Lumber I had been led by a regional association of independent lumber producers from the U.S. Pacific Northwest, but the next two rounds of the dispute would be led by large forest products firms in the United States, and the impetus would come from producers in North America's other major softwood lumber-producing region, the South.

In fall 1983, the Southeastern Lumber Manufacturers Association established a fund of $120,000 for publicizing the alleged Canadian lumber threat to the United States. The southern producers hoped to gain public support, persuade state and county authorities to enact "buy American" legislation, and obtain support from southern congressional legislators for action by the Reagan administration to pressure Canada to accept a voluntary quota on lumber exports to the United States (Jansen 1984).

Meanwhile, International Paper Company continued its campaign against Canadian lumber and tried to bring other large lumber producers along. Because the 1984 federal timber bailout did not cover large, financially solvent companies and because lumber prices did not increase much after U.S. housing starts picked up in 1983–1984, the U.S. lumber industry was faced with sustained low profit margins and even losses. Some sawmills inevitably shut down. It was at this juncture that several large forest products companies started to consider forming a new coalition to deal with the problem of rising Canadian lumber imports.

The Canadian industry was vigilant. Even though the Department of Commerce's 1983 negative determination on countervailing duties might have led some in the Canadian industry and government to believe that the case was closed, others realized that Canadian lumber exports to the United States were highly vulnerable to trade actions (Apsey and Thomas 1997). On March 13, 1984, the Canadian Forest Industries Council was established, and it provided a mechanism for Canadian forest companies to fight trade actions and raise the industry's profile in Ottawa, until it dissolved itself in 1998. The council was founded by 16 industry associations and represented more than 90 percent of the industrial forest users in Canada. It took over trade functions from the ad hoc Canadian Softwood Lumber Committee, and its first chairman was Adam Zimmerman, the committee's former cochair (Jansen 1984).

A New Section 332 Investigation

On October 22, 1984, a group of five companies—Georgia-Pacific Corporation, International Paper Company, Potlatch Corporation, Roseburg Forest Products, and Louisiana-Pacific Corporation (which subsequently dropped out)—met in Dallas and put up seed money to establish a new coalition. This group called on the U.S. trade representative (USTR) to undertake high-level negotiations with the Canadians. Its early efforts, although disorganized, generated one significant result: On March 6, 1985, the USTR, at the direction of the president, asked the U.S. International Trade Commission (ITC) to conduct another Section 332 investigation, updating its 1982 study and reporting all significant factors affecting the competitive status of the U.S. and Canadian softwood lumber industries.

The Coalition for Fair Lumber Imports was officially formed on May 14, 1985. As in any new organization, its participants wanted to proceed in different directions, and a perception existed that the new coalition could not win (Shinn 1987). Two separate events got the coalition off the ground and running.

First, Georgia-Pacific Corporation and the Washington, D.C.–based National Forest Products Association, neither of which had taken sides in Lumber I, joined the new coalition.[1] Stanley S. Dennison, executive vice president of Georgia-Pacific Corporation, served as the first chairman. Second, the coalition agreed to retain legal counsel. After a thorough search, it selected the Washington office of a New York firm—Dewey, Ballantine, Bushby, Palmer, and Wood (later changed to Dewey Ballantine LLP).[2] These two events ensured that the new coalition would be stronger than its predecessor. The latter move was described as "one of the smartest decisions the Coalition made" (Shinn 1987, 10).

A trade lawyer, Alan Wm. Wolff, from Dewey Ballantine, was the chief legal counsel to the coalition. Wolff had served as the U.S. deputy special representative for trade negotiations between 1977 and 1979 and held the rank of ambassador after having served as general counsel of the USTR from 1974 to 1977. He played an important role in the formulation and implementation of American trade policy in the 1970s. Although other lawyers also were involved, one young lawyer at the time, John Ragosta, showed great interest in the issue. He would gradually become the chief spokesman and counsel for the coalition as the lumber war continued in the next two decades.

Wolff, Ragosta, Dennison, and others, on behalf of the coalition, went to a public hearing conducted by ITC on its Section 332 investigation on July 23,

1985. Other witnesses appearing at the hearing included T. Mike Apsey of the Canadian Forest Industries Council, Lawrence A. Schneider (the Canadian council's counsel), and representatives from the National Lumber and Building Material Dealers Association. Senator Max Baucus (D-Montana) and Representatives Don Bonker (D-Washington), James Weaver (D-Oregon), and Larry Craig (R-Idaho), all from lumber-producing states, also made an appearance. The hearing had two panels: one on current conditions in the U.S. market, and the other to relate Canadian stumpage practices to market conditions.

The new Section 332 report (ITC 1985), issued in October, reached a conclusion similar to that in 1982: Canadian stumpage fees were lower than those in the United States. In addition, stumpage rates had risen about US$1/mbf (to US$11.84/mbf) in Canada between 1982 and 1984, while average U.S. stumpage prices had increased approximately US$10/mbf (to $US104.16/mbf). The report further noted that, in general, delivered wood costs, average variable costs, fixed costs, and residual unit values (profits) were lower in Canada than in the United States.

However, the difference in variable production costs was very small. In 1984, the U.S. industry's total aggregate variable cost to produce softwood lumber was only US$8/mbf higher than that of the Canadian industry. In the highest cost regions—the Pacific Northwest—the corresponding costs were US$265/mbf in coastal British Columbia and $251/mbf in Oregon and Washington (ITC 1985, *xi, 81–83*).

The report acknowledged that Canada had adequate softwood timber resources under the supply-and-demand conditions in Canadian markets. It stated,

> The current supply of timber in most regions of Canada is more than sufficient to meet the productivity capacity of the license holders. In the United States, the allowable cut [supply] from government lands and the offerings from private lands have been held at fairly constant levels in recent years, resulting in intense competitive bidding for sales of both government and private timber. (ITC 1985, *xi*)

Canadian sawmills also gained in productivity over U.S. sawmills in the same time period. The report noted, "Canadian employees produced about 100 board feet more softwood lumber per hour than U.S. employees" (ITC 1985, *x*). This conclusion, which favored Canadian producers, would be revised a few months later.

The Coalition's Grass-Roots Efforts and a Divided Opposition

The Coalition for Fair Lumber Imports did two things that were markedly different from its predecessor's work: It engaged in grass-root efforts, and it politicized its concerns on Capitol Hill. The grass-roots efforts increased membership. David Wang, a senior vice president of International Paper Company, commented in July 1986 that the coalition represented more than 70 percent of U.S. softwood lumber production (Shinn 1987). Since the coalition has never released a complete list of its members, however, it is not possible to verify this claim.

The coalition had the general support of the National Forest Products Association and several regional forest products associations. Not all these associations' members, however, actually supported the coalition. Weyerhaeuser Company and Boise Cascade—both members of the National Forest Products Association in the 1980s—stayed neutral, for example. Since only 3 of the 10 largest softwood lumber producers at the time—Georgia-Pacific (ranked 4th), International Paper (6th), and Rosenburg Forest Products (10th)—were members of the coalition and the other 7 companies were not (based on Shinn's 1987 interview of a dozen top U.S. lumber producers), it is unlikely that the 70 percent claim was true. On the other hand, foreign-owned companies in the United States or U.S. companies with substantial interest in Canada (such as Weyerhaeuser Company) would be legally considered neutral for trade actions.

Nonetheless, individual companies that stayed neutral on the issue—whether because they espoused the principle of free trade or because they had interests in Canada—did not become visible and vocal critics of the coalition. None of them spoke out against it or its 1986 petition for countervailing duties. The coalition, which was waging a vocal and political campaign against Canadian lumber imports, could take considerable satisfaction that no large U.S. lumber producer was presenting a contrary public position. It was thus able to freely lobby Congress and the Reagan administration as an industrial representative. This was probably important in the assessment of the issue by both the legislative and the executive branches.

The opposition to the Coalition for Fair Lumber Imports came primarily from Canada. In the forefront were the Canadian industry and federal and provincial governments. The Canadian Forest Industries Council, individual companies, and the Canadian federal and several provincial governments all had legal counsel in Washington, D.C. There were various communications between Prime Minister Brain Mulroney and President Ronald Reagan. The Canadians' lobby and the administration's appeals to Congress were based on a good bilateral relationship and Canada's support of U.S. positions in international arenas. But naturally, U.S. congressional representatives are less responsive to public sentiments and industry positions in Canada than they are to those at home.

Canadian producers do have natural allies in the United States—softwood lumber dealers and consumers. The National Lumber and Building Material Dealers Association and the National Association of Home Builders, along with other associations and individual firms, organized an ad hoc Coalition to Stop Unfair Wood Tariffs.[3] This group's primary concern was higher lumber prices as a result of a tariff on Canadian imports. However, it was not well organized and was ineffective in its lobbying efforts, and its members, in particular the National Association of Home Builders, had other, more important interests and priorities (Fox 1991). For example, proposed changes in tax provisions affecting homeowners and investors in rental housing were more important to the homebuilders than lumber prices, since lumber is a relatively small percentage of home construction costs, and Senator Packwood (R-Oregon) in particular was a major player in tax legislation. So, once the 1986 tax bill had been introduced on Capitol Hill, the association backed away from the Canadian lumber issue (Shinn 1987). Furthermore, as noted in Chapter 2, U.S. trade law does not consider consumer interests unless consumers are powerful enough that Congress cares and protects their interests.

The Canadian lobby was further hampered by different positions taken by provincial governments and industry associations once pressure from the U.S. industry, Congress, and the Reagan administration intensified. Canadian unity broke down naturally when the Coalition for Fair Lumber Imports decided to focus its 1986 countervailing duty case on the four major lumber-producing provinces, British Columbia, Québec, Ontario, and Alberta, which collectively accounted for more than 95 percent of Canadian lumber exports to the States. Governments and industry in the Maritime Provinces thus did not feel the need to fight the coalition.

A more significant development was that William Vander Zalm became the new premier of British Columbia, first appointed by the cabinet of the Social Credit Party (on August 6, 1986) and then elected (on October 22, 1986). Vander Zalm's predecessor, Bill Bennett, had taken a headline position on retaining the existing stumpage system. Because British Columbia was the largest softwood lumber producer in Canada, Premier Bennett's position was significant. Premier Vander Zalm adopted a different position. Faced with an annual budget deficit of more than C$1 billion, the new premier was eager to find more revenue from the Crown forest land base. On September 3, 1986, his Minister of Forests, Jack Kempf, announced a review of provincial forest management practices with a view to raising stumpage rates, stating, "I think rates at present are too low.... I have felt for many years now that we're not getting a good return from the industry" (Apsey and Thomas 1997, 22). Kempf's remark shocked the Canadian industry, and things began to go seriously awry for the Canadian defense.

* * *

Few people knew at the time that Kempf had secretly talked to a steering committee member of the Coalition for Fair Lumber Imports, Gus Kuehne, before he made his remark on September 3. Moreover, they had continued their communication before the two federal governments signed the memorandum of understanding (*Vancouver Sun* 1987c).

Kempf, who had first been elected as a member of the legislative assembly (MLA) in 1975 from the riding of Omineca in northern British Columbia, had been a manager of a small logging company and then mayor of Houston, British Columbia. He spent 10 years in the Social Credit Party backbenches before being elevated to Minister of Lands, Parks and Housing by Premier Bennett in February 1986. On August 14, Kempf was given the portfolio of Forests and Parks when Premier Vander Zalm assembled his first cabinet. He resigned and relinquished his cabinet portfolio on March 6, 1987, after the provincial comptroller-general started to investigate the financial administration of his office (*Vancouver Sun* 1987b). He later had to repay some C$14,000 of travel expenses and sit as an independent MLA for more than three years. In 1991, he was charged with breach of trust and fined $11,000 (*Vancouver Sun* 1992b). After an unsuccessful reelection campaign in 1991, he retired to Mexico. In 1992, he testified as an expert witness on behalf of the Coalition for Fair Lumber Imports at a Department of Commerce hearing of its countervailing duty investigation at the beginning of Lumber III.

As a backbencher, Kempf was known for his willingness to slam his own party (*Vancouver Sun* 1987a). On May 1, 1984, Kempf attacked the then-minister of Forests for his performance, inadequate reforestation, and sloppy regulation. But the most telling part of his lament was a direct attack on the big companies' near-monopoly of timber:

> We've allocated the resource of this province to a very few, and through having done so have hurt this industry.... There is no initiative to do better and to manufacture more of the available wood, no need to strive to attain better recovery from the cutting rights, *no initiative to pay better prices for the raw materials* or to seek out better markets or to produce a product that buyers are looking for. (*Vancouver Sun* 1987a; emphasis added)

On August 20, 1986, six days after Kempf was sworn in as Minister of Forests, Gus Kuehne was alerted by one of Kempf's friends and former business partner, Tom Forster, that Kempf wanted to meet him (Kuehne 2006). After receiving clearance from the coalition lawyer, Kuehne agreed to meet Kempf. On August 31, Kempf and his deputy minister, Robert Flitton, flew on a government plane to Bellingham, Washington, and met Kuehne in nearby Mount Vernon. The line of communication between Kempf and the coalition established that day was kept open "right up to the end of the negotiation" (*Vancouver Sun* 1987c). Kuehne would talk to either Kempf or Flitton on a weekly or even daily basis (Kuehne 2006), and he kept a record of these discussions, most of which were read in a defamation lawsuit (*Griffiths v. Pool*, Registry No. C871849, [1989], B.C.J. No. 2319; British Columbia Supreme Court, Vancouver) in which Robert Flitton was a codefendant.

At the time, however, the Canadian government and lumber industry were completely in the dark about these discussions. No wonder Trade Minister Pat Carney was upset when she learned of the talks from the media long afterward. T. Mike Apsey, president of the Council of Forest Industries in British Columbia, also said that he had known nothing about what Kempf was doing and was "absolutely shocked" (*Vancouver Sun* 1987c).

Premier Vander Zalm insisted that he did not know about the secret talks between Kempf and Kuehne, either. Initially, Kempf said that he did not inform the premier but defended his role as "acting on behalf of B.C." (*Vancouver Sun* 1987c). However, in his testimony in the aforementioned defamation lawsuit, Kempf stated that the premier was fully aware of his talks with the coalition and that "cabinet confidentiality was damned" (*Vancouver Sun* 1989). He went on to suggest a government investigation into the matter. Interestingly, Kempf was quickly exonerated of wrongdoing after an attorney-general investigation on his secret talks with the coalition ordered by the premier in 1987. The official findings of the investigation have not been released, but a press release concluded that although Kempf was indiscreet, he meant well and had told the Americans nothing (*Vancouver Sun* 1987d).

Later, Kuehne gave Kempf credit for making the memorandum of understanding possible. He said Kempf made it plain to the Coalition for Fair Lumber Imports that the B.C. government wanted to get more out of the industry. Kuehne further said, "Until Kempf got involved, Pat Carney was stonewalling us" (*Vancouver Sun* 1987c). Kuehne also commented that the coalition would give British Columbia relief if it increased its stumpage fees.

Kuehne might have given too much credit to Kempf with regard to the negotiation of the MOU. On the U.S. side, the "fix" was promised around mid-April 1986. The new government of British Columbia wanted to get more revenue from its forest industry, and the Canadian government placed a high priority on free trade negotiations with the United States. Thus, in retrospect, it is highly likely that a negotiated settlement similar to the MOU would have been reached even without the secret talks between Kempf and Kuehne. The secret talks, however, at a minimum put the Canadians in a difficult position in the negotiations, and the coalition kept one step ahead of the Canadians. The information asymmetry was so great that, in the months prior to the signing of the MOU, a reporter for the *Vancouver Sun*, Don Whiteley (2006), noticed that he could get more accurate information about Canada's position from the coalition than from the Canadian government.

It is perhaps not a coincidence that a few days after returning from his trip to Mount Vernon, Washington, Kempf said an increase in the stumpage rates would be a positive step in preventing tariffs from destroying the province's forest industry; the Americans, he continued, would take into consideration anything British Columbia did in this area and discount it from any tariff they might impose. He further said that if the review found stumpage rates too low, he was willing to admit to the Americans that the B.C. government was wrong and might have to open direct negotiations with the Americans if the federal government failed to persuade them to drop the tariff proposal. Premier Vander Zalm, too, said he was willing to listen to any complaints the Americans had: "If the Americans want to talk to us, we would welcome their advice ... It may be Americans are also quite keen on seeing this settled ..." (*Ottawa Citizen* 1986b).

* * *

Thus, it appears that the B.C. government took the position it did because it wanted to change provincial forest policy and saw the softwood lumber dispute not as a threat but as a convenient instrument. Canadian unity broke down even further after Vander Zalm took office in August 1986. The Canadian government, on the other hand, did not want to see the softwood lumber trade dispute jeopardize its ongoing free trade talks with the U.S. government. Despite the brave words from government officials about fighting for the lumber industry, Canada was probably glad to go along with the provincial officials of British Columbia (as well as those of Québec and Alberta) in facilitating the negotiation that ended with the MOU on December 30, 1986.

The Political and Legislative Tracks and the Bilateral Talks

The efforts by the Coalition for Fair Lumber Imports to politicize the issue were effective (Shinn 1987): It received critical legislative support from Congress, which in turn exerted political pressure on the Reagan administration. Gradually, the administration went along. The political and legislative tracks predated the legal track and then coincided with it once the countervailing duty investigation was initiated. The political track consisted of numerous meetings and contacts for which no public records are available. Consequently, it is difficult to document the linkage. Nonetheless, we can trace the process and major developments, using what records are available.

Because of a rising trade deficit and budget deficit in the middle 1980s, the general preference in Washington, D.C., was not for free trade but for rising protectionism in the name of "fair trade." Thus, it was not a time to stand up for foreign imports. For the most part, free traders on Capitol Hill chose to be silent. For example, Senator Dan Evans (R-Washington), a free trader from a lumber state, was uncomfortable with countervailing duties and urged both countries to search for a negotiated solution (Shinn 1987). Senators John Chafee (R-Rhode Island) and David Durenberger (R-Minnesota) expressed opposition to the preliminary countervailing duty determination by Commerce. They were concerned about an increase in lumber prices and the consequent construction costs of new houses.

The coalition found some good omens in a U.S. House of Representatives bill (H.R. 4784, Trade Remedies Reform Act) introduced by Sam Gibbons (D-Florida) on February 9, 1984, which contained a section on natural resource subsidies. Although neither was it concerned with lumber nor did it pass, it pointed out a legislative way for the U.S. lumber industry to put pressure on the administration and the Canadians.

In February 1985, Representative Weaver introduced the Canadian Softwood Import Control Act, H.R. 1088 (*Congressional Record* 1985a), which specifically called for a five-year restriction on Canadian lumber at a 25 (later 20) percent tariff.

In May 1985, Gibbons reintroduced his bill under a different title, H.R. 2451 Natural Resource Subsidy Amendments (*Congressional Record* 1985b). Senator Baucus introduced a companion bill (S. 1292) to the Senate (*Congressional Record* 1985c). Because these bills had a new definition of *subsidy* for the purposes of determining countervailing duties, they had implications for the softwood lumber dispute. H.R. 2451 specifies that a "resource input subsidy" is found to exist if

(1) (a) a product is provided or sold by a government-regulated or controlled entity within a country for input use within such country at a domestic price that is lower than the fair market value of the input product and is not freely available to U.S. producers; and (b) a product would, if sold at the fair market value, constitute a significant portion of the total cost of the manufacture or production of the merchandise in or for which the input product is used...

(2) under specified circumstances, the right to remove or extract such product is provided or sold by a government or a government-regulated or controlled entity within a country.

The bills also set forth the methods of calculation for the amount of a resource input subsidy and defined *fair market value* and *input use*. The methods include a comparison of prices paid in a foreign country with prices paid for the same materials by U.S. producers in a comparable region of the United States. These bills, if enacted into law, would have legalized the cross-country comparison method, which had been rejected by Commerce in Lumber I. Canadian stumpage programs seemed to meet the conditions set in these bills, and using a cross-border comparison method would likely find them a countervailing subsidy.

Other congressmen and senators who took an early and continued interest in the issue were all from lumber-producing states in the Northwest—Senators Steven Symms and James McClure (both R-Idaho) and Packwood, and Representatives Don Bonker, Jim Weaver, and Larry Craig—joined by southern Senators Trent Lott (R-Mississippi) and Strom Thurmond (R-South Carolina) and Representative Beryl Anthony (D-Arkansas). These senators and congressmen had their own bills, some of which directly pointed to Canadian lumber imports.[4]

In December 1984, Representative Weaver called a meeting in Portland to discuss the Canadian lumber problem. On June 25, 1985, Representative Craig organized the first of two "timber summits" on Capitol Hill (Shinn 1987). This closed-door session was attended by Commerce Secretary Baldrige, U.S. Trade

Representative Clayton Yeutter, and White House aide Max Freidersdorf. Sixty representatives and 12 senators made an appearance; some were outspoken in their criticism of Canadian lumber imports. On September 19, 1985, the Senate Finance Committee held a hearing on Canadian lumber; five congressmen from lumber states spoke in favor of restricting Canadian lumber imports. These two events got the attention of both the administration and the Canadians and reportedly convinced Yeutter that the lumber issue had to be reviewed on a priority basis (Shinn 1987).

On September 26, 1985, Prime Minister Mulroney formally requested, and President Reagan agreed, that the two countries start to negotiate a free trade agreement. On October 1, 1985, 10 members of the Senate Finance Committee, including Chairman Packwood, wrote a letter to Yeutter, stating,

> We understand that the Canadian Government has initiated exploratory discussions on a possible free trade agreement between the United States and Canada.
>
> We believe that the elected representatives of the people have a right to participate in this endeavor at the takeoff as well as landing ...
>
> In this connection, we reiterate our concerns about Canadian softwood lumber imports, which benefit from below-market government stumpage prices that enable Canadian producers to undersell more efficient U.S. producers ...
>
> ... Therefore, we believe that the Administration should seek an early resolution of the softwood lumber trade issue. This would facilitate Finance Committee consideration of any Administration proposals relating to the negotiation of a free trade agreement with Canada. (Packwood 1985)

The president needed the support of the Senate Finance Committee before the start of the free trade talks. Since Congress has jurisdiction over trade and commerce, he cannot rely upon his inherent foreign relations power to negotiate an international trade agreement and ensure that it will be faithfully implemented by Congress. So when the free trade negotiation process started, President Reagan made it clear to Congress that he wanted a "fast track" negotiating authority, under which Congress would not be allowed to offer amendments before voting to ratify the resulting agreement. If the request for a fast-track authority was approved by the committees of jurisdiction (the House Ways and Means Committee and the Senate Finance Committee), the president could proceed with negotiations and the resulting agreement would then be put to Congress for approval, which requires a simple majority.

Congressional authority in trade and commerce also includes the power to change the laws defining unfair trade. This authority helps explain the troubles between the two branches over trade legislation, including the ones directly targeted at Canadian lumber. There were at least three reasons the administration did not want protectionist legislation coming out of Congress in 1985–1986, whether it was on natural resource subsidies in general or Canadian lumber in particular.

The first was ideological. President Reagan believed that in general, more harm than good came from protectionism. The second was specific to Lumber II. With the free trade negotiations with Canada in the swaddling stage, the administration felt that protectionist legislation would be counterproductive (Dezell 1992). The third was self-interest. As Kalt (1988, *362,* emphasis original) notes, "if protection had to be delivered, the congressional, legislative route to protection for the U.S. lumber and timber industries was the *least* appealing course: it would be extremely difficult and time consuming to repeal tariff legislation and replace it with a policy that transferred wealth back to Canada."

On October 22, 1985, Yeutter (1985a) wrote a memo to the president's Economic Policy Council, which consisted of the secretaries of State, Treasury, Agriculture, Commerce, and Labor, the director of the Office of Management and Budget, the U.S. trade representative, and the chairman of the Council of Economic Advisers; it was chaired by the president, but Treasury Secretary James Baker served as chairman pro tempore in the president's absence. The memo summarized ITC's 1985 finding, congressional concerns, and possible options for the administration to respond. It stated,

> Since then [Commerce's negative decision in 1983] many members of Congress have been pressing for legislation that would change the subsidy definition to encompass the Canadian practices. This has become a major political issue with at least 50 Members with substantial timber interest in their states ... It is not one that the Administration can ignore ... (Yeutter 1985a, *2*)

The memo went on to list reasons why foreign government–controlled pricing practices on natural resources should be considered unfair by the U.S. government and why they should not. As for the possible avenues to deal with the Canadian lumber issue, it listed six options:

- negotiate with the Canadians to obtain elimination of their export ban on unprocessed logs and tariff reduction on U.S. wood products exports to Canada;
- pursue relief under Section 201 of the Trade Act;
- encourage industry to file a Section 301 petition;
- support legislation that would give the administration one year to negotiate with the Canadians, after which a legislated solution for stumpage only (not natural resources in general) would take effect unless Congress gave fast-track approval to a bill reporting the negotiated solution;
- encourage the industry to refile a countervailing duty case, indicating that application of the 1984 upstream subsidy provision of the Trade Act might yield a different result; and
- change the U.S. Forest Service's timber pricing and supply practices.

TABLE 4-1. Aggregate Variable Costs to Produce Softwood Lumber in the United States and Canada, 1984

	U.S. (US$)	Canada (US$)
Delivered wood costs (stumpage, harvesting, hauling)	156[a]	128[b]
Wages	81	65
Fuel and energy	9	11
Other (work contracted out to others, products bought and resold in the same condition, glues and packaging, operating and maintenance expenses)	25	33
Subtotal	271	237
Less residual unit value (chips, waste, bark)	−58	−32
Total aggregate variable costs, less residual unit values	213	205
Difference	8	

a. Includes average U.S. stumpage price of US$104.16.
b. Includes average Canadian stumpage price of US$11.84.
Source: Yeutter (1985a), from ITC (1985).

Interestingly, Yeutter's memo mentioned that the Canadian advantage in stumpage rates (and labor productivity) was partially offset by the U.S. advantage in lower harvesting costs for the timber and much lower transportation costs in moving the timber to mills. So the difference in overall variable costs was only about US$8/mbf, or less than 4 percent, but still tilted in Canada's favor. Yeutter's data are presented in Table 4-1.

The minutes of the Economic Policy Council meeting on October 24, 1985, noted,

> Ambassador Yeutter stated that Canadian lumber is a significant political issue in Congress. The Administration in the past has urged Congress to forgo any legislation affecting Canadian lumber, until the ITC report on Canadian lumber practices was completed. The report has been completed, and is not as useful as the Administration had expected in answering the basis questions regarding Canadian lumber ...
>
> The Council's discussion focused on the difficulty of determining whether the Canadians subsidize their timber, lumber and finished products industries, how that subsidy might work, and the degree of such as a subsidy. The Council agreed to continue discussion of Canadian lumber at a later date. (Economic Policy Council 1985a)

Another memo prepared for the same Economic Policy Council meeting showed that some members of the council were not in favor of strong action on Canadian lumber:

> Canada almost certainly does not meet the test for an anti-subsidy countervailing duty case.... According to the Appendix B of the USTR paper,

the net variable costs are comparable—$213 per ton[5] in the U.S. versus $205 in Canada.

The TPRG [Trade Policy Review Group] favors general negotiations with Canada on its trade practices in the lumber area rather than a specific position on stumpage. I think this makes sense ... All other options commit us to some form of protectionism in the name of heading off Congress. (Driggs 1985)

On October 29, 1985, 38 Republican members of the U.S. House of Representatives wrote a letter to the president, requesting a meeting with him to plan the administration's response to the Canadian lumber problem. The letter stated,

We, who are impacted by unfair Canadian trading practices, are no less committed in resolving this trade imbalance than what was evidenced in June of this year. When the call went out for a "Timber Summit" with Malcom Baldrige, Max Freidersdorf, and Michael Smith, Sixty Members of Congress attended to urge immediate action be taken. We who support you and have to run for election next year urge you in the strongest terms to act quickly and decisively to restore fairness to our lumber market. Also Ambassador Yeutter promised us he would act promptly after the ITC issued its report. Your pledge to insure fair trade will ring hollow indeed if you do not act now that the ITC has spoken. (Craig 1985; emphasis original)

On November 15, 1985, 64 members of Congress wrote to Secretary of State George Schultz, urging him to resolve the softwood lumber issue before commencing the free trade negotiations (Apsey and Thomas 1997). At this juncture, the Economic Policy Council (1985b) decided, on November 26, 1985, to endorse bilateral talks with Canada on the lumber issue, which would focus on the following issues:

- addressing the questionable elements in Canada's stumpage system;
- eliminating Canadian log export restrictions;
- reducing Canadian tariffs on imports of U.S. finished wood products;
- encouraging Canada to adopt satisfactory plywood performance standards; and
- working with Canada to open up third-country markets.

The Canadian government was amenable to discussing the lumber issue but was uncomfortable with calling these talks "negotiations." Subsequently, the two governments endured five rounds of talks until Canada left the table when the coalition filed its countervailing duty petition on May 19, 1986. The coalition said that it had delayed filing the petition for two weeks to facilitate the talks.

On December 10, 1985, President Reagan formally notified the Senate and House committees of jurisdiction that he intended to enter into negotiations with Canada for a free trade agreement. In the following months, U.S. interests with grievances against Canada intensified their lobbying in Congress to set conditions on the president's negotiating authority, as the political, legislative, and legal tracks were woven together in a strategy that eventually generated an understanding that the administration would "fix" the Canadian lumber problem, even before the coalition filed its countervailing duty petition.

On January 9, 1986, 11 days before the first round of bilateral lumber talks, Deputy Trade Representative Alan Woods, along with officials from Commerce, ITC, the State Department, and the U.S. Forest Service, met with the coalition's Task Group on Canadian Lumber. On January 14, officials from USTR, Commerce, the State Department, and the U.S. Forest Service, some of whom were on the U.S. delegation, met a second time with the coalition's lawyers, Alan Wm. Wolff, W. Clark McFadden II, and John Ragosta. In this meeting, the coalition made a presentation alleging that the stumpage subsidy in Canada was about US$50/mbf (Dewey Ballantine 1986).

The coalition eventually prepared an outline to Ambassador Woods for his presentation in the first round of bilateral talks in San Diego on January 20, 1986 (Lange 2003). No concrete solution was proposed in that round, or in the second rounds of talks, which took place in Prince George between February 12 and 14, 1986.

Perhaps frustrated with lack of progress in bilateral talks, Senator Baucus organized a "special order session" on Capitol Hill on February 26, 1986, at which some 39 senators, including 11 from the Finance Committee, spoke out against Canadian timber practices (Shinn 1987). Senator Packwood stated that a resolution of the lumber dispute "cannot wait until the conclusion of any free trade agreement" (Dezell 1992, 22). On March 5, the House of Representatives held its own special order session.

In this environment, in which the administration was eager to get the fast-track authority approved as well as to fend off protectionist legislation from Congress, it put forth four alternatives to Canada in the third round of bilateral talks on March 12, 1986:

- a Canadian reforestation tax on exports;
- higher stumpage fees based on an upward reassessment of Crown lands;
- a mill tax to increase costs to Canadian producers; or
- an auction system comparable to the U.S. method.

A few days later, on March 20, in the second timber summit organized by Representative Craig, Ambassador Woods said that the Canadians were "shell shocked" by the proposals and surprised by the forcefulness of the administration's position. The summit was also attended by Secretary Baldrige, Trade Representative Yeutter, Commerce Undersecretary Bruce Smart, and more than 20 senators and congressmen (Shinn 1987). Following the closed-door meeting, Representatives Weaver and Smith of Oregon stated that if within 60 days there was no action on the lumber issue by the administration, Congress would pass legislation aimed directly at Canadian lumber. Craig stated that he saw the administration's resolve to solve this problem.[6]

According to Representative Bonker, Baldrige attributed the lumber problem to oversupply in Canada and outlined some alternatives in the event that negotiations did not succeed, including filing a Section 301 petition and reexamining the subsidy charge in a countervailing duty case. Baldrige said that new information was now on hand that had not been available in 1983, and this could result in Commerce's coming up with a different answer (Olson 1986).

Baldrige hinted that Commerce had changed the interpretation of *subsidy* based on the *Cabot* decision (see later in this chapter), which was outlined in a memorandum from Deputy Assistant Secretary for Import Administration Gilbert B. Kaplan to Under Secretary Bruce Smart on March 8. The title of the memo was "Natural Resource Subsidies: Mexican Carbon Black (Cabot); Effect on Canadian Softwood Lumber." Although the main body of the memo was redacted when the Canadian Forest Industries Council made a Freedom of Information Act request in 1987, the visible part of the memo shows these sentences:

Our decision concerning general availability and preferentiality will have far-reaching effects on any future determinations involving natural resources, such as Canadian softwood lumber ...

The USG [U.S. government] is currently conducting talks with the Canadian government aimed at resolving the lumber issue. The talks may not be effective, and many would like to see the issue addressed in a new CVD [countervailing duty] investigation.... the following characterizes our current thinking ... (Kaplan 1986a)

This memo signaled to the congressional allies of the coalition that, should the coalition file another petition for countervailing duties, Commerce would be on its side based on a recent legal development. This had to please the members of Congress. Representative Bonker said after the second timber summit, "The whole U.S. government is now united. No amount of positive signs from the negotiations or suggested administrative remedies—short of actual resolution of the stumpage subsidy issue—will deter congressional action" (*Inside US Trade* 1986).

The House Ways and Means Committee did not act on the president's request for free trade negotiations with Canada, and thus granted its approval. The critical holdup was the Senate Finance Committee. Eight of the 20 senators on the committee were from lumber-producing states, and a few of them were facing reelection in 1986.[7] They were adamant about restricting Canadian access to the U.S. market (Apsey and Thomas 1997). These and a few other senators formed a bloc and insisted that the Canadian lumber problem be resolved before they would permit fast-track discussion to begin. After the Senate Finance Committee's straw vote on April 11, 1986, showed that a formal vote would deny the president fast-track authority, and then 12 committee members signed a letter to the president on April 17 saying they would not give the approval "unless the White House agrees to a new major trade bill and resolves some trade irritations with Canada" (*Globe and Mail* 1986), the administration began to make commitments before the formal vote of the committee, scheduled to take place on April 23.

On April 17, Trade Representative Yeutter met with representatives of U.S. pharmaceutical and lumber industries. He told the lumber people to "intensify your lobbying efforts with [Senate Finance] Committee members" and explained the new developments at Commerce regarding its reinterpretation of *subsidy* (Dezell 1992). In a handwritten annotation on a letter on behalf of the president to Senator David Pryor (D-Arkansas) on the same day, urging him to vote in favor of fast-track authority, Yeutter added the prophetic words, "We will get timber fixed ..." The letter further stated, "I hope you will carefully consider the economic and political ramifications of your decision ... Though the denial of fast track authority would provide some leverage for me, that leverage is irrelevant if there would be no negotiations ..." (Yeutter 1986).

Finally, on the day before the vote, President Reagan sent a letter to Senator Symms, stating, "I am strongly committed to finding a rapid and effective solution to the lumber and other pending problems between the United States and Canada ... I am optimistic that progress on lumber can be made before a comprehensive agreement with Canada" (Reagan 1986a). On the basis of these kinds of assurances, the Finance Committee relented and failed to disapprove the request for negotiations on free trade on a 10-to-10 vote on April 23, 1986. Later, another committee member, Senator Lloyd Bentsen (D-Texas), revealed that the vote could have just as easily been 11 to 9 or even 12 to 8 (Ritchie 1997). Congress was sending a message to the White House, and free trade was a card in this Washington power game.

The administration now needed to do its part. And it did. Committing himself to pay his debt, President Reagan sent a letter to Senator Packwood on May 8, 1986. The letter, bearing witness that the "fix" was indeed in, reads in part,

> I want you to know that I am committed to finding a rapid and effective solution to the Canadian softwood lumber problem which restores for the American lumber industry a fair opportunity to compete. To this end, I intend to press for an expedited resolution to this problem, independent of the comprehensive negotiations. If this cannot be achieved through bilateral negotiations with Canada, then I will take such action as may be necessary to resolve this problem consistent with U.S. law. (Reagan 1986b)

This is an important letter. One month later, a senior trade adviser to the Senate Finance Committee, Len Santos, said that the president made a "clear deal" to take action against Canadian lumber imports in return for a Senate Finance Committee green light on fast-track authority. Without the president's commitment on lumber, Santos said, the Senate Finance Committee would have killed the free trade discussion (*Ottawa Citizen* 1986a). In 1987, William Lange of the coalition said that once the coalition saw the president's letters, it knew that it had won. What was left "was just a question of how the commitment was going to be fulfilled" (Dezell 1992, 25).

For his part, Prime Minister Mulroney told the Canadian Parliament in May 1986 that Canada "will not accept their [Americans'] version of events and we will not sacrifice Canadian lumber or timber interest in this regard" (*Toronto Star* 1986). His government would change its stand shortly after Labor Day 1986, when British Columbia signaled that it wanted to settle.

The Shakes and Shingles Trade Dispute

When the Coalition for Fair Lumber Imports began to fight for restrictions on Canadian softwood lumber, the U.S. shakes and shingles industry, led by Gus Kuehne of the Northwest Independent Forest Manufacturers Association, submitted a petition for relief under Section 201 (the escape clause) of the Tariff Act and sought imposition of a temporary tariff on Canadian shakes and shingles imports. This petition, dated September 23, 1985, and preceding the softwood lumber countervailing duty petition by approximately nine months, alleged that imports of Canadian shakes and shingles surged 85 percent from 1975 to the first half of 1985, causing injury to the U.S. industry. It thus requested an 85 percent tariff on Canadian shakes and shingles. Although no Canadian foul play (in terms of subsidies or dumping) was alleged and most in the U.S. industry realized that the United States was running out of mature cedar trees for shakes and shingles, the development of the case had some relevance to the softwood lumber case.

On February 26, 1986, ITC voted 4 to 2, finding injury to the U.S. shakes and shingles industry. On March 18, ITC voted 2 to 1 for adjustment assistance and recommended to President Reagan a 35 percent tariff on Canadian shakes and shingles imports for five years (Fox 1991).

On May 22 (the same day that the U.S. House of Representatives passed H.R. 4800, which redefined *natural resource subsidy*), the president approved a relief for five years: a duty of 35 percent *ad valorem* for the first 30 months, a 20 percent duty for the following 24 months, and an 8 percent duty for the final 6 months. This was a victory for the U.S. shakes and shingles industry. It also demonstrated that the White House, like Congress, could be moved by pleas for protectionism, and Reagan might have been sending a signal that the White House intended to take a tough line in new trade negotiations with the Canadians (*Time* 1986). Canada retaliated by imposing a 10 percent tariff on books and computer parts imported from the United States.

Gus Kuehne was thrilled with his quick success in bringing in an estimated $225 million to the industry afforded by the five-year protection. Even more impressive was that he had not engaged a lawyer and had spent only some $60,000 from the industry. He was the first forester, nonlawyer, noneconomist, and non-Washington insider who had succeeded in petitioning the U.S. government for Section 201 relief for an industry (Kuehne 2006).

The Legal Track

Although the victory of the shakes and shingles industry boosted morale, the Coalition for Fair Lumber Imports would need a strong legal argument to persuade Commerce to reverse its own recent decision on countervailing duties. The critical help came from a legal case related to carbon black from Mexico (*Cabot Corp. v. U.S.,* 620, F. Supp. 722, CIT 1986), which led Commerce to change the interpretation of *specificity* and *preferentiality* in its investigations.

Carbon black, a chemical by-product from the oil refinery process, is primarily used in the rubber industry. A few months after Lumber I, Commerce rejected a petition by Cabot Corp., an American firm, which alleged that PEMEX, a Mexican government-owned petroleum company, had subsidized two Mexican carbon black producers through artificially low prices of a petroleum-derivative feedstock (commonly referred to as carbon black feedstock) and natural gas. The decision was based on the specificity and preferentiality tests similar to those used in the determination in Lumber I.

In *Cabot,* the U.S. Court of International Trade rejected Commerce's decision and broadened the interpretation of *specificity.* It looked at specificity as a requirement only to prevent the absurd result of countervailing "such things as public highways and bridges" or other public goods that "benefit society in a collective manner." It found that Commerce had failed to distinguish benefits extended de facto to a specific industry from benefits that were actually generally available and used broadly. Later, Gary Horlick (1991) stated that Commerce had done "de facto" tests with respect to specificity prior to *Cabot,* in Lumber I and several other cases, to which Ragosta (2006) commented by saying that he (Horlick) was simply defending his own decision in Lumber I.

In the eyes of the court, the inherent characteristics of resources and current level of technology could *de facto* make a foreign government program benefit a specific industry, irrespective of the activities of the government. The government program would thus be subject to the U.S. countervailing duty law.

The final barrier for Commerce to overcome before being able to find the Canadian stumpage programs specific to the lumber industry was that they were indeed available to at least one other industry, the pulp and paper industry; stumpage programs were little used by the furniture industry. Even though the statutory language read that the subsidy must be available to an "industry or a group of industries," the high degree of integration between wood products (which include softwood lumber, shakes and shingles, fencing, plywood, hardwood lumber, and hardboard) and pulp and paper was used in Commerce's (1986b) preliminary determination to justify the claim that the actual number of industries using timber was small.[8]

As for the preferentiality standard, the U.S. Court of International Trade held that Commerce's interpretation simply transposed its flawed "inherent characteristics" specificity argument into the language of the preferential provision of goods. The court asked Commerce to consider "the broader question of whether the Mexican pricing programs ... are additional benefits or competitive advantages." Commerce subsequently accepted the court's interpretation and reversed its decision by finding an affirmative subsidy.

In early 1986, when Commerce was conducting an administrative review of the carbon black case, it formally changed the interpretation of *subsidy* and proposed four alternative benchmarks to measure preferentiality in cases where producers under investigation were the only or the predominant users within a foreign jurisdiction. This was perhaps outlined in the aforementioned memorandum from Kaplan (1986a). From then on, the coalition was virtually assured of victory once it filed another countervailing duty case.

The four preferentiality benchmarks, ranked in order of priority, involve comparing the price of the alleged subsidized goods or services with

- the price charged by the same seller for a similar or related good;
- the price charged within the jurisdiction by other sellers for an identical good or service;
- the same seller's cost of producing the good or service; or
- external prices, such as export prices or a commercial price in an external market that resembles the market in question (DOC 1986a).

The ranking of those alternative tests reflects Commerce's stated belief that comparisons of prices within the foreign jurisdiction were the most appropriate measures of preferentiality. The use of external prices, alternative benchmark 4, is considered the "least desirable and most deficient because regardless of what external price is chosen for comparisons purposes, a domestic subsidy is no longer being defined by its effect on the domestic market. This test does not measure preference within an economy" (DOC 1986a, *13273*).

However, no matter how less desirable and deficient they are, external prices have since become part of U.S. law for the purpose of calculating a subsidy that triggers a countervailing duty. U.S. producer groups, including the coalition, have often viewed the cross-border comparison method as the most advantageous. The coalition subsequently asked Commerce to use a cross-border comparison of stumpage prices in Lumber II, III, and IV.[9]

This perhaps explains why, to the surprise of some Canadians, there could possibly be another petition for countervailing duties in merely two years. The

U.S. bureaucracy, much like the Canadians, thought initially it had seen the last of the issue (Shinn 1987). It was reportedly a wrenching experience for some of the working-level officials involved in Lumber I to look at it again so soon (Shinn 1987). Over time, as political pressure started to work, the coalition was able to find access to and get the cooperation of key officials in Commerce, ITC, and USTR. The Departments of State, Agriculture, and Treasury followed developments but played less important roles.

USTR took a lead in arranging fact-finding meetings with the Canadians. In an interview conducted in 2003, William Lange, the assistant to the president of the coalition in 1985–1986, stated that Deputy Trade Representative Alan Woods had been convinced that Canadian lumber producers were subsidized.[10] Had USTR decided at this early stage that there was no case to be made, the process might have taken a different course (Shinn 1987).

The involvement of USTR in the initial stage of Lumber II was understandable, since it was charged with starting negotiations with Canada for a free trade agreement, pending the approval of fast-track authority by Congress. It had to help the president clear the roadblocks and get the fast-track authority. Further, the countervailing duty case had not yet been filed.

Working-level officials from USTR, Commerce, and ITC drafted a position paper, dated March 12, 1986. This paper worked its way up the bureaucracy and reportedly solidified the U.S. government position. It convinced all the relevant players that some action on the Canadian lumber issue was merited (Shinn 1987).

The coalition's access to working-level officials was critical. The 1985 Section 332 report of ITC (1985) did find that Canadian mills had become increasingly more efficient between 1980 and 1984, producing as much as 60 percent more lumber per employee than did U.S. lumber mills in 1984. Although a recession could boost productivity, the interpretation by the Canadian interests was that the steady increase in market share resulted from greater efficiency, not subsidy. The coalition, on the other hand, pointed to other findings in the report: For example, when productivity was measured by the value added per production work hour, in most years the U.S. industry was the more productive.

The meaning of all these productivity measures was subject to debate. On the one hand, less value added per production work hour and more lumber produced per employee in Canada just meant that the Canadian industry was producing less value added per unit of lumber than the U.S. industry. Less value added generated by the Canadian industry implied that either it produced a less valued product mix or its costs were higher. The former is unlikely, since both industries sold their products in a single North American market. More likely, the latter was true. If so, how could the Canadian lumber industry be subsidized?

The coalition, however, argued that less value added generated in a period when prices collapsed—a recession—was caused by lower revenues. While U.S. producers shut down capacity, Canadian producers continued to operate even when they did not generate much value added in a recession environment.

When William Merkin of USTR told the coalition that the U.S. lumber industry was not competitive in productivity, the coalition, through its congressional allies, asked Trade Representative Yeutter to request that ITC look at the productivity issue in detail. Yeutter's request was based on the coalition's allegation that "the Commission calculated productivity using Canadian estimates of U.S. jobs based upon [U.S.] Bureau of Labor Statistics figures, which exceed [U.S.] Census figures by about 15,000 jobs" (Yeutter 1985b). Although reluctant, the commission agreed to look at the number again and produce a supplementary report (ITC 1986). This is the only instance in which the commission has ever taken the extraordinary step of issuing such a supplement to a completed report.

In the meantime, Lange got some sawmill production data from Tom Richards of Idaho Forest Industries and then made a cross-border comparison between Washington State and British Columbia. It was not enough, since the per-employee lumber production in Washington was lower. He then added Idaho and Montana. Close, but it still lagged that of British Columbia. Finally, he added Oregon and was able to get within a 6 percent difference. This comparison was given to Fred Ruggles at ITC, who used it in the commission's supplementary report (Lange 2003).

Similarly, Lange provided ITC with new estimates based on a cross-border comparison between other U.S. states and Canadian provinces. The commission used these data in its supplementary report but provided no state or provincial breakdown (Table 4-2). The report showed that Canadian mills were still more productive than the U.S. mills, but the level of difference was no longer increasing. The report concluded that "Canadian mills having similar output and product mix to that of U.S. mills generally have production per employee comparable to that of U.S. mills" (ITC 1986, 2).

Canada's Position

The Coalition for Fair Lumber Imports officially filed its petition on May 19, 1986, requesting a 27 percent duty on Canadian lumber imports. Although Canadian Ambassador Alan Gotlieb and the Canadian Forest Industries Council urged U.S. Commerce Secretary Baldrige to reject the petition, the investigation went ahead on June 5, 1986.

Initially, Canadians were prepared for a fight. On June 13, 1986, Canadian Minister of External Affairs Joe Clark stated in a federal, provincial, and industry meeting in Vancouver that the first step was a "determination to fight" the countervailing duty "on a united basis." The Canadian government requested that the GATT council consider the second petition harassment. It then requested two conciliations under Article 17 of the GATT Code. In July, Canadians received signals from the U.S. administration and Congress encouraging settlement of the lumber issue before the preliminary determination.

TABLE 4-2. Estimated Employee Productivity in the Softwood Lumber Industry in the United States and Canada, 1977–1984

| | ITC estimates, October 1985 | | | Revised ITC estimates, January 1986 | | |
| | mbf/employee/year | | | mbf/employee/year | | |
	Canada	U.S.	Canada/U.S.	Canada	U.S.	Canada/U.S.
1977	292	208	1.40	346	275	1.26
1978	286	207	1.38	330	292	1.13
1979	278	199	1.40	331	271	1.22
1980	285	185	1.54	348	248	1.40
1981	269	185	1.45	372	259	1.44
1982	299	209	1.44	401	318	1.26
1983	366	244	1.50	436	369	1.18
1984	382	239	1.60	464	368	1.26

Sources: ITC (1985, 1986).

Feeling the pressure, the Canadian Forest Industries Council started to conduct an unpublished study of various options for a negotiated settlement. The study was completed on July 15, 1986, with an export tax—which was both product and market specific and would preclude a stumpage increase—as the least of all "devils" and thus the preferred resolution. Shortly afterward, council leaders told Canadian trade officials that the political situation in the United States meant that a negotiated settlement might be necessary (*Globe and Mail* 1987).

On September 8, 1986, at the request of B.C. Premier Vander Zalm, Trade Minister Carney asked Secretary Baldrige to postpone the October deadline for a preliminary determination of whether stumpage fees constituted an unfair subsidy. This action was seen by opposition leader John Turner as a sellout of the forest industry. Carney, on the other hand, warned in a news conference on September 10 that if Canada won the case, retaliatory legislation in the U.S. Congress could be very painful for Canada: "If we win the countervail, we could lose in Congress, and if the U.S. wins the countervail, there will be a lot of emotion in Canada, so if there's a way to seek a technical deferment, both of us [Baldrige and Carney] agreed to explore it" (*Gazette* 1986a).

On September 9, 1986, Minister Carney stated in Parliament that she was simply seeing whether there was a way to defer the countervail ruling until later in the fall, after the U.S. election. This remark prompted coalition lawyer Alan Wolff on September 12, 1986, to send a note to Secretary Baldrige titled "Today's oxymoron: Canadian Government credibility on lumber" (Wolff 1986).

While Canada was signaling for a negotiated settlement, the coalition stepped up its pressure. On September 9, it asked for a 32 percent countervailing duty, and on September 26, 33 to 36 percent. In mid-September, Premier

Vander Zalm announced that his province had a solution in keeping any money that might be levied in a tariff in British Columbia (*Seattle Times* 1986).

It was at this point that Canadian producers, recognizing that their fight had been taken away from them, started to control damage. The Canadian Forest Industries Council, under the leadership of Zimmerman and Apsey, suggested that the Canadian government propose a "made-in-Canada" solution—an export tax until a better answer could be worked out (*Globe and Mail* 1987).

The attitude change by the Canadian Forest Industries Council leaders was welcomed by the Canadian federal and some provincial governments that wanted to find a quick way to end the lumber dispute, swallow the unavoidable tax on lumber in Canada, avoid the legal precedent of a ruling in favor of U.S. industry, and keep the free trade negotiations going. Although the council favored export taxes as the basis for a negotiated settlement, Vander Zalm and the Québec premier favored stumpage adjustment in lieu of an export tax because provincial governments own most forest lands, and they wanted any tax dollars to flow into provincial treasuries rather than go to the federal government.

On September 30, 1986, the Canadian government made a "final" but vaguely defined offer of provincial adjustment that would raise Canadian lumber prices in the United States by 10 percent, which amounted to C$370 million annually in the four major lumber-producing provinces. Minister Carney said that it was a nonnegotiable offer made on a no-prejudice basis to Canada's legal case.

The initial response from the coalition was that the Canadian move was "a good opening offer." However, on October 2, 1986, it rejected the offer, stating "the amount of the Canadian offer is still far too low, the changes won't be implemented for some time and, lastly, we don't have the necessary details of how the proposal could actually work." Minister Carney did not budge, stating that the pot of money was not unlimited (*Gazette* 1986b).

The Canadian "final offer" was intended to prevent Commerce from releasing its preliminary determination. It would not only fail to do so but also expose Canada's vulnerability. Ten percent became a floor for the coalition. Not surprisingly, it went to the Reagan administration and asked for more.

Commerce's Preliminary Determination and the Memorandum

On October 16, 1986, the Department of Commerce issued a preliminary affirmative determination that Canadian lumber was subsidized at "15.00 percent," 14.542 percent of which was from provincial stumpage programs. Because ITC had preliminarily found injuries to U.S. lumber producers in July, a 15 percent bond of countervailing duty was immediately placed on Canadian softwood lumber bound for the United States, contingent on a final determination to be made by December 30, 1986.

Although the affirmative finding would not be, by now, a surprise to those involved in the case, the method Commerce used to derive the rate of subsidy was contrary to economic theory. It double-counted by adding the alleged uncovered costs of administering timber resources to the imputed value of timber resources and then coming up with the so-called fair stumpage prices, resulting in a higher level of subsidy. So far, no refereed article has ever used this method to derive fair stumpage prices and level of subsidy. Commerce had not used it before or since. Commerce had never issued determinations with two zeros to the right of the decimal point prior to Lumber II, either.

The Commerce employee who did the calculations has declined a request for an interview. A person who was involved in Lumber II commented that this employee would not agree to an interview for the foreseeable future, perhaps ever. We must therefore find the logic behind the method on our own. Canada had already made a 10 percent offer. Under political pressure, the employee understood that she could not make a calculation that was less than 10 percent. It seems possible, if not likely, that she had received instructions, since the "fix" had been promised in April, and may have been told to come up with a stumpage number that, with other small programs, would add up to a total of "15.00 percent," even though the procedures adopted to measure the value of the alleged subsidy were seriously flawed.

The theoretical and empirical shortcomings of the Commerce method cast doubt upon the department's impartiality (Percy and Yoder 1987). A former coalition insider agreed that the calculation of the alleged subsidy was "double counting or even triple counting."

The four provincial governments in Canada were able to cover all expenditures for licensing timber rights to private enterprises and make a profit in the middle 1980s (Table 4-3). So under alternative 3 of the Commerce benchmarks, Canada should have passed the test easily. The question is whether the stumpage assessed by the Canadian provincial governments reflected the true market value of standing timber. The correct approach would be to compare stumpage values calculated administratively with those obtained through competitive bidding for timber stands with similar characteristics and management responsibilities. Since Commerce reasoned that private and public competitive bidding data were insufficient, it chose to impute the provinces' cost of producing stumpage.

The Commerce calculation of government "cost" in the alleged subsidy has two components. The first was an imputation for the "intrinsic value of land." In the case of British Columbia and Alberta, the competitive bid price obtained for the small portion of the government stumpage allocated in this fashion served as the proxy of the imputed value. For Ontario and Québec, prices from private sales in New Brunswick were employed as proxies. This imputation for the value of standing timber was then applied to provincial harvests.

TABLE 4-3. Canadian Provincial Expenditures and Revenues from Commercial Timber Operations, 1983–1986

Fiscal year	1983–84 (C$ million)	1984–85 (C$ million)	1985–86 (C$ million)
Alberta			
Expenditure	2.7	2.2	n.a.
Revenue	16.8	28.4	n.a.
Net income	14.1	26.2	n.a.
British Columbia			
Expenditure	74.7	81.2	82.3
Revenue	191.2	187.3	209.1
Net income	116.5	106.1	126.8
Ontario			
Expenditure	19.4	19.5	21.2
Revenue	46.7	59.4	68.6
Net income	27.3	39.9	47.4
Québec			
Expenditure	26.6	27.6	23.3
Revenue	34.9	47.5	45.8
Net income	8.3	19.9	22.5

Source: Percy and Yoder (1987).

If these proxies were close to the true value of stumpage on provincial land, they alone would be the true market value of timber harvested on government land. As economic theory indicates, the highest bidding price of a good is the market value. Commerce's imputed value of stumpage evaluated at bid prices totaled C$702 million.

Had Commerce used this value of standing timber, it would have at least made some sense in economics. The only questions would be how representative these proxies were and whether any differences in site and timber stand characteristics, location, and transportation costs were considered.

Instead, Commerce added a second component to the cost of the government—the costs that are directly related to providing timber to commercial users. These costs, by Commerce's reckoning, include virtually all expenditures by provincial forestry ministries, including administrative overhead, road costs, scaling and inventory costs, small business development programs, and reforestation costs. These direct expenditures by provinces on the provision of stumpage to commercial users exceeded revenues by more than C$543 million. This is the double counting.

The possible triple counting occurred because the "direct costs" of providing timber to commercial users included all road costs, even though some roads might be built primarily for recreational purposes. Similarly, a portion of the firefighting expenditure was used for fire suppression in provincial parks, recreational areas, and other noncommercial timber areas. A more problematic issue is the inclusion of reforestation expenditures as costs charged to the current commercial timber harvest. Reforestation, like all investment, should be included only if the present value of the future benefits from it is positive. Reforestation costs are a cost not to current timber stands, but to future timber stands.

As a result, Commerce calculated a total subsidy of C$1.245 billion (C$702 million plus C$543 million), or C$10.22/m^3 for the 122 million m^3 of timber harvested in 1985. The volume of sawlogs harvested was 90.2 million m^3, of which 77 percent was recovered as lumber. The 1985 total value of softwood lumber shipments was C$4.9 billion. The *ad valorem* subsidy of 14.542 percent per cubic meter of sawlogs was calculated after a lumber recovery factor and the portion of sawlogs in the total timber harvest was adjusted for. Had Commerce used C$702 million as the subsidy, the *ad valorem* subsidy rate would have only been 8.1 percent. This, plus the subsidy rate of 0.458 percent, was lower than the 10 percent that the Canadian government had offered.

The public response from the Canadian government was outrage. Minister Carney stated in a news release, "I deplore today's preliminary determination which could not be justified either under U.S. law or GATT rules." In the Canadian Parliament, she vowed to "fight this all the way," and Prime Minister Mulroney stated, "Action like this makes it extremely difficult for anyone, including Canadians, to be a friend of U.S. from time to time" (CBC News 1986).

On October 20–21, 1986, all participants in a federal, provincial, and industry meeting in Toronto agreed to a united front to fight to have the ruling thrown out rather than to negotiate. The Canadian Forest Industries Council sent a letter to Secretary Baldrige objecting to "double counting" in the preliminary decision. On October 30, the Canadian government delivered a note to the U.S. State Department, outlining in detail Canada's contention that the preliminary decision was seriously flawed in terms of U.S. law and economic logic.

Despite the public response and show of unity in fighting the preliminary determination, the Canadian government seemed unwilling to let the lumber issue disrupt the free trade talks. In a telegram sent to the U.S. State Department, Commerce, and USTR, the U.S. Embassy to Canada (1986) noted that on October 17, 1986, Minister Carney had said on a national TV program, "Canada A.M.," that the provinces might want to "top up their 10 percent offer to 15 percent." From this and other responses, the telegram concluded, "The Prime Minister has decided softwood lumber will be handled in a well modulated way that gives his government the necessary political cover but does not endanger the comprehensive trade talks."

On November 4, the Canadian Forest Industries Council decided to reject all options except to fight, and it made its position clear to the federal and provincial governments. It was too late, however: Neither the federal nor provincial governments were listening (*Globe and Mail* 1987). The Canadian government—with the support of British Columbia and Québec—wanted to explore the possibility of a suspension agreement—that is, suspension of the tariff for a period of time in exchange for reform in the stumpage charge. Ontario wished to continue the legal route only.

On November 19, 1986, Minister Carney proposed to Secretary Baldrige a settlement based on a 15 percent export tax (or stumpage adjustment) for withdrawal of the countervailing duty petition. This proposal did not have any input from the industry (*Globe and Mail* 1987).

Although some members of the Coalition for Fair Lumber Imports (International Paper in particular) wanted a high rate and made a counteroffer of a 23 percent export tax to Canada in early December, ultimately it decided to go with 15 percent, partly because it realized that Commerce could not win in court if it stuck with the method used in the preliminary determination—in fact, the coalition requested that Commerce abandon its method. Other possible reasons for the coalition to settle include risk and uncertainty, high legal costs, lack of supporting data, and fear of losing the administration's support if the U.S. government became reluctant to antagonize Canada and jeopardize the free trade negotiations. This was the basis on which the MOU was negotiated.

The U.S. and Canadian Industries' Economic Arguments

Although Lumber II was settled out of court, it is interesting to note the arguments presented or prepared by the industry in both countries.

The argument of the Coalition for Fair Lumber Imports was simple, direct, and easy to understand: Canadian timber was priced much lower than U.S. timber, and this difference in timber prices arose from an unfair subsidy to Canadian lumber producers. This contention is perhaps best captured in William Lange's presentation in January 1986 at a forestry symposium at Lakehead University. Lange worked for the National Forest Products Association and was on loan to the coalition in 1985–1986. A similar presentation was made by Deputy Trade Representative Alan Woods to Canadian government officials in the first round of bilateral lumber talks (Lange 2003).

Lange (1986) started with slides showing the increase in Canadian softwood lumber's share of the U.S. market and the difference in commercial timberland in both countries. A slide then showed that Canadian stumpage prices were only a fraction of U.S. stumpage, implying the existence of a Canadian subsidy. He then stated that U.S. lumber production grew only 20 percent between 1975 and 1985, while Canadian lumber production grew 103 percent. Since Canadian markets for lumber are small, most Canadian lumber went to the United States, taking away the share of U.S. lumber and depressing lumber prices. As a result, U.S. lumber prices had not been able to keep up with increases in consumption (Figure 4-1).

Lange stated that Figure 4-1 was an apparent contradiction of the law of supply and demand: The price of lumber in the United States had remained at

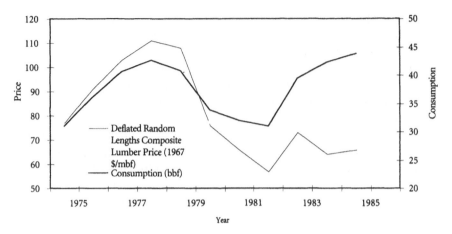

FIGURE 4-1. U.S. Softwood Lumber Consumption and Prices, 1975–1985

Source: Lange (1986).

near-Depression levels in the face of a boom market, forcing many U.S. lumber producers out of business.

What Lange did not say was that a thorough cross-border comparison of stumpage should involve variations in road conditions, transportation costs, log size, species, and labor costs. Further, all variable costs that covered delivered log prices were similar in both countries, as shown by ITC (1985) and Yeutter's (1985a) memo to the president's Economic Policy Council (Table 4-1).

Nor did he mention that the apparent violation of an economic law might be explained by several supply factors: (1) possible technological advance in Canadian sawmills, which would enable them to process small logs and thereby increase production; (2) increased timber supply from the U.S. South because of forest age class structure and insect outbreaks in that region; (3) differences in resource endowment (Canada has more timber resources in both relative and absolute terms than the United States) that would allow Canada to increase timber production at lower cost; and (4) variations in exchange rates that made Canadian lumber cheaper (Adams et al. 1986). So even if low stumpage fees leading to oversupply in Canada were a factor, they were by no means the only or even the dominant factor.

Yet Lange's message was appealing, and when it was repeated many times, it acquired the veneer of truth. Some politicians would rather cite the stated allegations (presented as fact) from a home industry than believe a foreign entity. Since Canadian lumber imports had "harmed" the U.S. lumber industry, these politicians believed that some action was needed. Finally, Lange's message created emotion. One U.S. congressman placed relative timber costs between the United States and Canada in this context: "Our companies pay $100, theirs pay $10; if that's not a subsidy I don't know what is" (cited in Melrose et al. 1986).

The Canadian Forest Industries Council's defense was based on three grounds: market forces (exchange rate and productivity) had caused the increase in Canadian share within the North America lumber market, provincial stumpage programs did not provide a subsidy, and the profit level between publicly traded firms in the two countries was in the U.S.'s favor. The Canadians argued that even if the provincial stumpage programs did not capture full economic rents, Canadian producers would not be able to produce more lumber than what the market dictated them to produce. The level of timber harvests was determined by the annual allowable cut, which was determined independent of timber pricing. Because U.S. forest products firms were more profitable than the Canadian forest products firms, it meant that timber was not priced "too low" in Canada, and if timber *was* priced lower than market value, the uncaptured rent dissipated in or was used to subsidize other factors of production (such as labor). In any event, the U.S. lumber industry could not have been injured by its Canadian counterpart.

Economic Impact of the Memorandum of Understanding

Figure 4-2 illustrates the structure of the North American softwood lumber market and the economic impact of the MOU. In the 1980s, bilateral trade between the two countries dominated the North American market. For illustrative purposes, we ignore multilateral trade in lumber and focus on these two markets in North America.

Figure 4-2 shows that under autarky (no trade), the Canadian domestic lumber price would be P_c, and the U.S. domestic price would be at P_u. When free trade takes place, the market price would be P_f; Canada would export EB amount (which equals JK) of lumber to the States. Compared to autarky, Canadian lumber producers would gain P_cABP_f amount of producer surplus; Canadian lumber consumers would lose P_fEAP_c. The net social welfare (gain from trade) for Canada is thus the area of ABE. Conversely, American producers would lose P_uHKP_f amount of producer surplus; American consumers would gain P_uHJP_f (amount of consumer surplus). The net social welfare gains for the United States in free trade would be the area of HJK.

Note that transportation costs are not considered here, for two reasons. First, because the Jones Act limits the transportation of goods from U.S. ports to American-owned ships, transportation costs between the two major ports in the Pacific Northwest—Seattle and Portland—and ports on the U.S. East Coast are usually higher than between Vancouver and the U.S. East Coast (Boyd and Hyde 1989). Second, there is no evidence that transporting lumber made from southern yellow pine is cheaper than transporting lumber from eastern Canada to the U.S. Northeast.

A stumpage adjustment of 15 percent *ad valorem* causes the supply curve of Canadian softwood lumber to rotate upward by 15 percent.[11] The newly estab-

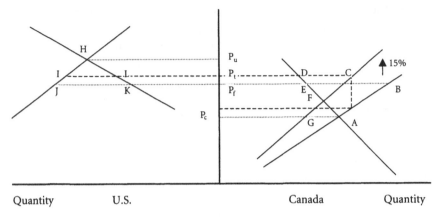

FIGURE 4-2. Structure of the Softwood Lumber Market in North America and the Impact of the Memorandum of Understanding: A 15 Percent Stumpage Adjustment

lished market price would be P_t, and Canadian exports to the States would shrink to DC (which equals IL). The exact location of P_t (and DC) depends on the elasticity of supply and demand in both the U.S. and the Canadian lumber markets.

The change in social welfare for the United States due to the export tariff is straightforward: U.S. consumers lose the benefits represented in the area of P_tIJP_f, and producers gain the area of P_tLKP_f. So the net welfare loss for the United States is the area of IJKL.

The change in social welfare for Canada is slightly more complicated. Consumers lose P_tDEP_f. The net change for producer surplus equals $P_fBAP_c - P_tCGP_c$. The net change in consumer and producer surplus is the area of ABE – the area of FCD. On top of this, government stumpage revenue increases by $15\% * P_t * P_tC$.

Wear and Lee (1993) provide estimates of the market and welfare impacts of the MOU. In 1987, it made lumber prices in the United States increase by US\$13.21/mbf (in 1982 dollars), or 10.62 percent $[(P_t - P_f)/P_f = 10.62\%]$ and lumber exports from Canada to the United States decline by 2.76 bbf, or 15.90 percent $[(P_fB - P_tC)/ P_fB = 15.90\%]$. It also made the total U.S. lumber production increase by 1.93 bbf or 5.71 percent. Consequently, total U.S. consumption declined by 0.82 bbf, or 1.59 percent.

Wear and Lee (1993) also point out that, in 1987, gains from such a policy for U.S. producers were US\$459 million in 1982 dollars, with an increase in consumer costs of \$806 million. For Canadian producers, profits fell by US\$136 million, but the provinces gained U.S. \$301 million in tax revenue. Although they have not provided an estimate of the loss in Canadian consumer surplus, the tax revenue should surpass the loss in both consumer surplus and producer surplus in Canada.

Over the full four-year period of the MOU (1987 to 1990), the Canadian share of the U.S. lumber market declined about 5 percent; U.S. producers gained about US$2.6 billion (in 1982 dollars), while U.S. consumers lost $3.8 billion. Thus, Wear and Lee (1993) place the net U.S. cost at $1.2 billion over the four-year period. U.S. consumers and Canadian producers were worse off; American producers and the Canadian treasury gained.

The MOU met the goal of the coalition and served as an effective rent-seeking mechanism for U.S. producers (Wear and Lee 1993). However, when on Canadian TV on December 31, 1986, it was suggested to him that the coalition must be happy with the restrictive measure against Canadian lumber, William Lange replied, "The Canadian people who are the owners of Canadian forest resources should be happy. They have secured a better return to their forest resources" (Lange 2003). He was right, at least from an equity point of view.

Notes

1. The National Forest Products Association later became part of the American Forest and Paper Association, which stayed neutral in Lumber III and Lumber IV, likely at the insistence of its Canadian members.

2. In this process, the coalition was surprised to find that most top trade law firms had been hired by the Canadians and thus could not work for the coalition because of conflict of interest (Lange 2003). The Canadians had strategically chosen their trade counsels by spreading their workloads among different law firms in Washington, D.C.

3. An undated release by this coalition lists among its members 42 associations consisting primarily of lumber dealers, homebuilders, at least two major unions, and nearly 600 individual companies, widely distributed over the country (Fox 1991).

4. These bills are the aforementioned Canadian Softwood Import Control Act, H.R. 1088, as well as the Softwood Lumber Stabilization Act of 1985, S. 1224 (*Congressional Record* 1985d), the Wood Products Trade Act of 1985, H.R. 1648 (*Congressional Record* 1985e) and S. 982 (*Congressional Record* 1985f).

5. Original. This should be per thousand board feet.

6. On May 22, 1986, the U.S. House of Representatives passed a bill (H.R. 4800) that contained a section on natural resource subsidies, borrowed from the Gibbons bill (H.R. 2451), by a wide margin (295 to 115). Both the Reagan administration and the Canadians were worried that forward movement on a companion bill in the Senate would jeopardize the free trade talks. If the Senate had passed the companion bill by the same margin (71 percent) as the House, President Reagan might not have been able to sustain a veto. However, the U.S. Senate did not vote on the companion bill, partly because the lumber issue was "fixed".

7. On October 3, 1985, Senator Bob Packwood, chairman of the Senate Finance Committee, invited Mike Apsey to his office and gave him 20 minutes to explain why "you Canadians think you are not subsidized." At the end, Packwood said, "Thank you Mike. That's the finest explanation I've ever heard as to why you Canadians feel that

you are not subsidized. And, I, Bob Packwood, am even prepared to believe that you are not, in fact, subsidized. But, Mike, I am going to get re-elected" (Apsey 2006, *249–50*).

8. Percy and Yoder (1987, *57*) note that only 22 percent of timber harvests in British Columbia was used in the production of dimension softwood lumber. The single largest use (23.5 percent) of softwood timber was in the production of bleached kraft market pulp, and the pulp and paper industry used about 35 percent softwood timber. Thus, Commerce (1986b) implicitly found the Canadian pulp and paper industry guilty of using a subsidized input, "underpriced" Crown timber. Percy and Yoder (1987) feared this was an invitation for a countervailing duty case against the Canadian pulp and paper industry.

Yet no such case against Canadian pulp and paper industry has been filed. When asked by the author in a 1996 interview why the coalition did not file such a case, John Ragosta replied, "We would love to file a [countervailing duty] case against the Canadian pulp and paper industry." He later said there was no stumpage subsidy to the Canadian pulp and paper industry (Ragosta 2006).

Other factors might have prevented lawyers from filing such a case (see Chapter 10).

9. Commerce used alternative benchmark 3 in Lumber II. The Canadian industry prepared for a cross-border comparison study in Lumber II, showing that after considering higher road-building costs, longer log hauls, and the cost of operating logging camps, the illusion of lower Canadian costs disappeared (McCloy 1986). As noted earlier, the coalition showed that there was a difference of US$50/mbf (Dewey Ballantine 1986).

10. Bill Lange would become a nonpolicymaking official in Commerce in Lumber III. He recused himself after the Canadian government protested.

11. A graph with a 15 percent export tax would be different from Figure 4-2. Export tax only applies to excess supply in Canada, while stumpage price adjustments rotate the Canadian supply curve upward. Nonetheless, Wear and Lee (1993) detect no significant change in the market impact of the policy shift (from export tax in 1987 to stumpage adjustments afterward) in the United States.

5

The Free Trade Agreement and Termination of the MOU, 1987–1991

Once fast-track authority to negotiate was granted to President Reagan in April 1986, the United States and Canada formally entered into negotiations for a trade agreement. The two-year-long initiation, negotiations, and signing of the Free Trade Agreement at midnight on October 4, 1987, were significant events in the U.S.–Canada trade relationship. The FTA was subsequently approved by the legislative bodies in both countries and formally took effect on January 1, 1989 (Hart et al. 1994).

Ostensibly, free trade and market access were the goals of the FTA for both countries. However, from the onset of the negotiations, Canada expressed as one of its primary negotiating objectives the elimination, on trade between the two countries, of the application of their respective antidumping and countervailing duty laws. In Canada's view, the U.S. system had become a complainant-driven and, in some cases, highly politicized and expensive method of harassing Canadian exporters (Apsey and Thomas 1997), and the solution was an exemption from U.S. trade remedy law for Canadian goods or the establishment of new institutions to oversee the operation of any agreement and arbitrate or otherwise resolve trade disputes. Prime Minister Mulroney said he would never sign a free trade deal with the United States unless Canada won special treatment under U.S. trade remedy law to prevent trade harassment. In March 1987, when the negotiations were in full swing, he stated in Parliament,

> Our highest priority is to have an agreement that ends the threat to Canadian industry from U.S. protectionists who harass and restrict our exports through the misuse of trade remedy laws.... Let me leave no doubt that first, a new regime on trade remedy laws must be part of the agreement. (*Toronto Star* 1992b)

The United States, on the other hand, did not see a problem and was not interested in constraining its trade remedy laws. The two countries compro-

mised by creating a new system for resolving disputes and committing to negotiate over the following five to seven years a code to determine which subsidies
would or would not be subject to U.S. trade measures. However, no progress has
been made on such a subsidy code.

The new dispute system retained existing domestic laws and investigative
procedures and set up a binational panel review mechanism for antidumping
and countervailing duty disputes. The two countries agreed, in Chapter 19 of
the FTA, to "replace judicial review of final anti-dumping and countervailing
duty determinations with bi-national panel review." The binational panel
would consist of five American and Canadian experts: two from each country,
who would collectively choose the fifth member. Thus, in place of national
courts, the panel would decide whether the importing country's "competent
investigating authority" had applied its antidumping or countervailing duty
laws in a particular investigation in accordance with its domestic laws. To ensure
the integrity of the panel, a roster of 50 individuals, half American and half
Canadian, was created. Candidates on the roster were to be of "good character,
high standing and repute" and were to be chosen strictly on the basis of objec-
tivity, reliability, sound judgment, and general familiarity with international
trade law. The review panel would not be a binational court, but its decisions
would be final and legally binding on both countries.

Questions were raised about how Chapter 19 would work in practice. For
example, how could lawyers schooled in the law of one country grasp the main-
stream principles of administrative laws of the other? In addition, the panel
roster could include nonlawyers. Could economists and political scientists do
the work that is often reserved for lawyers? Would the panel be able to discern
the relevant law and then apply it properly? Administrative law, although developed and voluminous in both countries, is imprecise. This is not an area of law
with clear, objective, and easily applied principles, and even experienced judges
are frequently confounded (Apsey and Thomas 1997).

A particular problem was a potential constitutional challenge to the panel
review mechanism. Article II of the U.S. Constitution requires Senate confirma-
tion of the president's appointees for "Ambassadors, other public Ministers and
Consuls, Judges of the Supreme Court, and all other Officers of the United
States..." Since the binational panel would replace U.S. federal courts, panelists
might be considered "other Officers of the United States." If so, the process of
appointing FTA panelists might not be constitutional.

Further, Article III of the U.S. Constitution guarantees "due process" in
court. If an FTA panel ruled against a U.S. industry or a firm and the ruling was
final under the agreement, the industry or firm would not be able to seek judicial relief in the U.S. courts.

The U.S. negotiators thought that a special appeals process to protect against
potential problems would reduce the chances of a successful constitutional
challenge to the FTA panel system. Consequently, the two countries agreed to
have an "extraordinary challenge committee" in case the panel process went

awry, even though the idea was not in the original "elements of agreement" document signed by negotiators on October 4, 1987.

Article 1904.13 thus provided that a party (either the U.S. or the Canadian government), within a month following a panel decision, could invoke an extraordinary challenge procedure if it could successfully pass the following three-pronged test:

1. the party alleges that (i) a member of the panel was guilty of gross misconduct, bias, or a serious conflict of interest, or otherwise materially violated the rules of conduct; (ii) the panel seriously departed from a fundamental rule of procedure; or (iii) the panel manifestly exceeded its powers, authority or jurisdiction set out in this Article [1904];
2. any of the above actions "materially affected the panel's decision"; and
3. such actions threatened the integrity of the binational panel review process.[1]

An extraordinary challenge committee could make one of three decisions. It could vacate the original binational panel decision, and a new panel would have to be established; remand the panel decision to the original panel; or if the grounds for review were not met, let stand the decision. The committee's decision would be binding on the parties with respect to the matter decided.

Debate about the Dispute Settlement System

Since the U.S. market is roughly 10 times the size of Canada's, it is no wonder Canadians are eager to have secure access to the American market. However, Canadian politicians, business leaders, and trade scholars have long debated the merits of a bilateral trade agreement with the United States in achieving such a goal. Some of Mulroney's predecessors—Mackenzie King, Louis St. Laurent, Lester Pearson, Pierre Trudeau—had traditionally relied on the multilateral trading system to liberalize world markets, thus avoiding Canada's possible loss of independence through a bilateral and continental trade deal with the United States. In his book, *Towards a Just Society*, Trudeau (1991) called the FTA "a monstrous swindle under which the Canadian government has ceded to the United States a large slice of the country's sovereignty over its economy and natural resources in exchange for advantages we already had, or were going to obtain in a few years anyway through the normal operation of the GATT."

Although it fell short of granting an exemption or special treatment for Canada from the U.S. trade remedy laws, Prime Minister Mulroney contended that the FTA would allow Canadian exporters "to compete in the U.S. market on a more secure, predictable and equitable footing." His justification was the establishment of the binational dispute settlement mechanism, which "guarantees the impartial application of U.S. anti-dumping and countervailing duty laws." Others saw it as a "Mickey Mouse" system (*Vancouver Sun* 1988a).

The question was whether the binational dispute settlement system was better than the existing system of dispute settlement within GATT (and later WTO). Crane (1988) argued that the GATT system was superior for three reasons (all of which now apply to the WTO process).

First, it assessed U.S. trade actions according to GATT rules, rights, and obligations, not the latest version of U.S. trade law. Because the GATT system dealt with rights and obligations that were negotiated multilaterally, it could not be changed unilaterally by the U.S. Congress.

Second, the GATT process, which could be initiated just 20 days after the Department of Commerce received a petition for a hearing, was faster than the FTA process. Under the new agreement, a review could not be launched until Commerce and ITC had handed down their final finding. GATT was returning findings in less than six months after initial meetings with the disputants; the FTA process would take about 10 months, after it was agreed there should be a panel and if no extraordinary challenge were launched.

Finally, the GATT system had worked well for Canada. In the 11 complaints Canada filed with GATT against trade measures adopted by other countries before 1988, only once did a GATT panel present findings against Canada. In six cases, GATT panels found in Canada's favor, and in four others, Canada settled with its trade adversary before the process was completed.

A few years later, Howse (1998) reached a similar conclusion, adding that the North American Free Trade Agreement process could be deprived of legitimacy by delays, high costs, divisions of panelists along national lines, and lack of consistency in decisionmaking.

However, the GATT system had at least two serious defects (which, again, apply to today's WTO process)—its rulings were hard to enforce, and duties paid prior to rulings were not paid back. The main GATT enforcement mechanism was retaliation if a losing country did not comply with its rulings. For countries like Canada, which are economically small, enjoy a trade surplus with the United States, and do not want to use their leverage (such as energy exports), finding an effective mechanism to ensure that the United States complied with GATT rulings was difficult. On the other hand, the FTA panel ruling would have the force of U.S. law, so the U.S. government would be legally obliged to abide by it. Further, U.S. courts have routinely required that duties be retroactively refunded to exporters if they were wrongly applied in the first place.

The Free Trade Agreement and the Memorandum of Understanding

Where did the softwood lumber trade dispute fit in the FTA negotiations? The dispute had already threatened to block the negotiations in early 1986, when President Reagan's request for fast-track authority was nearly denied by the

Senate Finance Committee. When the negotiations neared closure, the issue of how to deal with the MOU came up again. Given Carney's high exposure on this issue, as Canada's trade minister and a representative from British Columbia, she took personal responsibility for the negotiations on this point (Ritchie 1997). The result was that both sides agreed that the FTA "does not impair or prejudice the exercise of any rights or enforcement measures" arising out of the MOU.

This was a deliberately ambiguous formula under which both sides could claim victory. U.S. negotiators told their lumber producers and Capitol Hill that this meant the MOU was untouchable and they could keep the export tax on Canadian lumber forever. Canadian negotiators had a different view; they saw it as a mere postponement of the fight to another day (Ritchie 1997).

As noted earlier, softwood lumber consumers in Canada have not had a voice in the lumber dispute, and consequently, the media in Canada have reported on the MOU from the perspective of the forest industry. The industry detested the MOU in the first place; it saw lumber as a bargaining chip in the free trade negotiations. Apsey said that Canada's negotiators "sold their souls in a sense" because Canada would have to seek approval of "every move made in Canada that might affect the economics of the forest industry" (*Toronto Star* 1988a).

Now the FTA had been implemented. Would Canada be able to negotiate a new deal with the United States that replaced or eliminated the MOU? Suppose that all four provinces under the MOU replaced the export tax with other measures, such as higher stumpage fees; would the MOU still be valid? If the United States refused to negotiate a new deal and retaliated after Canada terminated the MOU, would the FTA dispute settlement system work in Canada's favor?

An Attempt to Renegotiate the MOU

The day of renewed fighting over the MOU would come soon. With the help of the government of British Columbia and the U.S. Department of Commerce on two separate fronts, the forest industry in Canada (especially in British Columbia) as early as November 1988 started lobbying for renegotiating or terminating the MOU.

On September 15, 1987, the B.C. government announced a new, province-wide forest policy with the following features:

- It shifted the responsibility for silviculture from the government to private companies.
- It immediately transferred 5 percent of the annual allowable cut from all replaceable licenses (tree farm, forest, timber sale, and timber sale harvesting licenses) to the provincial government, with another 5 percent to be

TABLE 5-1. Estimated Value of Replacement Measures in British Columbia, November 1987

	Reference year (1985–86) (C$ million)	Current (1987) (C$ million)	Increase (C$ million)	Factor[a]	Replacement value (C$ million)
Stumpage					
Coast	79.4	202.8	123.4	0.24	29.6
Interior	76.0	407.1	331.1	0.68	225.1
Royalty					
Coast	8.2	32.8	24.6	0.24	5.9
Interior	0.4	1.6	1.2	0.68	0.8
Forest renewal (silvicultural cost transfer)					
Coast	0.0	23.9	23.9	0.24	5.7
Interior	0.0	118.8	118.8	0.68	80.8
Total	164.0	787.0	623.0		347.9[b]

[a]Of the coastal timber harvest, 60 percent is processed in sawmills and 40 percent of lumber shipments are exported to the United States. Therefore, 24 percent (0.60 × 0.40) of the stumpage increase applies as a replacement measure. Of the interior timber harvest, 85 percent is processed in sawmills and 80 percent of lumber shipments are exported to the United States. Therefore, 68 percent (0.85 × 0.80) of the stumpage increase applies as a replacement measure.
[b]Between January 1 and September 30, 1987, the B.C. industry paid C$220.4 million in export charges. The annual payment would therefore be C$325 million.
Source: B.C. Ministry of Forests (1987).

taken upon renewal of the licenses (to provide more scope for the Small Business Forest Enterprise Program).
• It increased stumpage and other forest charges from $580 million to an estimated $680 million annually.

This policy change was supposed to be a replacement measure for the 15 percent export tax on lumber. It did more. The B.C. industry had collected C$787 million in 1987, C$623 million more than in the 1985–1986 reference year (Table 5-1). Approximately C$348 million was directly related to lumber exports to the United States, which was more than the C$325 million export tax paid without the replacement measure. The remaining C$275 million was attributable to domestic sales and sales to markets other than the United States. This is possible because the higher costs were imposed on all timber harvested from public lands in the province, regardless of the market, foreign or domestic, and whether in the form of lumber or other products. So a replacement of the export tax on lumber exported to the United States now became a tax on all forest products, no matter where the markets for these products were. This put British Columbia's forest industry at a disadvantage relative to its U.S. competitors in Japanese and European markets.

A subtle but important change in the new policy was the abandonment of the residual approach in calculating stumpage fees. Previously, stumpage payments were residuals obtained by subtracting costs of labor and capital inputs in timber harvesting (and processing of forest products, if delivered log prices were not available) from the market value of these products (logs or lumber). In other words, stumpage prices equal the end-product selling prices (log prices recorded in the Vancouver log market on the coast, lumber prices in the interior) minus operating costs for logging and transportation, profit allowance, as well as milling costs in the interior of the province. This residual approach was used in both the United States (where it is still used) and British Columbia and was exactly the exercise a forest products company had to perform in deciding how much to bid for timber in public or private auctions. It is largely a market-based approach.

The replacement measure, the so-called comparative valuation method, starts with the provincial government's setting an annual stumpage revenue target for the whole province, then target stumpage rates for the coast and for the interior, and finally the stumpage payment (and thus target rate) by each tenure holder based on timber species, grade, and timber stand location. If the adjustment for species, grade, and location is reasonable, the provincial stumpage revenue target must be set based on market conditions to begin with.

The nonmarket nature of this new method was the central focus of criticism from the industry. The revenue target was often set in consideration of a number of provincial objectives, the most notable being the government's desire to eliminate the export tax on softwood lumber exports, and possible provincial budget needs. The B.C. government had to convince and then negotiate with Commerce and the Coalition for Fair Lumber Imports that the initial stumpage revenue target was more than or about equal to the 15 percent export tax.

The Vander Zalm government had considered raising stumpage prices for some time. Since the federal export tax on lumber was returned to provincial governments, it did not have to resort to this replacement measure to fix its budget woes at the time. Possibly it had other motives: squeezing more from the forest industry,[2] securing tax revenues before the federal government took its share in corporate income tax[3], and then diverting the blame to the Americans.

Perhaps utilizing the MOU was the only way that the B.C. government could have concluded that, without any guidance from the market, the stumpage payment for future years should be C$680 million instead of C$580 million (both were estimates). From then on, stumpage payments would be decided by the financial and political needs of the provincial government, not the market. This was a triumph of politics over economics.

Interestingly, stumpage revenue had not reached C$500 million between 1981 and 1987, and the average stumpage revenue for the five years prior to March 31, 1987, was merely C$132 million. Under the new policy, average stumpage fees doubled in 1988. The total stumpage revenue in the fiscal year ending March 31, 1988, rose to C$483 million, more than double the amount of the previous year, C$215 million. Similarly, total government revenue generated from its forests was nearly C$600 million in the fiscal year ending March 31, 1988, rising from C$288 million the previous year (Table 5-2).

TABLE 5-2. Provincial Forest Revenues in British Columbia, 1981–1992

Fiscal year	Average stumpage (C$/m³)	Total stumpage (C$ thousand)	Rental, royalty, and other fees (C$ thousand)	Stumpage from SBFEP (C$ thousand)	Total (C$ thousand)
1981	5.16	309,794	51,044	711	361,549
1982	2.17	69,894	37,061	8,970	115,925
1983	1.79	48,091	39,239	9,384	96,714
1984	2.15	86,903	50,363	17,271	154,537
1985	2.12	144,321	43,028	25,450	212,799
1986	2.18	166,054	42,922	31,461	240,437
1987	2.88	214,558	31,608	42,168	288,334
1988	5.89	482,224	54,063	60,163	596,450
1989	6.68	393,663	95,523	134,456	623,642
1990	7.43	434,835	60,464	147,292	642,591
1991	7.34	395,040	66,648	111,482	573,170
1992	7.47	411,383	65,159	131,376	607,918

Note: SBFEP = Small Business Forest Enterprise Program.
Source: B.C. Ministry of Forests (various years).

The B.C. forest industry opposed the new stumpage system after the provincial Ministry of Forests published its white paper on July 10, 1987. The industry preferred to retain or modify the market-sensitive residual approach and the possibility and flexibility of lower stumpage fees when markets were down. It wanted the stumpage fees on timber destined for nonsoftwood lumber products and softwood lumber in non-U.S. markets unchanged. It requested that the export tax not be converted to a stumpage system, but rather be kept as a separate, visible, and potentially negotiable tariff. But neither of the two industry proposals—modifying the current residual approach by incorporating increased chip prices, increased lumber recovery factors, and revised profit and risk allowances, and using an export tax plus a modified residual approach—would satisfy the provincial government's desire for more revenue. In the end, the provincial cabinet overrode opposition from the Minister of Forests, Dave Parker, and implemented the new policy.

It would have been difficult for the B.C. government to implement the new forest policy earlier in the face of strong opposition from the industry and powerful unions. This "blame the Americans" strategy worked for the Vander Zalm government in fixing its budget woes but dismayed the industry. Mike Apsey expressed the industry's disappointment and frustration by saying, "We are dismayed. I mean, very dismayed" (*Financial Post* 1987).

Because any changes to this new policy would have to be done under the MOU and be sanctioned by Commerce and the coalition, the B.C. forest industry viewed the MOU as a barrier, even when it could convince the government that the market conditions could not support the government's stumpage revenue target or when a more sympathetic government returned to power a few years later.

In the meantime, both government and industry in Canada watched the U.S. Department of Commerce become increasingly intrusive. It created an office in its antidumping and countervailing duty operations to review Canada's performance under the MOU, and it seemed that no issue was too remote from the pricing of timber to justify not seeking an explanation from Canada (Apsey and Thomas 1997).

In mid-1988, sawmill owners in the most remote and perhaps the most forest-dependent region of the province, Prince George, were paying as much as C$17.50/m³ stumpage fees, up from C$2/m³ when the MOU was signed in 1986, plus a C$4/m³ reforestation cost. At the same time, Canadian dollars appreciated 16.7 percent (from C$/US$ = 0.72 to 0.84). On June 7, 1988, after being told by sawmill owners in the region that a slight dip in the lumber market would cause mill closure, the B.C. government announced that it would lower its stumpage in the region by C$1.75/m³, effective July 1. Even though this measure would save sawmills in the region some C$13 million, some mill owners said that it did not do much to solve the problem (*Vancouver Sun* 1988c). Nonetheless, the coalition argued that it was not allowed under the MOU.

Canadian and B.C. officials went to Washington, D.C., in late June to explain the provincial government's action. They met with officials from Commerce and the U.S. trade representative in Ottawa again in early July. Gus Kuehne of the coalition asked Commerce to investigate, contending that British Columbia had violated the MOU and arguing that if the province did not maintain the specified level of stumpage revenue, Canada would be required to reimpose an export tax or the United States would be required to impose a countervailing duty (*Wall Street Journal* 1988).

The coalition also alleged that British Columbia violated the MOU by refusing to implement an upward adjustment in the general fee scheduled on July 1. Apparently, economic conditions forced the provincial government to modify its scheduled fee adjustment. The coalition argued that the United States had to approve any change and that what British Columbia wanted to do was not allowed under the MOU. Senator Baucus urged the U.S. government to reimpose a duty on Canadian lumber imports and terminate the MOU. He said, in a hearing on the FTA,

> The province of British Columbia is now in open violation of the softwood lumber agreement ... Through a combination of uncollected taxes and underpriced stumpage, the province of British Columbia now appears to have violated the softwood lumber agreement [the MOU] to the tune of US$250 million to US$270 million. If this issue is not resolved quickly, I must urge the U.S. government in the strongest terms to consider re-imposing a duty on Canadian softwood imports and terminating the lumber agreement.[4] (*Vancouver Sun* 1988d)

Prior to the June–July meetings between government officials from the two countries, Commerce raised the issue of freight rate reductions announced in

March by Canadian National Railways and B.C. Railways for softwood lumber shipped from British Columbia and Alberta to eastern Canada, where some of it was shipped on to the United States. Joseph Spetrini, assistant secretary of Commerce for Import Administration, wrote to the Canadian government, demanding an explanation of how this would affect the MOU's operation.

Donald Campbell, a senior Canadian trade official, wrote back, stating, "I can assure you that the modest reduction in freight rates which you cite does not represent any attempt whatsoever to offset the effect of the export charge or the replacement measures since there is no government involvement in the setting of these rates." Although Commerce found this explanation "not satisfactory," it did not press the issue further (*Toronto Star* 1988b).

At a Senate International Trade Subcommittee hearing in April 1989, L.D. Broderick, president of Rivendell Forest Products Ltd. and chairman of the coalition, alleged that Canadian export companies in Alberta and Ontario, which were still required to pay 15 percent duty, were avoiding the export tax by falsely reporting their lumber as coming from tax-exempt British Columbia. Senator Baucus stated that the allegations suggested "outright customs violations" that "simply cannot be tolerated" and that illegal imports could have a disastrous effect on U.S. sawmills. He called on the U.S. Customs Service to prosecute the claims if proved true (*Seattle Times* 1989).

Senator Baucus also warned that Canadian officials were seeking to scrap the MOU, after learning that Frank Oberle, the Canadian Minister of Forestry, had said that finding a way to cancel the 1986 agreement was his top priority. The minister thought the MOU provided for its own cancellation "if and when the provinces and industry have developed offsets that would eliminate the perceived subsidy." Consequently, Canadian Trade Minister John Crosbie raised the issue, in early April 1989, with U.S. Trade Representative Carla Hills, who rebuffed him. Stanley Dennison, executive director of the coalition, said the Bush administration had reassured the industry "it is not going to reopen this treaty" (*Toronto Star* 1989a).

Preparation for Withdrawal from the MOU

As early as 1988, issues and possible withdrawal from the MOU were discussed among top Canadian forest industry leaders. In particular, Adam Zimmerman and T. Mike Apsey, chairman and trade coordinator of the Canadian Forest Industries Council, respectively, had sought the advice of the former Canadian deputy trade negotiator of the FTA, Gordon Ritchie, who became a trade consultant after the FTA negotiations, on the possibility of MOU withdrawal.

As the chairman of the Canadian industry group, Zimmerman was front and center in Lumber II. He was held responsible, by the Canadian Trade Department and by his industry, for much difficulty and perhaps the result, the MOU. Zimmerman did not like the interpretation of the FTA language on lumber—

there was no termination date for the lumber tax. It did not help that Zimmerman was a friend and supporter of opposition Liberal Party leader John Turner, and his relationship with the Mulroney-led Conservative government was rocky during the MOU and FTA negotiations (Ritchie 1997).

The top administrators in the government believed that Zimmerman had backed the original negotiations with the United States but changed his mind later. The government was less than pleased that during the final first ministers' meeting on a proposed deal based on a 15 percent export tax, Ontario Premier David Peterson, a Liberal, repeatedly left the negotiating table to speak by telephone with Zimmerman, who urged him not to accept the deal (*Vancouver Sun* 1988b).

For his part, Zimmerman said he reluctantly backed the government's negotiation efforts. He wanted the matter to be conducted on an industry-to-industry level. But he was convinced by the government that an import duty was inevitable and that the export tax would be kept under 10 percent. He said he changed his mind when the government broke its promise by offering a 15 percent export tax. Further, Zimmerman felt that increases in provincial stumpage fees in lieu of the federal export tax would be monitored and approved by the United States. This process, in his view, was controlled by the U.S. industry (*Vancouver Sun* 1988b).

Gordon Ritchie had not been a fan of the MOU to begin with. Although not directly involved in the negotiation of the MOU, he watched the unfolding of the lumber case with interest as he and his colleagues were preparing to negotiate the FTA. At one time, he passed a message to the Canadian government, a veiled threat from U.S. Commerce Secretary Baldrige: You [Canadians] "should not focus unduly on the facts and laws. The political reality was this: he [Baldrige] would have to determine that Canadian lumber should be penalized, or Congress would run amok and impose its own restriction, which could be much more damaging to Canadian interests. He really had no option" (Ritchie 1997, *199*).

After the FTA was signed, Ritchie stated, in a news conference, that if the agreement had been in place, the lumber case would have had a very different result. Ritchie believed that binational panels would have struck down Commerce's 1986 affirmative determination if it were made final. He advised Zimmerman and Apsey that they had a good chance of getting rid of the MOU under the FTA, and at least, "We should give the Americans the benefit of the doubt, unless and until they proved unworthy of this confidence" (Ritchie 1997, *201*).

Subsequently, the Canadian industry started lobbying for a change or termination of the MOU. One way to get rid of it was to enter into a new agreement with the U.S. government. That is, after all four major provinces implemented some replacement measures, as British Columbia had done, Canada could argue that the MOU had served its purpose and become irrelevant. With possibly reduced protectionist sentiment and a new trade focus on the European

Union and Japan in the U.S. Congress, the Bush administration might agree to negotiate a new deal.

The Canadian industry's hope for negotiating a new deal quickly vanished. On April 10, 1989, a U.S. trade representative spokesman stated, "If Canada wants to reopen the deal, the answer is no." In response, Trade Minister Crosbie said, "We have other alternatives," and he started to consult provinces and the industry to weigh the options (*Toronto Star* 1989b).

The other way left for Canada was to terminate the MOU. If the United States retaliated, which seemed likely, Canada could fight the battle under the FTA dispute resolution system, which gave Canada a better chance of winning the case than did the old system. Still, Canada needed to have a good case. So the Canadian Forest Industries Council started looking for political as well as empirical support for termination.

In 1989, the U.S. Forest Service, which administers most U.S. federal forest land (or more than 25 percent of total U.S. forest land), implemented a new accounting system, known as the Timber Sales Program Information Report System, after testing it since 1986. It was intended to document more fully the costs and benefits of sales of timber from public lands.[5] The Canadian Forest Industries Council decided that, to assist in demonstrating that Canadian lumber producers were not subsidized, the U.S. Forest Service's accounting system should be used rather than the flawed, result-driven method of calculating forestry costs and revenues employed by Commerce in Lumber II.

So the Canadian council studied the new accounting system extensively and hired American experts to assist in conducting a study of the four major timber-producing provinces in Canada. The American experts were instructed to be conservative when adjusting to Canadian circumstances. The results showed that each Canadian province was more than recovering the costs of its timber sales (Apsey and Thomas 1997).

In the summer of 1989, the Canadian government tried to encourage other provinces to find replacement measures for the export tax to demonstrate to the United States that the export tax was no longer necessary. Otherwise, it would be forced to defend them if a countervailing action was brought against them. Alberta and Ontario refused to come up with replacement measures. Québec took steps that substantially reduced the export tariff from 15 percent to 6.2 percent, which would be further reduced to 3.1 percent on November 1, 1991.

British Columbia and Québec together accounted for 73 percent of Canadian softwood lumber exports in volume and 89 percent in value to the United States in 1991. This, plus the export share (5 percent in volume, 2.3 percent in value) of provinces that were exempt from the MOU, meant that some 78 percent in volume and 91 percent in value of Canadian softwood lumber exported to the United States did not pay export tax anymore. Consequently, only C$40 million in export tax was collected in 1991, roughly a tenth of the collection in 1987 (Canadian Embassy to the U.S. 1991).

Given that British Columbia had probably done more than implementing the 15 percent export tax, Canada argued that on balance, it had adequately met the MOU requirements even with no replacement measure being implemented in Ontario and Alberta. Further, research based on the U.S. Timber Sales Program Information Report System showed that Canada did not subsidize its lumber industry, and Canada was going to continue to maintain the replacement measures, even though the calculation method used by Commerce in 1986 to derive the 15 percent subsidy was flawed. Third, Canadian dollars had increased in value against U.S. dollars and the Canadian share of the U.S. lumber market was falling. Finally, Canadian lumber producers' profits were low or negative because their access to the U.S. market was curtailed by the MOU.

Initial U.S. Reactions to the Possible Termination of MOU

News that the Canadian lumber industry was pressuring its federal and provincial governments to terminate the MOU brought actions from the Coalition for Fair Lumber Imports and its allies in the U.S. Congress. In a letter dated November 15, 1990, to U.S. Representative Ron Wyden (D-Oregon), chairman of the House Small Business Subcommittee, U.S. Commerce Secretary Robert Mosbacher pledged to enforce the MOU and protect the U.S. lumber industry. He stated,

> Events in Canada suggest that the government of Canada may be under increasing pressure to renegotiate or eliminate the 4-year-old MOU between the two countries ...
> We are firmly committed ... and will take any action necessary and appropriate to enforce the terms of the agreement, which has become a "political target" in Canada because of sawmill closures, a stronger Canadian dollar and fear of a market downturn ... While Canada's economic problems have an effect on its lumber industry, they don't affect the subsidies the agreement offsets. (*Seattle Post-Intelligencer* 1990)

After hearing that Canadian Trade Minister Crosbie wanted to scrap the 15 percent tax in late February 1991, the Wyden House subcommittee called in Marjorie Chorlins, a deputy assistant secretary of Commerce, to explain what the department would do in case Canada terminated the MOU. Chorlins said, "We stand firmly behind the Memorandum of Understanding, don't see any reason at the present time to change the terms of the agreement or to consider its termination ... The administration will use 'any tool which would be necessary and appropriate' to enforce the 1986 Memo of Understanding." Soon 32 U.S. senators voiced their opinions in a March 1991 letter to U.S. Trade Representative Carla Hills, urging her to "oppose 'any and all' attempts by the Canadian government to renegotiate [the MOU]" (*Vancouver Sun* 1991b).

In the meantime, Minister Crosbie had completed his consultation with provinces. All wanted to scrap the MOU except for the Atlantic provinces, which were exempt and did not want to jeopardize their special position. Provincial leaders who had not experienced previous rounds of the lumber war—like Ontario Premier Bob Rae, who was elected in 1990—were more enthusiastic about dropping the MOU. He sounded like he was in a political campaign, saying "Let's go for it. Let's get rid of it. Let's take the Americans on. We're not subsidizing our industry" (*Seattle Post-Intelligencer* 1991). Others who had dealt with the Americans under the MOU were more cautious but nonetheless supportive. B.C. Minister of Forests Claude Richmond said, "We think the time is right. We've got a good case to make. But I also caution you the Americans like the MOU and they will be fighting just as hard to keep it in place." Even if the MOU was scrapped, Richmond was against expecting a dramatically revised stumpage and lower government charges (*Vancouver Sun* 1991a).

Minister Crosbie then told the Canadian Parliament,

> We've had extensive research with respect to this question of whether provincial governments collect adequate ... revenues from the forestry sector or not. And the results of these studies are very clear. The methodology used by the U.S. Forest Service itself, we are quite confident it demonstrates that there is no subsidization involved ... Anyone who examines this question impartially and rationally would agree that the time has come for the MOU to be done away with. (*Vancouver Sun* 1991a)

Subsequently, Prime Minister Mulroney told President Bush, during his visit to Ottawa on March 13–14, 1991, that Canada wanted to get out of the MOU. Bush's visit to Canada was the first to a U.S. ally after the 1990 Gulf War. Representative Wyden was concerned that Canada would seek softwood lumber trade favors from the United States in return for its support in the Gulf War. He wanted the president to make a public response about defending the MOU and soon sent a letter to the president asking for assurance[6] (*Ottawa Citizen* 1991).

President Bush's exact response to Mulroney's request to terminate the MOU is unknown. The White House press officer and a Commerce spokeswoman said they had no information about what Bush said. But a spokesman for U.S. Trade Representative Carla Hills, on condition of anonymity, said Bush told Mulroney privately he would resist any changes. He said,

> The gist of it was that the United States isn't really interested in altering the agreement ... [Bush] respects Prime Minister Mulroney and I'm sure he must have listened to him very willingly and politely and will consult with the government about what if anything can be done, but essentially

his position is there will be no alterations any time soon. (*Ottawa Citizen* 1991)

The spokesman further stated that Bush did not rule out reconsidering the issue later (*Ottawa Citizen* 1991). Thus, it seemed that even if the president wanted to reward Canada (and his friend Mulroney), which he called "a staunch ally," he did not think the time was right.

If Canada was going to honor the MOU commitment anyway, why did it want to withdraw from the MOU and risk possible retaliation by the United States? Several possible reasons can be entertained. First, the MOU stood in the way of the B.C. government's considering the possibility of lowering its stumpage fees,[7] and second, Commerce had been too intrusive in monitoring and implementing the MOU, interfering with Canadian sovereignty in resource management. In addition, most forest business leaders believed that U.S. retaliation, if any, would not succeed under the Free Trade Agreement. At that time, the Canadian share of the U.S. market was declining because of the MOU, appreciation in the Canadian dollar, and a brief recession in both countries. The Canadian lumber industry wanted a break.

British Columbia's Final Push for Withdrawal

On April 2, 1991, Premier Vander Zalm was forced to resign after he was found by the province's conflict-of-interest commission to have mixed his political responsibilities with the sale of his Fantasy Gardens theme park in the Vancouver suburb of Richmond. The B.C. Social Credit Party picked Rita Johnston as the caretaker premier, and a provincial election was expected to be called in the fall. At that time, the main opposition to the ruling Social Credit government was the New Democrat Party, which was viewed as less friendly to the industry. Johnston, on the other hand, was apparently more sympathetic to the industry than Vander Zalm and the New Democrats.[8] Her government was receptive to the request from the industry to withdraw from the MOU and went as far as replacing the deputy minister of forests, Phillip Halkett, with Bob Plecas, who spoke strongly for the industry.

On August 7, 1991, the Johnston government made a bold political decision in a cabinet meeting to withdraw from the MOU—with or without the Canadian federal government's support. Lumber prices in interior British Columbia had risen significantly (about 20 percent) in May, June, and July of 1991 and then fallen to the previous level (Figure 5-1). Under the new system, stumpage prices in British Columbia would be adjusted upward, starting in October 1991. Forest industry leaders in the interior did not want to face higher stumpage prices, and the Coalition for Fair Lumber Imports would not give them a break under the MOU. The only way to avoid higher stumpage prices was to withdraw from the MOU.

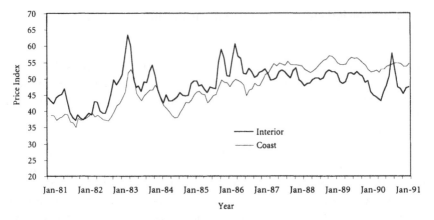

FIGURE 5-1. Softwood Lumber Price Index in British Columbia, 1981–1991

Source: Statistics Canada (http://cansim2.statcan.ca/). Series titles are British Columbia Interior, Lumber, softwood (Index, 1997=100); and British Columbia Coast, Lumber, softwood (Index, 1997=100).

Consequently, industry lobbied hard for a withdrawal from the MOU. Ike Barber, president of Slocan Forest Products Ltd., said that it was time Ottawa made the move, since the escalating charges had led to "major erosion in our confidence to do business in Interior B.C." Ross Gorman, past chairman of the Interior Lumber Manufacturers Association, stated,

> I think the provincial government is sort of caught between a rock and a hard place because of the MOU. They are required to collect so much … Southern interior lumber producers have been hit hard by recent increases in stumpage. You can't cope with it. The costs are rising so fast, and lumber prices are going down. There's no relationship of the increase [in stumpage] to the selling price [of lumber]. (*Vancouver Sun* 1991c)

The Johnston government did two things after it decided to withdraw from the MOU unilaterally. First, it sent Deputy Minister Plecas to Ottawa and Washington, D.C., to brief Canadian officials about the hardships that forest companies had continued to endure under the MOU. Johnston's minister of Forests, Claude Richmond, explained:

> We want to impress upon our Canadian representatives in the U.S. capital the seriousness of the situation of our forest-industry workers, because of [the MOU], and the critical need to get Canada–U.S. talks started on the agreement immediately. I am unwilling to wait for federal officials to begin discussions in Washington this fall. (*Vancouver Sun* 1991c)

Second, Premier Johnston turned up the heat on Prime Minister Mulroney, demanding that he be personally involved to ensure that the negotiation with the United States on lumber would start in the summer. In a letter dated August 14, 1991, to the prime minister, Johnston stated that the status quo was unacceptable and that "British Columbia is making every effort to get this issue addressed and our frustration is increasing with each delay" (*Vancouver Sun* 1991d).

Although certain Canadian officials resented the MOU because it infringed on Canadian sovereignty[9] and because they had to go to Washington, D.C., once a month to report and consult with Commerce, some senior diplomats worried that a withdrawal from the MOU, no matter how legitimate and right it was for Canada, would invite the United States to retaliate. It was not until the politicians in Ottawa saw the sheer determination of British Columbia that they took action in late August and pulled the trigger, in early September 1991.

The Formal Termination of the MOU

To avoid precipitating a dispute, the Canadian government tried to seek an American agreement to terminate. However, on August 18, 1991, Trade Representative Carla Hills once again rebuffed Canadian Trade Minister Michael Wilson's proposal to terminate the MOU (*Vancouver Sun* 1991e).

Finally, Prime Minister Mulroney raised the issue again with President George Bush when they met at Bush's vacation home in Kennebunkport, Maine, on August 25–27, 1991. All other bilateral issues were overtaken by a crisis in the former Soviet Union. Bush and Mulroney had three private meetings at which no other officials were present, so it is not known how the two heads of state discussed the lumber issue, which was Mulroney's "dominant" bilateral concern (*Toronto Star* 1991). At that time, the prime minister's chief of staff was Norm Spector, who was from British Columbia and had served as the deputy minister to the B.C. premier. He briefed the primer minister on the softwood lumber issue before he talked to President Bush alone (Plecas 2006).

There were several versions of how the conversation on the MOU might have gone between the leaders. One version holds that when Prime Minister Mulroney said that Canada was going to terminate the MOU, President Bush replied, "I think it's a good idea."[10] Mulroney and Canadian officials must have been pleased with President Bush's words and took them literally. Shortly after their meeting, officials in Ottawa prepared a diplomatic note to be transmitted to the U.S. State Department.

A final communication between Ottawa and the B.C. government occurred over the Labor Day weekend of 1991. Trade Minister Wilson called B.C. Minister of Forests Claude Richmond. Upon hearing that British Columbia still wanted to withdraw from the MOU, with or without the federal government's consent, Wilson said, "All right. Let's do it."

At midnight on September 3, 1991, Canada officially notified the United States that it would terminate the MOU one month later.

* * *

Canada's decision to withdraw from the Memorandum of Understanding was driven by industry demand, provincial politics, and province–federal dynamics. The MOU had brought some economic gains to Canada. Yet, at the request of lumber producers, particularly those in British Columbia, Canada chose to withdraw from it. A forthcoming provincial election in British Columbia and the desire of the Social Credit Party to hold on to power made the B.C. government determined to scrap it—even if it had to go it alone. At this juncture, the Canadian government had no choice but to withdraw from the MOU—lest it be embarrassed by a unilateral, provincial withdrawal from an international agreement. The B.C. government had perhaps initially overdone it by squeezing more from the industry than the MOU had called for. Now, the forest industry in that province had fought back, and Canadian provincial and federal governments had honored the industry's request. The episode inadvertently exposed a weak spot of the Canadian federation in forest products trade issues.

Notes

1. Unlike the panelists, members of the Extraordinary Challenge Committee must be judges or former judges of a federal court of the United States or a superior court of Canada, drawing from a 10-person roster (5 from each country). A committee would have 3 members; each country selects 1 member; and the third would be selected from the roster by the 2 members chosen by the countries or by a draw. Once selected, the committee would render a decision "typically within 30 days of its establishment."

2. With a modified residual approach, the Ministry of Forests calculated that it could generate C\$580 million revenue. Premier Vander Zalm thought that C\$580 million was fair but that the industry could afford an extra C\$100 million. Thus C\$680 million was set as a target (Plecas 2006).

3. Since stumpage revenue is tax deductible and the provincial share of corporate income tax is less than 50 percent, this replacement measure, in effect, secured the provincial revenue via stumpage charges while reducing the total amount of corporate income tax paid to both federal and provincial governments.

4. B.C. Forests Minister Parker said the "allegations by United States Senator Max Baucus are completely inaccurate and absolutely without justification ... Senator Baucus has provided erroneous figures to the media." Mike Apsey said that Baucus was apparently being briefed by the coalition coincident with talks then under way between Ottawa and Washington on technical issues of the MOU—issues brought up as a result of the new B.C. cutting fees (*Vancouver Sun* 1988d).

5. The new system was designed as a response to frequent complaints in Congress

about "below-cost" sales of federal timber. Below-cost sales had been seen by some environmentalists and fiscal conservative commentators as a subsidy to the U.S. forest industry. As noted earlier, the coalition believed that any domestic subsidy was legally irrelevant in its countervailing duty cases.

6. Trade Representative Carla Hills responded to Wyden in April 1991, writing, "in the event of violation or abrogation of the (agreement), we have not ruled out any options available under U.S. law, ... including section 301 [which allows the president to retaliate with sanctions in cases of unfair trading practices] if that were necessary.... The U.S. government remains firmly committed to the (agreement) and, as we have said, will take any action necessary and appropriate to enforce the terms of the agreement" (*Gazette* 1991).

7. There was no guarantee that replacement measures would not be rolled back without the MOU, notwithstanding the Canadian government's assurances to the contrary after the actual termination.

8. It was widely accepted that the industry did not want a New Democrat Party government in British Columbia. Therefore, there could be an implicit side deal accompanied by the industry's request for a withdrawal from the MOU: The industry would contribute to the election or reelection campaigns of candidates from the Social Credit Party in the forthcoming election in return for a low stumpage payment in the future if it eventually won the election and if the withdrawal did not bring retaliation from the United States.

9. On March 6, 1992, after learning of the preliminary affirmative determination of subsidy by Commerce, Canadian Trade Minister Michael Wilson said that he had no regrets about Canada's unilateral withdrawal from the MOU. "We had to reestablish our sovereignty here and I think that was the right decision" (*Vancouver Sun* 1992a).

10. The coalition contended that President Bush knew little about the softwood lumber dispute when he responded to the notice of withdrawal from MOU by Prime Minister Mulroney.

6

Lumber III

The War Intensifies, 1991–1994

To the surprise of Canadians, the Bush administration—from the White House to the Department of Commerce and the U.S. Trade Representative—said it was taken aback by the Canadian withdrawal from the Memorandum of Understanding in September 1991 (Ritchie 1997; Apsey and Thomas 1997). Ritchie (1997, *203*) stated, "It soon became clear that there had been a communications breakdown of majestic proportion within the Administration, as each of the officials the Canadians had alerted had kept the information to himself."

President Bush might have inadvertently not alerted his subordinates in Commerce and USTR because after his vacation in Maine, where he had met with Mulroney, he joined an informal meeting of leaders from G-7 countries on a major international issue before returning to Washington, D.C., on September 3, 1991. Or he may have changed his mind after his political advisers and subordinates convinced him that terminating the MOU would not be accepted by Congress. One might argue that the former scenario is unlikely, since most of Bush's cabinet secretaries were in Kennebunkport with him. But if it was true, Canadian officials could be blamed for not waiting for a few more days and pulling the trigger too soon.

The embarrassment quickly turned to outrage on Capitol Hill. Within hours of the announcement of withdrawal, Senator Baucus seemed to foreshadow the U.S. response: "The United States can't afford to let this action by the Canadians go unanswered. The United States must take action under U.S. trade laws to let the Canadians know we won't sit idly by as they backed out of the softwood lumber agreement." Representative Wyden suggested breaking off the free trade negotiations with Canada and Mexico. The USTR office said, "We will urgently review the situation. In consultation with Congress and our industry, we will be considering all options, including imposition of a U.S. import tax, if appropriate, to offset any existing subsidies" (*Wall Street Journal* 1991).

C.T. Howlett, chairman of the Coalition for Fair Lumber Imports and a vice president of Georgia-Pacific Corporation, warned that the MOU withdrawal "will inevitably lead to more subsidized lumber imports and a return to the devastation that subsidized Canadian lumber visited on the U.S. industry in the mid-1980s." He said that the coalition would vigorously pursue trade remedies under U.S. trade law, including import fees on Canadian lumber, and that the United States should make it perfectly clear that abrogation of subsidy agreements would not be tolerated (*Wall Street Journal* 1991). Later, he said that Canadian subsidies actually appeared to be rising and it would take a 25 percent U.S. duty to offset them (*Seattle Times* 1991).

In Canada, government officials and industry leaders predicted that the termination of MOU would have little impact on the stumpage fees set by the provinces for their timber, mainly because of domestic pressure. Apsey said,

> As far as we know, the stumpage system stays in place. What's been won is the ability for industry to do more than just complain to government about high stumpage charges. Canada has regained its ability to determine forest policy and timber pricing issues in this country without having to check with Washington.
>
> ... What we now have as an industry is the ability to discuss timber pricing questions with the B.C. government. We do that on a daily basis, have done that for decades, and will continue to do that for decades. But we had that pause where discussions were very hampered because the MOU was in place. Once it's gone, there will be direct discussion again. (*Vancouver Sun* 1991f)

With respect to sovereignty, Secretary Baldrige had stated on November 6, 1986, that Canada's sovereign right to manage its resources was not the issue, but any subsidy on lumber would have a large effect in the United States because a high percentage of Canada's lumber was exported to the States (Kaplan 1986b). The Canadian government asserted that it did not lose any sovereign rights by signing the MOU. Yet timber pricing policy is a significant part of the right to manage resources, and it has to be modified (or offset by other measures) if it is found to provide a subsidy. Consequently, some Canadians felt that the MOU and its enforcement mechanism peeled away some of their sovereign rights, while the U.S. government and the coalition thought they were just enforcing the MOU.

A flurry of diplomatic consultations ensued without much success. Canadians attempted to convince American officials that the financial impact of the replacement measures would not be undone by the termination, and that even if the U.S. position had had merit in 1986, the United States' own forestry accounting system showed that there was no subsidy for lumber producers in Canada. The two small lumber-exporting provinces (Ontario and Alberta) that had no replacement measures would not have a major impact in the market after the removal of export taxes. Therefore, any concerns that Canadian lumber might flood the U.S. market were simply ill founded (Apsey and Thomas 1997).

Soon, 66 U.S. senators wrote a letter to President Bush, urging him "either to press the Canadian Government to live up to its commitments or, if it refuses, to take immediate action under U.S. trade law in order to offset Canadian subsidy ... If these remedies are not pursued, we are prepared to find a legislative remedy to fully offset Canada's timber subsidies." This letter was delivered on September 20, 1991 (Zhang and Laband 2005). In any event, the action of Congress, led by Senators Packwood and Baucus, was swift. Packwood stated Congress would never have agreed to authorize former President Reagan to enter into free trade talks with Canada if it were not for the MOU. He said he discussed the issue with Bush on September 20, but the president did not indicate how he would respond (*Seattle Times* 1991).

As scheduled, Canada terminated the MOU on October 4, 1991. The Bush administration responded immediately by announcing that it would self-initiate a countervailing duty investigation and use Section 301 of the Trade Act to impose provisional duties. The duty on lumber from Ontario, Alberta, Manitoba, and Saskatchewan was 15 percent, and a 6.2 percent duty was placed on lumber from Québec before November 1, 1991, and 3.1 percent afterward. Lumber from British Columbia was exempt, since high stumpage fees imposed as a result of the MOU remained in effect. Bonds would be collected while the investigation was conducted (USTR 1991).

The use of Section 301 of the Trade Act by the Bush administration to impose liabilities even before any preliminary determinations of subsidy and injury were made astonished "America's Canadian friends," since such a measure is often brandished but rarely used against American allies. Canada appealed to the GATT, whose Subsidies Code Committee then established a panel to examine whether the imposition of interim bond and self-initiation of the investigation violated U.S. trade obligations.

Commerce's Preliminary Affirmative Determination

The official countervailing duty investigation started on October 23, 1991. The justification by Commerce for self-initiating the investigation was "(1) the special circumstances resulting from Canada's breach of the agreement between the two governments which had resulted in execution of the MOU and the termination of the investigation; and (2) information that the Department gathered regarding the extent of Canadian lumber subsidies and the likelihood that imports of these products resulted in material injury, or the threat of material injury, to the U.S. industry" (DOC 1991). By now, "Canada's unilateral breach of the agreement" and "Canadian lumber subsidies" were no longer words used only by Congress, but also by the investigating agency. These two descriptors became articles of faith in Washington (Ritchie 1997).

As an agency implementing U.S. trade laws, Commerce was the judge and adjudicator of a complaint it had itself brought against Canada. Although Commerce was under legal obligation to be impartial, its references to "Canadian lumber subsidies" were an indication that new subsidies would be found. Apsey and Thomas (1997) allege that Commerce prejudged the matter.

Commerce's notification of self-initiation of the countervailing duty investigation (DOC 1991, *56056*) further stated that as a result of Canada's termination of the MOU,

> ... the U.S. lumber industry will be denied the offset that had been provided by Canadian export charges against what in 1986 preliminarily had been found to be injurious Canadian subsidies ... the U.S. government and the U.S. industry will no longer have the ability to determine whether the timber fee increases instituted in some provinces to replace the export charge will remain in place because there will no longer be the exchange of information that occurred under the MOU.

Canadian officials argued that neither charge was true, pointing out that some 91 percent of Canadian lumber exports to the United States were no longer subject to an export tax and that replacement measures implemented under the MOU would not be diluted. Commerce and the Coalition for Fair Lumber Imports saw these words as a mere promise—unquantifiable, unreported, and unenforceable.

The notification also stated that it had gathered information on log export restrictions from British Columbia and manufacturing requirements in Québec, Ontario, and Alberta—restrictions that would likely lower domestic log prices. Although it lacked evidence demonstrating that export restrictions in Canada artificially had a measurable downward effect on log prices and thus was not sure whether the restrictions had met the threshold for initiation of an investigation, it invited interested parties to submit evidence and promised to be willing to investigate these programs.

Not surprisingly, the coalition submitted evidence that log export restrictions did indeed reduce the cost of raw logs and confer countervailable subsidies and therefore should be included in the investigation. Accordingly, Commerce expanded its investigation to cover log export restrictions.

Interestingly, Chapter 12 of the Free Trade Agreement exempted log export restrictions from the rules against export and import controls. Article 1203 states,

> The provisions of this Part (rules against export and import controls) shall not apply to
> a. controls by the United States on the export of logs of all species
> b. controls by Canada on exports of logs of all species ...

Canada therefore asked Commerce to exclude log export restrictions from its investigation. The department would not budge, however, citing domestic countervailing duty laws that FTA was supposed to uphold.

The U.S. International Trade Commission reported, on December 16, 1991, that it could not "conclude that there is clear and convincing evidence on the record of no material injury ... and *there is no likelihood that contrary evidence will be developed in the final investigation*" (ITC 1991, *20*, emphasis added). Although ITC noted that the standard of determination (of material injury) is different in the preliminary and final determination, it, too, seemed to have drawn its conclusions before conducting the final investigation.[1]

All signs pointed to adverse consequences for Canadian lumber exporters. Nonetheless, some Canadian industry executives hoped that, given that British Columbia and Québec had increased their stumpage fees and that Commerce could not use the discredited method it had used in Lumber II, the Americans might not be able to find much subsidy, if any.

Those who hoped for such a finding would be disappointed. After declaring that the investigation was "extraordinarily complicated" and extending the deadline twice, Commerce made a preliminary determination of subsidy at 14.48 percent on March 5, 1992. A provisional duty of 14.48 percent was placed on Canadian softwood lumber entering the United States from all provinces except the Maritimes and a few small firms on March 12, 1992 (DOC 1992a).

Commerce found subsidies mainly in two programs: stumpage programs and log export restrictions. With respect to the specificity test on provincial stumpage programs, Commerce gave little value to the precedent of its own negative ruling in Lumber I and stated that the government of Canada's appeal of the preliminary affirmative determination in Lumber II was "without legal force and effect." Commerce further stated, "As a general matter, there is no principle of administrative *stare decisis.* Administrative agencies are free to overturn prior precedent, provided they have a reasonable basis for doing so" (DOC 1992a, *8802*). It also cited relevant statutory provisions and court cases.

To establish a preferential rate, Commerce used the first two of the four alternative benchmarks (see Chapter 4; DOC 1986a)—the price charged by the same seller for a similar or related good (for British Columbia, Ontario, and Alberta), and the price charged within the jurisdiction by other sellers for an identical good or service (for Québec). The analysis by the Canadian Forest Industries Council based on the U.S. Forest Service's Timber Sales Program Information Report System was not used.

It is difficult to compare a competitively bid stumpage under one forest tenure with an administratively set stumpage under other forest tenures and find the difference, because the price-determining factors under these tenure arrangements are clearly different and adjustment has to be made. If administratively set stumpage fees in Canada were artificial, the adjustment made by Commerce was necessarily also artificial. Might the adjustment be wrong? If administratively set stumpage fees deviated from market-based stumpage prices and the adjustment was wrong, would two wrongs make the right stumpage price?

To illustrate, I use British Columbia as an example. Commerce determined that the stumpage prices under the Small Business Forest Enterprise Program, which accounted for about 10 percent of softwood sawlog sales in the province, were determined solely by market forces and were thus nonpreferential. All other stumpage prices were administratively set. There were, however, differences in road building and maintenance costs and management costs between the small enterprise program and the so-called major forest tenures, and adjustments had to be made.

One of the adjustments was silvicultural costs. Major forest tenure holders were required to perform certain activities pertaining to reforestation. These activities, referred to as silviculture, are broken down into two types—basic and incremental. Major tenure holders must perform the former; the small enterprise tenure holders are not required to perform either. As a result, Commerce added basic silvicultural costs incurred by major tenure holders to the stumpage fees. It made no adjustment for incremental silvicultural costs because no tenure holders, whether large or small, were required to perform these activities.

Although major tenure holders were not required to do incremental silviculture, some of them did. Zhang and Pearse (1996) find that, *ceteris paribus,* holders of timber licenses and tree farm licenses invest 26 percent and 14 percent more in silviculture, respectively, than the holders of forest licenses in British Columbia. The difference arises because timber and tree farm licenses are more secure property rights arrangements than forest licenses. The study covered the period between 1989 and 1993, roughly coinciding with the period of investigation for Lumber III (fiscal year 1990–1991). This study, which had nothing to do with the lumber dispute, shows the arbitrary nature of Commerce's adjustment: The incremental silviculture performed by the holders of timber and tree farm licenses should have been added to their stumpage rates but was not.

Since provincial governments do not provide direct financial contributions to lumber producers in Canada under log export restrictions, Commerce relied on the "indirectly" language in Section 771(5)(A)(ii) of the Tariff Act of 1930, as amended (see Chapter 3), to conduct the specificity test.

Commerce cited two studies by Canadian scholars (Margolick and Uhler 1986; Percy 1986) as evidence of preferential rates under B.C. log export restrictions. These restrictions affect domestic log prices, and many economists have called for their removal (Zhang 1995), but powerful labor unions in British Columbia want to keep them.

Table 6-1 shows the breakdown of Commerce's calculated rate of subsidies by province. British Columbia, which had implemented the highest stumpage hike under the Memorandum of Understanding, was found to be subsidizing its industry the most.

TABLE 6-1. U.S. Department of Commerce Calculated Rate of Subsidies in Canada, 1992

	B.C.	Québec	Ontario	Alberta	Other[a]	Canada
Preliminary determination						
Stumpage program	6.88%	3.78%	5.21%	4.16%	6.25%	6.25%
Log export restriction	10.54	0.00	0.00	0.00	0.00	8.23
Total	17.42	3.78	5.21	4.16	6.25	14.48
Final determination						
Stumpage program	3.30	0.01	5.95	1.25	2.91	2.91
Log export restriction	4.65	0.00	0.00	0.00	0.00	3.60
Total	7.95	0.01	5.95	1.25	2.91	6.51

a. Manitoba, Saskatchewan, the Northwest Territories, and the Yukon Territory.
Source: DOC (1992a, 1992b).

* * *

The coalition, which had asked for a 30 percent duty against Canadian lumber, was pleased with the preliminary determination by Commerce. The National Association of Home Builders, on the other hand, alleged in a letter to Commerce that each 10 percent added to the wholesale cost of lumber would increase the price of a new home by US$1,000, and imposition of a countervailing duty would needlessly harm the housing industry and impede economic recovery and homeownership.

In Ottawa, Trade Minister Wilson said, "This fight will continue and we'll use every weapon at our disposal. [Washington must be made to understand] that these sorts of actions on their part can't be taken with impunity.... If our log exports can be challenged, so can theirs." Prime Minister Mulroney, advised of the ruling, said, "There's an American election going on, there's a recession in the United States, there are protectionists running for office down there lobbying hand grenades at the White House everyday. What you've got going on is politics, it's not law. Ultimately, this is going to be decided in a court of law ..." He later likened U.S. trade actions to those of a "tinpot dictator" (*Vancouver Sun* 1992a).

The Bush administration stayed out of the rhetorical fray, but Trade Representative Carla Hills admitted that the recession had brought "protectionists out of the woodwork." She defended U.S. countervailing duty laws as being fairly applied and said that "sensible rhetoric" was needed to resolve trade disputes, including softwood lumber (*Ottawa Citizen* 1992). Meanwhile, the coalition's supporters in Congress returned some of the Canadian fire. Senator Baucus lashed out at Ottawa for bringing "political pressure to bear on a quasi-judicial decision." He charged that Canada had hired 12 law firms and spent more than US$20 million in an attempt to sway the decision (*Asian Wall Street Journal* 1992).

On April 6, 1992, four U.S. lawmakers from the Northwest lumber-producing states (Senators Packwood and Baucus, Representative Wyden, and Representative Bruce Chandler, R-Washington) sent a letter to the Canadian ambassador to the United States, Derek Burney, indicating that the U.S. investigation into the alleged Canadian subsidies had become "a major trade irritant" and that they wanted to offer what they considered a reasonable compromise: that Canadian provinces adopt a competitive bidding system and allow log exports in return for avoiding a trade war (*Seattle Times* 1992). The offer was described as "trade blackmail" and a "resource grab" and not taken seriously by the Canadian government (McCarthy 1992).

Canada's Challenge to the Determinations by Commerce

The Department of Commerce made its final determination in May 1992. Since the preliminary affirmative determination in Lumber II had not been contested, the preliminary and final affirmative determinations in Lumber III were the first test of the ruling on lumber. Not surprisingly, they were hotly contested by the government of Canada and its provincial governments, the Canadian lumber industry, and the Coalition for Fair Lumber Imports, on behalf of the U.S. lumber industry. Cases and rebuttal briefs from interested parties were sent to Commerce, which then held a 22-hour public hearing on the matter on April 29 and 30, 1992. The final affirmative determination, released on May 15 and printed in the *Federal Register* on May 28, ran 55 pages. Of the many issues raised, I note the following items, which either were important in Lumber III or resurfaced in Lumber IV.

Scope of investigation. The Canadian government requested that Commerce exclude from the investigation the following: products manufactured from western red cedar, eastern white and red pine, and clear and shop grades of lumber. Softwood lumber produced from these six species and grades would differ from dimensional lumber in appearance, strength, and resistance to insects, diseases, and fungi and would be priced accordingly. Furthermore, the Canadian government requested that remanufactured softwood lumber products be excluded from the scope of the investigation. Commerce denied both requests.

Calculation and application of country-wide rate issues. These issues include how to appropriately derive the denominator and numerator in calculating province-wide or country-wide rates (by including and excluding certain items) and how to appropriately identify sawtimber and pulpwood. Québec, in particular, wanted to have a province-wide rate, which was denied.

Specificity and preferentiality. Commerce went to great lengths to demonstrate that stumpage programs and log export restrictions were specific to the primary timber-processing industry group (which includes solid wood products and pulp and paper industries). As for the preferentiality test, the Canadian government relied on the economic rent theory of William D. Nordhaus, professor of economics at Yale University and a former member of the U.S. Council of Economic Advisers. In essence, Nordhaus argued that stumpage charges were economic rents, which could not result in increased production (that is, a market distortion) unless the provinces conferred net harvest-related benefits on tenure holders. Canadians said there was no evidence in this case that stumpage charges conferred such net benefits.

Citing a Commerce determination in a case involving carbon steel wire rod from Poland, Canadian interests argued that the department should conduct a "market distortion test." Citing legislative history and other cases, Commerce rejected the suggestion for calculating the net benefit and conducting a market distortion test when the alleged subsidy occurs in a country with a market economy. The Canadian industry's study based on the U.S. Forest Service's timber sales program system was ruled irrelevant to the investigation.

The Nordhaus analysis. The economic analysis by William Nordhaus began with stumpage harvest, which is set, under provincial stumpage programs, on a sustained-yield basis such that harvests can be maintained at that level in the future. Since private markets seek to maximize value, the harvest under provincial stumpage programs must be less than under a competitive situation because the stumpage programs are constrained to follow sustained-yield policies. Therefore, timber harvest from the stumpage programs in effect cannot exceed that of a competitive market. Furthermore, the price of stumpage under these programs would be higher than what would prevail in a system where stumpage prices were set competitively.

Commerce refuted his analysis, stating "any price determined in this [competitive market] fashion will almost always be higher than an administered stumpage charge." It further stated,

> Depending on the objectives of either a provincial stumpage program or a private owner, a forest can be managed to provide a high or low level of sustained harvest. For example, provincial stumpage programs managed under a policy of sustained yield tend to use biological criteria for choosing rotation lengths, which is the time period between the establishment and the harvesting of a timber stand. The use of such criteria tends to give a higher level of timber harvest than the economic criteria which many private forest owners use to set rotation lengths. (DOC 1992b, *22589*)

That statement is flawed. Forest economists would agree that the correct economic method for determining rotation length is the Faustmann formula and that, under most circumstances, using biological criteria such as sustained yield would postpone timber harvesting and increase rotation length. The final harvest level under a longer rotation would be higher than that using the economic criteria. But over a period of time, the average timber harvest per year using the biological criteria (under which timber stands are harvested less frequently) would be lower than that using the economic criteria. Furthermore, postponing timber harvests under the biological criteria would impose economic losses on landowners. Since the provincial governments incurred a loss by sticking to the biological criteria, where was the alleged subsidy coming from?

Commerce cited the brief submitted by the Coalition for Fair Lumber Imports and stated,

> Neither the rent theory nor the related appraisal procedure involve consideration of stumpage production costs or the possibility of a reservation price on the part of forest owners. It is implicitly assumed that the supply of all productive factors other than timber is perfectly elastic, that the supply of timber offered is perfectly inelastic with response to price, and that the forest owner is in a position to extract rent. With these assumptions, the rent-based appraisal method of stumpage pricing provides little resistance for analyzing the effect of changing timber supplies and/or production costs on either stumpage prices or product prices.
>
> ... The validity of the economic rent model proposed by Dr. Nordhaus depends on whether the supply of stumpage varies with price.... Consequently Dr. Nordhaus' assumption that the supply of timber does not vary with price appears to be at odds with the very way in which stumpage market behaves. (DOC 1992b, *22589*).

Commerce had a point here. However, the rent theory can be dynamic and is applicable when the supply of all productive factors other than timber is not perfectly elastic and when the supply of timber offered is not perfectly inelastic with respect to price. Under the provincial stumpage programs, tenure holders are assigned an annual allowable cut, which in the short run is inelastic (but not perfectly inelastic). Timber harvest can change within 10 percent of the cut for any given year and within 50 percent over a five-year period. Since the annual allowable cut can vary to a certain extent, stumpage supply is responsive to price to a degree. If the actual harvest and the allowable cut diverge too much, the cut's even-flow constraint would be ineffective.

Finally, Commerce denied the linkage between the alleged subsidy and rates of return among Canadian forest products companies. Canadian interests had argued that because Canadian forest products companies had lower rates of return relative to other Canadian companies, they were not receiving net benefits as defined by Nordhaus under provincial stumpage programs. Therefore, if no net benefit was being provided, no subsidy was transferred; if these firms were receiving preferential treatment, presumably they would have supranormal profits. Commerce stated that it did not consider a comparison of rate of return between industries to be relevant in determining whether a particular industry had received a subsidy.

Preferentiality hierarchy. Commerce defended its use of the two benchmarks in calculating the preferential rate as appropriate and consistent with statutes and past cases. In addition, while British Columbia advocated the use of the cost recovery method adopted by the U.S. Forest Service for its timber sales program, other provinces were against it. So even the Canadian provinces could not agree on which method was best. The department cited lack of appropriate price-based benchmarks in explaining its decision to use the "established cost" method in Lumber II. Furthermore, "the fact that cost-based replacement measures for static negotiated export rates were allowed under the MOU is immaterial to the department's subsidy analysis in a countervailing duty investigation" (DOC 1992b, *22591*).

Reasons and methods of adjustment. Commerce commented on various submissions from interested parties on subsidy calculation such as why some adjustments (on prices, road-building costs, silvicultural expenses) should be made and which method should be used. In the end, it determined that the subsidies from stumpage programs were 5.95 percent in Ontario, 3.30 percent in British Columbia, 1.25 percent in Alberta, and 0.01 percent in Québec, with a country-wide rate of 2.91 percent (Table 6-1).

Log export restrictions in British Columbia. Notwithstanding the rejection of a market distortion test for specificity and preferentiality in stumpage, Commerce used a market distortion test in measuring the alleged subsidy rate in log export restrictions. In its words,

> ... We have established that proof of market distortion is not, as a matter of law, a prerequisite to a finding of a subsidy. Nor can market distortion defined as an increase in output or a decrease in price, be the measure of a subsidy. Nonetheless, we have relied upon a supply-and-demand analysis for purposes of the log export restriction issue, because this analysis is the only method by which we could determine whether BC softwood lumber manufacturers receive countervailing benefits as a result of BC's log export restrictions. (DOC 1992b, *22605*)

There is not much consistency regarding the application of a market distortion test to the stumpage and log export restriction programs. Commerce perhaps did not have much room to maneuver here. Market distortion tests make sense in economics, but not necessarily in law. Log export restrictions in British Columbia were found to convey a subsidy of 4.65 percent for softwood lumber producers in that province, yielding a country-wide weighted average rate of 3.60 percent.

Note that the calculated subsidy for Québec was *de minimis*. Should a province-wide rate be used or if Québec were on its own, Québec would be exempt from the countervailing duty investigation or the case would be dropped. But Québec was part of the broader case against the four major lumber-producing provinces. This meant that exporters from Québec would have to pay the average countervailing duty—a price of being a part of Canada. Ritchie (1997, *206*) stated,

> This deeply angered those Canadians, all the way up to the Prime Minister, who were fighting to keep the country together during a difficult period of constitutional disagreement ... My blood still boils when I think

back on this part of the decision. In order to serve their domestic industry clients, the Commerce Department was prepared to take steps deliberately designed to put Quebec against the rest of Canada. Such a cynical action could surely not have been taken without the knowledge and sanction of the top levels of the administration, including the White House itself. This was the single most dishonorable and contemptible action the Americans have taken in my thirty years of observation.

In the end, the final affirmative determination printed in the *Federal Register* had only a country-wide rate. But the damage was done. At a minimum, the final determination was seen as an attempt to further split the common front of the four provinces—just as it split the Maritime Provinces from the four major lumber-producing provinces.

If a promise to lower stumpage prices had ever been made by the Rita Johnston–led Social Credit Party government, B.C. lumber producers were caught and penalized—along with producers in the other provinces—before their provincial government had a chance to fulfill its promise. For one thing, the Social Credit government was defeated in the fall election of 1991. Worse was yet to come for the forest industry in British Columbia: The newly elected New Democratic Party government would unilaterally increase its stumpage by 75 percent in 1994, irrespective of Commerce's actions.

* * *

The American response was mixed. C.T. Howlett of the coalition called the final determination a disappointment. American homebuilders and some timber companies with interests in Canada opposed a higher tariff on Canadian lumber. Jerry Connors, president of the Manufactured Housing Institute, said a tariff could prolong the recession by affecting "one of the greatest catalysts to our recovery—the building industry" (*Oregonian* 1992a).

In a sign of how politically sensitive the issue was, the final affirmative determination by Commerce was moved ahead five days from its scheduled announcement on May 20, 1992. Otherwise, the announcement would have coincided with Prime Minister Mulroney's one-day official visit to Washington. In a joint news conference with President Bush, the prime minister said,

> For some time, Canadians have been troubled and angered by the attitude adopted by some people in Washington on major trade issues.... Rather than move quickly to resolve or prevent irritants, the tendency was to retaliate against Canadian products by threatening to impose demonstrably unfair penalties on Canadian imports. And these actions create uncertainty for investors and exporters and undermine the fundamental intent of the Free Trade Agreement.... The kinds of harassment that we've seen must stop. And I think that the President understands that. (*Wall Street Journal* 1992)

President Bush chose to stress the positive aspects of the U.S.–Canada trade relationship. Noting that trade between the two countries had reached almost $200 billion annually, the president said, "I believe that this trade is of enormous benefit to the two economies and demonstrates vividly the value" of the FTA. He promised to "work with our administration to see that these disputes receive the proper high level consideration before they go to some form of action" (*Wall Street Journal* 1992).

Bush's conciliatory comments got mixed reviews from U.S. lawmakers from the northwestern and southern states. A spokesman for Representative Wyden said, "We wish he had made a stronger statement." Senator Mark Hatfield (R-Oregon), on the other hand, backed a conciliatory approach. He said he had advised Commerce Secretary Barbara Franklin to separate the log export issue from the question of government subsidies for public timber in Canada because the United States had its own log export restrictions. That step would have reduced the amount of the proposed tariff by nearly half. On the prospect for a prolonged dispute, Hatfield added, "I just don't think the whole exercise is helping Canadian–American relations" (*Oregonian* 1992b).

The Canadians immediately filed a request for panel review pursuant to Article 1904 of the FTA on the same day the final determination was published in the *Federal Register*, May 28, 1992. This panel (hereafter referred to as the FTA Subsidy Panel, since it was charged with reviewing the subsidy determination) would convene on July 29, 1992, shortly after the ITC determination that Canadian lumber imports had materially injured the U.S. industry based on a vote of 4 to 2 on July 9, 1992 (ITC 1992). Another FTA panel (hereafter referred to as the FTA Injury Panel) was requested, on July 24, by the government of Canada to review ITC's injury determination.

Motion to Dismiss

Although confident that Canada would win under FTA, from the onset of Lumber III, there were concerns among Canadian officials about the Bush administration's commitment to the FTA binational panel dispute settlement system if the United States lost. In an editorial published in the *Wall Street Journal*, Ritchie (1993) wrote, "Obviously fearing this result, senior officials in the administration have hinted the United States may refuse to be bound by the decision of the bi-national panels—or may even refuse to allow the case to go before them. This would be tantamount to tearing up the Free Trade Agreement." In the end, these concerns seemed to be unfounded, at least in Lumber III.

The Coalition for Fair Lumber Imports filed with both FTA panels, in December 1992, a "notice of motion to dismiss for lack of jurisdiction." The coalition argued that the self-initiation of the countervailing duty investigation was an enforcement measure arising out of the MOU and thus should be exempt from the consideration by the panels. Commerce, ITC, and the Canadians argued in opposition to the coalition. In the end, both panels denied the coalition's motion and concluded that they had the authority to review the contested determinations.

GATT and FTA Challenges

On February 19, 1993, the GATT panel examining Canada's challenge to the U.S. imposition of interim import bonds on Canadian lumber upon the MOU's termination and the self-initiation of the countervailing duty investigation issued its report, stating that the United States acted properly in its self-initiation of the investigation, but improperly in the imposition of interim bonds prior to a preliminary affirmative determination of subsidy and injury. Thus, it recommended that the United States be requested to refund any cash deposits made when the bonding requirements were in effect. In addition, the panel agreed with Canada that the special circumstances cited by the United States were inapplicable to the log export restrictions, which were not part of the MOU.

In April 1993, President Clinton held a "forest summit" in Portland, Oregon, to discuss forest-related issues in the U.S. Pacific Northwest, where reductions in federal timber harvesting due to environmental regulations were causing social and economic hardships. The president was scheduled to travel to Vancouver to meet Russian President Boris Yeltsin and Canadian Prime Minister Jean Chrétien. There were rumors, at the time, that President Clinton might eliminate the countervailing duty. However, the rumors were quickly dismissed, since the Coalition for Fair Lumber Imports would have to give its blessing before the duty could be rescinded—and the coalition had made it clear that it was not about to do so.

The Canadian response to Commerce's preliminary and final affirmative determinations of subsidy, ITC's determination of injury, and eventually the two FTA panels in Lumber III was markedly different than in the previous cases. First, Canadians had confidence in the FTA panel review process. From Canada's perspective, the process was designed with the 1986 softwood lumber case in mind, to curtail the excessive politicizing and arbitrary treatment of trade disputes between the countries. It thus provided a better chance of success than the U.S. investigating agencies. The record of previous binational panels had been quite favorable to Canada (Apsey and Thomas 1997).

Second, unlike Lumber I and Lumber II, when the industry conducted most of the defense, all major parties in Canada were involved and largely united. Ted Boswell, president of E.B. Eddy Forest Products Ltd., told the Canadian Lumbermen's Association on February 13, 1992, that the American action was a "massive intrusion into Canada's sovereignty" and threatened the Free Trade Agreement. Furthermore, it was "bloody minded" but had galvanized the Canadian industry, Ottawa, and the provinces, which were all prepared to fight an adverse ruling by Commerce (*Toronto Star* 1992a).

All interested Canadian parties—including the federal government, the governments of the four major lumber-producing provinces, the Canadian Forest Industries Council, the Québec Lumber Manufacturers' Association, and several firms—retained legal counsel. All Canadian parties involved realized that there had to be a commitment to see things through to the end. They would share information, coordinate, and participate in the defense on an equal basis. This united approach, which would necessitate greater expense and complexity in case management but yield more careful consideration of evidence and legal analysis, turned out to be effective and contributed to the Canadians' ultimate victory in the FTA panel review process (Apsey and Thomas 1997).

Third, knowing they were fighting against the coalition, which had strong political allies on Capitol Hill and in the Bush and Clinton administrations, Canadian parties were proactive and better prepared on both legal and economics fronts.[2] Some Canadians saw the third countervailing duty case as an opportunity to demonstrate certain facts that they believed had not been fully understood or just ignored by Commerce, which in their view had subverted economic sense and the law in 1986 (Apsey and Thomas 1997).

As mentioned earlier, the defense on economic grounds was provided by William Nordhaus of Yale University, with the assistance of Robert Litan, a senior fellow at the Brookings Institute and a consultant for Steptoe and Johnson, a law firm working for the Canadian industry. In essence, they used the rent theory to argue that changes in stumpage rates could not confer a trade-distorting subsidy because the changes did not affect production of logs (and thus lumber and lumber exports) and thus would not injure the U.S. industry. In other words, they argued, the supply of harvested timber was very inelastic. They wrote,

> The important point to note about normal stumpage is that at any level between zero and the excessive rate, stumpage has no distortionary effect upon the harvest. Because there would be no impact upon the price or output of logs, there would be no impact on the marginal cost, on supply, on the price of the output, or on the export of manufactured forest products. Hence for normal stumpage, there would be no impact on the industries of other countries. (Nordhaus and Litan 1992, *18–19*)

They backed up their claims with empirical evidence from British Columbia, where the four-year experience with the MOU replacement measures provided an unusual experiment. They demonstrated that except at the very outer margins, a change in stumpage rates—either upward or downward—did not significantly change production of total lumber and hence exports.[3]

The legal defense for the Canadians was based on case law in which both Commerce and the U.S. courts indicated that the purpose of the U.S. countervailing duty law was to offset the distortion in a nation's economy that resulted from a subsidy. A subsidy would exist only when a government program had the effect of distorting the country's comparative advantage in a particular good by lowering the price or increasing the supply of that good. If a government program did not distort a country's comparative advantage, there was no subsidy. This was known as the market distortion test, which Commerce rejected.

The FTA Subsidy Panel Decision

On May 6, 1993, the FTA Subsidy Panel rendered its first decision. The panel found that "the Department both misunderstood the theoretical analysis developed by the Canadians of a national resource market, and ignored the crucial empirical evidence offered by the Canadians to corroborate their theory about the softwood lumber market in that country" (FTA Subsidy Panel 1993a, *52*). On most of the major points, the panel unanimously found that Commerce had failed to act in accordance with U.S. law.

First, the panel concluded that Commerce had failed to consider all four relevant factors (number of users and range of products, existence or lack of dominant or disproportionate use of stumpage by the softwood lumber industry, exercises of government discretion, and extent of government discretion in conferring benefits) in making its determination that stumpage programs were "specific" to certain enterprises or industries. It directed Commerce to consider all the evidence (FTA Subsidy Panel 1993a).

Second, the panel concluded that Commerce should conduct a market distortion test with respect to stumpage preferentiality "before concluding that these governmental policies involve the type of 'preferential' pricing that constitutes a countervailing subsidy within the meaning of the Tariff Act" (FTA Subsidy Panel 1993a, *59–60*).

Third, the panel agreed with the Nordhaus analysis that "the price set for the natural resources does play a key role in determining how the financial value— the economic rent—of the resource will be divided between owner and purchaser. It does not, however, have any market distorting impact on the output of the resource or the amount of price of downstream products" (FTA Subsidy Panel 1993a, *53*). The panel examined Commerce's treatment of Nordhaus's theoretical analysis and related empirical evidence and rendered this opinion, which supported the Nordhaus thesis:

> As the Canadians demonstrated through their analysis on the Record for the purpose of this appeal, not only was there no substantial analytical rebuttal of the Nordhaus thesis, but only the Canadians offered any empirical evidence relating specifically to the relationship between provincial stumpage programs and the corresponding lumber market.

Furthermore,

The Nordhaus/Litan study was made possible by, in effect, a natural experiment about the relationship between stumpage rates and log output occasioned by the preliminary determination in Lumber II and the MOU between the United States and Canada. The MOU required British Columbia to raise its stumpage rates by an average of 15 percent in order to get relief from the export tax. British Columbia chose to raise its stumpage rates by very different amounts—ranging from zero to 700 percent—for six different species produced in eight different regions. Thus, Drs. Nordhaus and Litan had a total of 48 observations for each of the two different time comparisons through which to investigate whether higher prices in fact generated lower output. The fact there were such sharply different price increases for different lots made it possible for the first time to conduct such a price-output test while implicitly controlling for any external variables that affected demand for softwood lumber products (and thence softwood lumber logs) from all regions and species.

Dr. Nordhaus' theoretical hypothesis was that higher prices in the normal range would produce no variation in output (contrary to the Coalition's position, which is that higher prices would always generate corresponding lower output). The actual finding from the study was that timber production showed virtually no response to stumpage changes. In particular, a 100 percent increase in price was associated with only a 2.8 percent decline in output. As Dr. Nordhaus put it, this was "essentially zero from a financial point of view and insignificantly different from zero from a statistical point of view." *However, in its decision Commerce did not even mention, let alone try to refute, such a crucial piece of evidence on this issue—the only empirical evidence available in these proceedings about the softwood lumber market that was the subject of this case.* (FTA Subsidy Panel 1993a, 58–59; emphasis added)

Finally, with regard to log export restrictions, two panelists dissented, holding that they did not believe that the countervailing duty remedy was intended to reach export restrictions that did not involve government financial contributions. However, the majority found that Commerce did have authority to countervail restrictions on log exports. The majority of the panel noted that in arriving at a finding of subsidy, the department had employed a "market distortion test." The panel unanimously remanded the matter on log export restrictions to Commerce for clarification on the legal standards it had used and on the cause–effect linkage between log export restrictions and lumber production.

* * *

The FTA Subsidy Panel's remand decision was harshly criticized by the coalition but welcomed by Canadian parties. Mike Apsey called it "a step—a very powerful step—towards vindication." Similarly, Trade Minister Wilson said, "It is a very positive decision. It's the best result we could have had." B.C. Forests

Minister Dan Miller went further, saying, "One could conclude that a second look (by Commerce) will either totally eliminate the 6.5 percent tariff or dramatically reduce it" (*Vancouver Sun* 1993a). He would be proven to be too optimistic.

It was around this time that a controversy about logging and logging practices on Vancouver Island erupted (Stanbury 2000),[4] and several environmental groups, including the Natural Resources Defense Council, decided to join the U.S. forest industry in fighting for a tariff on Canadian lumber imports. Environmental groups had battled the U.S. forest industry in the Pacific Northwest for years, succeeding in putting the northern spotted owl on the U.S. endangered species list and forcing the U.S. federal and state governments to reduce timber harvesting on public forests in the region by some 80 percent. They now became allies and supporters of the U.S. industry for imposing restrictions on Canadian lumber, because to the extent that the restrictions would reduce Canadian domestic lumber prices, they would ease demand for Canadian logs and save some old-growth forests in Canada. However, these groups had to be careful, since the U.S. industry also called for lifting log export bans, which would increase log prices and potentially lead to more timber harvesting in Canada.

The FTA Injury Panel Decision

On July 26, 1993, the FTA Injury Panel released its first decision, concluding that ITC's determination of material injury was not supported by substantial evidence. In the panel's view, ITC had not presented evidence ("requisite causation") to substantiate the assertion of injury caused by Canadian lumber imports (FTA Injury Panel 1993).

In addressing whether a domestic industry has been materially injured by subsidized imports, ITC is required by the Tariff Act of 1930 to consider three factors: (1) the volume of the imported products subject to investigation; (2) the effect of such imports on prices of like products in the United States; and (3) the impact of such imports on domestic producers of like products (19 U.S.C. Section 1677(7)B(i)).

Each of those factors is further explained in the statute. For example, the statute specifically requires that ITC assess "volume" by considering "whether the volume of imports, or any increase in that volume, either in absolute terms or relative to production or consumption in the U.S. is significant" (19 U.S.C. Section 1677(7)C(i)). With respect to the effect of imports on U.S. prices, ITC must consider whether there has been significant price underselling by the imported products and whether "such products otherwise depress prices to a significant degree or prevent price increases, which otherwise would have occurred, to a significant degree" (19 U.S.C. Section 1677(7)C(ii)). Finally, the assessment of the imports on domestic producers requires ITC to evaluate all

TABLE 6-2. Volume of Canadian Softwood Lumber Imports and U.S. Lumber Price Index, 1986–1991

| | Canadian imports | | | | U.S. softwood lumber price | | |
| | Four major provinces | | Total imports[a] | | | | |
Year	Volume (mmbf)	Share of U.S. consumption (percentage)	Volume (mmbf)	Share of U.S. consumption (percentage)[a]	Eastern species index	Western species index	Spruce–pine–fir price[b]
1986	13,535	28.5	14,161	29.8	81.3	69.2	269
1987	14,058	27.8	14,821	29.3	88.8	73.7	293
1988	13,317	27.5	13,806	28.5	88.9	77.3	277
1989	12,817	26.7	13,378	27.9	87.5	84.3	273
1990	11,364	25.3	11,964	26.6	89.5	80.6	273
1991	11,026	26.1	11,588	27.4	88.7	82.2	270

a. These numbers are slightly different from those reported by ITC (1992, A-24). The differences, however, are very small.
b. US$/mbf for eastern, spruce-pine-fir, kiln-dried, 2x4, standard and better, delivered to Great Lakes.
Source: Canadian Forest Service (various issues).

"relevant economic factors which have a bearing on the state of the industry in the U.S.," within the context of the "business cycle and conditions of competition that are distinctive to the affected industry" (19 U.S.C. Section 1677(7)C(iii)) (cited in FTA Injury Panel 1993, *29–30*).

ITC had no problem finding that the volume of Canadian lumber imports was significant relative to U.S. production or consumption, although an increase in volume was not apparent during the period of investigation (Table 6-2). More difficult was demonstrating that imports of Canadian lumber had prevented price increases, since lumber prices are influenced by many factors, such as housing starts and domestic lumber supplies. ITC had collected pricing information from industry sources and the U.S. Bureau of Labor Statistics, but it decided not to use any of them. It stated that although pricing information was "accurate and reflected pricing trends in the market, its usefulness for reflecting comparative prices of domestic and imported lumber was limited" (ITC 1992, *30*).

Instead, ITC had employed an analytical framework to facilitate its evaluation of the relationship between injury to the domestic industry and imports of Canadian lumber. The framework states that the impact of imports on domestic sales and prices is greater when (1) the imports are significant in volume, whether absolutely or relative to total consumption; (2) demand is inelastic; and (3) the products are considered close substitutes (ITC 1992, *27*).

The Canadians contested item (3) and argued that the framework could not be used. The FTA Injury Panel sided with ITC, indicating that it could work. However, the panel pointed out "even if the analytical framework's conditions are satisfied, in order to reach an affirmative determination the Commission must make findings supported by substantial evidence, with respect to all three statutory factors (the volume of imports, the effect of the imports on domestic prices, and the impact of the imports on the domestic industry)" (FTA Injury Panel 1993, *30*).

The panel was critical about the lack of actual pricing data to support the ITC conclusion. It noted, "At the outset that the Commission has not supported its affirmative determination in this case on any of the grounds traditionally relied on by it (i.e., increased imports by volume or market share, decreased prices, underselling, confirmed lost sales, or price leadership). The unreliability of the pricing data in this case made certain of these traditional tools unavailable to the Commission, while other indicia, particularly increased imports (by volume), simply did not exist" (FTA Injury Panel 1993, *18–19*).

The panel agreed with ITC's findings that softwood lumber products from Canada and the United States were highly substitutable and that the volume of Canadian imports during the period of investigation was "significant." However, it found, "the mere presence of a significant volume of unfairly traded imports is not sufficient to support an affirmative injury determination" (FTA Injury Panel 1993, *19*).

With respect to ITC's finding that imports of Canadian lumber (mainly species of spruce, pine, and fir species) limit potential increases in U.S. softwood lumber prices (price suppression),[5] the panel found that the evidence cited by ITC did not rise to the level of "substantial" (FTA Injury Panel 1993, *20*). Lacking such causal evidence, the panel did not agree that Canadian imports were limiting potential increases in U.S. softwood lumber prices. Rather, it unanimously concluded that the ITC assertion of price suppression was based solely on a handful of broad statements that did not begin to satisfy the criterion that an injury determination be supported by rationally based findings (FTA Injury Panel 1993, *53*).

Finally, the panel had concerns regarding ITC's legal authority to conduct a cross-sector (lumber versus other wood products) comparison between an investigated industry and noninvestigated industries. It also found that ITC's methodology in conducting the cross-sector comparison was seriously flawed and that the results did not produce substantial evidence of significant price suppression. Apparently, ITC used the coalition's idea of comparing the performance of U.S. producers in their softwood lumber operations with their operations in other wood products and materials to assert that "the recession and timber supply constraints were not the sole causes of material injury to the domestic industry" (FTA Injury Panel 1993, *55*).[6]

Commerce's Remand Determination

On September 17, 1993, the Department of Commerce issued its first remand determination to the FTA Subsidy Panel. It strongly criticized the panel's decision, stating that it was "incumbent upon it to note a few aspects of the Panel's decision that it considers to be reflective of a fundamental misapprehension of the specificity standards" (DOC 1993, *2*). It further stated, "The Panel appears to have reached its conclusion on specificity by constructing a straw man, debunking an argument which Commerce never made" (DOC 1993, *4*). It then proceeded to justify its specificity determination, concluding again that a finding of specificity was justified.

Commerce responded to the request that it consider all four factors in determining that stumpage programs provided specific subsidy. First, it found that users of stumpage in 1990 accounted for 0.41 percent of all Canadian enterprises, between 2.63 percent and 3.95 percent of all industries at the two-digit level of Standard Industry Classification aggregation, 3.14 percent of all industries at the four-digit level of aggregation, 3.25 percent GDP, 9.18 percent of manufacturing GDP, and an estimated 9.02 percent of the commodities produced in the Canadian economy. Thus, these numbers fell "at the 'too few' users end of the specificity spectrum"; they were "small" and therefore "too few" not to be considered specific (DOC 1993, *11, 25*). It provided several court cases to support that the users of stumpage were few.

Second, Commerce found that 74 percent of all softwood timber harvested in the four provinces passed through sawmills as evidence of predominant use of stumpage by lumber producers. Third, it found government actions to limit the availability of stumpage programs to the primary timber-processing industries to be evidence of government limitation. However, it found no evidence that government discretion was exercised in favor of one class of users over another.

Commerce (1993) was equally critical about the panel's acceptance of Canada's argument that a market distortion test was required to find the existence of a subsidy. It stated, "Market distortion, albeit a conceptual rationale for the statute, is nowhere mentioned in the statute as a separate, distinct factor to be considered, much less proved, and is not a term used either to identify or measure a countervailing benefit." Nonetheless, it then attempted to use the marginal cost theory as well as empirical evidence to support its market distortion analysis.

Commerce's empirical evidence was a reworking of the Nordhaus–Litan empirical study of stumpage supply in British Columbia. It found that there was heteroscedasticity in the Nordhaus–Litan regression analysis and made a correction by "weighing the observations." In addition, it added new data for later years and found log supply elasticity with respect to stumpage price in British Columbia to be around −0.08. It concluded that timber harvests were sensitive to stumpage prices and that lower stumpage prices under administered systems would result in excess timber harvests and thus generate a market distortion.

In the end, Commerce recalculated the subsidy as 11.54 percent, almost double the previous 6.51 percent, to the liking of the coalition and its supporters in the U.S. Congress. Some observers saw the tone of the remand determination and the recalculated level of subsidy as "intended to snub the Panel" (Apsey and Thomas 1997, 53).

* * *

At this time, in the fall of 1993, NAFTA had been negotiated and was await-ing ratification. In an apparent attempt to persuade Congress to vote for a law implementing the agreement, the U.S. trade representative issued a statement of administrative action on November 5, 1993, urging U.S. industry to use the broader powers the United States had negotiated to challenge FTA (and soon NAFTA) binational panels. The statement encouraged "private parties to notify USTR when a bi-national panel has taken action that the private parties believe may warrant (challenges).... Private parties are urged to provide information and arguments that might be used to invoke an extraordinary challenge." Thus, the Clinton administration made a promise to Congress to assist and facilitate challenges to adverse rulings by FTA or NAFTA binational panels.

Gordon Ritchie saw that expanding the grounds a country could use to chal-lenge a ruling as contrary to the spirit of FTA, in which challenges were intended only for exceptional circumstances. The appropriate action for the U.S. administration, he said, was to end the misbehavior of its Commerce Department and ITC in becoming the tools of the protectionist Congress, not side with industry in a case against which the FTA panel had ruled (*Ottawa Cit-izen* 1993).

ITC's Remand Determination and the FTA Injury Panel's Second Decision

On October 25, 1993, ITC issued its first remand determination (ITC 1993). With a four-to-two vote, ITC again found that domestic industry had suffered material injury as a result of Canadian lumber imports.

ITC used an analysis of the supply and demand in the softwood lumber market to support its finding of price suppression. It characterized this market as highly competitive and subject to inelastic demand. In such circumstances, log cost increases experienced by the softwood lumber industry, all else being equal, should cause an inward shift in the industry's supply curve and an increase in the equilibrium price of softwood lumber. In a market characterized by inelastic demand, such a shift should cause the equilibrium price to rise rel-atively substantially, and domestic producers should have been able to "pass cost increases along to customers almost dollar for dollar" (ITC 1993, 11). Thus, the failure of prices to keep up with cost increases, *ceteris paribus*, indicated price suppression.[7]

Three evidentiary findings were submitted to support ITC's conclusion that price suppression of U.S. softwood lumber products had been caused, in part, by Canadian imports. First, Canadian prices tended to rise more slowly and fall more rapidly than domestic prices. Second, the price of subsidized Canadian imports, particularly of spruce, pine, and fir, had a dominant impact on lumber prices in the U.S. market. Finally, the weighted average composite U.S. price in the northern markets, where Canadian imports penetration was highest, was lower than prices in the southern markets, where import penetration was lower (ITC 1993).

The first evidentiary finding was based on a cross-country comparison of trends in composite price indices (producer price index, PPI) for U.S. and Canadian lumber. The second finding was based on a survey of lumber producers, importers, and purchasers. The third relied on data collected early in the investigation for the purpose of comparing the economic health of western U.S. softwood lumber producers with the remainder of the country.

On January 28, 1994, the FTA Injury Panel (1994a) unanimously found that ITC's remand determination was still not supported by substantial evidence. It declined to pursue the supply–demand model, although it did not consider that ITC had in fact established that the circumstances of the lumber market were such that the model would operate. It instead focused on the three evidentiary findings and concluded that ITC "has not met the substantial evidence standard in support of its conclusion that significant price suppression was *caused* by Canadian imports of softwood lumber" (FTA Injury Panel 1994a, *10*, emphasis original).

With respect to the first evidentiary basis, the panel found that although a fully developed "price trend analysis" could be used in support of a causation finding, the ITC analysis was unsupported by substantial evidence. The panel noticed that the price trend graphs had come from the coalition and had not been previously mentioned by ITC. The panel indicated "apparently relying on the graphs developed by the Coalition, the Commission simply treats the conclusion that prices of imported Canadian lumber rose more slowly and fell more quickly than domestic prices as self-evident. But the Commission must support its conclusion by reasoned analysis, not revelation" (FTA Injury Panel 1994a, *17*).

The panel found no ITC or court precedent utilizing producer price indices (PPIs) for the specific and precise purpose of establishing underselling, price depression, or price suppression. PPIs normally have a much broader purpose and are constructed using different deflators, even though the exact same product series is involved in both countries. Since PPIs are designed to measure only the change in prices received for the output of domestic industries, they do not measure prices at all, but rather, the average change in prices. Thus, the coalition had to normalize the price trends data by reference to a specific base date (1988), which was critical because figures showed the relationship of Canadian and U.S. prices in the light of the price difference that existed between them as of that time. "What is not indicated is whether that differential was typical of the price relationship throughout the period of investigation. Nor is there any indication of the point at which any change in that differential has an impact on sales" (FTA Injury Panel 1994a, *17*).

The panel further noted,

> Even in light of adequate information about the base date selection, and the verification that any change in the differential between domestic and imported lumber would be insignificant, it is not self-evident that on average Canadian prices fell more quickly and rose more slowly than domestic prices throughout the period of investigation. A cursory glance at the slopes on the graphs relied on by the Commission might suggest that prices of imported lumber fell more quickly and rose more slowly about half the time, and rose more quickly and fell more slowly the other half of the time. Further information on a more precise analysis clearly is needed.
>
> ... If the market had functioned as the Commission asserts, then Canadian market share would have increased. ... But this did not occur, and in fact over the period of investigation the Canadian market share declined slightly. (FTA Injury Panel 1994a, *18*)

In regard to the finding of the effect of Canadian imports on the U.S. market, the panel noted that ITC's conclusion that spruce, pine, and fir as a product could constitute a "reference point for pricing" had been rejected by 59 percent of respondents in an ITC survey of producer, importer, and purchaser groups, and ITC had not explained why it accepted the minority view. Since the responses to the ITC survey indicated that at least 16 (and very likely more) items were involved in the pricing of softwood lumber, the panel concluded that the term "reference point" seemed to mean "little more than the [spruce–pine–fir] prices could be expected to be included among a list of items that a producer, importer, or purchaser might (or might not) refer to when focusing on a particular purchase or sale of [spruce–pine–fir], or some other species of softwood lumber." Finally, the panel stated,

> ... the fact that [spruce–pine–fir] prices are or may be included on a list of factors that a member of the domestic softwood lumber industry might refer to for purposes of establishing his own transaction prices is legally insufficient, without more, to sustain a finding that Canadian [spruce–pine–fir] has caused price suppression, to a significant degree, of domestic softwood lumber prices. (FTA Injury Panel 1994a, *28*)

In regard to ITC's regional price comparisons, the panel found that in producing such comparisons, the commission had relied upon data that it had initially rejected in its original injury determination, without explanation. Furthermore, the panel noted that ITC's analysis entailed a very low degree of statistical certainty. In fact, the variation between the prices (US$262.48 and US$270.40, a difference of US$7.92) ITC had relied on was less than one-quarter to one-third of the standard deviation involved. Thus, the panel concluded "that the regional analysis conducted by the Commission is insufficient to support its affirmative determination" (FTA Injury Panel 1994a, *33–36*).

In summary, the FTA Injury Panel found that the ITC remand determination, like the original determination, seemed to "rely heavily on the volume of Canadian softwood lumber import ... as probative" of causation. Yet "causation cannot be proved by volume alone." Thus, evidence relied upon by ITC in its remand determination "do(es) not constitute substantial evidence of price suppression by reason of imports of softwood lumber from Canada or are otherwise not in accordance with law" (FTA Injury Panel 1994a, *36*).

Subsidy Panel Decision on Commerce's Remand Determination

On December 17, 1993, the FTA Subsidy Panel issued its second remand determination. This time, the panel split three to two, along national lines, in ordering Commerce to reverse itself and enter a negative determination. The Canadian majority continued to hold the position taken by all five panelists in the first remand. The two American panelists, however, reversed themselves, finding that a recent decision by the Federal Circuit Court of Appeals in *Daewoo (Daewoo Electronics Co. Ltd. et al. v. U.S.*, 6 F.3d 1511 (Fed. Cir. 1993)) forced them to conclude that the majority had committed major errors in applying existing U.S. laws.[8]

Daewoo involved judicial review of Commerce's enforcement of the antidumping laws by the U.S. Court of International Trade. In reversing the decision of the trial court, the court of appeals said that the trial court erred in overturning the department's accounting methodology and in requiring it to do an econometric analysis of tax incidence in calculating dumping margin. The court of appeals indicated that accounting methodology should be deferred to the investigating agency and an econometric analysis was an "onerous burden" upon the agency.

To the majority of the FTA Subsidy Panel, this was not a "new" or "expanded" standard of deference to the exercise of agency discretion; the panel must use the "substantial evidence" standard. The majority cited the FTA Injury Panel's decision and an FTA Extraordinary Challenge Committee in *Live Swine from Canada* (ECC-93-1904-01USA, April 8, 1993) in supporting their decision that "The deference to be afforded to an agency's findings and conclusions is therefore not unbounded" (FTA Subsidy Panel 1993b, *15*); Commerce's construction must be "permissible" and applied in a rational manner. A panel standing in the place of a reviewing court may "not permit the agency under the guise of a lawful discretion or interpretation, to contrive or ignore the intent of Congress" (FTA Subsidy Panel 1993b, *17*).

With respect to specificity, the majority of the panel found fault in two factors considered by Commerce—the number of stumpage users and dominant or disproportionate users. It found that Commerce "engaged in conclusive analysis" (users of stumpage programs were "small" and thus "specific"), which "is not legally sufficient to support the ultimate finding of specificity" (FTA Subsidy Panel 1993b, 29). Furthermore, none of the cases cited by the department actually supported the level of industry aggregation, since they concerned export subsidies, regional subsidies, or only a few enterprises. Thus, the majority concluded, "The lack of reasoned analysis of the number of industrial users in finding them to be 'too few' reveals a mechanical and arbitrary exercise that is not supportable under U.S. law" (FTA Subsidy Panel 1993b, 37).

As to the finding that lumber producers were the predominant users of stumpage programs, the majority of the panel concluded that sawmilling is a necessary first step in the production of many forest products, and actual use of sawmills for the production of lumber was between 28 and 37 percent, but actual use by the other "industry" was in the range of 40 to 50 percent. Thus, "sawmills are neither the largest users of softwood stumpage nor disproportionate users" (FTA Subsidy Panel 1993b, 41).

With respect to preferentiality, the majority defended the panel's unanimous decision in its first remand, saying that requesting Commerce to conduct a "market distortion test" was in accordance with U.S. law. The "marginal cost theory" supported by Commerce and the "economic rent theory" advanced by Nordhaus were complementary, they said, but "neither of which provide support for [Commerce's] conclusion that where lower stumpage prices exist in an administrated system, output will be increased beyond the level that would otherwise prevail in a normal competitive market" (FTA Subsidy Panel 1993b, 59). They faulted the department's failure to explain the reasons or assumptions behind its decision to weigh by volume instead of using other methods to correct heteroscedasticity and to run regressions on data for additional years. They reasoned that, based on the results, it would take a 100 percent increase in stumpage prices to produce a mere 8 percent increase in output. This was entirely consistent with rent theory, which incorporated the possibility that a change in stumpage fees might push those fees either from the normal to the excessive range, or vice versa, and thereby affect output. Nonetheless, "the presence of some very limited elasticity cannot, without an unreasoned leap in logic, be stretched to support the finding that lower stumpage fees result in output being pushed beyond the competitive norm" (FTA Subsidy Panel 1993b, 64).

Thus, the majority of the panel remanded to Commerce for a determination that provincial stumpage programs were not specific and did not distort normal competitive markets for softwood lumber and therefore were not countervailable. They used similar logic to direct Commerce to find that the beneficiaries of log export restrictions were nonspecific. They agreed with the department, however, that log export restrictions provided "direct and discernible effects" on log purchasers and thus were countervailable, if specific.

The minority of the panel agreed on the standard of review, including that the panel "may not permit the agency under the guise of lawful discretion of interpretation, to contravene or ignore the intent of Congress." However, when the intent of Congress was not clearly stated in substantive laws, the minority believed that the panel must ask whether the department's interpretation was based on permissible construction of the laws and regulations. The minority stated that Commerce's construction in this case was permissible and thus must be affirmed. They stated that "the Majority has applied review standards not to U.S. law, but to what the Majority believes U.S. law should be" (FTA Subsidy Panel 1993b, Minority Opinion, 7). The minority quoted *Daewoo*: "a court may not substitute its own construction of a statutory provision for a reasonable interpretation made by the administrator of an agency" (FTA Subsidy Panel 1993b, Minority Opinion, 9–10).

The minority viewed *Daewoo* as "a case of extraordinary importance for this Panel's task, yet one which, in our view, the Majority misconstrues and underestimates." Specifically, the minority saw *Daewoo* as reinforcing "the posture of deference that United States administrative law accords to agency review" and "the posture of deference owed to methodologies developed by the agency to implement its statutory mandate when the statute itself does not indicate them" (FTA Subsidy Panel 1993b, Minority Opinion, 15).

With respect to the specificity test for stumpage and log export restrictions, the minority believed that one factor (instead of all four factors) could be relevant and dispositive. It then indicated that Commerce's tests on the number of stumpage users and predominant or disproportionate users were sufficient to conclude that stumpage was specific. Again, the minority believed that the Congress had not stipulated a methodology in specificity tests, and Commerce had to come up with an appropriate methodology. A court engaged in administrative review could not superimpose its own methodology, and that was "what the Majority is doing." The minority further alleged that "the Majority's real grievance is with the Regulations and the Statute," and "the Panel is acting *Ultra Vires*," or beyond its powers (FTA Subsidy Panel 1993b, Minority Opinion, 35).

With respect to stumpage preferentiality, the minority viewed that a market distortion test was not required by U.S. law in a market economy, and thus making it a prerequisite to a formative determination by Commerce might impose an "onerous burden" because "Commerce must undertake some type of econometric analysis." The minority noted, "Were we not strongly persuaded that Daewoo trumps our earlier instruction on market distortion, we would concur in most of the Majority's reasoning on stumpage preferentiality in the present opinion" (FTA Subsidy Panel 1993b, Minority Opinion, 50).

Setting the Stage for an Extraordinary Challenge

A split vote along national lines and the opinions of the two Americans on the FTA Subsidy Panel set the stage for a possible extraordinary challenge.

Canadian interests hoped that the subsidy panel's ruling would persuade the United States to bring this case to a close. But the Coalition for Fair Lumber Imports vowed to appeal to an extraordinary challenge committee to overturn the panel's decisions. Senator Baucus, chairman of the Senate International Trade Subcommittee, called the FTA Subsidy Panel's decision an outrage, a political decision, and not one based on merit (*Seattle Post-Intelligencer* 1993). He later urged the Clinton administration to challenge it.

On January 6, 1994, Commerce, in a terse report to the FTA Subsidy Panel, reluctantly gave up its fight, saying it "strongly objects" to the panel's imposition of its own interpretation of U.S. trade law, but it had no other choice.[9] Soon thereafter, James Holbein of the FTA Binational Panel Secretariat in Washington said that Canadian producers could get their duty deposits back soon if no appeal was launched.

Although a few politicians in Canada—including B.C. Premier Mike Harcourt, who said, "I think the pressure I have relentlessly applied both in Washington and in Ottawa has brought success"—rushed to claim credit, some seasoned observers, such as Mike Apsey and IWA-Canada economist J.D. Smyth, saw the trade row over softwood lumber as being far from over (*Vancouver Sun* 1994a).

Canada needed to win only one of the two rulings from the two panels to have the duty scrapped. Although the FTA Injury Panel of three Americans and two Canadians unanimously ruled, for the second time, on January 28, 1994, that ITC had not provided enough evidence to show injury to the American industry, the split along national lines in the FTA Subsidy Panel made its decision more interesting than that of the Injury Panel.

On December 30, 1993, the coalition wrote to the U.S. FTA Secretariat, complaining about the FTA Subsidy Panel chairman's relationships with Canadian forest companies. A few weeks later, it added another panel member. The coalition said both Richard Dearden and Lawson Hunter had personally or through their law firms represented Canadian lumber producers in other cases and therefore serving as panelists "presented an appearance of bias."

In late February, U.S. Trade Representative Mickey Kantor formally demanded that the FTA Subsidy Panel be reconvened. Ottawa's refusal to remove the two panelists and to reconvene another panel led Kantor to announce, on February 24, 1994, that he would file an extraordinary challenge because "it is essential that both the public and litigants are able to have complete confidence in the integrity and credibility of the bi-national panel process" (*Toronto Star* 1994a). John Ragosta had his spin, saying, "The gross errors of law committed by the Canadian panelists alone compel an appeal. The appearance of bias makes an appeal absolutely necessary and the results even more certain" (*Vancouver Sun* 1994b).

Lumber consumer groups pressed for the U.S. government not to fight the Canadian softwood lumber war any more. Kent Colton, executive vice president of the National Association of Home Builders, said, "Softwood lumber prices have generally risen 60 to 70 percent since July 1993, largely because endangered-species protection in the Pacific Northwest has cut logging. It's just crazy for Washington to be attacking Canadian imports when prices are so high." His organization and the National Lumber and Building Material Dealers Association wrote to Kantor, urging him to drop the trade dispute with Canada over softwood lumber duties (*Oregonian* 1994).

Even Laura Tyson, chair of the president's Council of Economic Advisers, supported the U.S. builders' position. In a February 28, 1994, memo, she argued that the administration should back off because a U.S. timber shortage was driving up lumber costs in the housing industry. "We do not believe that the U.S. should be doing anything at this time to discourage Canadian imports of lumber" (*Ottawa Citizen* 1994a).

On April 6, however, the United States formally requested an extraordinary challenge committee for an appeal of the FTA Subsidy Panel's decisions. A committee was formed on April 25.

* * *

In a separate move, the B.C. government announced on April 14, 1994, that it would increase provincial stumpage fees. At then-current lumber prices, the increase in the target stumpage and royalty payments amounted to C\$12.30/m^3 for interior producers (81.1 percent) and C\$10.83/m^3 for those on the coast (64.4 percent) (British Columbia Ministry of Forests 1994). This represented a 75 percent hike in stumpage fees. At a price of US\$350/mbf for the bellwether spruce–pine–fir lumber and with the then-current annual allowable cut, the increase would amount to C\$562.5 million/year.[10] Most of the money would be used to fund a government forest program, Forest Renewal B.C.

Because stumpage fees were deductible for the purposes of federal and provincial income taxation, the costs and revenues from the new fees were shared among tenure holders, the provincial government, and the federal government. Assuming a 40 percent corporate tax rate, and spruce–pine–fir prices of US\$350/mbf, the after-tax impact on the tenure holders would be C\$337.5 million/year (0.6 × \$562.5 million). Since the cost of capital for the B.C. forest sector was 11 percent (McCallum 1997), the total capitalized cost of the stumpage fee increases to all tenure holders would be about C\$3.1 billion.

The stock prices of publicly traded B.C. forest products companies fell the day of the announcement. Binkley and Zhang (1998) estimate that the total decapitalization of the industry amounted to about C\$2.4 billion—roughly the capitalized after-tax cost of the higher stumpage fees. Hence, the capital investments made by Forest Renewal B.C. do not represent new capital to the sector, but rather a shift of capital from private investors to the public sector for different purposes. By shifting the timber rent from companies to Forest Renewal B.C., the government eliminated from the forest sector an amount of private capital roughly equal to the then-current market capitalization of the province's leading forest products company, MacMillan Bloedel.

The financial burden of this and other government policies (such as the Forest Practice Code) put on the B.C. forest industry would be felt in the coming years in the form of low and negative profitability for the industry in the late 1990s, when the U.S. and Canadian economies were booming and the U.S. forest industry was more profitable.

The coalition called the move "an extremely important step in the right direction in an effort to establish fair timber fees in Canada" (Random Lengths 2004). However, it was not yet ready to withdraw its contention that the provincial government was subsidizing its industry. Since this stumpage hike was a unilateral move, the new stumpage fees would become a new floor under the Softwood Lumber Agreement that was signed two years later.

* * *

On March 14, 1994, the U.S. International Trade Commission reaffirmed for the third time, by a vote of three to two, its earlier finding that the U.S. industry had been injured by Canadian lumber imports.

On July 6, 1994, the FTA Injury Panel unanimously ruled that ITC's determination of material injury was not yet supported by substantial evidence. It then "affirms in part and remands in part" ITC's finding of injury, and sent the issue back, for the third time, to ITC for further consideration. The panel affirmed its standard of review in its deliberation, stating,

> Indeed, the recent Daewoo decision simply reaffirms the standard of review as understood and applied by the Panel.
>
> The Panel also recognizes, as pointed out by the Commission counsel, that its review must be based on the grounds invoked by the agency. The Panel is not empowered to draw its own conclusions from the record. While it must presume that the Commissioners have considered all of the evidence presented, evidence not fairly encompassed in the discernable 'path of reasoning' is not properly before the Panel for review. (FTA Injury Panel 1994b, 4–5)

The panel agreed with four of six ITC "specific findings and judgments" in support of its affirmative second remand determination:

Finding 1. The domestic industry was currently experiencing material injury.

Finding 2. The market for lumber was a commodity market supplied almost exclusively by U.S. and Canadian producers, with thousands of transactions each day, rapid dissemination of information about these transactions to buyers and sellers, and volatile prices.

Finding 3. Subsidized Canadian imports accounted for one-quarter of the U.S. softwood lumber market and had even larger shares in some local markets.

Finding 5. The effect, if any, of the price of the subsidized Canadian imports on the price of softwood lumber in the United States could not be determined on the basis of the information on the record.

The panel did not accept the conclusion ITC drew from Finding 4 (that the volume of Canadian imports was significant)—that a "finding of significance" also amounts to a finding that "subsidized Canadian imports were causally linked to the material injury being suffered by the domestic softwood lumber industry" (FTA Injury Panel 1994b, *12*).

Nor did the panel accept ITC's Finding 6 (that no other causes fully explained the injury being experienced by the industry) because ITC "has not adequately responded to the Panel's concerns regarding the statutory validity of such a comparison, and the methodology employed by the ITC in reaching its conclusion" (FTA Injury Panel 1994b, *16*). The panel concluded,

> ... the plurality has demonstrated the "likelihood" of injury by reason of imports—but "likelihood" created by the conditions of competition (analytical framework) and the "significant" but decreasing volume and generally stable market share are not, alone, enough to support an affirmative determination. These factors may indicate that, depending on its probative value, not very much additional evidence may be necessary to sustain an affirmative determination. However, it is for the Commission to meet the substantial evidence standard by providing the additional support that the Panel has indicated is required. (FTA Injury Panel 1994b, *16*)

By agreeing with Finding 1, the panel allowed ITC to reopen the record. And the panel's conclusion might suggest that a coalition victory was close, since "not very much additional evidence may be necessary to sustain an affirmative determination." But the real battle for Lumber III was in the Extraordinary Challenge Committee, which would soon make its decision under the FTA timeline. Thus another vote by ITC on the injury question did not occur. Instead, the FTA Injury Panel relieved ITC of further obligations to pursue the case in light of the forthcoming decision by the Extraordinary Challenge Committee.

The Extraordinary Challenge Committee's Decision

On August 3, 1994, by a vote of two to one along national lines, the FTA Extraordinary Challenge Committee rejected the appeal by the U.S. government (the requestor) and the Coalition for Fair Lumber Imports (the nonparty participant), which had asked it to vacate the FTA Subsidy Panel's decisions (of no subsidy) of December 17, 1993, and of May 16, 1993.

The U.S. government (DOC 1994) had listed four specific reasons in its request for an extraordinary challenge:

1. Two of the panelists materially violated the FTA's rules of conduct by failing to disclose information that revealed at least the appearance of partiality or bias and, in the case of one panelist, a serious conflict of interest.
2. The panel in its May and December 1993 decisions manifestly exceeded its power, authority, and jurisdiction by failing to apply the appropriate standard of review and general legal principles that a U.S. court would apply when it ruled that Commerce must determine that the preferentiality treatment in timber pricing led to an increased output of lumber.
3. In its analysis of Commerce's determination that provincial stumpage programs in fact benefited an industry or group of industries, the majority manifestly exceeded its power, authority, and jurisdiction by failing to apply the appropriate standard of review and by misapprehending the U.S. substantive law it was required to apply. Instead of determining whether Commerce's finding was a permissible exercise of its discretion under U.S. law, the majority systematically substituted its own judgment for that of Commerce as to interpretations of the law and fact.
4. The above-mentioned defects in the majority's approach in the stumpage context also applied to the context of specificity of log export restrictions.

The U.S. government alleged that those actions materially affected the FTA Subsidy Panel's decisions and threatened the integrity of the binational panel review process.

All three judges sitting on the committee wrote their own opinions regarding the committee's role as well as about the four counts charged by the U.S. government.

The role of the Extraordinary Challenge Committee. Citing FTA and opinions of two previous cases that went through an extraordinary challenge, Justice Gordon L.S. Hart argued that the committee did not serve as an ordinary appellate court but should be perceived as a safety valve in those extraordinary circumstances where a challenge was warranted to maintain the integrity of the binational panel process. Similarly, Justice Morgan stated that "Our duty is solely to determine whether the Panel acted within its mandate" (FTA ECC 1994, *19–20*).

The dissenter, Judge Malcolm Wilkey, voiced concern "that an Extraordinary Challenge Committee will have no role at all." Wilkey saw that Hart's word was "technically true; neither 'Panel' nor 'Committee' is called a 'Court'; but they are the complete and only substitute for the U.S. appellate system. If this substitute appellate system had not been intended to achieve similar results in applying U.S. law, the United States would have never agreed to it. The United States never contemplated that United States law would be changed by a binational body. If the substitute appellate system does not achieve similar results in applying U.S. law, it may not be long continued." He criticized the Canadian counsel, who, he said, "obviously thought they were addressing, in brief and orally, three judicial eunuchs [on the committee], powerless to change the outcome of any Panel decision" (FTA ECC 1994, *10*).

Allegation of violation of the FTA rules of conduct and conflict of interest. In Hart's and Morgan's view, the principle of the FTA code of conduct was that a candidate or member must disclose the existence of any interests or relationships that were likely to affect his or her independence and impartiality or that might reasonably create the appearance of bias.

Hart did not see the two Canadian panelists' industry ties as sufficient grounds to justify their removal. He raised three related issues. First, no allegation was raised against these two panelists until they had twice decided the issue against the position of the United States, even though there had been ample opportunity to do so. Second, "without even waiting for all the facts, and before the Parties had consulted on the issue as required by FTA Annex 1901.2(6), the United States publicly announced its intention to bring this extraordinary challenge based upon misconduct allegations." Third, "it was also known that one of the American members of this Panel was associated with a firm that billed over $3,800,000 to an American government agency during 1992–1993. Neither party considered it necessary to treat these facts as an indication of bias on the part of any panelists and did not do so. It was only when the final decision was in that the matter was raised" (FTA ECC 1994, *46–53*).

Similarly, Morgan concluded, "Suffice it to say at this stage that none of them [the subsequent disclosures] related to the specific issue before the Panel nor did they differ in any material respect from those initially disclosed and found acceptable to the United States Government" (FTA ECC 1994, *26*).[11] Thus, the two panelists' nondisclosure at least did not materially affect their decision and the integrity of the FTA dispute resolution system.

Wilkey believed that the two panelists were in breach of the code of conduct. After conducting a chronological analysis of the two panelists' affiliations, he stated that the United States would have requested one of the two panelists (Lawson Hunter) to leave the panel had it been revealed earlier that he had once been retained by the attorney general of Canada (for a short period of time and for an unrelated matter, in the fall of 1992). Wilkey believed that it was also highly questionable that the United States would have accepted Chairman Dearden had it known all the additional information that Dearden disclosed in February 1994. He stated,

> The key is—the United States had the absolute right to accept or to reject
> Hunter and Dearden. Corollary to this, the United States had the absolute
> right to know the complete truth as to their and their firm's affiliations,
> on which to base its decision. The United States was denied these rights
> guaranteed under the FTA. The United States had no recourse except to

ask for the vacating of the Panel judgment and opinions to which the votes of Hunter and Dearden were essential. (FTA ECC 1994, 76)

Allegations of failing to apply the appropriate standard of review in Commerce's preferentiality determination. After citing cases under the FTA and in the U.S. Court of International Trade and the legal arguments from both parties, along with their readings of supporting cases such as *Daewoo*, Justice Hart stated,

> On the assumption that this recent pronouncement by the [Court of International Trade] represents the law of the United States it is difficult to say that the Panel majority did not apply the appropriate standard of review when reaching its conclusions.... I cannot say that an appellate court in the United States could not reach the same conclusions as the unanimous Panel of May 1993 and the majority of the Panel in December 1993. The arguments made on both sides had a solid foundation in court precedents and the *amount of deference extended to the agency was in tune with the novelty of the exercise.*
>
> I would like to point out that in reality the replacement of court adjudication by a five member panel of experts in international trade law may very well reduce the amount of deference to the Department in the future. When the Court of International Trade reviews the determinations of Commerce it would be expected to bow to the expertise within the Department. When the parties to the FTA agreed to replace that court with this type of panel they must have realized and intended that a review of the actions of Commerce or of the Canadian agency would be intense. The panels have been given the right to make a final determination of the matters in dispute between the two countries in a relatively short period of time without any judicial review. Apparently each government felt that this system was more satisfactory than the one which was replaced.
>
> In my opinion the Panel followed an appropriate standard of review and properly interpreted United States law when it ruled that Commerce in this unique situation was required to assess whether or not there was any competitive advantage or market distortion created by the Canadian stumpage systems on the British Columbia [log export restrictions] ... Furthermore, having determined that there was no such distortion according to the evidence there was nothing to countervail. (FTA ECC 1994, 28–29, emphasis added)

Similarly, Justice Morgan found himself "unable to conclude that the Majority did not conscientiously apply U.S. law in requiring Commerce to consider market distortion nor in its conclusion that Commerce's finding of market distortion in its Redetermination was not supported by substantial evidence on the Record."

Judge Wilkey agreed with the two dissenters in the panel that the statute is silent on the market distortion test and that whether it is necessary to conduct such a test in the present case should be deferred to Commerce. But he believed that the majority of the panel had usurped the function of Commerce:

> This is precisely the situation when deference to administrative agency discretion and expertise should be at its highest. Confronted with a comparatively new economic situation to be addressed, *it is the ITA [International Trade Administration] of the Commerce Department—not the courts (or the substitute Panel)—to whom Congress have given discretion to formulate policy and methodology adequate to the circumstance.* Unless the Panel majority or my two colleagues can show that Commerce acted contrary to a specific provision of the governing statute—and neither has even pretended to assert this—Commerce's Redetermination must prevail.
>
> ... Even if another reasonable conclusion could be reached on the same evidence, the agency is entitled to have its interpretation validated. (FTA ECC 1994, *35–38*, emphasis original)

Wilkey cited legislative history—in particular, Senate Joint Committee Report 103-189 (published on November 19, 1993) and House Ways and Means Committee Report 103-361 (published on November 15, 1993) on the North American Free Trade Agreement Implementation Act[12]—to support his position. He acknowledged, "The basic problem on accepting these Reports in this case is that the English Courts accept no legislative history at all and the Canadians follow closely in their footsteps" (*40*).

Allegations of failing to apply the appropriate standard of review in Commerce's specificity determination. Hart stated,

> It is apparent that the panelists articulated the proper standard of review and in my opinion the entire panel in its May decision and the majority in their December decision conscientiously applied the appropriate law. There can be differences in view concerning that law but there is nothing in the record which appears to me to be an attempt to avoid the standard of review required by law... in my opinion it cannot be said that the majority decision was clearly wrong. (FTA ECC 1994, *41*)

Morgan found that "it's passing strange that any administrative tribunal can state that a decision of a court of appeal of the Federal Circuit or indeed any Federal court is wrongly decided, and that it did not propose to follow it, as in this case." He was referring to PPG IV, *PPG Industries, Inc. v. United States*, 978 F.2d (1232) (Fed. Cir. 1992), one of the precedents on which the panel had relied in requiring Commerce to consider all the factors on which a determination of specificity is based. He said, "It cannot be said that the Panel did not conscientiously apply U.S. law" (FTA ECC 1994, *18*).

With respect to specificity, Wilkey again found a gap in statute. He stated, "In our case, it is the ITA [International Trade Administration], not the Binational Panel, which is authorized to say how many factors it will consider on specificity" (FTA ECC 1994, *30*).[13]

Wilkey reasoned that Commerce's "Redetermination findings and conclusions were in conformity with and were in no way violative of the statute and normal administrative procedure," and "basically the Panel opinion attempts to redo, to reevaluate the evidence, to redetermine the technical issues before the administrative agency." Further, "the Panel places its own interpretation and makes its own evaluation of the weight of the evidence. In addition, the Panel insists upon its own methodology, thus violating the principle that where there is a gap in the statute, ... this is confided to the Agency's expertise and discretion." (*32–35*)

In short, Wilkey believed that not enough deference (in both preferentiality and specificity tests) was paid to Commerce. Hart inferred that Wilkey was demanding almost absolute deference and leaving almost no breathing space for a reviewing tribunal. He stated, "If this is correct law to apply there is no need for a binational panel under the FTA" (FTA ECC 1994, *54*).

Wilkey concluded that the panel proceeded to violate the standard of review for administrative agency action and that "to see how review of administrative action should be done, in this case, it is necessary to read the 83 page opinion of the two dissenters, particularly pages 5–38 and 43–50" (FTA ECC 1994, Opinion of Judge Wilkey, *37*).[14]

* * *

Judge Wilkey's criticism of the binational panel and the extraordinary challenge process. Wilkey further alleged that trade experts in the binational panel were not likely to become expert in the judicial review of administrative agency action. He sarcastically asked why panel members should be expected to defer to administrative agency action when they were the experts who "know better than the lowly paid 'experts' over in the Commerce Department." He also saw that neither panel members nor Canadian judges sitting on extraordinary challenge committees understood the intricacies of U.S. administrative law and, therefore, would not be capable of applying the proper standard of review. In his view, the FTA Chapter 19 review system was so riddled with problems that it could not be fixed (Macrory 2002, *12*).

On the future of NAFTA, Wilkey stated,

> All of this has occurred in the operation of this innovative scheme of appellate review between Canada and the United States, two common law countries with similar legal traditions and antecedents. Now we have

Mexico as a third member of NAFTA, and in the near future perhaps Chile and other Ibero-American countries. Mexico has no legal system or traditions in common with the United States whatsoever; it is proudly a civil law country.... If Canadians on the Panels and [extraordinary challenge committees] have failed—as in my judgment here they have—to comprehend the United States standards of judicial review of administrative agency action, what can we expect from lawyers and judges schooled in the Civil Law?

This brings up a point so large that it cannot be dealt with here, only noted. Early in the negotiations a United States constitutional problem was identified: Could litigants in the United States be deprived of their right to appeal from administrative action to a hierarchy of life-time Article III judges, i.e., to the Court of International Trade, then as of right to the Federal Circuit, and then possibly seek certiorari in the Supreme Court, by the device of a Binational Panel composed of ad hoc non-judges, and then a special review of Panel decisions by another binational tribunal [an extraordinary challenge committee] composed of ad hoc judges? (FTA ECC 1994, 63–68, emphasis added)

This last statement seemed designed to invite a constitutional challenge to the FTA binational panel process. The coalition subsequently accepted Judge Wilkey's invitation and filed such a challenge in the U.S. Court of Appeals for the District of Columbia on September 14, 1994.

* * *

Canadian interests hailed the Extraordinary Challenge Committee's decision; the coalition and its allies in Congress planned to continue the fight. Harold Maxwell, chairman of the coalition, said that U.S. companies could not rely on the FTA panel process and needed to persuade Congress to legislate limits on Canadian softwood. Senator Baucus said the ruling would jeopardize thousands of U.S. sawmill jobs and "calls into question the very efficacy and integrity of the bi-national panel process" set up under the FTA (*Buffalo News* 1994). A few days later, he wrote a letter to President Clinton, stating that the panel members had "exceeded their jurisdiction and usurped Congress's right to make U.S. law" (*Toronto Star* 1994b).

Because the committee's decision in August 1994 was final, the United States seemed to be running out of options. But Lumber III did not end with that decision.

Notes

1. "While the definition of 'material injury' is the same in both preliminary and final investigations, the standard of determination is different. In preliminary investigations an affirmative determination is based on 'reasonable indication' of material injury or threat, as opposed to the finding of actual material injury or threat required for an affirmative determination in the final determination" (ITC 1991, *14*).

2. In the last three rounds of the lumber war, the Canadians have arguably not done enough on the political front. The political effort in Lumber II consisted of hiring Walter Mondale, the former majority leader of the U.S. Senate and losing candidate in the prior presidential election, to lobby the Reagan administration. In Lumber III and Lumber IV, Canada hired some lobbyists but did not do grass-roots work (Horlick 2006).

3. Ignoring the equity issue (the distribution of income between resource owners and users) for a moment, this conclusion—that production might not change with stumpage charges—may be true in the short run because stumpage is a residual payment. In the long run, profits and hence investment could be affected, which in turn affects production, unless the profit levels for Canadian producers are similar to or lower than those of U.S. producers.

4. Environmental groups led many protests against logging of old-growth forests in Carmanah Valley, Tsitika Valley, and Walbran Valley on Vancouver Island in the late 1980s and early 1990s. Their protests culminated in the summer of 1993, after a government decision to allow timber harvesting in Clayoquot Sound on Vancouver Island. The blockades in Clayoquot Sound resulted in nearly 800 arrests (Stanbury 2000, *73*).

5. Three statutory elements that are probative of causation are price underselling, price depression, and price suppression. The panel noted that ITC was unable to make any finding concerning underselling or price depression by Canadian imports, and therefore it relied on price suppression (FTA Injury Panel 1993, *35*).

6. The panel noted that the argument for doing the comparison was first raised by the counsel for the coalition, who said, "Other building products subject to the recession and supply concerns but insulated from subsidized Canadian competition have performed much better than softwood lumber during this period of recession." In its final determination, ITC stated that such a comparison of the softwood lumber industry with the "wood products and building materials" industries was relevant (FTA Injury Panel 1993, *55*).

7. Most empirical studies show that demand for softwood lumber in the United States is highly inelastic (with price elasticity between –0.11 and –0.17) and that supply of softwood lumber in the United States is more elastic (about three to four times more, or around 0.4 to 0.8) than demand in absolute terms. Therefore, consumers would share more of the burden of a lumber price increase caused by an increase in log price. However, producers would not be able to "pass cost increases along to consumers almost dollar for dollar." In addition, producers could substitute other inputs for logs in case of a log price hike, resulting in less of a price increase in lumber markets (than when the substitutability between logs and other inputs are not considered). See Li and Zhang (2006).

8. Critics (Apsey and Thomas 1997) charged that the reversal of position by the two U.S. panelists was an about-face, since even the dissenting judge in the subsequent Extraordinary Challenge Committee and the FTA Injury Panel noted that *Daewoo* simply restated existing law and did not create new precedent. The dissenting judge in the extraordinary challenge defended the two panelists by stating that *Daewoo* had awakened them.

9. This report was accepted by the FTA Subsidy Panel on February 23, 1994, and on March 7, the NAFTA Secretariat issued a notice that concluded the FTA review process.

10. On May, 20 1994, the Canadian government deferred C$30 million of the increased timber license royalties after consultation with licensees.

11. In his detailed response to the concerns raised by the coalition, Dearden first listed other parties that his firm had represented and explained in detail the nature and the type of advice given. He then stated that far from being partisan toward Canada, he had represented the U.S. trade representative office in the past, he had worked closely with Commerce in connection with the negotiation of the FTA itself, and several members of his firm had represented and were currently representing the U.S. government in various matters unrelated to this proceeding (FTA ECC 1994, *22*).

12. These two reports criticize the binational panel's decision on almost all cases when its decision was against the position of Commerce. For example, the Senate report stated,

> In several cases, binational panels have misinterpreted U.S. law and practice in two key substantive areas of U.S. countervailing duty law—regarding the so-called "effects test" and regarding the requirement that subsidy must be "specific" to an industry.

> In [Softwood Lumber Panel, 6 May 1993] the binational panel misinterpreted U.S. law to require that, even after the Department of Commerce has determined that the subsidy has been provided, the Department must further demonstrate that the subsidy has the effect of lowering the price of increasing the output of goods before duty can be imposed.

> Such an "effects" test for subsidies has never been mandated by the law and is inconsistent with the effective enforcement of the countervailing duty law....

> ... Congress had explicitly rejected the use of "effects" tests in the Trade Agreements Act of 1979 ...

> From a policy perspective, the Committee believes an "effects" analysis should not be required. (cited in FTA ECC 1994, Opinion of Judge Wilkey, *46–47*)

13. With respect to specificity, the Senate Joint Committee Report stated,

> The Committee agrees with current Department of Commerce practice with respect to specificity ... the department set forth four factors that may be considered whether specificity exists. Under current practice ... Commerce may base the finding against a subsidy is specifically provided on one or more relevant factors.

> ... One factor alone could be sufficient for a de facto specificity finding. (cited in FTA ECC 1994, *48*)

14. Judge Wilkey repeated this message at least twice in his opinion. He stated, on page 39, "It is not necessary for us to rehash what has been written by Commerce, by the three-man majority, and by the two dissenters. Just read the dissent. I would affirm the Commerce Department Redetermination based on that opinion." He stated, on page 62, "If one has a solid background in principles of United States judicial review of agency action, it is not even necessary to have read the Determination to see how far astray the Panel majority went. But for the clincher, read the Panel dissent, particularly pages 5–38 and 43–50."

7

A Temporary Truce

The Softwood Lumber Agreement of 1996

Following the Extraordinary Challenge Committee ruling under the Free Trade Agreement, several events motivated the Canadian government and industry to resume their positions around the bargaining table with their U.S counterparts, even though they just won the legal case. Some seasoned observers saw this development as an indication that as long as the U.S. industry and its congressional allies turned up the political heat, Canadians would give in.

Impetus to Engage in a Consultative Process

Withholding of the refund. On August 5, 1994, John Ragosta, counsel for the Coalition for Fair Lumber Imports, said that FTA panel decisions were not retroactive, and the Department of Commerce hinted that it was exploring legal options that would allow the United States to keep the C$800 million lumber duties it had collected. The United States did, however, refund duties it collected in a previous trade case Canada had won on pork, and it agreed to refund duties paid on or after March 17, 1994, the date of publication of the FTA Subsidy Panel's final decision on softwood lumber (*Ottawa Citizen* 1994b).

On August 16, 1994, several senators and representatives, calling themselves the Fair Trade Caucus of Congress, wrote a letter to President Clinton, complaining about the "outrageous" FTA panel decision that had overturned the 6.5 percent tariff on Canadian softwood lumber. They stated that the administration had no legislative authority to return the duties and that "legal authority to return those funds to Canada must be sought from Congress and should be granted only if the long-term problem of Canadian [softwood] subsidies is resolved" (*Toronto Star* 1994b).

It is doubtful that Canadian FTA negotiators foresaw that the duty refund would be a problem. Otherwise, U.S. industry groups such as the Coalition for Fair Lumber Imports would have a strong financial incentive to keep seeking high countervailing duties on Canadian exports, even if such duties were later ruled illegal. In mid-September, the Canadian lumber industry filed a petition in the U.S. Court of International Trade to preserve a right to appeal if the United States did not refund all the duties, insisting that there was absolutely no legal basis or precedent for the United States to withhold the duties (*Toronto Star* 1994c).

The constitutional challenge. When, in September 1994, the Coalition for Fair Lumber Imports filed its lawsuit challenging the constitutionality of the FTA panel system,[1] it alleged that it had been denied due process in the panel process, and that the FTA process violated the Appointments Clause of the U.S. Constitution, the separation of powers requirements under the Constitution, the Fifth Amendment's due process requirements, and the guarantee of equal protection under the law (Apsey and Thomas 1997).

At that time, the North American Free Trade Agreement had been implemented for nine months. Like FTA, NAFTA has a binational dispute panel system. Not willing to see the courts determine the fate of FTA and NAFTA or to be seen as against its own lumber industry, the Clinton administration did not welcome this constitutional challenge. Although the coalition had its allies in the Department of Commerce and Congress, the constitutional challenge questioned a law that had been passed by Congress in December 1993, thus raising important issues of principle that the U.S. Justice Department would defend vigorously.

It was also reported that some coalition members did not endorse this constitutional challenge, since they realized that a court victory would destroy not only Canadian lumber imports but also the market opportunities NAFTA had opened in Mexico and Canada (*Vancouver Sun* 1994d). Thus there were doubts about how far the constitutional challenge could go. Nonetheless, the challenge provided leverage for the Clinton administration to persuade the Canadians to come back to the bargaining table.

Legislative actions. The coalition also sought help on Capitol Hill, where Congress was considering legislative action to implement the recently completed Uruguay Round of multinational trade negotiations, which among other things established the World Trade Organization. This allowed the coalition to seek statutory amendments or legislative history that would support its continuing complaint and facilitate the withholding of the duties.

Congress indeed amended, on December 8, 1994, the United States' countervailing duty law as part of the Uruguay Round Agreements Act. Two of the amendments were explicitly designed to reverse the major panel findings in Lumber III. One provides that Commerce can base a finding of specificity on just one of the four factors; the other is that Commerce is not required to consider the effect of a subsidy in considering whether one exists.[2]

Because the Uruguay Round bill was going to become a U.S. law, U.S. Trade Representative Mickey Kantor hinted that the United States could use it to squeeze concessions out of Canada over the longstanding softwood lumber dispute. He stated, "It's clear that we're in a position today where we can resolve this quickly," and he linked "underlying issues" in suggesting that Ottawa might have to give a little more to get what the Extraordinary Challenge Committee had ruled Canada was owed. He further stated, "The underlying issues involve subsidization and other kinds of practices which would put the Canadian industry in a preferred position versus its U.S. counterparts or competitors ..." (*Vancouver Sun* 1994c).

Although Trade Minister Roy MacLaren said Canada was not prepared to negotiate anything and demanded a full refund of the duties, the significance of the new U.S. trade legislation was noticed. Based on it, the Clinton administration invited Canada to enter into a new consultative process. On December 15, 1994, the coalition withdrew its constitutional challenge to FTA and NAFTA, which paved the way for refunding the remainder of previously collected duties.

Canada maintained that there would be no talks until the duties were refunded in full. When USTR confirmed that the duties would be returned in full, Canada agreed to a consultation process on December 15, 1994.[3] Minister MacLaren stated, "With this U.S. action, we can now put this case behind us ... The creation of a consultative process is an important step in moving from a litigious to cooperative bilateral relationship on lumber" (Canadian Foreign Affairs and International Trade 1994). He went on to describe the purpose of the consultations as being to enhance bilateral cooperation in areas of mutual concern and interest within the forestry industry.

The Canadian forest industry saw this development as a victory. John C. (Jake) Kerr, president of Lignum Ltd., a company in interior British Columbia that would play a critical role in the next episode of the lumber trade dispute, was happy to get the money back but concerned about the consultation process. He stated,

> The only restraint we have had in our position is that we did not want it to be deemed negotiations because we don't feel there is anything to negotiate. We very much support sharing data, discussing how the industries work and issues like how we value timber.... There is continuing misunderstanding, we believe, in the issue of subsidy. We would like the opportunity to sit down and talk. (*Vancouver Sun* 1994d)

Jake Kerr's concern was real. Trade Representative Kantor's view was quite different from that of Minister MacLaren regarding the purposes of the consultations. USTR stated, "From the U.S. standpoint, a key purpose of the consultations is to try to address the problem of injurious subsidies" (USTR 1994).

Thus, Kantor and the coalition considered the consultative process as negotiation. Coalition Chairman Mack Singleton stated, "If the talks are successful, as we expect, litigation is completely unnecessary. If the talks prove unproductive, the Coalition will reassess its strategy, including the possibility of new litigation and recourse to trade remedies." He further stated that the group withdrew the constitutional challenge "in an effort to make the atmosphere less contentious for the talks." For his part, Senator Max Baucus said he supported the decision of the United States and Canada "to enter into formal consultations in order to reach a permanent resolution to the long-standing softwood lumber dispute" (*Toronto Star* 1994d).

At this juncture, all parties involved—the two industries, two national governments, and provincial governments in Canada) wanted to try a different avenue rather than have another countervailing duty case. For the coalition, insisting on the constitutional challenge to FTA and NAFTA would antagonize the Clinton administration and some lumber producers; it probably did not really want to tear apart NAFTA; consultations might bring a negotiated settlement in its favor. The Clinton administration did not want the courts to decide the fate of NAFTA, and consultations might secure an agreement that would make the domestic industry happy while not jeopardizing overall trade relations with Canada. For Canadian governments and industry, the consultation process could allow them to avoid, at least temporarily, another countervailing duty case, which they could lose under the Uruguay Round Agreements Act. The costs and uncertainty of litigation presented problems for all sides. In short, the consultation process was, at the moment, preferable to slugging it out in the courts and trade tribunals.

According to the "Elements of a Consultative Process," the parties agreed to initiate a dialogue on a range of issues, including current and future policies and practices and barriers that affected trade in softwood lumber and other obstacles identified by industry in either country. They would seek to work together to resolve problems, ensure that progress was not eroded, and explore alternative mechanisms for resolving disputes without resort to litigation. Consultations would commence no later than March 1, 1995 (Apsey and Thomas 1997).

The Consultative Process

A staff-level meeting of government officials from both countries was held in March 1995, and the first round of consultation, which included industry executives, took place May 24–25 in Washington, D.C. On both occasions, no lawyer working for the industries was allowed to be present. The idea was that foresters and business leaders might be able to craft a resolution so that litigation could be avoided. Participants at the meeting in May 1995 included Deputy Trade Representative Ira Shapiro and his Canadian counterpart, John Weekes. The

U.S. lumber industry was represented by, among others, Dick Bennett, president of Bennett Lumber Company of Idaho; Mike Suwyn and Lyn Withey, vice presidents of International Paper; and John Turner, vice president of Georgia-Pacific. The Canadian lumber industry was represented by, among others, Jake Kerr and Mike Apsey of the Canadian Forest Industries Council and Carl Grenier of the Québec Lumber Manufacturers' Association. The meeting produced no resolution, but both sides agreed to meet again in July to consider the current market situation in North America and issues, policy, and forest management practices.

In the first half of 1995, U.S. housing starts declined, and demand for lumber was down; yet the Canadian share of the U.S. lumber market increased from 28 percent in 1992 to 36 percent. Some Canadian lumber that had gone to Europe was diverted to the United States because of new European Union regulations on lumber implemented in 1992.

Not happy with the increasing Canadian share, the Coalition for Fair Lumber Imports renewed its efforts to curb Canadian lumber imports. On June 5–6, it brought a group of industry representatives—about 25 industry and association executives—to Washington, D.C., to discuss strategy. It was the first gathering of industry groups on Canadian lumber in nearly 10 years. The attendees of the meeting, while preferring some trade restriction measures, were divided about specific strategy. John Turner, for example, did not favor the litigation route and later asked Deputy Trade Representative Shapiro to find an alternative to litigation (Shapiro 2006). Others thought that litigation was the only way to wring concessions from Canada. Ultimately, a strategy of negotiation with the threat of litigation was pursued.

Shortly after the industry gathering, somebody in the coalition leaked a fundraising letter signed by its chairman, Mack Singleton, indicating that it was seeking commitments of support—financial and otherwise—to "proceed with litigation and legislative efforts as appropriate, probably including a new countervailing duty case." The apparent need for legislative efforts was necessary to "seek to remove the threat that, after winning our case, a binational panel will steal from us." The leak was apparently calculated to impress on Canadians the coalition's serious intent to return to litigation and to pressure both governments to speed up the consultation process. The coalition "plan(s) to make it very clear to our government and the Canadian government that absent real, concrete progress in the July Consultation, the U.S. industry will have no choice but to pursue other action" (Singleton 1995).

The letter indicated that the coalition would proceed with its efforts only if it had "financial commitments from at least 10 BBF of U.S. softwood lumber production at 25c/MBF annually for an anticipated 3 years of litigation and 3 months of preparation"—a minimum of US$75 million. The letter reasoned, "Of course, litigation and legislative efforts are also very expensive. We know that the Canadian industry spent from $50–100 million in the last case to protect its subsidies" (Singleton 1995).

The letter further indicated that the U.S. lumber industry should pursue this course. The calculus of benefits and costs for the industry was clear and expressed forthrightly in the letter: "If we reduce artificial price suppression caused by subsidized Canadian lumber by even 1 percent for one year, we will pay for a three-year effort four times over" (Singleton 1995).

That was the bottom line. The coalition wanted to raise the price of lumber in the United States to a level that it deemed to be fair, accompanied with a fair market share. Countervailing duty cases were a means of achieving its goals.

The institutional arrangements in the United States are such that despite the recent defeats under the FTA, the U.S. lumber industry was able to lobby and change U.S. laws that made any future Canadian legal victory less likely. With a sympathetic Department of Commerce and U.S. Congress, the threat of another countervailing duty case, along with a likely coalition victory, was all too real.

The demand for lumber in the United States is cyclical. When demand falls and prices decline (which could be caused in part by increased Canadian lumber exports to the States, whether the lumber is subsidized or not), U.S. producers can try to get some relief by forcing up the cost of Canadian lumber. The easiest way to do that is by claiming unfair competition. An interim duty is imposed while investigations of the validity of the claim proceed.

The letter from Singleton (1995) indicated that even though "the statutory timetable for preliminary relief is 3–5 months after bringing a case," there was no down side for the U.S. industry. During the investigations, the prices of Canadian lumber would be raised by the level of the interim (and final) countervailing duty during the protracted appeals procedure started by the losing side (which would be much longer than the investigation period). In the worst scenario for the U.S. industry—if at the end of all this the U.S. producers' claims were found to be without merit and the duties collected were eventually returned to Canada—the U.S. producers would have achieved their objectives in the meantime. The prices raised by the interim and final duty would be more than the legal costs of bringing such a case forward.

* * *

It is no wonder that some U.S. companies find litigation an attractive option. Canadian producers lose production and competitiveness to their U.S. counterparts. But the biggest loser in all this is the U.S. consumer, who pays a higher price than under free trade.

This is why public choice theory is so relevant to the U.S.–Canada softwood lumber trade dispute: A small but highly organized and focused group of potential beneficiaries can achieve economic gains at the expense of widely spread, politically unorganized, and less focused consumers. Because U.S. lumber producers face rationally apathetic consumer groups whose individual gains are too small to warrant a fight and who collectively have higher priorities than lumber, they have had some U.S. lawmakers on their side against "unfairly competing" foreigners. Under congressional pressure, the president and his subordinates in the Department of Commerce sometimes cater to the producers rather than to the larger, more diffuse, and less responsive consumer groups. This provides a compelling explanation for the longevity of certain trade disputes, such as softwood lumber.

Foreigners cannot sue U.S. industries for launching vexatious claims of unfair trade. Nor can foreigners vote in U.S. elections. Thus, it is unlikely that Congress would enact provisions to discourage the filing of claims alleging unfair trading on the part of foreigners.

Unless U.S. consumers or businesses dependent on trade become more vocal against protectionism and gain credence in U.S. politics, U.S. industries will continue to launch trade actions against foreign competitors that increase their market share in the United States. Trade disputes are thus likely to be inevitable for Canada and other countries, and some of them might continue for many years. Regional or global trade institutions, such as WTO and NAFTA, might help resolve certain trade disputes. But for large, politically sensitive trade disputes such as softwood lumber, domestic politics plays a significant role.

* * *

The second round of consultation took place July 11–12, 1995, in Kelowna, British Columbia. In the meeting, Mack Singleton of the Coalition for Fair Lumber Imports and Deputy Trade Representative Ira Shapiro demanded resolution of "the injurious subsidy problem." Shapiro said, "Obviously we have a concern about some of the harm that has been done in the United States, some of the damage that has been inflicted within the industry." Singleton presented various proposals that had been floated in private discussions, including changes in stumpage price systems, imposition of an export tax, voluntary volume restrictions, and a combination of these measures (*Vancouver Sun* 1995a).

Jake Kerr emerged from the talks feeling optimistic. Apparently, he and his Washington, D.C., lawyer, John Reilly, of Baker and McKenzie LLP, realized that although the United States could not meet its domestic demand for lumber, the coalition would not tolerate too high a Canadian share of the U.S. lumber market. What the coalition really wanted was volume control. A voluntary export control or quota would meet the coalition's demand and thus was deemed acceptable (Kerr 2006).

It took a while for Canadian industry leaders to recognize that volume was the key, since the coalition's stated objective was to have a competitive timber sale system in Canada. In the Kelowna meeting, Jake Kerr and Dick Bennett of the coalition had the following conversation, as recounted by Kerr (2006):

Kerr: "I understand that you [the coalition] want to have a competitive timber sale system in Canada that is similar to the one used by the U.S. Forest Service. What will happen if stumpage prices fall after we implement such a timber sale system in British Columbia?"

Bennett: "We will sue you again [if that happens]."

Having earned a bachelor's degree in economics and a master's degree in finance and having worked in the forest industry for decades, Kerr understood that under a quota system, Canadian producers would lose some export volume, but gain quota rents, which could compensate and even surpass the loss in producer surplus associated with volume loss when demand is high. If demand was low, the quota might not be met and the industry would not suffer from paying any tax. Unlike an export tax or stumpage fee increase, the industry would not be harmed under a quota system when demand was low and could benefit from quota rents when the demand was high.

In this way, the Canadian industry, instead of the government, would collect quota rents. Undoubtedly, the Canadian industry would lose competitiveness to the U.S. industry under a quota system instead of free trade. But if the quota system could be designed to be acceptable to the coalition, the Canadian industry could avoid costly litigation. Further, British Columbia would avoid new hikes in stumpage rates, which were already the highest on record as a result of increases in 1987 and 1994. Coastal producers that exported to Asia and Europe and producers of other forest products in the province would avoid penalty from a stumpage hike or export tax.

Later, as the actual quota was allocated, some industry leaders charged that Kerr had other motives for proposing a quota system. Lignum Ltd., a lumber producer in interior British Columbia, had a lumber wholesale operation that had historically exported high volumes to the United States (in contrast to producers in coastal British Columbia and other provinces). Therefore Lignum Ltd. and other interior lumber producers would receive a large share of the quota.

Kerr and his supporters did not foresee two other problems—the Asian economic crisis in 1997–1998 that would dampen Asia's demand for coastal lumber and a surge of export to the United States from other provinces and countries after the Softwood Lumber Agreement of 1996 was signed. Because some coastal lumber producers did not have much quota to export to the States, losing the Asian market was particularly damaging. A surge of exports from other countries and provinces that were not subject to the quota system would replace the four major lumber-producing provinces' share in the United States. Nonetheless, these two problems were not in prospect back in 1995. A third problem was that high lumber prices under the quota system would induce U.S. producers to build additional capacity and increase their production. But in 1995 no one had a good estimate about the expected price level under a quota system and the expected production capacity increase in the United States.

Few other options were available if some trade restrictions had to be implemented. Both an export tax and a stumpage hike had been tried under the 1986–1991 Memorandum of Understanding. The Canadian industry was not prepared to go back to either measure. A quota system seemed to be a logical choice.

Since the U.S. industry could not ask Washington to impose a quota on Canadian lumber imports, the coalition was happy to see the Canadians offer it. Singleton insisted that the coalition was there not to dictate but to discuss what might be possible. Shapiro said, "There is some confidence being built. We are involved in a serious and constructive process that in my mind holds more promise than endless rounds of litigation" (*Vancouver Sun* 1995a).

After intensive negotiations with USTR and with the blessing of the coalition, Jake Kerr sought to persuade the Canadian industry to go along with his voluntary quota idea. Industry offered various opinions, from "do not do it" to "support it with reservation." Mostly, the comment was that if Canada was forced to do something in order to have peace with the United States, it ought to get a commitment from the U.S. industry that it would not launch another countervailing duty case.

On August 8, 1995, Senator Larry Craig stepped up his attack on "cheap, subsidized Canadian lumber" in a speech to the U.S. Senate. He said that in May 1995, Canada had 39 percent of the U.S. softwood lumber market, "an all-time record for foreign market share of lumber in the United States." He said Canadian subsidies were to blame, especially in British Columbia, where producers paid about US$100/mbf of timber while producers in Idaho, Oregon, and Washington paid US$365 for the same amount and type of timber. He further stated that unless Canada changed its timber pricing system, the United States might have to legislate changes to the NAFTA. Referring to the forthcoming third round of consultation between the two countries, he said it "must accelerate and complete efforts to produce a concrete framework for permanently reforming Canadian pricing schemes in order to eliminate the subsidies provided to the Canadian producers" (*Congressional Record* 1995a).

On September 25–26, the third round of consultations was held in Washington, D.C. Some progress was reported, and the United States urged all provinces, especially British Columbia and Québec, to make settlement proposals. All other issues, such as forecasting timber supply, environmental regulations, and forest practices, fell by the wayside and proved not to be important to the U.S. side. Canada responded that it was prepared to explore solutions to the U.S. concerns so long as its concerns of ensuring security and predictability of market access were also met. Canada sought to have an agreement on a "ceasefire" on any future trade remedy investigations and on a consultative process that would be used to discuss any allegations of unfair trade practices before a complaint was filed (Apsey and Thomas 1997). Apparently, the bottom line for Canada was no more countervailing duty cases, and for the United States, it was limits on the Canadian share of the U.S. lumber market.

When the proposals did not come quickly, Trade Representative Kantor stated on October 12, "Our patience is running thin; so far the provinces of British Columbia and Québec have not responded" (*Vancouver Sun* 1995b). On November 3, 1995, Senator Baucus introduced a bill—S. 1392 (Emergency Lumber Act of 1995)—calling for the imposition of a 25 percent duty on imports of Canadian softwood lumber and requiring Commerce to initiate a countervailing duty investigation (*Congressional Record* 1995b).

On November 15, 1995, British Columbia officially proposed an agreement that contained a tariff-rate quota system, under which an export tax would be imposed for lumber exports exceeding a certain quota. In return, Canada demanded a written guarantee from the U.S. industry that no new countervailing duty case would be filed. The agreement would also stipulate some form of mandatory dispute resolution and would remain in effect a minimum of five years. Québec expressed an interest in modifying its stumpage system, but after considerable discussion, the B.C. proposal emerged as the front runner.

The coalition and U.S. officials wanted the proposal to be more specific, so U.S. and B.C. officials met in Chicago on November 27–28, 1995, to hammer out details. Kantor named a deadline of December 15, after which the consultative process would be over and the U.S. industry would be free to litigate. British Columbia then put out specific numbers, promising to reduce its share of the U.S. market to 18 percent from the then-current 21 percent. Because the proposal was a substantial movement, Kantor set a new deadline, the end of January 1996.

On December 18, 1995, a bill (H.R. 2802) similar to S. 1392 was introduced in the U.S. House of Representatives. On December 20, a group of 12 senators and congressmen held a hearing on Canadian lumber, where Kantor said he was prepared to levy an import tariff on Canadian lumber if Canada failed to make concessions soon to help U.S. producers. Senator Craig said Kantor "saw the strong resolve of Congress to deal with this in a bipartisan way; Senator Baucus said, "A gathering this large should show the Canadians how serious the timber issue is" (*Bangor Daily News* 1995).

In the first four months of 1996, Canadian politics took center stage as discussion and debates on province-specific proposals and quota allocations went on. The United States wanted to reduce Canada's total market share to 30 percent from 36 percent. British Columbia had already offered to reduce its share to 18 percent from 21 percent, but it wanted other provinces to go along. Otherwise, those provinces would simply take the B.C. share.

Québec, on the other hand, offered to raise its per-unit stumpage fee to about half of what B.C. producers paid, the lower amount reflecting the inferior timber quality in Québec. It regarded British Columbia's solution as a sellout (*Gazette* 1996). Québec argued that under WTO, a quota would be deemed illegal, and it set a bad precedent in trade disputes. Alberta and Ontario supported Québec's position.[4]

The Canadian government had the unenviable task of trying to craft a solution based on divided interests and proposals made by these provinces. Québec's proposal was simpler and did not require federal monitoring and tax collection. On the other hand, British Columbia was the largest softwood lumber-producing province, and its proposal had been accepted by the coalition. If the B.C. quota proposal were implemented, the tax would have to be applied Canada-wide to be enforceable and effective, since neither the coalition nor British Columbia would agree to a deal that might see British Columbia's export replaced by other provinces. However, if the export tax were applicable across Canada, Québec could make a cause out of it, which would give credence to the province's separatist government. Trade Minister MacLaren favored no negotiation at all, and if he had to choose, he would have preferred the Québec approach. He warned that caving in to U.S. pressure on lumber would set "an extremely dangerous trade precedent" (*Toronto Star* 1996). He was replaced by Art Eggleton in January 1996. Soon, Rob Wright, a deputy minister of International Trade, became Canada's chief lumber negotiator.

Knowing that the lion's share of Canadian lumber exports to the United States came from British Columbia, the coalition was happy to see the B.C. proposal. Soon the coalition joined British Columbia in attacking Québec. John Ragosta said that British Columbia was no longer the problem; Québec was holding up the process and its offer was "totally unacceptable" and "totally inadequate, as well as Ontario's and Alberta's" (*Gazette* 1996).

As the January 31 deadline approached, Québec would not back down. Deputy Premier Landry said Québec would do everything it could to defend its cause if there was a new inquiry over softwood lumber. After a meeting with Canada's ambassador in Washington, D.C., Kantor said the United States would delay taking any action until after his mid-February meeting with Canada's new trade minister (*Gazette* 1996).

The issue of a separate deal with British Columbia was raised despite the questionable legality of a quota. Kerr said there would be no Canada-wide settlement that did not include the B.C. proposal. Québec contended that its proposal had been acceptable to U.S. negotiators until British Columbia came up with its quota proposal.

The negotiations between Deputy Trade Representative Shapiro and his Canadian counterpart, Rob Wright, broke down on February 14, 1996. The sticking point was that the Canadian government, with support from Québec, Ontario, and Alberta, did not want a quota arrangement; the United States preferred British Columbia's proposal. Since Trade Representative Kantor had threatened to use Section 301 to sanction Canada if no agreement was reached on February 15, and Canada would retaliate, things could get nasty (Shapiro 2006).

On the next day, Shapiro arranged a phone call with Canadian Ambassador Raymond Chrétien and the White House (the chair of the Council of Economic Advisers, Larry Tasso). Ambassador Chrétien assured both negotiators that the Canadian government wanted a negotiated deal, and the White House promised that the United States would not use Section 301 immediately. Under this kind of promise, both negotiators went back to work (Shapiro 2006).

In the end, a compromise was worked out. An agreement-in-principle signed by Trade Representative Kantor and Minister Eggleton on February 16, 1996, had the solutions from both British Columbia and Québec. British

Columbia would reduce by an estimated 14 percent the amount of free lumber arriving in the United States annually, which would result in a duty-free quota of 9 bbf. An export tax of US$50/mbf applied to an additional 250 million board feet (mmbf) and $100/mbf for any amount over 9.25 bbf. Québec would raise its stumpage fees by $100 million. Ontario and Alberta would increase stumpage fees as well. The agreement was for five years, beginning April 1, 1996.

In a news conference, Kantor praised the two countries' "tremendous commitment" in maintaining a strong trading relationship. He said that the 14 percent reduction in the amount of lumber arriving in the United States from British Columbia was impressive and that the agreement would "provide necessary relief and the level playing field that U.S. companies and workers have sought for so long." He further stated that the agreement would have "negligible, if any" effect on the prices of houses in the United States. Senator Craig said he anticipated the tariff would have been set at about 15 percent. Senator Baucus said the agreement "means that our mills and the people who work in them can compete fairly" (*Seattle Post-Intelligencer* 1996).

In March, Québec, Ontario, and Alberta turned around and agreed to the quota system instead of the stumpage adjustment. These provinces realized that because the two federal governments had accommodated British Columbia's quota proposal, they would be better off trying to secure more quota. On April 2, after 11 hours of intense negotiations in Washington, D.C., the two countries agreed on the size of the quota. On May 29, the Softwood Lumber Agreement was officially signed.

The Softwood Lumber Agreement of 1996

Under the Softwood Lumber Agreement, Canada agreed to impose an export control regime on shipments of softwood lumber from the four major lumber-producing provinces to the States. In return, the United States agreed not to bring any trade action (including antidumping or countervailing cases, Section 201 or safeguard cases, or Section 301 or retaliation cases) against Canadian lumber imports. In this regard, written commitments were to be received from the U.S. industry and labor unions that they would not petition for trade restrictions during the agreement period.

The main points of this complicated agreement follow.

Fee-free export limit and fee level. Annual fee-free exports from British Columbia, Québec, Ontario, and Alberta, which collectively accounted for more than 95 percent of Canadian softwood exports to the United States in 1995, would be limited to 14.7 bbf. The next 650 mmbf exports would initially be subject to a US$50/mbf export fee. Additional covered exports would be subject to a $100/mbf fee.[5] Thus, softwood lumber exports from these four provinces to the United States would be under a two-tier tariff-rate quota system. The fee level would be adjusted annually for the difference in inflation rates between the two countries.

Fee collection. A fee-free quota would be allocated to individual Canadian exporters with annual softwood production of 10 mmbf or more. "Quarterly band fees" would be collected when an exporter exceeded 28.75 percent of its annual fee-free quota. The fees could be refunded if the total exports from the four provinces were less than 28.75 percent of the annual fee-free quota (4.226 bbf). Similarly, the fees could be refunded if the total annual export was less than the fee-free export quota.

Trigger price mechanism. The trigger price was defined as the average for a calendar quarter of the price reported by Random Lengths Inc. for eastern spruce–pine–fir, kiln-dried 2x4s, standard and better, delivered to the Great Lakes area. If the trigger price met or exceeded US$405/mbf in any quarter during the first two years, or $410/mbf thereafter, 92 mmbf of additional fee-free exports would be allocated in the subsequent quarters within one year of issuance. This arrangement made it possible to increase the fee-free export limit.

The agreement also covered customs procedures, reporting, monitoring, and dispute settlement systems.[6] Under the agreement, individual firms reported their export volumes each month to the Canadian government, but their quotas were set annually. Since the agreement was at the country level, the effectiveness and actual market impact of the Softwood Lumber Agreement relied on whether Canada as a whole exceeded its fee-free quota and on the amount by which it exceeded that quota in a particular quarter or year.

The Economic Impacts of the Agreement

In 1995, the four provinces exported 16.2 bbf of lumber to the United States. Had the Softwood Lumber Agreement been in place that year, it would have reduced the duty-free export by 1.5 bbf, or about 9.3 percent of the 1995 level. Assuming that the trigger price mechanism was not used, the Canadian government would have collected US$117.5 million export tax (Table 7-1), which represented about 2 percent of the total value (some US$5.7 billion) of the lumber exports originating from these provinces in 1995.

Note that the market and economic impacts of a tariff-rate quota are quite different from those of an export tax. A tariff-rate quota that generates a 2 percent export tax on the total value of exports is much more significant—in terms of the market (price and quantity) and welfare impact—than an export tax scheme that applies a 2 percent tax on all exports.

To see how tariff-rate quota works, refer to Figure 7-1, which shows a one-tier (US$50/mbf after the quota at Q_1) tariff-rate quota for export supply of Canadian lumber and a per-unit export tax of $50/mbf irrespective of export quantity, respectively. Under the tariff-rate quota system shown in Figure 7-1a, the Canadian export supply curve would kink twice and become oabcd from oS_c.

TABLE 7-1. Export Tax That Would Have Been Collected Had the Softwood Lumber Agreement of 1996 Been Implemented in 1995

	Volume (bbf)	Tax rate (US$/mbf)	Tax (US$ million)
Duty-free quota (established base)	14.70	0.0	0.0
Low fee base	0.65	50.0	32.5
Upper fee base	0.85	100.0	85.0
Total export volume/total tax revenue	16.20		117.5

The effectiveness of the tariff-rate quota system depends on Canadian export supply and U.S. demand. If the demand and supply curves cross below point a, then Canadian exports will be less than Q_1, and price will be less than P_1. Consequently, the tariff-rate quota will have no market or welfare effect. If the Canadian export supply curve shifts to left (up)—for example, because of changes in the exchange rate—the Canadian export supply could be priced out before reaching the tax-free quota (Q_1). A U.S. demand curve shift to the left (down), could lead to the same result, as would a combination of these changes in supply and demand.

The tariff-rate quota becomes effective when the demand and supply curve cross at or above point a. Between points a and b, Canadian producers get a quota rent that equals $50 \times Q_1$ and pay no export tax. The quota rent comes from U.S. consumers of Canadian lumber. The price impact would be $50/mbf. When the supply and demand curve cross above point b, say at point c, Canadian producers still enjoy the quota rent (which is equal to $[(P_2-P_1)] \times Q_1$) and pay the export tax, which is equal to $50 \times (Q_2-Q_1)$. The price impact would be less than $50/mbf ($P_2-P_3 < 50$).

Under a $50/mbf export tax system (Figure 7-1b), Canadian producers pay $50 \times Q_2$ amount of export tax, irrespective of what the market price is, which is always more than what they pay under the tariff-rate quota system (either $[$50 \times (Q_2-Q_1)]$ or 0). Thus, under this system, Canadian producers instead of the Canadian government retain the quota rent.

Furthermore, the price impact of the export tax system would be always less than $50/mbf unless demand is perfectly inelastic, but the price impact under a tariff-rate quota system could vary from $0 to $50/mbf. Finally, when demand changes, lumber prices would be more volatile than under an export tax system because the former made the supply curve kinked and more inelastic around the two kink points.

Note also that after the quota is reached, the price impact under a tariff-rate quota system (Figure 7-1a) is equal to that of a pure export tax system (shown in Figure 7-1b). In other words, the difference between P_2 and P_3 in Figure 7-1a is equal to the difference between P_2 and P_3 in Figure 7-1b. Similarly, the impact on supply and demand quantity in Figure 7-1a (Q_2-Q_3) is equal to that of the

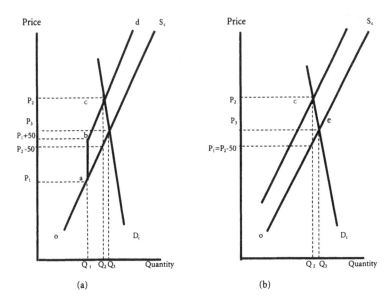

FIGURE 7-1. The Market Impact of a Tariff-Rate Quota and an Export Tariff

export tax shown in Figure 7-1b ($Q_2 - Q_3$). The only difference between a tariff-rate quota system after the quota is reached and a flat export tax system is that Canadian exporters retain the quota rent in the former, but not in the latter.

In sum, if the quota is binding and is reached, the price impact is similar under both systems. However, Canadian producers retain quota rents under a tariff-rate quota system, which would have been taxed away by the government under the export tax system. And when demand and supply change, lumber prices are more volatile than under an export tax system (Zhang and Sun 2001). Finally, the welfare impact for the U.S. consumers under a tariff-rate quota system would be (1) zero and thus lower (than under an export tax system) when demand and supply curves cross each other below point a (the quota limit); (2) higher when demand and supply curves cross between points a and b, because they pay for the full quota rent to Canadian producers; and (3) the same as under the export tax system between points b and d. Table 7-2 summarizes these impacts.

Under the Softwood Lumber Agreement, the Canadian export supply curve kinked four times. Adding the Canadian export supply curve to the U.S. supply curve would produce a total supply curve of softwood lumber in the U.S. market that also kinked four times. In theory, there were five possible price (and welfare) scenarios at any given moment.

Table 7-3 presents the theoretical fee-free quota for and the actual exports of Canadian producers under the agreement. It indicates that Canadian producers as a whole paid a $50/mbf fee for export volume exceeding Q_1 in the last four years of the agreement and that their total exports were just about equal

TABLE 7-2. Comparison of Tariff-Rate Quota System and Export Tax System

Impact on	Tariff-rate quota ($50/mbf beyond Q1)[a]	Export tax (US$50/mbf)[a]
Price (ΔP)	Vary between $0 and $50/mbf: • $0 when demand and supply curves cross below point a in Figure 7-1a. • $50/mbf when they cross between points a and b. • Less than $50/mbf (and equal to impact under equivalent export tax system). • Price more volatile than under export tax system.	• Always less than $50/mbf unless demand is perfectly inelastic. • Price less volatile than under tariff-rate quota system.
Equilibrium quantity(ΔQ)	Vary from no impact to same impact under export tax system	$= \eta \times \Delta P \times Q/P$, where η is demand elasticity, P and Q are market price and quantity under export tax system, $\Delta P = P_3 - P_1$
Canadian producer welfare	• Retain quota rent $=\$50 \times Q_1$ whenever equilibrium quantity is equal to or greater than Q_1; pay export tax $[=50 \times (Q_2-Q_1)]$. • Indifferent from free market when equilibrium quantity is below Q_0.	$=(50-\Delta P) \times (Q_2+Q_3)/2$. Have to pay $50/mbf export tax on all quantity exported irrespective of market conditions.
Canadian government tax revenue	$=\$50 \times (Q_2-Q_1)$. Less than export tariff system.	$=\$50 \times Q_2$. More than tariff-rate quota system.
U.S. consumer welfare	• $0 when demand and supply curves cross below point a in Figure 7-1a. • $50 \times Q_1$ when they cross between points a and b. • Equal to impact under equivalent export tax system after Q_1 (the quota limit) is reached.	$= \Delta P \times (Q_2+Q_3)/2$.
U.S. producer welfare	• No impact when demand and supply curves cross below point a in Figure 7-1a. • Positive when demand and supply cross between points a and b. • Positive gains equal to impact under equivalent export tax system after point b in Figure 7-1a.	Positive irrespective of market conditions.

a. See Figure 7-1.

TABLE 7-3. Theoretical Fee-Free Quota and Actual Canadian Softwood Lumber Exports to the United States under the Softwood Lumber Agreement of 1996

Year	Theoretical fee-free quota[a]			Actual export[a,b]					
	EB	Bonus	Total fee-free export	EB	Bonus	LFB	UFB	Total	Difference[c]
1996–97	14,700	276	14,976	14,581	161	503	474	15,719	743
1997–98	14,700	276	14,976	14,559	320	541	137	15,557	581
1998–99	14,700	0	14,700	14,582	38	617	186	15,423	723[d]
1999–00	14,700	368	15,068	14,577	175	598	330	15,680	611
2000–01	14,700	92	14,792	14,677	305	207	72	15,263	471

a. EB= established base, LFB=lower fee base, UFB=upper fee base; all in mmbf.
b. Under the agreement, Canadian exporters are allowed to pay export fees for certain lumber exported to the United States even if they collectively have not exhausted all quota allocated.
c. Volume theoretically subject to fee.
d. 73 mmbf of the 723 mmbf is counted as low-fee export for the previous year.
Source: Canadian Forest Service (various issues).

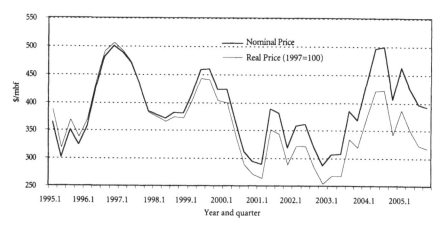

FIGURE 7-2. Quarterly Softwood Lumber Prices, 1995–2005

Note: For eastern spruce-pine-fir, kiln-dried, 2x4, standard and better, delivered to the Great Lakes.
Source: Random Lengths, Inc. (various years).

to or slightly greater than Q_2 in the first year (1996–1997). Therefore, Canadian producers as a whole paid a \$50/mbf fee for the amount of export volume between Q_1 and Q_2. In the first year they paid a \$100 fee for export volume exceeding Q_2.

Zhang (2006) estimates a price impact of the Softwood Lumber Agreement of US\$29.6/mbf, or 7.4 percent, in the U.S. market in the first four years. This would translate to an 11.6 percent export tax. In the fifth year, the price impact was negative. For the full five years, the price impact in the U.S. market was about US\$16.7/mbf, or 3.8 percent, because lumber prices declined by more than 40 percent compared with the first four years (Figure 7-2).

* * *

Why did softwood lumber prices collapse in the U.S. market in the fifth year under the Softwood Lumber Agreement? One reason may be declining demand. Levels of housing starts during the first quarter of the fifth year were approximately equal to the previous year's level but then declined 6.42 percent in the three ensuing quarters. For the whole year, housing starts declined 4.57 percent. *Ceteris paribus*, based on the lumber demand elasticity of –0.17, a decline in demand of 4.57 percent would translate to a decline in price of 26.89 percent.

Excess capacity in the U.S. lumber industry caused by high lumber prices during the first few years of the agreement is likely a second factor.[7] In the short run, U.S. producers could continue to utilize the excess capacity as long as they could cover at least a portion of their variable costs. Strategically, while they continued to use the excess capacity (thus contributing to the price decline) in the fifth year, they could use the fact that prices were low in that year to play a blame game with U.S. lumber consumers and Canadian exporters and demand more stringent trade restriction measures before and after the agreement expired.

Third, the structure of the agreement might have contributed to oversupply in the U.S. market from Canadian exporters. Under the agreement, Canadian firms were allocated certain quotas that they were required to either use or lose. Canadian firms consequently had incentive to fill the entire quota regardless of the then-prevailing market conditions. Perhaps more importantly, quota allocations in the future were based on historical export volumes. This creates an incentive to export more lumber than a firm would without the quota and pay the export tax on such exports, hoping for gains in future quota allocation. The fact that Canadian firms' collective export volume exceeded the tax-free quota for the fifth year despite that year's depressed market conditions seems to support this observation.

Finally, the scheduled expiration of the Softwood Lumber Agreement on March 31, 2001, and a breakdown in talks between the U.S. and Canadian governments in February 2001 might have prompted some lumber buyers to postpone their purchases in anticipation of lower prices after the expiry date. This would further reinforce the price decline.[8]

The collapse of lumber prices in the fifth year under the agreement could thus be seen as both a natural and a human-made anomaly. The demand for both U.S. and Canadian lumber was naturally down, and the demand for Canadian lumber could even have been lower than the fee-free quota. Yet U.S. companies continued to produce more than they would have without the agreement, and Canadian exporters continued to export because of its structure. The agreement had unintended consequences from the perspectives of producers in both countries.

* * *

Based on the estimated price impacts and actual production, consumption and price data, and equations and elasticities documented in Zhang (2001), Zhang (2006) simulated the market and welfare impacts. Tables 7-4 and 7-5 present the market impacts and welfare impacts, respectively.

Table 7-4 shows that Canadian lumber exports to the United States fell 3.2 bbf annually under the Softwood Lumber Agreement compared with the otherwise open market solution. U.S. production increased by 1.9 bbf, and imports from other producers—including firms in Canadian provinces not covered under the Softwood Lumber Agreement and firms in other countries—increased by 70 mmbf. The consequent change in U.S. consumption is an annual reduction of 1.2 bbf.

Table 7-5 shows that U.S. lumber producers received the gains anticipated from such policy—producer surplus increased by approximately US$2.6 billion (in 1997 dollars). The costs to the U.S. consumer were about US$4.3 billion. Net social loss to the United States was therefore roughly US$1.8 billion. Canadian

TABLE 7-4. Estimated Market Impact of the Softwood Lumber Agreement of 1996

Year	Price[a] (1997$/mbf)	U.S. consumption[a] (mmbf)	Canadian exporting supply[a] (mmbf)	Other supply[a,b] (mmbf)	U.S. production[a] (mmbf)
1996–1997	77.05	−1,357.8	−3,547.0	119.7	2,069.5
	(19.05)	(−2.7)	(−18.4)	(6.4)	(6.4)
1997–1998	11.39	−239.8	−633.1	28.1	365.1
	(2.83)	(−0.5)	(−3.9)	(1.1)	(1.1)
1998–1999	7.61	−179.0	−476.4	24.4	273.0
	(2.05)	(−0.3)	(−3.0)	(0.8)	(0.8)
1999–2000	22.33	−496.9	−1,336.0	82.1	757.0
	(5.59)	(−0.9)	(−7.9)	(2.1)	(2.1)
2000–2001	−34.82	1,033.2	2,759.7	−184.2	−1,544.7
	(−10.67)	(2.0)	(22.2)	(−4.6)	(−4.6)
Average/total[c]	16.71	−1,240.3	−3,232.8	70.1	1,920.0
	(3.77)	(−0.5)	(−4.0)	(0.5)	(0.5)
Average/total[d]	29.59				
	(7.38)				

a. Numbers in parentheses are percentages.
b. Other supply includes exports from Canadian provinces that are not covered by the agreement and from other countries.
c. Accounts for the negative price impact in 2000–2001.
d. Without accounting for the negative price impact in 2000–2001.
Source: Zhang (2006).

producers lost some because their export volume was curtailed and they paid taxes, but they gained a little more with higher lumber prices. The net results were a small gain in producer surplus—US$305 million for Canadian producers and $243 million in export taxes for the four provincial governments in Canada.[9] Thus, the net gains to Canada were about US$548 million. Other suppliers to the U.S. market gained US$232 million. The overall impact of the Softwood Lumber Agreement was a net loss of US$1.0 billion. Although the overall impact was small, the welfare impacts for U.S. producers, consumers, and the United States as a whole were large. Canadian producers were estimated to have gained a much smaller amount than their U.S counterparts.

After adjusting for inflation (the U.S. consumer price index increased 1.68 times between 1982 and 1997), the welfare impact of the Softwood Lumber Agreement on U.S. consumers, U.S. producers, and the United States as a whole is similar to that under the Memorandum of Understanding (Wear and Lee 1993). Furthermore, Canadian producers gained slightly under the agreement but lost slightly under the memorandum. The difference in Canadian producer welfare stems from the fact that these producers had to pay taxes on all lumber exported to the United States under the MOU but paid only for export volume exceeding their fee-free quota and enjoyed the quota rent under the Softwood Lumber Agreement.

TABLE 7-5. Estimated Welfare Impact of the Softwood Lumber Agreement of 1996

Year	U.S. producer surplus	U.S. consumer surplus	Total U.S. impact	Canadian producer surplus[a]	Canadian export fee[b]	Total Canadian impact[a]	Other producer surplus[c]	Net impact
1996–97	2,412.4	–3,899.6	–1,487.2	947.3	72.6	1,019.9	139.5	–327.8
1997–98	376.1	–585.9	–209.8	101.3	40.8	142.1	29.0	–38.7
1998–99	257.9	–400.2	–142.3	21.7	49.5	71.2	23.1	–48.0
1999–00	794.6	–1,329.6	–535.0	232.9	62.9	295.8	86.2	–69.2
2000–01	–1,187.9	1,809.2	621.3	–998.2	17.6	–980.6	–141.7	–501.0
Total	2,653.1	–4,406.1	–1,669.2	305.0	243.4	548.4	136.1	–984.7

Note: In millions of 1997 U.S. dollars.

a. This estimate covers only the U.S. market.

b. Calculated based on data in Table 7-3.

c. Other producer surplus is the gain of exporters from Canadian provinces that are not covered by the agreement and other countries.

Source: Zhang (2006).

U.S. Consumer Group Actions

The Softwood Lumber Agreement was largely an agreement between two dominant producer groups, similar to a "market sharing agreement" by a bilateral duopoly (Zhang 2001). Any efforts undertaken by U.S. and Canadian lumber producers, through their governments, to secure this trade regulation would be rational from the standpoint of political economy.

As such, consumer groups did not have much influence in the initiation, negotiation, or structure of the agreement. The National Association of Home Builders had a presence in several rounds of the softwood lumber trade dispute and opposed the MOU and Softwood Lumber Agreement. However, Michael Carliner, staff vice president for economics of the association, admitted that it "lacked expertise in international trade disputes, and was completely outmaneuvered by the lumber producers." The association did not have a countermeasure when the Coalition for Fair Lumber Imports challenged the constitutionality of the NAFTA dispute resolution process. He added, "Except for saying 'just do not do it [the agreement],' we could not offer the administration or Congress anything" (Carliner 1996).

The Softwood Lumber Agreement has pitted two traditional allies in the United States—the timber industry and home builders—against each other. When environmental restrictions limited logging in the Pacific Northwest in the early 1990s, the two groups teamed up and fought unsuccessfully against logging cutbacks. As noted earlier, environmental groups, which favored logging restrictions, became the timber industry's allies in advocating restrictions on Canadian lumber imports.

Under U.S. antitrust law, U.S. producers cannot curtail their production collectively or divide market share among themselves to raise prices and profits. The Softwood Lumber Agreement shows that with the help of their government, U.S. producers could craft a market-sharing agreement with foreign competitors to curtail foreign imports and thus enhance their profitability. U.S. consumer groups acting alone could not stop it.

What consumer groups could hope for was to team up with disgruntled Canadian producers to thwart any market-sharing agreement. They did not succeed in preventing the agreement, however, primarily because in 1996 the disgruntled Canadian producers did not have a critical mass. Since the majority of Canadian lumber producers and U.S. consumers had different interests, cooperation between them broke down.

After the agreement was implemented, not only did lumber prices rise, they also became more volatile. Lumber prices could swing as much as 30 percent in a few weeks. Price volatility was a risk for homebuilders contracting for new home construction before buying the materials. Subsequently, U.S. lumber consumer groups, led by the National Association of Home Builders, in November 1996 called on the Clinton administration to renegotiate the agreement and ease soaring lumber prices by allowing more Canadian lumber imports. Their congressional allies introduced a bill (Americans for Affordable Housing Act, H.R. 1526), which called for an elimination of the treatment of timber sales from public lands as subsidies to justify countervailing duties (*Congressional Record* 1997). By May 1997, the bill had 59 sponsors and cosponsors. These efforts produced some media coverage but had no impact on the continuation of the Softwood Lumber Agreement.

Meanwhile, the disgruntled Canadian producers grew in number. Some of these producers might have been true believers of free trade who disliked managed trade. Others might have been merely unhappy about the quota they received. Initially, most of the disgruntled Canadian producers were in Québec and Ontario, and collectively, they produced less than half of Canadian lumber. Their opponents in Canada, obviously, were producers that happened to have an adequate quota, mostly located in interior British Columbia.

In 1998, however, a group of British Columbia producers joined the producers in eastern and central Canada to protest the Softwood Lumber Agreement. The leaders in the group were two of the largest forest products firms in Canada—MacMillan Bloedel Ltd. and Canfor Corporation. Suddenly, the disgruntled producers became a powerful faction in Canada.

What caused MacMillan Bloedel and Canfor and other producers in western Canada to change their position was a seemingly unrelated event, the 1997–1998 Asian economic crisis. Traditionally, producers in coastal British Columbia exported a significant share of their lumber—in the case of MacMillan Bloedel, it was 51 percent—to Japan and other Asian countries. Since historically not much of their exports had gone to the United States, they received relatively low quotas. The Asian economic crisis significantly curtailed Asian demand for their lumber. Now these firms could not ship their lumber to Asia, nor could they export it to the States, for lack of quota. To these producers, the Softwood Lumber Agreement was enemy No. 1 at the time. In fall 1998, they teamed up with producers in eastern and central Canada to form the Free Trade Lumber Council.

As a pan-Canadian organization and private advocacy group, the Free Trade Lumber Council sought free access to world markets, most notably to the U.S. market, for Canadian softwood lumber. In 1998, council members accounted for about half of the Canadian lumber production covered under the Softwood Lumber Agreement. After MacMillan Bloedel (purchased by Weyerhaeuser in 1999) and Canfor (about to merge with another firm in 2002) withdrew from the group, it represented some 30 percent of Canadian softwood lumber exports to the United States.[10]

Soon U.S. consumer groups teamed up with the council to fight for free trade in lumber between the United States and Canada. In 1998, U.S. consumer groups organized a lobby organization—the American Consumers for Affordable Homes, headed by Susan Petniunas. The Free Trade Lumber Council became a member of this group, along with the American Homeowners Grass-roots Alliance, Catamount Pellet Fuel Corporation, CHEP International, Consumers for World Trade, Fremont Forest Group Corporation, Furniture Retailers of America, Home Depot, International Sleep Products Association, Manufactured Housing Association for Regulatory Reform, Manufactured Housing Institute, National Association of Home Builders, National Black Chamber of Commerce, National Lumber and Building Material Dealers Association, National Retail Federation, Retail Industry Leaders Association, and the United States Hispanic Contractors Association.

American Consumers for Affordable Homes and the Free Trade Lumber Council have essentially been working in tandem since 1998. The consumer organization mobilizes consumer groups in the United States, engaging in lobbying and public relations. The industry group coordinates producers in Canada. The goals of these two organizations were first to make sure that the Softwood Lumber Agreement expired as scheduled and then to lobby and fight for free trade in lumber.

For 1998–1999, the cochairs of the Free Trade Lumber Council were Frank Dottori, CEO of Tembec Inc., and Tom Stephens, CEO of MacMillan Bloedel. Stephens had been CEO of Denver-based Manville Corporation, which was a member of the Coalition for Fair Lumber Imports in the 1980s. From Lumber II, he knew well how the political game was played in the United States. He was one of the architects of American Consumers for Affordable Homes and its go-between with the Free Trade Lumber Council.

Stephens engaged in battles with Jake Kerr, Canada's industry representative in negotiating the Softwood Lumber Agreement, who favored some kind of negotiated agreement or managed trade after its expiration. On October 13, 1999, after reading Kerr's comments to the *Vancouver Sun* calling the Council of Forest Industries in British Columbia and other industry organizations a "sham" and its members "poor woebegone guys here with nowhere else to go," Stephens wrote an open letter to Kerr. He stated, "These words display a degree of arrogance and lack of respect for the people you [Jake Kerr] are supposed to represent. They also ring of someone who is losing his grip on reality." He went on:

> How can you possibly advocate that we again follow you down the path of rolling over to the U.S. timber companies before the debate [on what to do after the agreement ends] even starts? The industry followed your leadership during the last round and the results speak for themselves. How could we possibly make the same mistake again in light of the enormous support we have gained from American consumers, who are telling Washington it's time to abandon the managed trade concept? How can we fall on our swords now when most realize that the result of another Softwood Lumber Agreement will be more unemployed Canadian workers, fewer homes for American families, and a group of competitors in the U.S. that have learned that all they have to do is rattle their swords and we will fall all over ourselves to compromise. Don't do it.

... Do we really want to give away any chance for future growth in B.C. and in Canada and future jobs for our kids just to protect companies like yours that have quota? Is this an issue of trade policy or is this just protecting a few "haves" to the detriment of the "have-nots"?

We did not agree two years ago and we still do not today. To make a mistake once is forgivable; to make the same mistake a second time is just plain stupid. (Stephens 1999)

In a public response dated October 14, 1999, Jake Kerr apologized for his words and then defended his position:

I was widely quoted last week as saying a renewal of the current Softwood Lumber Agreement was not an option.... the B.C. Lumber Trade Council adopted the following consensus position which I will repeat as that organization's co-chair.

"There is NO appetite for renewal of the [Softwood Lumber Agreement] as it currently exists, however, there is a desire to consider all options, only disregarding those that were considered impractical."

Free trade would be great, and as an owner and operator of an efficient and productive mill in B.C., I can tell you I would welcome operating in a free trade context. However, in the more than 100-year history of this dispute, free trade in lumber has never been attainable.

Protectionist sentiment in the [U.S.] Congress is strong, especially going into an election year ...

... the consistent counsel from the Canadian government, the B.C. government, our own industry experts in Washington DC, and independent advice, clearly indicate that free trade at this time is not a realistic option.

... We do not wish again to suffer through the enormous cost of memoranda of understanding and countervailing duties. If and when Canada engages in trade talks with the U.S., the position advanced will be in the best long-term interests of the B.C. industry as a whole.

Will it be different from the current deal? Absolutely. Will it be free trade? Probably not. Will it lead to free trade? I certainly hope so in the long term. (Kerr 1999)

So Jake Kerr's logic might look like this: Free trade is not a realistic option and can be considered impractical and thus disregarded; negotiation for a new agreement is the way to go. His preference order would be free trade, then negotiated settlement, and finally litigation.

* * *

So it seemed, at least by the summer of 1999, that free-traders and disgruntled producers in Canada had made their voice heard. The very first hint of the Canadian government's position on the Softwood Lumber Agreement appeared on March 8, 1999, when then-Trade Minister Sergio Marchi said he was uncomfortable with the American penchant for wanting to manage Canadian trade in several major sectors, including lumber (*Vancouver Sun* 1999a).

Partly because of the strong opposition to the agreement from American lumber consumers and some Canadian producers, the U.S–Canada negotiation that started in July 1999—conducted between Peter Scher, U.S. special trade ambassador, and Doug Waddell of Canada—went nowhere. On September 24, 1999, Scher wrote a letter to Canadian Trade Minister Pierre Pettigrew, indicating that the United States did not intend to renew the Softwood Lumber Agreement. Both the U.S. and Canadian governments, he said, should get out of the business of regulating lumber trade. Nonetheless, the United States would continue applying pressure if Canada failed to address the issue of subsidized logging. He wrote, "The United States will not be inclined, nor well-positioned, to resist U.S. lumber industry's urging to return to addressing Canada's unfair trade practices through whatever means deemed appropriate at the time" (*Wall Street Journal* 1999).

Trade Frictions

That the Softwood Lumber Agreement expired as scheduled was also partly due to several frictions related to U.S. Customs' reclassification of lumber-related products as well as a change in stumpage fees in British Columbia. These trade frictions further frustrated some U.S. and Canadian producers. The Coalition for Fair Lumber Imports charged that Canadian producers had tried to find loopholes in the agreement. The Canadian producers charged that the U.S. Customs' reclassification was politically motivated and denied them an opportunity to export lumber products not covered by the agreement.

Because a softwood lumber quota means money (quota rents), it was inevitable that somebody would try to find a way to get more quota. As W.C. Fields once said, "A thing worth having is a thing worth cheating for." Indeed, the Softwood Lumber Agreement created incentives for Canadian producers to get higher quotas and thus more quota rent by circumventing its provisions.

The first lumber-related product to be reclassified was drilled studs. In February 1997, the U.S. Customs Service classified 2x4 and 2x6 studs with holes drilled to accommodate wire as "joinery and carpentry," not as regular lumber. Such a classification exempted the predrilled studs from the Softwood Lumber Agreement, along with other finished wood products, such as windows and door frames. In April 1998, when the U.S. Customs Service reversed itself and ruled that predrilled studs were regular lumber (and thus subject to the agreement), Canadian exports of drilled studs were about C$20 million a month.

Does drilling holes in lumber make it a value-added product that should be exempted from the Softwood Lumber Agreement? The U.S. lumber producers did not think so and thus asked for a reclassification. The National Association of Home Builders charged that several major U.S. lumber producers pressured the Clinton administration and Congress in an effort to put the predrilled studs under the Softwood Lumber Agreement and that the reversal of policy by the U.S. Customs Service had been triggered by political considerations.

In a *Wall Street Journal* editorial, Rushford (1998) shed some light on the Customs Service's reclassification move. He stated that Deputy Treasury Secretary Lawrence Summers, who was otherwise occupied with weighty macroeconomic issues, such as plunging Asian currencies, cared about the reclassification because he had heard complaints from a dozen-plus lawmakers from timber-producing states, including Senators Baucus and Richard Shelby (R-Alabama). Now, pressed by Summers, Customs had complied.

Several days later, Assistant Secretary of the Treasury Howard Schloss (1998) responded by stating that Rushford's column "was misleading ... and personalized an issue about the enforcement of U.S. law.... In the context of these facts presented by the Treasury Department, Summers asked Customs to revisit its initial classification decision, a review that was already under way. After a full public process, Customs concluded that as a matter of law, the initial classification of drilled softwood lumber was in error." Had politics played a role in Summers' intervention?

After the U.S. Customs Service ruled that predrilled studs were regular lumber, Canadian producers sought higher quotas under the Softwood Lumber Agreement, which American producers vigorously opposed. The coalition even sought to take away quotas retroactively, but decided not to pursue it. A group of affected Canadian lumber producers, along with the National Association of Home Builders and the National Lumber and Building Material Dealers Association, initially applied for a court injunction against the U.S. Customs Service on the application of the reclassification on predrilled studs. Two weeks later they dropped the bid for an injunction in exchange for a speedy trial and challenged the reclassification before the U.S. Court of International Trade. On December 17, 1998, that court upheld the U.S. Customs Service's second decision (*Vancouver Sun* 1998b). Canada appealed the ruling at the Brussels-based World Customs Organization, which voted 21 to 1 in May 1999 that the United States had not correctly classified Canadian predrilled studs. The ruling merely amounted to a moral victory to Canada, since it was not binding.

The other frictions involved notched studs and rougher headed lumber. Notched studs are lumber notched for electrical wires and have a similar use to predrilled studs. Rougher headed lumber is roughened on one side to appear rough-sawn or rustic and is used in siding and fencing. In March 1999, the U.S. Customs Service wanted to reclassify both products and make them covered by the Softwood Lumber Agreement, pending a public comment period. It was estimated that this would affect more than C$300 million annually of products shipped under this classification.

By this time, the coalition was lobbying to expand the ruling to include more than a dozen other products, such as exterior siding and trim. Frank

Dottori and Tom Stephens of the Free Trade Lumber Council urged Canadian government officials to seek immediate, high-level talks with U.S. Treasury and trade officials over the U.S Customs Service's reclassification move. For the council, the reclassification was just one more reason to move the Canadian lumber industry to free trade. It warned that the U.S. industry was flexing its muscles and giving the Canadian lumber industry a foretaste of the kind of hardball it could expect as both countries headed toward a new round of negotiations.

Jake Kerr, however, saw things differently. He believed that the coastal companies, which produced most of the products under the reclassification investigations by the U.S. Customs Service, were pushing the boundaries of duty-free lumber to the point of forcing a U.S. trade challenge. He said that some of the products U.S. Customs wanted to delist were poorly disguised unprocessed two-by-fours, and "the problem is, we have been slightly creative and the American Customs have some justification for saying, 'We're going to look into this.' It's not quite as simple as it sounds." Fears that the reclassification ruling would be a springboard for dozens of other Canadian products to be struck from the duty-free list were unfounded, he said, and it was not time to panic (*Vancouver Sun* 1999b).

On June 9, 1999, the U.S. Customs Service indeed reclassified notched studs and rougher headed lumber as regular lumber. This time, not only the Free Trade Lumber Council and Canadian trade officials protested, but also B.C. Premier Glen Clark vowed not to sign a new softwood lumber deal with the United States (*Vancouver Sun* 1999c).

After the reclassifications took effect in August 1999, Canada challenged the reclassification of rougher headed lumber by requesting an arbitration procedure under the Softwood Lumber Agreement. A binational panel was set up in October 1999 and was expected to make a ruling in a year. However, the ruling was avoided when the two countries reached an agreement on October 6, 2000. Under it, Canada withdrew the arbitration procedure against the United States. In return, Canada was allowed to export 72.5 mmbf of rougher headed lumber, free of export permit fees, between October 6, 2000, and the expiration of the agreement. The negotiation was conducted secretly between the B.C. Lumber Trade Council and the coalition. American Consumers for Affordable Homes and the Free Trade Lumber Council were unhappy about the secret deal. But since the product under discussion was mostly from British Columbia, the Canadian government eventually signed off on it. No more reclassifications took place; there was not much time left under the Softwood Lumber Agreement. More importantly, American Consumers for Affordable Homes got U.S. Representatives Jim Kolbe (R-Arizona), chairman of a subcommittee responsible for the Treasury budget, and Steny Hoyer (D-Maryland), a ranking Democrat, on its side. These two congressmen told Treasury to stop the reclassification (Horlick 2006).

The biggest friction surrounding the Softwood Lumber Agreement, however, was related to a stumpage change in British Columbia.

As early as November 1997, when the ramifications of the Asian economic crisis became clear, the government of British Columbia came under pressure to lower its stumpage fees. In a November 25 letter to the B.C. government, the USTR office warned that the proposed actions could violate the Softwood Lumber Agreement.

John Ragosta of the Coalition for Fair Lumber Imports argued that Washington and Oregon sawmills were facing the same problems as B.C. mills because of plummeting Asian markets. The difference between Washington and Oregon sawmills and B.C. sawmills, however, was that the former had a U.S. market while the latter was limited by the quota. B.C. forestry companies also pointed out that previous increases in stumpage fees and environmental restrictions had more than doubled the average cost of timber in the province since 1992. Stumpage payments amounted to C$1.7 billion in 1996, rising from some C$500 million in 1988, and C$215 million in 1987.

In late January 1998, the B.C. government sent a delegation to Washington, D.C., trying to persuade USTR and the coalition to go along with its stumpage rate reduction plan. Neither would endorse the province's plan.

On January 26, 1998, the B.C. government announced a reduction of stumpage fees of C$293 million, which was about $5/m^3, or 16 percent. The proposed reduction would be split evenly between the two regions of the province: about $8.10/m^3 on the coast and $3.50/m^3 in the interior. The proposal still needed the approval from USTR. When that approval did not come, the B.C. government delayed stumpage relief for two months. Finally, in May 1998, it decided to honor its proposal and reduced the stumpage rates, starting in July 1998.

The coalition immediately called the action by the B.C. government a violation of the Softwood Lumber Agreement and requested talks with Canada's Trade Ministry on July 3, 1998. Under the agreement, if no solution is found within 35 days, the United States can take the dispute to an independent arbitration panel and then walk away from the agreement.

B.C. Premier Glen Clark led another delegation to Washington, D.C., in the second week of July 1998, attempting to sell the coalition on the hard-luck story of the province's financially strapped forest industry. He told the coalition that the B.C. industry needed a break—perhaps another C$300 million stumpage reduction—to survive the Asian economic crisis, and that stumpage relief would compensate the industry only for a miscalculation in government-imposed environmental protection measures. But the coalition refused to give him a break. Ragosta said, "We can't reach an agreement with him. We're not going to negotiate with him. We know what British Columbia's position is. From our perspective, it's straightforward: if there is any change to stumpage they have to be balanced changes. But agreeing on what that balance is, is something he has to deal with the U.S. government on" (*Vancouver Sun* 1998a).

Soon an independent arbitration panel was set up. In July 1999, before the panel had released its ruling, the B.C. government approached the U.S. government to make a deal, fearing not only that the panel would find the stumpage fee reduction illegal but also that the remedy might be worse than a negotiated settlement. The deal, signed by the U.S. and Canadian governments, called for a super export tax of $146/mbf on B.C. lumber that exceeded "historical levels" under the Softwood Lumber Agreement.

The calculus for the B.C. industry was that it expected the panel to add the reduction in stumpage fees, about C$14/mbf, to the price of B.C. lumber, something that would have cost the industry about $22 million. This negotiated settlement, however, would cost the industry only $8 million [= (total B.C. export to the United States – tax free quota – lumber export paid for lower- and upper-bound fees) × $146/mbf] a year based on actual lumber exports to the States under the Softwood Lumber Agreement. In addition, the industry would keep the $230-million-a-year savings in stumpage fees.

The deal infuriated the National Association of Home Builders, which saw it as yet another piece of evidence that timber barons in the United States and lumber mills in British Columbia were trying to squeeze more from U.S. lumber consumers. The deal would be illegal if the U.S. government did not sign on. American Consumers for Affordable Homes asked Congress to overturn it, to no avail.

The Expiration of the Softwood Lumber Agreement

In the fall of 2000, Canadian lumber producers who favored managed trade were in the minority. Only the British Columbia Lumber Trade Council, which was dominated by producers in the interior, favored a transitional deal that would move both sides to some sort of free trade. American Consumers for Affordable Homes was able to get a bipartisan group of 118 members of the U.S. Congress to sponsor a resolution calling for the termination of the Softwood Lumber Agreement when it expired.[11] Government officials in both countries were also frustrated with the constant wrangling between lumber producers in the two countries, and at least three of them—Peter Scher of the USTR office, Canadian Trade Minister Sergio Marchi, and B.C. Premier Glen Clark—publicly called for the termination of the agreement.

Equally important was that lumber prices were falling, starting in the beginning of the fifth year under the Softwood Lumber Agreement. The Coalition for Fair Lumber Imports, too, seemed to think the agreement in its current form was not tough enough and was difficult to enforce at times. The coalition contended that Canadian firms had used so-called value-added products, such as predrilled studs, to circumvent the agreement. Moreover, it said, the Maritime Provinces—which were exempt from the agreement—exported all of their lumber production (and sometimes more than their lumber production) to the

States and used lumber from Québec to meet their domestic needs.[12] Consequently, the coalition demanded a new, tough agreement that covered all Canadian producers, or it would wage legal war.

In a March 2000 interview with the *National Post* (2000), W.J. "Rusty" Wood, the newly appointed chairman of the coalition and president of Tolleson Lumber Co. Inc., repeated the coalition's call for a truly competitive market in Canada. Otherwise, he said, the coalition's lawyers would take over, and that would likely mean that US$6.4 billion a year in Canadian lumber exports to the States would soon be hit with huge and punitive countervailing duties.

The last few months before the expiration of the Softwood Lumber Agreement witnessed various players jostling for position. In September 2000, Jake Kerr threatened to go alone (he later tempered his comments) and make a deal between British Columbia and the United States if the issue continued to be bogged down by regional differences in Canada and a slow response on the part of Ottawa. Frank Dottori of the Free Trade Lumber Council said Kerr's idea weakened Canada's negotiation position; his group preferred to fight the American protectionists in WTO and under NAFTA. If the two countries were to negotiate, a united front for all Canadian producers would get Canada a better deal. The B.C. government and a group of leaders from forest-dependent communities in the province did not endorse Kerr's idea (*Vancouver Sun* 2000).

One person who was among the strongest advocates for Canadians to seek free trade in lumber (even at the cost of fighting lengthy legal and political battles) was Tom Stephens. On March 7, 2001, at PriceWaterhouseCooper's 14th Annual Global Forest Industry Conference, Stephens told the audience that he was more convinced than ever that free trade in lumber must be achieved. He urged Canadian industry to take a firm stand and said it had a powerful ally in U.S. consumers. He suggested that Canada ensure during trade discussions that the U.S. need for energy was not separated from possible restrictions on trade in lumber and other commodities, since Canada's energy resources provided a potent bargaining chip and President George W. Bush wanted a continental trade deal on energy that included Canada and Mexico. He added,

> Canada has its hand on the American light switch ... If we really want to call a spade a spade, I'd tell the U.S. trade rep that what's good for the goose is good for the gander ... A dollar per dollar surcharge on gas that matches any countervailing duty on lumber will make any politician think twice before they screw the American homeowner twice, once when they drive up the cost of housing and second when they force an energy tax. I would remind U.S. policymakers that without Canada's energy, they better learn to speak Arabic and read by candlelight.... My advice: Don't blink. (*Canada Newswire 2001*)

Retaliation or linkage between energy and lumber has not happened. Neither the premier of resource-rich Alberta nor the members of Calgary's Petroleum Club were interested in being used as pawns in a trade war over lumber. In addition, Canada had a trade surplus with the United States and had sent some 85 percent of its exported goods and services to the States in the 1990s. Therefore, linkage of trade issues was seen by some as a dangerous game, and trade retaliation would be at best a lose–lose situation for both countries, and at worst could hurt Canada more. Shortly after hearing Stephens's remarks, Canada's Natural Resource Minister Ralph Goodale said the Americans are "dead wrong" in their plan to punish Canada over a softwood lumber dispute, but the natural gas or hydroelectricity sectors should not be drawn into a damaging trade war. Goodale described energy as a "positive dimension" in relations between the two countries and wanted to have good relations with the United States across the broad front of trading interconnections (*Vancouver Sun* 2001c).

The B.C. Lumber Trade Council wanted to negotiate a deal, citing uncertainty, costs, and loss of jobs if the American industry's threat materialized. If such a deal were going to be made, it ought to be a Canada-wide deal. The Maritime Provinces wanted to keep their special status of being exempt from any duty or quota. In mid-March 2001, the B.C. council accused Atlantic Canada of provoking the Americans by drastically increasing exports in recent years under the umbrella of the special exemption. The president of the Maritime Lumber Bureau, Diana Blenkhorn, immediately responded, suggesting that the B.C. industry was subsidized, just as U.S. competitors alleged (*Ottawa Citizen* 2001). A Bloc Québécois leader, Gilles Duceppe, too, alleged in a Parliament debate that B.C. producers were unfairly subsidized. He stated, "Forestry industries in Québec have been severely penalized because of the [B.C.] subsidies" (*National Post* 2001a).

The Canadian government had again to build a pan-Canadian position and choose a best route from all options presented by producers in various parts of the country—negotiation or litigation, free trade or some form of managed trade, a deal that covered the whole country or just the four major lumber-producing provinces, a temporary export tax until a long-term solution could be found or no temporary tax at all for fear of making it permanent. In the end, it chose not to negotiate for a managed trade deal, at least not immediately.

Prime Minister Chrétien raised the lumber issue with President Bush in their first meeting in early February 2001. In a follow-up meeting between Trade Minister Pierre Pettigrew and U.S. Trade Representative Robert B. Zoellick in late February, Pettigrew rejected Zoellick's request for a 20 percent or more export tax on lumber exported to the States after the Softwood Lumber Agreement expired. After the meeting, which lasted for nearly four hours, Pettigrew was apparently frustrated with the unrelenting U.S. drive to maintain or even increase high duties on Canadian lumber. He said, in reference to the contention by the U.S. industry that Canada was subsidizing its lumber, "I find it annoying time and again to reinvent the wheel, especially when we win every time. When will they learn?" (*Washington Post* 2001).

Minister Pettigrew pushed the idea of an "eminent persons group" to tackle the chronic, rhetoric-charged lumber issue, but the Coalition for Fair Lumber Imports found the proposal too fuzzy and feared it could be a Canadian stalling tactic. Ragosta said, "We can negotiate while we litigate." Although the coalition did not oppose the idea of having prominent special envoys sort out the dispute, it did not want to stop its litigation process (*Financial Post* 2001).

The Canadian government filed a request, in early 2000, to WTO for a ruling on an American "Statement of Administrative Action," under which another country's ban on exports of a material can be treated as a subsidy for goods made from that material. This request was viewed as a preemptive strike on Canada's log export restrictions—which would surely be alleged to be a source of subsidy in future lumber litigation. On June 29, 2001, a WTO panel ruled that export restraints do not provide a financial contribution and thus do not confer countervailable subsidies. The panel also found that the dispute was not "ripe." Neither Canada nor the United States appealed the decision. The Department of Commerce has not explicitly countervailed Canadian log export restrictions since.

On March 1, 2001, the Canadian government held consultations with Commerce over the consistency of Section 129 of the Uruguay Round Agreements Act with the Americans' WTO obligations. Section 129 applies in cases in which the WTO dispute settlement body has ruled that a U.S. antidumping or countervailing duty order is inconsistent with its obligations under the antidumping agreement or the Subsidies and Countervailing Measures Agreement, and USTR could direct either Commerce or the U.S. International Trade Commission to make a new determination. This new determination (called Section 129 Determination or Review) might apply only to entries of imports made on or after the date on which USTR directs Commerce to amend or to revoke the original antidumping or countervailing duty order.

Canada alleged that Section 129 Review could have the effect of preventing future reimbursement of duty deposits on products and of allowing the United States to assess WTO-incompatible duties long after the date for compliance (with a WTO panel ruling) had passed. Canada believed the duties should cease promptly once a WTO panel had ruled against the United States.

The consultations did not yield the results that Canada wanted. On July 24, 2001, Canada requested the establishment of a WTO panel and sought a ruling on Section 129. The WTO panel would issue its ruling in 2002 (see next chapter).

The coalition was well prepared politically and legally before the expiration of the Softwood Lumber Agreement. In February 2001, 51 senators sent a letter to President Bush, urging him and his administration "to make resolving the problem of subsidized lumber imports from Canada a top trade priority" (Zhang and Laband 2005). In releasing the letter to the public, Senator Baucus held a news conference on March 2, 2001, demanding that the Bush adminis-tration put new restrictions on Canadian softwood lumber after the agreement expired. Two weeks later, he held another news conference, this time with U.S. environmental groups, such as the Northwest Ecosystem Alliance, at his side, charging that Canadian lumber companies were being subsidized through lax environmental regulations (*Toronto Star* 2001a).

Canadian interests and U.S. consumer groups refuted these charges. Citing the U.S. government's 1998 filing with WTO that subsidies to its forest indus-try amounted to more than US$600 million per year (mostly in tax breaks), Consumers for World Trade pointed out that it was the U.S. government that subsidized its forest industry. In addition, the U.S. Forest Service reported that it collected US$546 million from its auction of tracts of timber in 1998 but spent US$672 million in reforestation, road construction, wildlife restoration, and payments to state authorities. Thus the Forest Service had an annual deficit of US$126 million. However, the U.S. General Accounting Office put the cost of the federal logging program closer to US$400 million per year (*Vancouver Sun* 2001b). Cashore and Auld (2003) show that Canadian provinces rank ahead of U.S. states in forest practice and environmental regulations and in exempting forests from commercial development.

On March 7, Coalition Chairman Rusty Wood dropped all equivocation during a speech to the Canadian–American Business Council, a bilateral busi-ness group, suggesting there was no way a trade war could be avoided. He stated, "On April 2, we're going to file a countervailing duty and an antidump-ing duty." The coalition's case would be built, in part, on information quietly obtained by disgruntled Canadian mill operators. He said, "We've got five or six independent Canadian producers that are calling us and telling us some dirty little secrets" (*Toronto Star* 2001b).

A week later, Wood said that Québec's stand in the lumber dispute was going to hurt sawmills in British Columbia: "We recognize that British Columbia is approaching this problem in a more mature manner," referring to a willingness by producers in that province to work out a negotiated settlement. But British Columbia producers were drawn into the fight despite their efforts to address U.S. concerns. He accused Québec sawmillers of cheating by creating a "free-dom trail for wood" from that province to New Brunswick to the United States (*Vancouver Sun* 2001d).

For the moment, B.C. lumber producers were the friends of the coalition. Some of them were pleased with this position. Jake Kerr said that the coalition "has figured out who their target is and it isn't us. And frankly we are glad of that.... You look at our market share in Canada. It has gone down. You look at the eastern provinces. It has gone up. I am not trying to breed discontent in the country, but the flip side is that all of Canada is in this for the next round and the Eastern guys should at least realize this risk" (*Vancouver Sun* 2001d).

On March 2, Ragosta indicated that the coalition's calculations of subsidy were around 40 percent, and that did not include dumping (*Vancouver Sun*

2001a). On March 7, the Bush administration sent a strong signal it would back the trade war; Trade Representative Zoellick had previously warned Minister Pettigrew during their meeting in February how politically charged the issue was in the United States. He said, "The concerns here are volatile to explosive, and I urged him to consider any other steps that they might take as the agreement ended so that we don't make the problem worse." He also indicated that he initially favored extending the current agreement, but "they [U.S. lumber producers] preferred to have us basically get out of the way so they could file the anti-dumping and countervailing duty suits. And I told them that I would be supportive of that process" (*Toronto Star* 2001b).

Apparently the coalition's legal documents against Canadian lumber imports had been prepared in March 2001. Realizing that litigation was unavoidable, all Canadian lumber producers agreed to make a financial contribution to collectively fight the allegation of injury under the umbrella of the Canadian Lumber Trade Alliance while leaving the federal and provincial governments to defend in the countervailing duty case and individual firms to defend themselves in antidumping cases.

The Byrd Amendment

Several months earlier, the Coalition for Fair Lumber Imports had received a legislative boost from Congress when it passed the so-called Byrd Amendment. On October 16, as Congress wound down its 106th legislative session, Senator Robert Byrd (D–West Virginia) offered a rider to the Agriculture Department appropriations bill during a House–Senate conference committee meeting. The amendment permitted antidumping and countervailing duties collected by U.S. Customs to be paid to the companies that petitioned for the duties, rather than to the U.S. Treasury. The agriculture bill passed, and neither house debated the amendment. And on October 28, 2000, President Clinton signed the agriculture bill, with the Byrd Amendment, into law.

The idea contained in the Byrd Amendment had floated around through congressional sessions for some 20 years. The tactic that Senator Byrd used to get it passed by the Congress (by offering it as a rider bill, which was unlikely to derail the agriculture appropriations bill, during a period called the "silly season" inside the Washington Beltway) was also not surprising. Nonetheless, its impact on trade is far reaching.

First, it encourages domestic companies to file antidumping and countervailing duty complaints. Under the existing law, an antidumping complaint has to get the support of companies representing at least 50 percent of the domestic production of the same product. With the Byrd Amendment, support for antidumping complaints could increase because companies have a financial incentive to do so.

Second, U.S. companies that bring trade remedy cases to U.S. authorities stand to benefit not only from the imposition of antidumping and countervailing duties on competing imports, but also from direct payments from the U.S. government when those duties are disbursed. President George W. Bush said that the Byrd Amendment offered "a double dip of benefit" to U.S. companies.

Third, it is not consistent with U.S. commitments to WTO and invites foreign retaliation against U.S. exports. In September 2001, 11 WTO members, including Canada, challenged the Byrd Amendment in WTO. In September 2002, a WTO panel determined that such payments were WTO-inconsistent. Following a U.S. appeal, in January 2003, a WTO appellate body upheld the primary panel findings against the Byrd Amendment. A WTO arbitrator subsequently gave the United States 11 months (until December 27, 2003) to be into compliance. The United States failed to meet this deadline. And in early 2004, the 11 countries started to implement retaliation measures against U.S. exports.

So a seemingly inconsequential bit of trade legislation tacked on as a rider to the agriculture appropriations bill provided added incentives for protectionism and resulted in international trade retaliations. But for the coalition waiting to start Lumber IV in early 2001, the Byrd Amendment was a gift, since it brought stronger support for its complaint against Canadian lumber imports.

Notes

1. In July 1998, the United Steel Workers of America brought a federal suit, charging that NAFTA was unconstitutional because it was by definition a treaty and therefore required a two-thirds vote of the U.S. Senate before being implemented. The court ruled against the union in 1999. In 2001, the union filed a certiorari petition with the U.S. Supreme Court, which declined to hear the case.

2. The Uruguay Round Agreements Act (Public Law 103-465) Section 251(a)(5)(C), which amends Section 771(5) of the Tariff Act of 1930 (19 U.S.C.1677), states,

> ... The determination of whether a subsidy exists shall be made without regard to whether the recipient of the subsidy is publicly or privately owned and without regard to whether the subsidy is provided directly or indirectly on the manufacture, production, or export of merchandise. *The administering authority is not required to consider the effect of the subsidy in determining whether a subsidy exists under this paragraph.*
>
> ...Where there are reasons to believe that a subsidy may be specific as a matter of fact, the subsidy is specific if *one or more of the following factors* exist:
>
> (I) The actual recipients of the subsidy, whether considered on an enterprise or industry basis, are limited in number.
>
> (II) An enterprise or industry is a predominant user of the subsidy.
>
> (III) An enterprise or industry receives a disproportionately large amount of the subsidy.
>
> (IV) The manner in which the authority providing the subsidy has exercised

discretion in the decision to grant the subsidy indicates that an enterprise or industry is favored over others. (emphasis added)

3. Canadian government officials and industry insisted that the refund was not linked to the consultation process, and Mike Apsey said there was no tit-for-tat in the start of discussions between the two countries. He stated, "Our stand is that there is no connection between the case which Canada has won and the return of the funds as a result of that. On the other hand, both countries wish to enter into consultations to see whether we can bring peace in the lumber trade ... The two are not linked" (*Vancouver Sun* 1994d).

4. Nonetheless, making the American producers happy was the prevailing goal of the Canadian industry at the moment. Pat Kelly of Vancouver-based futures brokers Global Futures Corp. said, "If we ... have 36.5 percent of their industry, even though we are legally right, there is another issue—it's the difference between what they call law and equity in the legal profession. We would very much like to have this thing [lumber trade dispute] out of the way" (*Gazette* 1996). Jacques Robitaille, deputy minister of Québec's Department of Natural Resources, said, "We want to keep the U.S. happy. It is not a cheap deal right now and we do not necessarily agree, but we want to avoid another [trade] war" (*Oregonian* 1996).

5. The formal terminologies of these three export levels are the established base (EB, 14.7 bbf), the lower fee base (LFB, the next 650 mmbf), and the upper fee base (UFB).

6. Any disputes over volumes were referred to an auditor, and other disputes were resolved under a dispute settlement mechanism derived from NAFTA's Chapter 20.

7. Henry Spelter (2000), a U.S. Forest Service economist, stated that the initial boost given to lumber prices by the Softwood Lumber Agreement sent an artificially amplified investment signal to producers in both the United States and Canada. Lumber capacity of both the traditional kind and the composite engineered variety increased substantially. The result was that, since the beginning of 2000, prices had been in a free fall, and in late August, six months before its expiration and the possible resumption of unconstrained Canadian imports, prices were lower than when the agreement had been implemented four and one-half years previously.

8. The change of behavior by some U.S. producers, Canadian exporters, and U.S. consumers in the fifth year also may be explained, in part, by the gaming strategy they used in playing the final period game with incomplete information. When information is incomplete among players (it was unclear whether there would be a new trade restriction measure after the Softwood Lumber Agreement and if so, what type of measure it would be, and players were ignorant about the associated payoff for each other player in various situations), there could be a qualitative switch in player behavior near the end of a finite game. This is explored in depth in "reputation" models by Milgrom and Roberts (1982), Kreps et al. (1982), and Kreps and Wilson (1982).

9. In theory, the four provincial (and Canadian federal) governments could gain at least another US\$120 million from income taxes on incremental producer profit because corporate income tax rates exceed 40 percent in all of these provinces. Note that Zhang (2001, 2006) covers only the U.S. market and does not count the loss that Canadian producers suffered in their domestic and other foreign markets under the Softwood Lumber Agreement.

10. Interestingly, Canfor's chief executive officer, David Emerson, who would later become an industry minister in the Martin government between 2003 and 2005 and minister of international trade in the Harper government since 2006, had briefly served as cochair of the B.C. Lumber Trade Council before he entered federal politics in 2003. Because the B.C. organization favored some kind of negotiated settlements, Canfor's withdrawal from the Free Trade Lumber Council might also reflect Emerson's thinking at the time that free trade was not working or could not work.

11. At this juncture, a study of the impacts of the Softwood Lumber Agreement by the Cato Institute, a free-market and free-trade think tank in Washington, D.C., was released. The study, titled "Nailing the Homeowners" (Lindsey et al. 2000), documented the price impacts of the Softwood Lumber Agreement in its first three years, costs to consumers, benefits to U.S. lumber producers, jobs lost in the construction industry, as well as number of households that could not afford to buy a house. The coalition called the study methodology flawed and distributed its objection commentary to the study on Capitol Hill.

12. This observation is consistent with economic theory. Producers in the Maritime Provinces enjoyed the quota rent freely by exporting all of their lumber to the States while importing lumber from Québec. As long as the per-unit lumber transportation cost from Québec to these provinces was less than the US$50–100/mbf tax, Québec and the Maritimes would have an economic incentive to continue to do so.

8

Lumber IV

The Battle through Litigation, 2001–2006

Indeed, the Coalition for Fair Lumber Imports wasted no time in delivering, on April 2, 2001 (April 1 was a Sunday), in two trucks, a petition and more than 5,000 pages of evidence to the Department of Commerce and U.S. International Trade Commission to support two claims against Canada's "predatory practice of subsidizing softwood lumber and dumping it into the United States." It alleged a subsidy rate of 39.9 percent and a dumping rate of 28–38 percent. In its news conference on Capitol Hill, which was attended by a half-dozen U.S. senators, it blamed the Canadians for not negotiating. According to Rusty Wood, chairman of the Coalition for Fair Lumber Imports, "Canada's stubborn intransigence has left us with no choice but to pursue litigation" (*Vancouver Sun* 2001e).

At the ITC hearing on the allegation of injury to the U.S. industry on April 23, an interesting dialogue occurred between an ITC staff lawyer and coalition counsel John Ragosta. The ITC lawyer stated that as part of the Softwood Lumber Agreement, U.S. lumber companies had indicated, in writing, that during the agreement there had been no material injury or threat of injury, and yet one day after it expired, the coalition was alleging that there *had* been material injury. Ragosta replied that the statements in question were merely a "legal fiction" needed to secure Canadian support for the agreement and that the final sentence in these letters stated that all the above representations and commitments "shall have no force or effect after the term of the Agreement." A lawyer representing the Canadian lumber industry asked ITC to treat these letters as part of the factual record in the case.

On May 18, by a vote of four to zero, ITC determined that there was "reasonable indication" that the U.S. industry "is threatened with material injury" by Canadian lumber imports. Commerce continued to conduct its subsidy and dumping investigations against Canadian lumber producers.

This chapter covers the legal context, rulings by North American Free Trade Agreement and World Trade Organization panels and U.S. courts, and the responses from Commerce, ITC, the coalition, and the Canadian government and industry during Lumber IV. In many instances, appeals and challenges were made by the industry and/or government from each country in NAFTA, WTO, or U.S. courts. Thus, the litigation track was a complicated, interlocking process that produced some results that permitted the industry in each country to claim victory. Nonetheless, the results of litigation determined the course of negotiation, which eventually succeeded in generating a "framework agreement" between the two governments on April 27, 2006 (next chapter). At the time the Framework Agreement was signed, there had been some 30 separate legal actions and challenges, several of which had concluded; others still were ongoing. Some of these ongoing cases had to be terminated as a condition of the 2006 U.S.–Canada Softwood Lumber Agreement.

Since there were many NAFTA and WTO panels, I name them by combining the name of the international body and the substantive issue they were charged to look into. For example, the NAFTA Injury Panel is the NAFTA panel that looked into the injury allegation, and the WTO Subsidy Panel is the WTO panel that investigated the alleged subsidy. Similarly, the WTO Subsidy Compliance Panel is the WTO panel that ruled on the compliance of the United States or Canada to the WTO Subsidy Panel ruling, and the WTO Subsidy Compliance Appellate Panel is the WTO appellate panel that looked into an appeal to the WTO Subsidy Compliance Panel ruling. Furthermore, since dumping allegations are company-specific, I only note the significant issues, such as zeroing and the antidumping duty deposit refund, that have broad implications in Lumber IV. Finally, although most of this chapter covers major cases that were concluded prior to April 27, 2006, and guided the negotiation of the Framework Agreement, other significant cases that concluded afterward or were still ongoing when this book was written are presented in the last section. These latter cases have broad implications for the operation of NAFTA (and WTO) dispute settlement mechanisms, as well as the 2006 Softwood Lumber Agreement. In fact, had the rulings in these latter cases been available before April 27, or had the two countries not implemented the 2006 agreement on October 12, it is not certain that a negotiated settlement would have been reached.

Commerce's Countervailing and Antidumping Duty Determinations

The coalition's petition and Commerce's initial investigation covered all of Canada. However, an intense lobbying effort by the Maritime Lumber Bureau and J.D. Irving Ltd., among other parties, resulted in exemption of the Maritime Provinces from the countervailing duty investigation. On August 9, 2001, Commerce issued a preliminary affirmative countervailing duty determination and a preliminary affirmative critical circumstance determination (DOC 2001a). The latter would entitle the United States to impose a countervailing duty retroactively to May 19, 2001, one day after ITC made its preliminary affirmative threat of injury determination.

The preliminary affirmative critical circumstance determination was a surprise to Canadians, since Canada's lumber exports to the United States had increased only 11.3 percent between April and June (the comparison period), compared with the previous quarter (the base period)—safely below the 15 percent threshold that Commerce was expected to use in determining whether to make the countervailing duty retroactive. However, Commerce calculated a seasonal adjustment factor (12 percent) based on the six-year period from 1995 to 2000 and used it to find that lumber imports from Canada, net of the Maritime Provinces, increased by 23.3 (12 + 11.3) percent in the comparison period. Therefore, the countervailing duty would have been applied retroactively if ITC had an affirmative injury determination.

On the other hand, Commerce's affirmative countervailing duty determination might not be surprising, given its track record in Lumber II and Lumber III. Commerce found the provincial stumpage programs were de facto specific and made a financial contribution to the Canadian lumber industry.[1] It then went to great lengths to explain and justify its use of cross-border comparison of stumpage prices to determine the financial contribution that provided a benefit (DOC 2001a).

Commerce noted that under Section 771(5)(E) of the Tariff Act of 1930 implemented by the Uruguay Round Agreements Act, a benefit is conferred by a government when it provides the good or service for less than adequate remuneration. Section 771(5)(E) further states that the adequacy of remuneration "shall be determined in relation to prevailing market conditions for the good or service being provided ... in the country which is subject to the investigation or review. Prevailing market conditions include price, quality, availability, marketability, transportation, and other conditions of ... sale."

Accordingly, Commerce interpreted "adequate remuneration" as "remuneration that is market-based," and therefore the benchmarks used in Lumber III would not be appropriate in Lumber IV. It further noted that Section 351.511(a)(2) of the countervailing duty regulations set forth three benchmarks, in hierarchical order, for determining whether a government good or service is provided for less than adequate remuneration:

1. market prices from actual transactions within the country under investigation;
2. world market prices that would be available to purchasers in the country of exportation; or
3. an assessment of whether the government price is consistent with market principles.

Finally, Commerce stated that private stumpage markets in the four major lumber-producing Canadian provinces were distorted by the large share of timber harvest from public lands and could not be used. As for comparison

TABLE 8-1. Results of the U.S. Department of Commerce's Preliminary and Final Countervailing Duty Determinations

| Province | Preliminary (8/9/2001) | | | Final (5/22/2002) |
	Subsidy rate	Export weighting	Weighted rate	Weighted rate
Alberta	64.74%	6.82%	4.42%	2.24%
Saskatchewan	39.21	2.21	0.87	0.56
Ontario	20.61	9.22	1.90	1.47
Québec	15.43	21.99	3.39	4.98
British Columbia	14.50	57.90	8.40	9.17
Manitoba	13.81	1.70	0.23	0.28
Northwest Territory	0.00	0.04	0.00	0.00
Yukon Territory	0.00	0.12	0.00	0.00
Total stumpage			19.21	18.70
All other programs			0.10	0.09
Total			19.31	18.79

Sources: DOC (2001a) and http://www.trade.gov/ia.

between stumpage sold competitively under the Small Business Forest Enterprise Program in British Columbia with those nonbidding sales, Commerce reasoned the small business program was distorted and not market based.

Although Commerce agreed that there was no unified North American market for stumpage because each individual stand of timber was unique, it reasoned that cross-border comparison was acceptable. Consequently, it chose to use stumpage prices from border states as the benchmark prices, and after various adjustments, it preliminarily determined the subsidy rate was 19.31 percent for Canada (net of the Maritime Provinces) (Table 8-1).

On October 31, 2001, Commerce issued its preliminary affirmative antidumping determination. Commerce's antidumping investigation focused on the six largest Canadian softwood lumber producers: Abitibi-Consolidated Inc.; Canfor Corporation; Slocan Forest Products Ltd.; Tembec Inc.; West Fraser Timber Co. Ltd., and Weyerhaeuser Canada (Weyerhaeuser). For each firm, Commerce calculated the export price and constructed export price and compared one of them with normal value or cost of production to come up with a dumping margin. All other producers were assigned a margin that was equal to the weighted average of margins for these six firms.

"Export price" was defined as the price at which the subject merchandise was first sold before the date of importation by the exporter or producer outside the United States to an unaffiliated purchaser in the States or to an unaffiliated purchaser for exportation to the States. "Constructed export price" was the price at which the subject merchandise was first sold in the United States before or after the date of importation, by or for the account of the producer or exporter of the merchandise, or by a seller affiliated with the producer or exporter to an unaffiliated purchaser. "Normal value" was the price at which the foreign-produced, similar product was sold in the home market, provided that the product was sold in sufficient quantities or value and that there was no particular market situation that prevented a proper comparison with the two export prices (DOC 2001b).

If one has an export price (or constructed export price) and a price for a similar good in the home market (the normal value), it should be straightforward to determine whether either export price is below the normal value, and if so, what the dumping margin is. Why would Commerce then calculate the cost of production for each firm? It turned out that Commerce analysts "believe or suspect that softwood lumber sales were made in Canada below the cost of production" (DOC 2001b, *56068*). Commerce disregarded the below-cost sales—defined as sales in Canada below the cost of production—and used the remaining sales to determine the normal value. For example, if a firm has two products in both the home and export markets, 2x4 and 2x6, and if Commerce finds the firm's sale price of 2x4 in home market is below cost, it would disregard 2x4 and look only at 2x6 in its dumping margin analysis.

Furthermore, Commerce used a "zeroing" method in calculating the dumping margin. Zeroing is the practice of assigning a margin of zero to goods in transactions for which the export price exceeds the home market price. This difference is also referred to as a negative dumping margin. Zeroing prevents a firm's dumping margin from being offset by negative dumping margins, resulting in a higher overall antidumping margin.

Commerce determined the dumping margins as shown in Table 8-2. As of late 2001, the combined preliminary countervailing and antidumping duty amounted to 31.89 percent.

Unlike a countervailing duty case, individual companies facing dumping allegations have to defend themselves. The practical way for individual companies to get rid of the antidumping duty is to lower their unit production cost until they can pass Commerce's annual administrative review. Other alternatives, such as selling the product at a higher price in foreign markets or selling the product at a lower price in domestic markets, are either impossible (not allowed by the market) or impractical (damaging to the companies' bottom line). Since average variable cost does not change much with production level, and average fixed cost does, companies can increase production to reduce their unit cost. Thus, an antidumping duty could have consequences that had not been intended by the coalition: an increase in Canadian production that decreased lumber prices in the United States.

This is indeed what happened. In 2002, lumber prices reached the lowest level in 10 years despite an uptick in housing starts fueled by the lowest interest rates in decades (Figure 7-2). On November 20, 2002, Steven Rogel, CEO and president of Weyerhaeuser Company, said, "Clearly, the anti-dumping duty doesn't work. In fact, it's back-fired as Canadian firms have increased production to lower their unit costs. The anti-dumping duty has aggravated the over-supply situation and driven prices lower" (Weyerhaeuser Company

TABLE 8-2. Results of the U.S. Department of Commerce's Preliminary and Final Antidumping Duty Margin Determinations

Exporter or producer	Weighted-average margin		
	Preliminary (10/31/2001)	Final (4/2/2002)	Amended final (5/22/2002)
Abitibi	13.64%	14.60%	12.44%
Canfor	12.98	5.96	5.96
Slocan	19.24	7.55	7.71
Tembec	10.76	12.04	10.21
West Fraser	5.94	2.26	2.18
Weyerhaeuser	11.93	15.63	12.39
All others	12.58	9.67	8.43

Sources: DOC (2001b) and http://www.trade.gov/ia.

2002).[2] Other factors—such as oversupply in the United States and an increase in imports from other countries—also contributed to the record low lumber prices in 2002 (*Washington Times* 2003).

On March 21, 2002, Commerce made its final affirmative determination of a 19.34 percent countervailing duty and 9.67 percent antidumping duty on Canadian softwood lumber imports (for a combined rate of 29.01 percent). Interestingly, Commerce did not find critical circumstances in this final determination, noting that the increase in Canadian imports during the six-month period immediately after the initiation of the case was less than 15 percent compared with the six-month period immediately before.[3] On May 22, Commerce further amended the rates to 18.79 percent and 8.43 percent, respectively (for the combined tariff rate of 27.22 percent), citing clerical errors in the previous calculation.

A Few Inconclusive Rulings

Two separate WTO rulings related to the lumber dispute came out in the summer of 2002. In June 2002, a WTO panel declined to rule on a U.S. trade law (Section 129 of the Uruguay Round Agreements Act) that effectively prevented the prompt reimbursement of antidumping and countervailing duties imposed in cases where WTO panels ruled against the United States. The panel viewed U.S. law as not necessarily mandating that duties collected after an adverse ruling could not be reimbursed, implying that the law gave sufficient discretion to the U.S. government to promptly revoke duties (*Inside US Trade* 2002b).

In July, the WTO panel looking into Canada's challenge to Commerce's preliminary affirmative determination issued a confidential interim ruling. It stated that Canadian provincial stumpage programs might provide a financial contribution and could be considered a subsidy to the lumber industry. On the other hand, the United States had used an illegal method (cross-border comparison) to calculate the subsidy rate, since Article 14(d) of the Uruguay Round Subsidies Agreement required that price comparisons "shall be determined in relation to the prevailing market conditions ... in the country of provision or purchase." When the final ruling was published in September 2002, neither country appealed, primarily because it was on a preliminary determination and the United States had already returned the bonds collected between May 19, 2001, and May 22, 2002.

In May 2003, the WTO Subsidy Panel (2003) issued an interim ruling on Commerce's final affirmative countervailing determination, which was similar to a previous WTO panel ruling on its preliminary countervailing duty determination issued in 2002. The panel ruled that the stumpage rights sold by provinces to Canadian lumber firms were specific and could confer a subsidy. However, the panel stated that the United States had not proven that a benefit had been conferred because its cross-border comparison methodology violated WTO rules. When the ruling was made final and published in August 2003, the United States appealed to the WTO Appellate Body for Dispute Settlement, seeking to overturn the ruling on the cross-border comparison method. Canada appealed as well, seeking a different ruling on specificity.

On July 17, the NAFTA Dumping Panel (2003) ruled that the United States had correctly initiated an antidumping investigation on softwood lumber from Canada. It also upheld Commerce's practice of zeroing. The panel reasoned that although the zeroing practices conflict with WTO antidumping agreements obligations and WTO cases, it was a permissible application of U.S. laws and the application has been upheld by various reviewing courts. But the NAFTA Dumping Panel found that Commerce had erred by not considering physical differences between various lumber imports when comparing these products with U.S. products for the purpose of calculating fair market price and the eventual antidumping margins.

On August 13, the NAFTA Subsidy Panel, comprising three Americans and two Canadians and including an American judge—the only judge on the NFFTA panel roster from the two countries in 2003—ruled unanimously that the timber rights sold by Canada to private firms could be a subsidy, but Commerce had failed to prove that a benefit had been conferred because the methodology used to determine the alleged subsidy was not justified. The decision largely mirrored an earlier decision of the WTO Subsidy Panel. However, whereas the WTO panel ruled that the cross-border comparison method was illegal and that Commerce could consider only prices in Canada, the NAFTA panel did not fault Commerce's rejection of private prices in Canada as an inadequate benchmark. As for the cross-border comparison, the NAFTA panel stated that Commerce could have compared stumpage prices in Canada with stumpage prices outside Canada had it shown that there was a world price on stumpage (which there was not). The panel noted that the preamble to Commerce regulations for determining the adequacy of remuneration stated that

Commerce could compare prices outside the border of the country only where the benefit was allegedly conferred for commodities that were commercially available across borders. The panel found that standing timber in the United States was not a good that was commercially available across borders and that Commerce had not provided substantial evidence that market conditions in the two countries were comparable (NAFTA Subsidy Panel 2003).

Industry representatives in both countries were encouraged. The coalition claimed a victory in the WTO and NAFTA panels' rulings that stumpage was countervailable. The Canadian industry claimed a victory in that the way Commerce calculated its duties had been found flawed.

The NAFTA Injury Panel Decision

If the last few WTO and NAFTA panel rulings sparked claims of victory from both industries, the NAFTA Injury Panel of three Americans and two Canadians would give Canadian industry a resounding victory on September 5, 2003, when it unanimously ruled that ITC had not proved that U.S. producers were threatened with injury from rising Canadian imports.[4] It said,

> The Panel is particularly *troubled by the extensive lack of analysis undertaken by the Commission* of the factors applicable to a determination of whether there is a threat of material injury to the domestic softwood lumber industry. This has inexorably led us to the opinion that the Commission did not exercise "special care" in making its threat determination in this case. To the contrary, *the Commission made its threat determination on the basis of considerable speculation and conjecture, the result of which conflicts not only with the agency's statutory mandate, but also with the rationale underlying its present material injury determination, as well as the record evidence.* (NAFTA Injury Panel 2003, *107*, emphasis added)

What makes this NAFTA Injury Panel ruling pivotal is that it was an all-or-nothing decision. If a final ruling finds no threat of injury, then all the arguments about subsidy or no subsidy become academic—the duties have to be removed. Such was the prevailing thought of Canadian industry and government officials.

Some background and analysis on ITC's threat of injury determination and on the NAFTA Injury Panel's (first remand) decision are warranted. In making its threat of injury analysis, ITC (2002) predicted that imports from Canada were likely to increase substantially from the period of investigation (1999 to 2001). ITC evaluated the following six statutory factors:

- "Such information as may be presented to it by the administering authority as to the nature of the subsidy, and whether imports of the subject merchandise are likely to increase" (19 U.S.C. Section 1677(7)(F)(i)(I)) ("nature of the subsidy" threat factor).

- "Any existing unused production capacity or imminent, substantial increase in production capacity in the exporting country indicating the likelihood of substantially increased imports of the subject merchandise into the United States, taking into account the availability of other export markets to absorb any additional exports" (19 U.S.C. Section 1677(7)(F)(i)(II)) ("capacity" threat factor).
- "A significant rate of increase of the volume or market penetration of imports of the subject merchandise indicating the likelihood of substantially increased imports" (19 U.S.C. Section 1677(7)(F)(i)(III)) ("volume" threat factor).
- "Whether imports of the subject merchandise are entering at prices that are likely to have a significant depressing or suppressing effect on domestic prices, and are likely to increase demand for further imports" (19 U.S.C. Section 1677(7)(F)(i)(IV)) ("price" threat factor).
- "Inventories of the subject merchandise" (19 U.S.C. Section 1677(7)(F)(i)(V)) ("inventory" threat factor).
- "The actual and potential negative effects on the existing development and production efforts of the domestic industry, including efforts to develop a derivative or more advanced version of the domestic like production" (19 U.S.C. Section 1677(7)(F)(i)(VIII)) ("development and production" threat factor).

The NAFTA Injury Panel (2003) ruled that the nature of the subsidy threat factor was a neutral point, and that the development and production threat factor was entitled to little weight because ITC "chose not to rest its threat determination on this factor." With respect to the other four threat factors, the panel held that ITC's finding that they indicated a threat of material injury "is not supported by substantial evidence."

On the volume threat factor, the NAFTA Injury Panel (2003, *68–70*) noted that ITC presented in its final determination the following findings:

- The volume of subject imports from Canada increased by 2.8 percent from 1999 to 2001, which is neither significant nor substantial; the relevant U.S. statute defines "imports from a country of merchandise to a domestic like product identified by the Commission are 'negligible' if such imports account for less than 3 percent of the volume of all such merchandise imported into the United States (19 U.S.C. Section 1677(24) (A)(i)) and the ITC recently acknowledged that imports that account for less than 3 percent of all such merchandise imported into the U.S. shall be deemed negligible."
- As a share of apparent domestic consumption, subject imports from Canada increased from 33.2 percent in 1999 to 34.3 percent in 2001.

- In its discussion of finding no present material injury, ITC noted the "relatively stable market share maintained by subject imports over the period of investigation."

All those findings, in the panel's view, did "not equate to the Commission finding—nor a claim that it found—'a significant increase of the volume or market penetration' that the 19 U.S.C. Section 1677(7)(F)(i)(III) requires to permit an inference of 'the likelihood of substantially increased imports.' *The record evidence relied upon by the Commission that is before this Panel is simply devoid of any support for the proposition that there has been 'a significant rate of increase of the volume or market penetration of imports of the subject merchandise'*" (NAFTA Injury Panel 2003, 68–69, emphasis added).

The panel also considered four other factors that ITC relied on to reach its affirmative finding in the volume threat factor: export orientation of Canadian producers to the United States, effects of the expiration of the Softwood Lumber Agreement of 1996, subject import trends during periods where there were no import constraints, and forecasts of strong and improving demand in the U.S. market. The panel concluded that not one of these factors presented by the ITC advanced its finding that "subject imports are likely to increase substantially."

As for the price threat factor, the panel noted the statutes require ITC to assess "whether imports of the subject merchandise *are entering at prices* that are likely to have a significant depressing or suppressing effect on domestic prices." In other words, "the focus of this statutory provision is on actual current prices for predicting future price effects." Yet ITC "explicitly acknowledged that it lacked sufficient record evidence regarding the current prices at which subject imports 'are entering' from which it could draw conclusions regarding any likely current effect on domestic prices, much less any likely future effect on domestic prices" (NAFTA Injury Panel 2003, 71, emphasis original).

Instead, ITC tried to use (1) "likely significant increases in the subject volumes" and (2) its finding of "at least moderate substitutability between subject imports and domestic product." The panel regarded this as an unlawful action by ITC, and "even if the focus of this statutory threat factor was properly on volume and/or substitutability, we find that the Commission's conclusion that 'subject imports from Canada are entering at prices that are likely to have a significant depressing or suppressing effect on domestic prices' would still not be supported by substantial evidence" (NAFTA Injury Panel 2003, 73).

Without a showing of rising market penetration or depressing price impacts by Canadian imports, the panel reasoned that even if the volume of Canadian imports rose slightly, U.S. producers would not be threatened with injury because of a corresponding increase in demand and market size.

The NAFTA Injury Panel (2003) instructed ITC to conduct six new analyses to provide evidence that the panel would accept, as a minimum:

- the impact of other (non-Canadian) lumber imports;

- the actions of its own domestic industry;
- the impact of engineered wood products in the market;
- the impact of insufficient domestic timber supply;
- the impact of the cyclical nature of the forest industry; and
- the impact on domestic research and development.

Complicating ITC's task was another directive requiring it to rebuild its case using only the evidence already in the record within 100 days. ITC issued its first remand determination and upheld its injury finding by a vote of five to zero with one abstention on December 15, 2003.

In its second remand decision, issued on April 29, 2004, the NAFTA Injury Panel again unanimously rejected most of the arguments that ITC had put forward. Specifically, the panel concluded that ITC's finding that subject imports would increase substantially in the imminent future was unsupported by substantial evidence for the following reasons:

- ITC failed to tie any unused (or even "imminent, substantial increase") in Canada's production capacity to "the likelihood of substantially increased imports of the subject merchandise into the United States, taking into account the availability of other export markets to absorb any additional exports" (capacity threat factor) (NAFTA Injury Panel 2004a, *16*).
- ITC "still has not explained how projected minimal increases in absolute Canadian exports to the United States, combined with projected decreases in the percentage of total Canadian shipments that were exported to the United States, provided support for its finding that there is a likelihood of substantial increases in subject imports" (export orientation of Canadian producers to the U.S. market factor) (*20*).
- The increase in subject imports over the period of investigation (market share) is neither significant nor substantial (*23*).
- Although the Softwood Lumber Agreement had some restraining effect, the difficulty remains that it is not possible to appraise the magnitude or impact of that effect (*26*).
- ITC did not examine the market conditions in reaching its conclusion that evidence during periods when there were no import restraints showed a likelihood of substantial increases in subject imports (*28*).
- ITC failed to explain why it changed from "forecasts of strong and improving demand" to "forecasts for strong and stable demand" in the U.S. market.

Similarly, the panel concluded that ITC's finding that the prices of subject imports were likely to have a significant depressing or suppressing effect on domestic prices in the imminent future was not supported by substantial evidence, for the following reasons:

- ITC's price trend clearly demonstrated that prices rose steadily since the fourth quarter of 2001, in contrast to ITC's own statement that "prices declined substantially at the end of the period of investigation" (NAFTA Injury Panel 2004a, *35*).

- The record evidence did not support ITC's finding that U.S. producers had curbed their production. Thus, in a "strong and improving" U.S. market, even a slight increase in volumes of Canadian imports—one of the two bases ITC relied upon in concluding that "subject imports from Canada are entering at prices that are likely to have a significant depressing or suppressing effect on domestic prices"—could not actually have such a depressing or suppressing effect on domestic prices (*36–38*).
- Regardless of the degree of substitutability, ITC still "fail[s] to consider whether, and to what extent, its predicted increase in imports from Canada would likely serve segments of the U.S. market *where purchasers do not consider Canadian and U.S. lumber to be close substitutes*" (*41*, emphasis original).

Consequently, the panel found that ITC's remand determination of threat of injury was not supported by substantial evidence. The panel ordered ITC to conduct further proceedings within 21 days and with existing record. Later, ITC twice requested additional time and reopening the record. The panel extended the deadline to June 10, 2004, but ordered ITC not to reopen the record.

Mark R. Joelson, one of the three Americans on the panel, wrote a separate and concurring opinion. He agreed with the panel's conclusion. In addition, he noted that ITC had changed its position in two related determinations. In its (no) material injury determination, ITC reasoned that price declines in 2002 were the result of too much supply in the market, an access supply condition to which both Canadian and domestic producers contributed. Yet in its threat of injury determination, ITC concluded "that U.S. producers had curbed their production, but that overproduction remains a problem in Canada." He held that ITC provided no substantial evidence to support its conclusion that U.S. producers had curbed, for the foreseeable future, their production of softwood lumber (NAFTA Injury Panel 2004b, *45–50*).

On August 31, 2004, the NAFTA Injury Panel unanimously ruled on ITC's second remand determination, stating,

> In its Second Remand Determination, *the Commission has refused to follow the instructions in the First Panel Remand Decision.* The Commission relies on the same record evidence that this Panel not once, but twice before, held insufficient as a matter of law to support the Commission's affirmative threat finding. By the Commission's so doing, this Panel can reasonably conclude that there is no other record evidence to support the Commission's affirmative threat determination. *The Commission has made it abundantly clear to this Panel that it is simply unwilling to accept this Panel's review authority under Chapter 19 of the NAFTA and has consistently ignored the authority of this Panel in an effort to preserve its finding*

of threat of material injury. This conduct obviates the impartiality of the agency decision-making process, and severely undermines the entire Chapter 19 panel review process.

... The Panel has thoroughly analyzed the Commission's views in the *Second Remand Determination,* and concluded that the Commission's decision has added nothing to its views expressed in its first remand determination. In light of the fact that there is no other record evidence to support the Commission's affirmative threat determination, *this Panel further concludes that it would be an exercise in futility to remand the case to the Commission to, yet again, consider and undertake an analysis of the substantive issues.* This is unfortunately the case because *the Commission has made it clear that it refuses to make a negative threat finding based on the record evidence.*

Accordingly, in the face of the Commission's regrettable position, this Panel specifically precludes the Commission on remand from undertaking yet another analysis of the substantive issues.

... Upon analyzing the Commission's Second Remand Determination, this Panel determines that a remand on the substantive issues would be an 'idle and useless formality,' as it would not result in anything but another insupportable affirmative threat of material injury finding. Hence, this case is one of those 'rare circumstances' in which a remand is not warranted. (NAFTA Injury Panel 2004b, 3–5, emphasis added)

Thus, the panel unanimously "*remands this case to the Commission to make a determination consistent with the decision of this Panel that the evidence on the record does not support a finding of threat of material injury* and to make that determination within ten (10) days from the date of this Panel decision" (NAFTA Injury Panel 2004b, 7, emphasis added).

On September 10, 2004, ITC voted five to one to accept the panel's order to enter a negative threat of injury determination. After criticizing the panel in many aspects (such as ignoring ITC's substantial evidence, substituting its own judgment for that of ITC, not allowing ITC to reopen the record, exceeding its power, refinding the facts, and giving ITC insufficient time to respond to the panel's decisions), ITC concluded,

The Panel's Decision and Order of August 31, 2004, can only be seen as a reversal of the Commission's affirmative determination of threat of material injury, despite the fact that neither the NAFTA nor U.S. law gives the Panel authority to reverse the Commission's determination in these circumstances. As such, the Panel's decision signals the end of this Panel proceeding.

Because the Commission respects and is bound by the NAFTA dispute settlement process, we issue a determination, consistent with the Panel's decision, that the U.S. softwood lumber industry is not threatened with material injury by reason of subject imports from Canada. In so doing, we disagree with the Panel's view that there is no substantial evidence to support a finding of threat of material injury and we continue to view the Panel's decisions throughout this proceeding as overstepping its authority, violating the NAFTA, seriously departing from fundamental rules of procedure, and committing legal error. (ITC 2004, *13–14*)

ITC further noted that because the panel had precluded it from engaging in any analysis of substantive issues, it had not reached and could not reach any determination regarding whether there was substantial evidence to support this negative determination.

On October 12, the NAFTA Injury Panel affirmed ITC's third remand determination. On November 24, the U.S. Trade Representative launched an extraordinary challenge.

NAFTA Extraordinary Challenge Committee's Injury Decision

Even before the second remand decision of the NAFTA Injury Panel was released on April 29, 2004, an allegation of conflict of interest surfaced. This allegation eventually became one of two main reasons cited by the U.S. government for launching its challenge. The facts and issues related to the allegation were documented in detail in the *Opinion and Order of the Extraordinary Challenge Committee* (NAFTA ECC 2005), published on August 10, 2005.

Specifically, an American panelist, Louis S. Mastriani, as counsel, appeared on behalf of a client in ITC's investigation on another antidumping case on November 26, 2003, some two and a half months after the panel made its first remand on lumber. He filed a brief to the NAFTA Secretariat on December 10, 2003, about his role in this new antidumping case.

The Coalition for Fair Lumber Imports became aware of Mastriani's involvement in the new case. In both the softwood lumber and the new cases, the question of export orientation as a factor to be considered in determining threat to a U.S. industry was an issue. Furthermore, when both producers' projections and historical data are available, which one should ITC (or the NAFTA Injury Panel in the lumber case) choose? Mastriani's submission to ITC on the new case relied on producers' projections. The coalition reasoned that Mastriani might have been motivated to find that Canadian producers' projections, rather than historical data, should be the basis for export orientation finding and that he could rely upon that finding as a precedent in the new case.

The coalition raised this issue with USTR, which in turn raised it with the Canadian government. Under relevant NAFTA guidelines, parties can remove panelists only by agreement. The U.S. government was of the view that Mastriani's involvement in the new case suggested an appearance of impropriety or an apprehension of bias, but the Canadian government did not concur. Consequently, there was no agreement that Mastriani should be removed.

On April 19, 2004, the coalition filed a notification with the U.S. NAFTA Secretariat, alleging that Mastriani's involvement in the new case created an appearance of impropriety and asking that he be recused. The coalition also made a similar allegation concerning Mastriani's involvement in a third case, which was later ruled by USTR a nonissue.

Also on April 19, the panel transmitted its second remand decision to the U.S. NAFTA Secretariat. The parties asked the secretariat to refrain from publicly releasing the decision during the process dealing with the allegation against Mastriani.

On April 26 the U.S. NAFTA secretary wrote to Mastriani, seeking his response to the allegation; he was given until the end of business on April 28 to respond.

On April 27 a reporter from Canada's major newspaper, *The Globe and Mail*, contacted Mastriani, seeking his comments on the allegation. The NAFTA Extraordinary Challenge Committee reported that both the United States and Canada agreed that it was likely that during their discussions, the reporter informed Mastriani that the coalition was the source of the allegation.

On April 28 the reporter's article in *The Globe and Mail* described the allegation against Mastriani and named the coalition as the source of the allegation. On the same day, Mastriani submitted his response, vigorously denying the accusation of impropriety. He pointed out that he had made his decisions on the softwood lumber case months before the other two cases were launched, and months before his law firm took them on. He said he had no intention of resigning from the panel. He further stated,

> I find the allegation against me to be an improper and likely illegal attempt by the Coalition to prevent the release of the NAFTA remand opinion. *This conduct by a participant in a Chapter 19 NAFTA proceeding is disturbing and disgraceful.* It does violence to the letter and spirit of Chapter 19 and the NAFTA treaty.

Mastriani's spirited defense was seen by the coalition as intemperate and cited as another reason for creating "an appearance of impropriety and a reasonable apprehension of bias." Mastriani would later be vindicated on both counts by a NAFTA extraordinary challenge committee consisting of two Americans and one Canadian.

In addition, the United States based its challenge (and asked the Extraordinary Challenge Committee to vacate the NAFTA Injury Panel's decisions and its order of October 12, 2004) on four grounds:

- the panel's refusal to permit ITC to reopen the record;

- the panel's failure to provide adequate time for ITC to respond to the issues raised in Panel Decision II (the panel's second remand decision, issued on April 29, 2004);
- the panel's failure to apply the substantial evidence standard when reviewing ITC's determinations that the importation of softwood lumber presented a threat of material injury to domestic producers; and
- the panel's direction to ITC in Panel Decision III to enter a negative threat determination (NAFTA ECC 2005).

On August 10, 2005, the NAFTA Extraordinary Challenge Committee (2005, 2, emphasis added) unanimously ruled that except for a subsidiary issue, the United States failed on all of these grounds[5] and decided "*to deny this challenge and to affirm the order of the Panel of October 12, 2004.*"

Specifically, the committee determined, on the issue of not permitting ITC to reopen the record, that the applicable U.S. law "cannot be said so clearly to preclude the Panel from ordering the Commission to conduct its reconsideration on the basis of the existing record that its order manifestly exceeded its jurisdiction." Further, the committee "tend[s] to agree with the submission advanced at the hearing by counsel for the Coalition that binational NAFTA panels have a residual discretion to remand to the Commission for reconsideration on the record." Thus, the committee "does not agree that the panel exercised its discretion on the facts before it in a manner that can be characterized as manifestly in excess of its authority" (NAFTA ECC 2005, 14–18).

Similarly, the committee concluded that the panel did not manifestly exceed its power, authority, or jurisdiction in setting a time limit within which ITC had to respond to the panel's second remand decision or in ordering ITC to enter a negative threat determination.

On the issue of whether the panel exceeded its jurisdiction by failing to apply the substantial evidence standard when reviewing ITC's findings of fact, the committee found that the panel failed to apply the substantial evidence standard of review in one subsidiary issue (export orientation). Nonetheless, it concluded that the panel did not exceed its powers, authority, or jurisdiction by failing to apply the appropriate standard of review "because the Panel's error did not materially affect its decision."

In all other subsidiary issues, the Extraordinary Challenge Committee pointed out the deficiency of ITC evidence in supporting its threat of injury finding. Regarding the volume threat factor and the impact of the Softwood Lumber Agreement (SLA), the committee stated,

To satisfy the statutory Volume Threat Factor in 19 U.S.C. Section 1677(7)(F)(i)(III), the Commission's finding must support a conclusion of a 'likelihood of substantially increased imports.' It was open to the Panel to assess whether the Commission's findings met that legal test. The adverb "substantially" in the legal test implies a consideration of magnitude. Because the Commission originally found that the SLA *appeared* to have restrained imports and because it subsequently found that the SLA only had *some* effect without any indication of magnitude, it was not impermissible for the Panel to determine that the Commission's finding did not support its conclusion that the SLA had a *substantial* effect on imports or that its removal would likely cause imports to increase *substantially*. (NAFTA ECC 2005, *30–31*; emphasis original)

Regarding whether a 2.8 percent increase in volume was significant, the committee confirmed that the panel gave ITC the opportunity to explain why it considered 2.8 percent significant, but ITC failed to do so. Similarly, on the issue of substitutability, ITC failed to respond whether and to what extent its predicted increase in imports from Canada would likely serve segments of the U.S. market where purchasers did not consider Canadian and U.S. lumber to be close substitutes.

On the issue of forecasted lumber demand in the United States, the committee noted,

The fundamental question asked by the Panel was how strong and improving demand (or even strong but stable demand) in the United States would cause subject imports to increase substantially, which is a consideration that goes to the conclusion of whether there is a material threat to the United States industry. Neither the Commission's forecast of demand nor anything else in *Commission Remand Determination II* provides such an explanation. In our view, the Panel was justified in *Panel Decision III* to find that the Commission had refused to follow the Panel's instructions in *Panel Decision I*. As a result, the finding in *Panel Decision I*, that there was no substantial evidence for the Commission's finding in its *Final Determination* that strong and improving demand in the United States would be a cause for "subject imports to increase substantially" remains justified. There has been no failure to apply the correct standard of review by the Panel on this issue. (NAFTA ECC 2005, *42*)

Thus, in the eyes of the Extraordinary Challenge Committee, it was the sloppy work by ITC, especially its response to the panel's remand decisions, that led the panel to issue an order of negative threat of injury.

The WTO Injury Panel Decision

On December 19, 2003, the WTO Injury Panel released a confidential interim report finding that ITC violated WTO rules with its determination that Canadian softwood lumber threatened to injure the U.S. industry. However, USTR stated that the ruling had no practical implications because it concerned an ITC determination that was no longer in place; because of the NAFTA Injury Panel ruling, ITC made its first remand determination on December 15, 2003. This interpretation by USTR was seen by some Canadians as the U.S. government's shifting the target so that the coalition could continue its legal battle.

The WTO Injury Panel's ruling was made public on March 22, 2004. Its stated reasons for reaching its conclusion were similar to those of the NAFTA Injury Panel. First, ITC did not find any significant price effects. Furthermore, ITC's conclusion that imports would increase substantially could not have been reached by an unbiased investigating authority based on an objective examination of evidence concerning relevant factors in the investigation. Finally, ITC's causal analysis was flawed (WTO Injury Panel 2004).

On the other hand, the WTO panel decided not to honor Canada's request that it recommend that the United States revoke the final determination of threat of injury, cease to impose antidumping and countervailing duties, and return the cash deposits imposed because "the U.S. could appropriately implement our [the panel's] recommendation."

However, the United States was not prepared to implement the WTO Injury Panel's decision. On April 26, 2004, the WTO Dispute Settlement Body adopted the WTO Injury Panel report. Rather than appeal to the WTO Appellate Body, on June 14, 2004, U.S. Trade Representative Robert B. Zoellick sent a letter, pursuant to Section 129 of the Uruguay Round Agreements Act, to ITC requesting an advisory report as to whether ITC would be able to implement the WTO Injury Panel decision.

On July 14, ITC replied that it would be able to render its determination "not inconsistent" with the WTO Injury Panel decision. On July 24, USTR requested that ITC issue a determination not inconsistent with the WTO Injury Panel findings, pursuant to Section 129 of the Uruguay Round Agreements Act (CIT 2006c). This move allowed ITC to make another affirmative, so-called Section 129 threat of injury determination.

Subsequently, ITC voted five to one on November 24, 2004, that the U.S. lumber industry was threatened with injury. This Section 129 determination came just two and a half months after it issued exactly the opposite determination under the direction of the NAFTA Injury Panel. The coalition asserted that the new determination meant that duties were justified, but the Canadian Lumber Trade Alliance saw it as ITC's attempt to resurrect the affirmative threat finding that the NAFTA Injury Panel had found illegal under U.S. law and that the WTO Injury Panel had found inconsistent with WTO rules.

On February 9, 2005, two weeks after the "reasonable time" for the United States to comply with the March 2004 WTO Injury Panel ruling ran out (on January 26), Canada announced that it would seek authority from WTO to impose C$4.1 billion in retaliatory sanctions against the United States for its refusal to comply with the WTO Injury Panel decision. Canada also requested the formation of a WTO compliance panel to determine whether the United

States had complied with the WTO Injury Panel ruling. For Canada, compliance meant, at a minimum, lifting the countervailing and antidumping duty orders. The United States, on the other hand, argued that it complied with the WTO panel decision in November 2004 when ITC issued its affirmative Section 129 threat of injury determination.

Several weeks earlier (in January 2005), Tembec, along with the Canadian Lumber Trade Alliance and the Canadian government, filed a request for a NAFTA panel review of ITC's Section 129 determination. Tembec also filed a case in the U.S. Court of International Trade, alleging that the United States illegally continued to enforce the antidumping and countervailing duty orders following the illegal implementation of ITC's Section 129 determination. They argued that the United States should lift the countervailing and antidumping duty orders in the wake of the NAFTA Injury Panel decision and could only reimpose duties after new investigations that were affirmative for both subsidy (and/or dumping) and injury.

In a twist-and-turn fashion, the WTO Injury Compliance Panel made a confidential interim decision on August 29, 2005, upholding ITC's Section 129 determination. Perhaps additional information resulting from reopening the record lent greater support to ITC's Section 129 threat of injury determination. The final decision of the WTO Injury Compliance Panel (2005), published on November 15, affirmed that ITC's Section 129 threat of injury determination was consistent with international trade rules and thus gave the U.S. industry a legal victory.

Canada appealed the WTO Injury Compliance Panel's decision to the WTO Appellate Body. On April 13, 2006, the WTO Injury Compliance Appellate Panel ruled that the WTO Injury Compliance Panel was too deferential to ITC and employed an incorrect standard of review. It reversed the WTO Injury Compliance Panel's decision that the United States had complied with an earlier panel decision. However, it did not make a ruling on whether ITC's Section 129 determination was consistent with U.S. obligations under WTO rules, in part because it did not have enough information to make a decision (WTO Injury Compliance Appellate Panel 2006). As a result, it did not make a recommendation to the WTO Dispute Settlement Body and did not leave Canada with the possibility of requesting for authority to retaliate. The decision, in effect, let stand ITC's Section 129 determination of threat of injury.

The NAFTA Subsidy Panel Decision

Because the NAFTA Subsidy Panel (2003) held that there was no "world market price" for timber and that the use of U.S. timber prices as a benchmark was improper, Commerce was directed, in effect, to apply the third-tier benchmarks—that is, an assessment of whether government price was consistent with market principles.[6]

TABLE 8-3. Results of the U.S. Department of Commerce's Remand Determinations of Countervailing Duty in Response to NAFTA Subsidy Panel Decisions

	1st remand (1/24/2004)	2nd remand (7/30/2004)	3rd remand (1/24/2005)	4th remand (7/7/2005)	5th remand (11/23/2005)
Alberta	2.56%	0.45%	0.31%	0.31%	0.31%
British Columbia	4.69[a]	5.77[a]	0.08[b]	0.08[b]	0.08[b]
Manitoba	0.89	0.03	0.03	0.01	0.00
Ontario	0.61	0.15	0.04	0.03	0.02
Québec	2.79	1.28	1.29	0.69	0.33
Saskatchewan	1.69	0.14	0.13	0.09	0.06
Country-wide	13.23	7.82	1.88	1.21	0.80

Note: Weighted average country-wide calculation of countervailing duty rates (percentages).
a. Includes a 0.09% subsidy rate in programs other than stumpage.
b. Includes a 0.08% subsidy rate in programs other than stumpage.
Source: http://ia.ita.doc.gov/remands/index.html.

In its first remand determination issued on January 12, 2004, Commerce complied with the NAFTA Subsidy Panel's decision by using a derived demand method to calculate the alleged subsidy rates. Specifically, it used imported log prices and private log prices in various provinces as the benchmarks and then deducted logging and transportation costs and profits to derive the value for standing timber. Commerce found a subsidy rate of 13.23 percent (Table 8-3).

In its second remand decision, the NAFTA Subsidy Panel accepted Commerce's methodology but faulted details of its calculation, such as simple average versus weighted average, species-specific benchmarks versus stand-level benchmarks, advertised prices versus actual market transaction prices, use of appropriate import and private log price data, profit allowance, and regional versus provincial aggregation. The panel remanded the matter to Commerce four more times (on June 7, 2004; December 1, 2004; May 23, 2005; and October 5, 2005), and each time Commerce returned with a different rate of subsidy (Table 8-3).

In its third remand determination, Commerce found a rate of subsidy of 1.88 percent. Not satisfied, Undersecretary of Commerce Grant Aldonas commented that in this determination, the United States had "acquiesced" to the NAFTA Subsidy Panel's demands, but it was "academic." He said, "Since the decision is largely academic, I don't feel uncomfortable saying 'fine, let's let the decision go,' because the prevailing rate is going to be ... 17 percent"[7] (*Inside US Trade* 2005a).

This remark revealed a strategy of Commerce for complying with the NAFTA Subsidy Panel decision: As long as the subsidy rate was higher than *de minimis*, it could rely on administrative reviews to get a different, potentially higher duty rate.

In its fourth remand determination, Commerce was able to find a subsidy rate of only 1.21 percent, slightly above the *de miminis* threshold of 1 percent. Yet the NAFTA Subsidy Panel still found additional errors. Whether Commerce would find a *de minimis* rate of subsidy in its fifth remand determination, which was due on October 28, 2005, became critical.

However, on October 28, Commerce requested a clarification of the NAFTA Subsidy Panel's decision and an extension. This move may have been related to a letter to Commerce Secretary Carlos M. Gutierrez from 21 U.S. senators, led by Baucus, dated October 20. The senators demanded that Commerce "ensure that it calculates the duties in a way that sufficiently offsets pervasive Canadian subsidies." They further urged the department, "in responding to this flawed NAFTA decision, to fully consider and utilize any legal and appropriate alternative that would allow for this essential trade law relief to stay in effect" (Baucus 2005).

Commerce's request was denied, and the NAFTA Subsidy Panel ordered it to submit its fifth remand decision before November 23, 2005. Despite a call from five U.S. senators to preserve the countervailing duty, Commerce rendered a country-wide subsidy rate of 0.80 percent, which was *de minimis*.

Commerce (2005c) declared three times, in the first paragraph alone of a 10-page determination, that it "disagrees" with the NAFTA Subsidy Panel, and repeated this sentiment throughout the document. It also accused the panel of inconsistency but acquiesced: "Notwithstanding the objections noted above, we have implemented the Panel's decision."

As a reminder, Commerce warned in its press release on the remand determination, "The filing of this remand has no immediate effect on the cash deposit and assessment rates. Cash deposits will continue to be required at the rates currently in place, with an average combined antidumping/countervailing duty of 20.96 percent" (DOC 2005d).

On March 17, 2006, the NAFTA Subsidy Panel accepted Commerce's fifth remand determination that the rate of subsidy in Canadian lumber was *de minimis*. The United States had until April 27, 2006, to decide whether to file an extraordinary challenge. Although few expected that the NAFTA Subsidy Panel's decision would be overturned, the United States could prolong the fight by making an appeal. On the other hand, if the decision were not appealed, it would signal that the United States was ready to settle through negotiation. It was at this juncture that the two governments reached the Framework Agreement (see next chapter).

However, to the dismay of some Canadian officials, the United States did file an extraordinary challenge on April 27 after the Framework Agreement was reached. USTR stated such a move was to preserve the U.S. right if the Framework Agreement did not work out. On May 11, the United States suspended such a challenge. Two Ontario forestry associations challenged the suspension of the NAFTA extraordinary challenge process in the U.S. Court of International Trade, which dismissed the case on August 2, 2006, saying that both governments were involved in the suspension.

Administrative Reviews

The United States has a "retrospective" assessment system under which the final liability for antidumping and countervailing duties is determined after merchandise is imported. Although duty liability may be determined in the context of other types of reviews, the most common procedure for determining the final duty liability is an administrative review under Section 751(a)(1) of the Tariff Act of 1930, as amended.

Under the regulations, Commerce normally announces an opportunity to request an administrative review of countervailing and antidumping duty orders. An interested party (such as an interest group or a Canadian firm, or the government of Canada), as defined in the Tariff Act, may request that Commerce conduct an administrative review each year during the anniversary month of the publication of an antidumping or countervailing duty order. Commerce then conducts the review and publishes the preliminary and final results. The final results have the force of law; that is, U.S. Customs will use the antidumping and countervailing duty rates specified in the administrative review. If the duty rate differs from that in a countervailing or antidumping duty order or previous administrative review, Canadian lumber exporters not only get an adjustment in the duty rate paid in the period covered in the administrative review, but also pay the new duty rate until another administrative review is conducted or the countervailing or antidumping duty order is lifted.

Thus, other than trying to get the antidumping and countervailing duty orders revoked, the second-best option for Canadian lumber exporters would be seeking lower duty rates through administrative reviews. The Coalition for Fair Lumber Imports, on the other hand, would defend the duty rates specified in the antidumping and countervailing duty orders or even try to increase them. Indeed, in May 2003, it brought new allegations of 12 additional subsidy programs and charged that Canadian federal and provincial governments had increased their level of subsidy. The Canadian government and some 290 Canadian companies argued that there was no subsidy in the period under review, from May 22, 2002, to March 31, 2003.

Interestingly, Commerce used a first-tier benchmark in its first administrative review—private stumpage prices in New Brunswick and Nova Scotia—to determine the subsidy rate in other provinces after adjusting for differences in timber quality. In so doing, Commerce rejected the coalition's position that these prices were unsuitable benchmarks to assess the adequacy of remuneration from provincial stumpage programs. On June 14, 2004, Commerce published the preliminary results of the first administrative review, indicating a subsidy rate of 9.24 percent, which was about half the rate specified in the countervailing duty order (Table 8-4).

However, Commerce changed its benchmarks in its first final administrative review and used the cross-border comparison method to find a large subsidy

TABLE 8-4. Results of the U.S. Department of Commerce's Administrative Reviews of the Countervailing Duty Order on Canadian Softwood Lumber

	First			Second		Third
	Preliminary results (6/14/2004)	*Final results* (12/14/2004)	*Amended final results* (2/24/2005)	*Preliminary results* (6/7/2005)	*Final results* (12/14/2005)	*Preliminary results* (6/12/2006)
Alberta	0.83%	0.56%	0.50%	0.46%	0.58%	0.42%
British Columbia	5.40	14.13	13.52	6.01	6.07	8.55
Manitoba	0.09	0.10	0.09	0.09	0.10	0.07
Ontario	0.97	0.92	0.82	0.55	0.65	0.69
Québec	1.37	0.89	0.77	0.72	0.97	0.98
Saskatchewan	0.20	0.20	0.19	0.14	0.16	0.17
Total stumpage	8.86	16.80	15.89	7.97	8.53	10.88
All other programs	0.38	0.38	0.48	0.21	0.17	0.35
Country-wide	9.24	17.18	16.37	8.18	8.70	11.23

Note: Weighted average country-wide calculation of countervailing duty rate (percentage).
Source: http://www.trade.gov/ia.

rate for British Columbia. As a result, the new countervailing duty was set at 17.18 percent, roughly twice the rate set in its first preliminary administrative review and only slightly below the rate specified in the original countervailing duty order.

The Canadian industry saw the change of methodology as a bowing to political pressure from 14 U.S. senators who wrote a letter to Commerce Secretary Don Evans. The November 23, 2004, letter demanded that Commerce use the cross-border comparison method (and keep cash deposits) to give the president much-needed "negotiating leverage" (Craig 2004). The Canadian industry and governments asserted that the cross-border comparison method was illegal and vowed to appeal. Indeed, the Canadian government announced its challenge to Commerce's first final administrative review on January 13, 2004. It also challenged Commerce's second final administrative review in NAFTA.[8]

The problem was that although the Canadian producers were appealing the first final administrative review, the second administrative review would likely supersede the first. Thus they would be constantly chasing their tails. The top priority for Canadian producers, accordingly, was to get the antidumping and countervailing duty orders lifted.

The WTO Subsidy Appellate Panel Decision

A big win for the U.S. producers came on January 19, 2004, when the WTO Subsidy Appellate Panel (2004) ruled that if Commerce could show that Canadian domestic timber prices were distorted, it might use a benchmark other than private prices in Canada for calculating subsidy rates. Nonetheless, it stopped short of giving the United States a green light to pursue its case using U.S. prices as benchmarks, since it did not have enough information to determine whether Commerce was justified in using cross-border comparison method in this case.

Since the ruling came from an appellate body, its decision was final. Canada could take some consolation only in the fact that the appellate panel stopped short of endorsing use of the cross-border comparison method. To pursue that point, however, Canada would have to start the entire WTO process again.

However, the WTO appellate panel's decision was not entirely in favor of the United States. It found that Commerce had failed to conduct a pass-through analysis for arm's-length sales of logs by tenured harvesters and sawmills to unrelated sawmills (WTO Subsidy Appellate Panel 2004). The panel required Commerce to analyze whether the subsidy conferred on products of certain enterprises in the production chain was "passed through," in arm's-length transactions, to other enterprises producing the countervailed product. Theoretically, this analysis is needed to avoid inflating the duty rate (that is, calculating duty on both logs and lumber).

The WTO Subsidy Appellate Panel's report was adopted in February 2004. On December 17, 2004, the United States informed the WTO Dispute Settlement Body that it had complied with the panel's recommendations and rulings. This was based on yet another Section 129 determination (this time, by Commerce) on December 6, 2004.

Canada disagreed, charging that this revised determination failed to address the WTO Subsidy Appellate Panel rulings. As such, on December 30, 2004, Canada requested that a WTO compliance panel review Commerce's revised determination as well as the results of Commerce's first countervailing duty administrative review of December 14, 2004, which, in Canada's view, had also failed to demonstrate the existence of a subsidy in certain log purchases.

On August 1, 2005, the WTO Subsidy Compliance Panel (2005, *32*) found that measures used by Commerce in both its Section 129 determination and first final administrative review were flawed. As a result, the department "included in its subsidy numerator transactions for which it had not demonstrated that the benefit of subsidized log inputs had passed through to the processed product" and thus inflated the calculated subsidy rate.

This was a small technical victory for Canada. Had the United States properly implemented the WTO Dispute Settlement Body recommendations, it might have resulted in a reduction of some C$200 million in countervailing duty, which was a small portion of the total antidumping and countervailing duties it collected. To protect its retaliatory rights, Canada sought authority to retaliate on a maximum of C$200 million of U.S. imports on December 30, 2005.

On September 6, 2005, the United States filed an appeal of the WTO Subsidy Compliance Panel's ruling of August 1, 2005. On December 5, 2005, the WTO Subsidy Compliance Appellate Panel upheld the WTO Subsidy Compliance

Panel's ruling and asked the United States to bring its measures (a finding of subsidy in certain arm's-length purchases of logs by certain Canadian producers) into compliance with WTO rules. The ruling was a nominal victory for the Canadian industry.

Dumping: A Salvo over Duty Deposits

On October 15, 2003, Commerce responded to the NAFTA Dumping Panel's (2003) decision by finding an average Canada-wide rate of 8.38 percent, roughly equal to the original rate (8.43 percent) found in May 2002.

On March 5, 2004, the NAFTA Dumping Panel (2004) ruled, in its second remand decision, that on 8 of 11 issues, the United States had correctly implemented U.S. antidumping laws on Canadian lumber imports. The panel turned down a Canadian appeal to defeat the tariff but ruled that Commerce should lower the antidumping duties for some 25 Canadian companies and remanded three company-specific antidumping duty calculations back to the department.

One of those three companies was West Fraser, whose dumping rate fell below the 2 percent *de minimis* level that would trigger antidumping duties. Commerce confirmed that in an April 13, 2004, draft remand determination that reflected the panel's decision: "We noted that as a result of the revised calculations the margin for West Fraser is *de minimis*. Therefore, if this remand determination becomes final, subject merchandise produced and exported by West Fraser will be excluded from the amended [antidumping] order" (cited in NAFTA Dumping Panel 2005, 3).[9]

The next day, West Fraser requested that Commerce make clear "that its amended final determination in this case will have retroactive as well as prospective effect." In addition, West Fraser asked Commerce to issue a determination releasing and refunding all estimated antidumping duties deposited pursuant to the final antidumping order of May 22, 2002, plus interest (cited in NAFTA Dumping Panel 2005, 3–4).

Commerce rejected West Fraser's request in an April 21 NAFTA dumping remand determination and its June 8 brief to the NAFTA Dumping Panel. Instead, it reasoned, any refund on the cash deposits would have to be based on U.S. administrative reviews, not the NAFTA panel decisions, and once the NAFTA process was final, West Fraser would be excluded from the antidumping order only prospectively (cited in NAFTA Dumping Panel 2005, 4).

Commerce argued that unlike a U.S. Court, the NAFTA panels had no equity power to retroactively implement changes to final determinations and that this fact was clear from U.S. statute and the applicable legislative history, in particular the Statement of Administrative Action for the U.S.–Canada Free Trade Agreement that preceded NAFTA.

Specifically, Commerce argued that according to 19 U.S.C. Section 1516a(g)(5)(B), entries were to be liquidated or returned from deposits into a final assessment of actual duties in accordance with the original determination as long as they entered the United States before publication of the notice of a NAFTA panel decision that changed the results of that determination. This was the intent of the statute, Commerce said: according to the Statement of Administrative Action, NAFTA panels "will not have equity powers" and "the injunctive remedy" provided by a separate part of the statute "will not be available to prevent liquidation" (*Inside US Trade* 2004b).

In contrast, the Canadian government argued, in its May 14, 2004, brief to the NAFTA Dumping Panel in support of West Fraser, that 19 U.S.C. Section 1516a(g)(5)(B) was procedural in nature and was only intended to implement Commerce's authority to assess antidumping duties while a NAFTA panel's work was ongoing and entries were subject to liquidation (cited in NAFTA Dumping Panel 2005).The U.S. position, Canada said, contradicted previous Commerce actions when determinations were invalidated and deposits were returned to Canadian companies. The Canadian brief gave three examples: the 1991 pork case, the 1995 corrosion-resistant steel case, and the 1994 softwood lumber case (*Inside US Trade* 2004b).

In its June 8 brief, Commerce countered that even though the United States had refunded deposits in previous disputes, such refunds were not made pursuant to NAFTA panel directives. Commerce cited the 1994 softwood lumber case as an example in which the United States refunded deposits only after Canada agreed to negotiate for a settlement that led to the Softwood Lumber Agreement of 1996. The Coalition for Fair Lumber Imports introduced briefs in support of Commerce, arguing that no U.S. statute authorized Commerce or U.S. Customs and Border Protection to return the deposits to Canada and that both agencies were forbidden to return duty deposits unless expressly authorized to do so by U.S. statute (*Inside US Trade* 2004b).

By this action, Commerce signaled it would take the position of refusing to return deposits collected even if the NAFTA Subsidy Panel later found the Canadian subsidy *de minimis* or the NAFTA Injury Panel found no threat to U.S. industry. Clearly realizing the implication of Commerce's position, Trade Minister James Peterson wrote a letter to Secretary Don Evans, criticizing the United States for undermining the NAFTA by refusing to return deposits collected from West Fraser. He wrote,

> The NAFTA Chapter 19 dispute settlement mechanism is intended to replace domestic judicial review of countervailing and anti-dumping duty actions in the United States, Mexico and Canada. The U.S. statute implementing NAFTA Chapter 19 requires the United States to refund duty deposits where panel review leads to a negative determination in an investigation. The statute and legislative history make clear the unequivocal intent of Congress that panel decisions be given effect, including the refund of duties with interest.

In making its determination, the Department of Commerce has interpreted U.S. law in such a way as to deny binational panel decisions the legal effect of equivalent U.S. court decisions ... The assessment of duties on imports determined not to be dumped contradicts the basic provisions of U.S. trade law and *seriously undermines NAFTA* ...

The Department of Commerce's decision to deny the refund of duty deposits *strikes a blow to the credibility and legitimacy of NAFTA dispute resolution proceedings.* Were Canada and Mexico to be afforded lesser protections that are available through judicial review in U.S. courts, *the binding binational panel review that made the Free Trade Agreement and NAFTA possible would be called into question.* (Peterson 2004, emphasis added)

Canadian lumber producers perceived a U.S. government strategy to pressure them to negotiate. This objective was expressed by Senator Mike Crapo (R-Idaho, chairman of the International Trade Subcommittee), when he joined six other U.S. senators on October 5, 2004, in attacking the NAFTA Injury Panel's (2004b) decision that ordered ITC to find no threat of injury. He stated, "Of course, the deposits could always be returned as part of a negotiated settlement that preserves the interests of U.S. workers and sawmills, as was done in 1994 ..." (*Congressional Record* 2004a).

Thus the fight for deposits began. It was a dispute within a dispute that exposed a gap in NAFTA. In less significant trade cases, the United States complied with the trade agreement panel rulings by refunding all cash deposits. Now, in Lumber IV, it decided to deny Canada's request for a refund. The NAFTA Chapter 19 dispute settlement mechanism was at stake.

Zeroing

On April 13, 2004, shortly after the NAFTA Dumping Panel made its second remand decision, the WTO Dumping Panel (2004) rendered its decision and sided with the United States on most challenges brought by Canada. But the WTO panel said the zeroing methodology used by Commerce to set the margin of antidumping duties at 8.43 percent violated the WTO antidumping agreement, and the United States should bring its measure into conformity with WTO rules.

The United States and Canada both appealed. On August 11, 2004, the WTO Dumping Appellate Panel upheld the panel's ruling on "zeroing" as inconsistent with WTO.

On November 4, 2004, the U.S. trade representative requested that Commerce issue a Section 129 review (its second, or third by the United States, counting ITC's). On April 15, 2005, Commerce issued such a determination, stating that it "is precluded in this instance from not offsetting non-dumping sales in making weighted average-to-weighted average comparisons ..." (DOC 2005a, *22639*). Yet Commerce used the zeroing practice in its new calculations, albeit in a modified way.

Specifically, Commerce chose to use the transaction-to-transaction methodology (instead of the weighted-average to weighted-average comparisons), which did not offset for nondumped sales. Commerce's justification for using this new methodology was that it was permitted under U.S. law for nonnormal cases, and the volatility of softwood lumber prices during the period of investigation distinguished this case from the norm. However, the true justification might have been this: "because the Appellate Body Report requires the offset for no-dumped sales only for the weighted-average-to-weighted-average comparison, we have not applied the offset for nondumped sales in our analysis" (DOC 2005a, *22639*).

In other words, Commerce abandoned the weighted-average to weighted-average comparisons because it was precluded from using zeroing in that calculation. It then seized another calculation method that it thought would permit it to continue to use zeroing.

This new method is complicated. Commerce began with transactions in the United States that had certain characteristics. It then attempted to find an identical match in the home market at the same level of trade on the same day or within seven days before or after a U.S. sale. There were six criteria, in order, for identifying the single most appropriate match:

- variable cost;
- quantity;
- customer category;
- channel of distribution;
- movement expenses; and
- number of days between payment and shipment.

After considering those criteria, Commerce still found a small number of U.S. sales that had more than one equally comparable home market match. In these cases, Commerce would simply let the computer select the first observation on the short list of equally comparable sales. The result was that the new Section 129 determination established a dumping rate of 11.54 percent (Table 8-5), an increase from the original rate of 8.43 percent.

By now, Commerce had used two different methods in calculating the dumping margins and four different methods in calculating the countervailing duty rates. The Canadian industry alleged that Commerce was trying to evade the United States' international obligations by continuing to use the zeroing method in its transaction-to-transaction calculation.

Canada asked the WTO Dumping Compliance Panel to consider the U.S. practice of zeroing in its Section 129 determination and a WTO authority to retaliate against the United States for up to C$400 million. However, on April 3, 2006, the WTO Dumping Compliance Panel ruled that the Section 129 deter-

TABLE 8-5. Results of the U.S. Department of Commerce's Antidumping Duty Margin Calculation: Remand Determinations in Response to the NAFTA Dumping Panel Decisions and Section 129 Determination

Exporter or producer	Original remand (10/15/2003)	2nd remand (4/21/2004)	3rd remand (7/13/2005)	Section 129 (5/2/2005)
Abitibi	11.85%		8.88%	13.22%
Canfor	5.74		8.29	9.27
Slocan	8.77	8.56%	13.32	12.91
Tembec	6.66	6.28	9.08	12.96
West Fraser	2.22	1.79	3.19	3.92
Weyerhaeuser	12.36		17.59	16.35
All others	8.07	8.85	10.52	11.54

Sources: http://ia.ita.doc.gov/remands/index.html and DOC (2005a).

mination was not inconsistent with WTO rules. This ruling was overturned by the WTO Dumping Compliance Appellate Panel on August 15. Relatedly, on April 18, the WTO Appellate Body for Dispute Settlement ruled, in a challenge brought by the European Union, that the use of transaction-to-transaction "zeroing" practices in 16 administrative reviews by Commerce was illegal (*Inside US Trade* 2006a). Therefore, it seems justifying the use of zeroing in the future would be difficult.

* * *

On June 9, 2005, the NAFTA Dumping Panel (2005), in its third remand decision, directed Commerce to render a negative less-than-fair-value determination and to revoke the antidumping order with respect to exports by West Fraser. The panel further stated that the United States should return all the duties it had collected (about US$24 million) from West Fraser, since the United States had no authority to keep deposits collected pursuant to an invalid order and the duties should never have been imposed in the first place.

Specifically, since Commerce found that West Fraser should have been excluded from the antidumping order, given the *de minimis* finding, the panel stated, "*it follows that no estimated antidumping duties should have been collected with respect to the company's imports and, to the extent deposits were taken, they are subject to refund upon proper application to West Fraser*" (NAFTA Dumping Panel 2005, *18*, emphasis added).

The panel further criticized Commerce for suggesting that the duties should be kept "in accordance with a discredited final administrative determination" and not returned to importers, because that "would render review by a court of competent jurisdiction or a bi-national panel meaningless." The panel said that if this were the case, agencies would have little incentive to perform their tasks correctly and might even be inclined to err on the side of imposing higher dumping margins, or to impose dumping margins where none should exist. Nonetheless, the NAFTA Dumping Panel refrained from ordering Commerce to refund deposits by West Fraser and directed West Fraser to request this relief directly from the department or from any court or panel reviewing its final determination respecting its entries (NAFTA Dumping Panel 2005).

Interestingly, the NAFTA Dumping Panel reversed its position on the practice of zeroing in light of the decision of the WTO Dumping Panel and an appellate body that the practice was inconsistent with U.S. international trade obligations. The panel subsequently ordered Commerce to recalculate the dumping margins for Canadian companies without resorting to zeroing.

Commerce responded in its third remand determination in a similar fashion as in its antidumping Section 129 determination—it continued to use zeroing but in transaction-to-transaction comparisons, which resulted in a 3.21 percent dumping margin for West Fraser and 10.52 percent margin for "all others." As a result, the antidumping order on West Fraser stayed. Canadian industry charged that both decisions (using a different method and refusing to lift the antidumping order on imports from West Fraser) violated NAFTA rules and were motivated by the U.S. desire to extend the legal battle.

The results of the antidumping margin calculation in the first three remand determinations and its Section 129 determination are presented in Table 8-5. Even though the third remand determination (to NAFTA) and the Section 129 determination used the same methodology and both determinations covered the same period, the calculated antidumping margins were different (see the last two columns of Table 8-5). Commerce explained this difference by saying it "continued to include changes made to the margin calculations that were made as a result of the prior NAFTA remand determinations" (DOC 2005b, *12*).

The results of the antidumping margin calculation in its administrative reviews are presented in Table 8-6. The major difference in the margins between the administrative reviews and the remand determinations resulted not only from the difference in the period of investigation but also in the methodologies that Commerce used in these reviews and determinations.

The Fight for a Full Refund

The call for refunding antidumping duty cash deposits to West Fraser when it was found to be dumping at a *de minimis* level was the precursor to a much bigger fight—the refund of all duty deposits after the NAFTA Extraordinary Challenge Committee (NAFTA ECC 2005) upheld the NAFTA Injury Panel's ruling of no threat of injury to the U.S. lumber industry and the NAFTA Subsidy Panel's ruling of a *de minimis* subsidy margin.

On July 14, 2003, the U.S. Bureau of Customs and Border Protection (CBP 2003) published a notice in the *Federal Register* indicating that, as required by the Byrd Amendment, it intended to distribute assessed antidumping or countervailing duties for fiscal year 2003. The notice also provided the instructions for affected domestic producers to file claims. Companies that believed they had

TABLE 8-6. Results of the U.S. Department of Commerce's Administrative Reviews of the Antidumping Duty Order on Canadian Softwood Lumber

Exporter or producer	First[a]			Second[b]			Third[b]
	Preliminary (6/14/2004)	Final (12/14/2004)	Amended final (1/12/2005)	Preliminary (6/7/2005)	Final (12/12/2005)	Amended final (2/14/2006)	Preliminary (6/12/2006)
Abitibi	2.97%	3.12%	3.12%	2.53%	2.52%	2.52%	3.47%[c]
Buchanan	4.80	4.76	4.76	2.49	2.86	2.76	3.47[c]
Canfor	2.06	1.83[d]	1.83	1.42[d]	1.36	1.35	3.47[c]
Slocan	1.64						
Tembec	10.21	10.59	9.10	3.16	4.02	4.02	1.85
Tolko	3.68	3.85	3.72	3.22	3.09	3.09	0.90
West Fraser	1.08	0.92	0.91	0.51	0.61	0.61	1.47
Weyerhaeuser	8.38	8.70	7.99	4.74	0.51	0.51	2.38
All others	3.98	4.03	3.78	2.44	2.11	2.10	3.47[c]

a. The first administrative review covered May 22, 2002, to April 30, 2003.
b. The second administrative review covered May 1, 2003, to April 30, 2004, and the third covered the following year.
c. Review-specific rate applied to many other producers as well.
d. Canfor and Slocan merged in late 2003. Canfor's margin is based on the weighted average of the premerger Canfor and Slocan margins.
Source: http://www.trade.gov/ia.

suffered as a result of competition from less expensive Canadian lumber were invited to apply for a share of the duties thus far collected.

Although the Canadian government and most Canadian companies had launched appeals in U.S. courts and under NAFTA that protected the duties, some small companies, mostly in the Atlantic provinces, had neglected to file appeals. The antidumping duties paid by these small companies would be redistributed to the Coalition for Fair Lumber Imports and U.S. lumber producers (*National Post* 2003b).

To prevent Customs from distributing the duty deposits to U.S. lumber producers, the Canadian government, along with several forestry associations, filed a lawsuit in the U.S. Court of International Trade on April 29, 2005. The suit asked the court to issue a permanent injunction prohibiting U.S. Customs from further distribution of duty deposits.

Specifically, the legal challenge pointed out that according to Section 408 of the NAFTA Implementation Act of the United States, any amendment made to Section 303 or Title VII of the Tariff Act of 1930 would apply to goods from a NAFTA country only to the extent specified in the amendment. Canadian interests argued that because the Byrd Amendment did not mention Canadian goods specifically, Customs could not distribute any duties collected from the antidumping or countervailing duty orders on Canadian goods.

Canadian interests also argued that NAFTA signatories that amended their trade remedy laws must notify other NAFTA partners, and that the United States had not taken this step. Finally, the lawsuit stated that changes to trade remedy laws affecting NAFTA partners could not be inconsistent with the WTO ruling that the Byrd Amendment was not in compliance with international trade rules.

The coalition, entering the case as an intervener, argued that the Byrd Amendment was not the type of amendment to the Tariff Act that was referred to by the NAFTA Implementation Act. It asked the court to toss out the lawsuit.

On April 7, 2006, the Court of International Trade ruled that the Byrd Amendment violated U.S. law implementing the NAFTA and, as a result, should not be applied to goods from Canada or Mexico (CIT 2006a). On July 14, the court issued a permanent injunction prohibiting the U.S. government from distributing duties collected on softwood lumber (as well as magnesium and wheat) to U.S. producers under the Byrd Amendment (CIT 2006b).

On a separate front, Congress enacted a law in December 2005 that repealed the Byrd Amendment. However, the law would not take effect until October 2007. Thus, without the court ruling in April and July, duties collected prior to October 2007 could still be distributed to U.S. producers under the Byrd Amendment.

* * *

Shortly after the NAFTA Extraordinary Challenge Committee affirmed the negative threat of injury determination on August 10, 2005, Canadian Trade

Minister Peterson called on the United States to stop collecting deposits on softwood lumber imports entering the United States and to return all deposits collected thus far to the importers of record, most of whom were affiliates of Canadian exporters.

However, on the same day, the United States indicated that it would not revoke the orders. A USTR spokeswoman stated that the ruling would have no impact on the current antidumping and countervailing duty orders, given ITC's November 2004 Section 129 determination that U.S. lumber producers were threatened with injury from Canadian imports.

ITC's November 2004 determination was issued on the same day that the United States called for a NAFTA extraordinary challenge committee. The U.S. government held that this determination was a new basis for keeping the countervailing and antidumping duty orders in place after the NAFTA Injury Panel and the committee had overturned ITC's initial threat of injury determination.

Canadian interests argued that the United States could not use a new threat of injury determination to support antidumping and countervailing duty orders after the original determination had been thrown out as unjustified. It did not make sense to them that all deposits collected under the initial orders, justified by the original threat of injury determination, would remain in the United States. As noted earlier, Tembec filed a lawsuit challenging the use of ITC's Section 129 determination in the U.S. Court of International Trade, which had not ruled before the two countries reached a Framework Agreement that eventually led to the Softwood Lumber Agreement of 2006.

The Canadian government went on the offense in trying to secure a refund of all duty deposits. On several occasions in August 2005, Prime Minister Paul Martin stated that the United States was maintaining an unacceptable position by insisting that antidumping and countervailing duty orders against Canadian lumber would remain in place and deposits would not be returned in the wake of the Extraordinary Challenge Committee decision. On September 6, the prime minister addressed the Economic Club of New York. He said,

...The softwood lumber issue is basically a disagreement between special interests in the U.S. and your national interest. Canada provides about one-third of your softwood lumber supply. We trade this commodity fairly and within the agreed rules of NAFTA. But in the last several years our firms have been charged a total of $5 billion in tariffs.

This, in spite of the fact that Canada has won panel decision after panel decision under NAFTA's process for the settlement of disputes. Recently, we won a unanimous decision which confirmed these findings—this, in NAFTA's "Final Court of Appeal," which included a majority of U.S. judges. The problem is, instead of honoring this decision, the United States has decided to ignore it.

Forgive my sudden departure from the safe language of diplomacy, but this is nonsense. More than that, it's a breach of faith. Countries must live up to their agreements. The duties must be refunded. Free trade must be fair trade.

In any business relationship, you're going to have differences of opinion, but you establish a mechanism to settle these differences, you accept the verdict, and move on. NAFTA established such a mechanism, and ignoring it hurts not just Canadians, but Americans.

... *It's clear that the U.S. approach to softwood brings into question the integrity of NAFTA in general, and the efficacy of the dispute resolution mechanism in particular.*

... The point I would make here, is that *where rules are established and agreed upon, they should be followed.* Both because it's in our mutual interest, and because of the example we can set in a world that needs the rule of law. The fact is plain: the United States itself depends as much as we do—as much as any nation does—on a liberalized global economy governed by rules that everyone can rely on. And the world is watching. No-one wants the emerging economies to emulate our worst practices. They are a bounty on trade. (Martin 2005, emphasis added)

The prime minister spoke with President Bush on the lumber issue on October 14, 2005. He again urged the United States to honor the NAFTA ruling, and if not, Canada would go to court and to the American consumers. President Bush suggested that both countries return to the negotiating table and find a solution; he also emphasized the U.S. commitment to NAFTA (McClellan 2005).

The Constitutional Challenge

On another front, the Coalition for Fair Lumber Imports carried out its threat to challenge the constitutionality of the NAFTA dispute settlement system and filed a suit with the U.S. Court of Appeals for the District of Columbia on September 13, 2005.

Both the U.S. and the Canadian governments announced their opposition to the suit. Some observers saw it as a tactical move by the coalition to pressure the Canadian and U.S. governments to negotiate. However, the coalition did not withdraw the suit after the Softwood Lumber Agreement of 2006 was implemented, even though the U.S. government thought it had a promise from the coalition to withdraw it.

Some said that the challenge should be allowed to proceed through the legal process because the U.S. administration and Canada should not surrender automatically whenever the coalition rattles its saber. Should the coalition lose, NAFTA would finally gain its authority and live up to its promise of promoting trade in North America. And if the NAFTA dispute resolution system were ruled unconstitutional, so be it—it is already effectively dead if the United States continues to take the positions it took in Lumber IV.

Summary of the Litigation

Table 8-7 summarizes the main results of litigation and issues that remained unresolved before and after April 27, 2006, when the Framework Agreement was reached. As of that date, the Canadian lumber industry had won resounding victories under NAFTA on almost all critical issues (threat of injury and subsidy) but lost or at least did not win clearly when some of the same issues were heard by the WTO panels. In particular, it did not clearly win the subsidy and the threat of injury cases in WTO. On dumping, Canadian industry won in its challenge to weighted-average to weighted-average zeroing practice in the WTO. Canada, along with other nations, won the right to retaliate if the United States did not repeal the Byrd Amendment. It also won a case in the U.S. Court of International Trade that the Byrd Amendment violated U.S. law. As of April 2006, the court had yet to make a ruling on Canada's request to compel the Bush administration to honor the rulings of the NAFTA panels and Extraordinary Challenge Committee and to refund all duty deposits collected (it did so in October 2006).

Issues that the Canadian industry did not clearly win meant victories for the Coalition for Fair Lumber Imports. Citing WTO rulings and three subsequent Section 129 determinations, the U.S. government refused to honor all rulings by NAFTA panels and the NAFTA Extraordinary Challenge Committee to revoke the countervailing and antidumping duty orders, as well as to refund duty deposits to Canadian exporters.

There were several new developments in the litigation track after April 27, 2006.

First and foremost, the court ruled twice in a challenge brought by Tembec in January 2005 on whether the United States could use ITC's Section 129 determination to refuse to revoke the original antidumping and countervailing duty orders. It said in its first ruling on the *Tembec v. United States* case, on July 21, that "the May 22, 2002 Orders are not supported by an affirmative finding of injury" (CIT 2006c, 67) and that the United States should return all of the deposits collected since November 4, 2004, plus interest. Further, the court stated in its second ruling, on October 13, 2001, that "all of Plaintiffs' unliquidated entries, including those entered before, on, and after November 4, 2004, must be liquidated in accordance with the final negative decision of the NAFTA (Injury) Panel" (CIT 2006d, 20).

The latter ruling, if it stands, means that Commerce must revoke the original countervailing and antidumping duty orders and return all duty deposits retroactively to Canadian exporters. If so, the coalition would have lost almost completely in Lumber IV. Had the ruling come out prior to April 27, the majority of Canadian industry might not have endorsed the Framework Agreement reached by the two governments.

In a news release, Deputy Assistant Trade Representative Gretchen Hamel made this statement:

> ... We believe the entry into force of the Softwood Lumber Agreement (SLA 2006) should render the case moot ...
>
> It should also be kept in mind that if there were no settlement, today's decision would certainly have been appealed, which could have meant more than another year of litigation. During that time, the United States would have continued to collect antidumping and countervailing duty deposits. Furthermore, even if the court's decision became final, the U.S. industry would almost certainly have filed new unfair trade cases. Given the soft market and the strong Canadian dollar, the margins could change significantly. As we have said all along, without the settlement, the cycle of litigation would continue with no end in sight.
>
> However, under the terms of the settlement agreement, antidumping and countervailing deposits will no longer be collected, and the duty deposits collected to date will start to be returned immediately. (USTR 2006)

The Framework Agreement notwithstanding, the U.S. government has requested that the Court of International Trade dismiss the case and vacate these rulings, while the Canadian government has argued that the rulings should stand. Concurrently, the U.S. government filed an appeal to the Court of Appeals for the Federal Circuit.[10] If the Court of International Trade does not vacate its rulings and the U.S. government loses its appeal, Canadian producers' right to a refund of full duty deposits in the future would be established. They could go straight to NAFTA in future disputes. If the court rulings are overturned by a high court, the NAFTA dispute settlement mechanism will be undermined and become impotent.

Second, as noted earlier, on July 14, 2006, the court issued a permanent injunction preventing the U.S. government from distributing duties collected on softwood lumber to U.S. producers. Third, on August 15, 2006, the WTO Dumping Compliance Appellate Panel reversed a previous WTO panel decision and ruled that transaction-to-transaction zeroing was inconsistent with WTO. These three rulings all favor the Canadian lumber industry.

Finally, on December 12, 2006, the U.S. Court of Appeals for the District of Columbia dismissed the coalition's constitutional challenge to the NAFTA dispute settlement mechanism, citing a lack of jurisdiction. The court said that, after the Softwood Lumber Agreement of 2006, there was "no determination left on which to hang our hat." The elimination of countervailing and antidumping duty orders as a result of the agreement makes the coalition's challenge a free-standing challenge to NAFTA that "Congress chose expressly not to permit." The U.S. and Canadian governments had asked the court to dismiss the case. The coalition had asked the court to make a ruling on the case (*Inside US Trade* 2006b), as did the Canadian Lumber Trade Alliance and the Ontario government—each side hoping for a different result.

There are several lessons to be learned from the legal fight in Lumber IV.

First, litigation is a long, complicated process that sometimes produces uncertain results. Lumber IV had gone on for five years, longer than the first three rounds. The U.S. investigating agencies were innovative and up to the challenge in choosing their calculation methods in responding to the WTO and NAFTA panel rulings as well as in conducting their own investigations and administrative reviews. Different rules, legal standards, and constituents in WTO, NAFTA, and U.S. courts on various issues (subsidy, threat of injury, zeroing, Byrd Amendment, constitutionality, compliance) were behind the wins and losses. No quick victory to either side contributed to the prolonging of the dispute.

Second, the NAFTA panel system is being tested. The United States used a weapon that it had not used before—restricting the power of NAFTA panels. If the current U.S. interpretation that a NAFTA panel decision has only prospective effect is not reversed by the court, U.S. industry will have an added incentive not to launch countervailing or antidumping duty petitions. Similarly, if the best they can get is to stop paying duty after a NAFTA panel rules against the United States, no Canadian or Mexican firms will go to NAFTA panels any more. Thus, without teeth, the whole NAFTA panel system will cease to be an effective and efficient avenue to settle trade disputes among the three North American countries. NAFTA Chapter 19 will be dead. On the other hand, if the two Court of International Trade rulings in the *Tembec v. United States* case stand, NAFTA Chapter 19 will be alive and well. Further, Canadian and Mexican producers likely will choose to take trade disputes with the United States straight to NAFTA.

Third, unlike other cases and contrary to some scholars' belief, WTO did not end Lumber IV, but NAFTA might. In hindsight, had Canada gone only to NAFTA panels, the United States would not have been able to use Section 129 of the Uruguay Round Agreements Act to secure a new threat of injury determination and ignore the decisions by the NAFTA Injury Panel and the Extraordinary Challenge Committee. It would have had to revoke the countervailing and antidumping duty orders after the NAFTA Injury Panel ruled in August 2004 or the Extraordinary Challenge Committee made its decision in August 2005, and the only possible costs to Canadian firms would be if the NAFTA panels' decisions were ruled by a U.S. court to have only prospective effect. Granted, the coalition could still try to get the administration to keep the duty deposits through a constitutional challenge on NAFTA. But such a challenge will not have the support of the administration and may not succeed.

Fourth, WTO tests U.S. government actions against its international obligations while the NAFTA panels ask whether the U.S. government follows its own laws. Because WTO has a much larger constituency (some 150 members), it has looser rules than NAFTA. Thus the WTO dispute settlement mechanism may not be as efficient and stringent as NAFTA's. In addition, the only remedy if Canada wins a case against the United States in WTO is to retaliate. In a country that is relatively small in economic size and has a large trade surplus with the United States, retaliation is impractical.

Finally, the softwood lumber dispute involves many producers and their legal counsels. Does the industry on either side of the border really want the dispute to continue into the foreseeable future? Is there an element of legal moral hazard? What was the lumber war all about? If Canadian lumber producers are indeed subsidized and keep some windfall profits, it might be financially better for U.S. lumber producers to buy more Canadian sawmills than to fight legal battles.

Notes

1. The coalition also alleged that a ban on the export of logs provided a benefit to Canadian softwood lumber producers. However, Commerce decided not to address this allegation in the preliminary determination because any conceivable benefit provided through a log ban would already be included in the calculation of the stumpage benefit based upon the department's selected market-based benchmark prices for stumpage, which were U.S. prices (DOC 2001a).

2. Another unintended consequence is that American duties have made Canadian firms more efficient than ever. The duties certainly hit Canadian producers hard. But with production now concentrated at the more efficient mills, Canadian producers maintained their share of the American market while still turning a thin profit. As lumber prices stayed low, the duties did not shield American producers from pain. Many U.S. producers admitted that the duties had failed and wanted to replace them with export quotas (*The Economist* 2003).

3. Since ITC found a threat of injury instead of material injury in its determination on May 2, 2002, duties could not be applied retroactively even if Commerce chose to stick with its seasonal adjustment factor and found critical circumstances in its final determination.

4. The panel unanimously ruled in ITC's favor on several technical issues. It confirmed that ITC had correctly ruled western red cedar and eastern white pine as part of a continuum of softwood lumber products, that ITC did not have to make a separate injury determination for the Maritime Provinces, and that ITC was not required to determine that the threat of injury was caused through the effects of subsidy or dumping. It remanded to ITC on whether squared-end bed frame components and flange stock were softwood lumber and requested that ITC find a better justification in considering the cross-cumulate dumping and subsidized imports in its analysis. The panel later accepted ITC's justification on these issues.

5. Therefore it was not necessary for the committee to determine whether, if the panel had committed any of the errors alleged, they would have been material to the panel's decision or threatened the integrity of the binational panel review process.

6. The panel, in its second remand decision, denied the coalition's request to allow Commerce to use the cross-border comparison method and also denied the Canadian industry's request to direct Commerce to use the first-tier benchmarks (domestic prices).

7. This rate was determined by Commerce in the first final administrative review of its countervailing duty order (see next section).

8. Both cases were later withdrawn as a condition of the Softwood Lumber Agreement of 2006.

9. Commerce's first preliminary review of the antidumping order for the period between May 22, 2002, and April 30, 2003, confirmed that West Fraser's dumping rate was *de minimis* and the rate for "other" Canadian firms was 3.98 percent (Table 8-6).

10. By filing an appeal before the Court of International Trade decides whether to vacate its rulings, the U.S. government may in fact deprive the court of its jurisdiction in the case.

TABLE 8-7. Results of the Litigation Track: What Has Been Decided and What Has Not?

Subject	Avenue	Results and further actions
		Preemptive strike
Log export restrictions	WTO	*June 2001*: Panel ruled that such restraints do not constitute "financial contribution" under definition of "subsidy" in Subsidies and Countervailing Measures Agreement and thus are not countervailable.
Section 129 of Uruguay Round Agreements Act	WTO	*June 2002*: Panel declined to rule on U.S. trade law that effectively prevents prompt reimbursement of antidumping and countervailing duties imposed in cases where WTO ruled against United States. Panel viewed U.S. law as not necessarily mandating that duties collected after adverse ruling cannot be reimbursed, implying that law gave sufficient discretion to U.S. government to promptly revoke duties. Panel did not rule whether Section 129 violated WTO rules in absence of specific instance in which it has been applied.
		Legal challenge to preliminary determination
Commerce's preliminary affirmative critical circumstance and countervailing duty determination	WTO	*September 2002*: Panel ruled against cross-border price comparison method used by Commerce in calculating countervailing duties on softwood lumber from Canada and critical circumstance determination, but upheld that Canadian stumpage was specific financial contribution to its lumber industry and thus countervailable.
		Legal challenge to final determinations
Threat of injury	NAFTA	*August 2004*: NAFTA Injury Panel, in its third ruling, ordered ITC to find negative threat-of-injury determination; ITC complied in September 2004.
	NAFTA ECC	*August 2005*: NAFTA Extraordinary Challenge Committee upheld NAFTA Injury Panel's decision (ordering ITC to reach negative threat-of-injury determination).
	WTO	*March 2004*: WTO Injury Panel found that ITC's threat-of-injury determination violated WTO rules. United States did not appeal ruling.
	ITC	*November 2004*: ITC issued new Section 129 determination (of threat of injury).
	WTO	*November 2005*: WTO Injury Compliance Panel affirmed that with ITC's Section 129 threat-of-

TABLE 8-7 (continued). Results of the Litigation Track: What Has Been Decided and What Has Not?

Subject	Avenue	Results and further actions
Threat of injury	WTO	injury determination, United States had complied with WTO Injury Panel's ruling of March 2004. *April 2006*: WTO Injury Compliance Appellate Panel reversed finding by WTO Injury Compliance Panel that United States had complied with WTO Injury Panel ruling of March 2004. However, it did not make ruling on whether ITC's Section 129 determination was consistent with U.S. obligations under WTO antidumping and countervailing rules, because it did not have enough information to make such decision.
	NAFTA	*February 2005*: Canada filed challenge to ITC's Section 129 threat-of-injury determination under NAFTA. Case was withdrawn after Softwood Lumber Agreement of 2006 was implemented.
	U.S. Court of International Trade	*January 2005*: Tembec filed challenge to ITC's Section 129 threat-of-injury determination. *July 2006*: Court ruled that Commerce's May 22, 2002, antidumping and countervailing duty orders were not supported by affirmative finding of injury and that United States was obliged to return all deposits collected since November 4, 2004, with interest. *October 2006*: Court ruled that all duty deposits collected before, on, or after November 4, 2004, be returned in accordance with final negative decision of NAFTA Injury Panel.
Countervailing duty (subsidy)	NAFTA	*August 2003*: NAFTA Subsidy Panel affirmed Commerce's findings that stumpage was actionable subsidy but questioned cross-border price comparison method Commerce used. *November 2005*: Commerce made *de minimis* subsidy determination in its fifth remand determination. *March 2006*: Panel accepted Commerce's fifth remand determination of *de minimis* subsidy. *April 2006*: United States filed NAFTA extraordinary challenge. *May 2006*: NAFTA extraordinary challenge process was suspended.

TABLE 8-7 (continued). Results of the Litigation Track: What Has Been Decided and What Has Not?

Subject	Avenue	Results and further actions
Countervailing duty (subsidy)	U.S. Court of International Trade	*May 2006*: Two Ontario forestry associations challenged suspension of NAFTA extraordinary challenge process. *July 2006*: Court dismissed case brought by two Ontario forestry associations challenging suspension of NAFTA extraordinary challenge process.
	WTO	*August 2003*: WTO Subsidy Panel ruled in similar way as another WTO panel on Commerce's preliminary affirmative countervailing duty determination of August 9, 2001 (see above). *January 2004:* WTO Subsidy Appellate Panel found that if domestic prices in Canada were distorted, Commerce could seek alternative price benchmark if new benchmark were informative about Canadian market conditions. However, it did not issue findings on whether Canadian domestic prices were distorted or whether cross-border prices used by Commerce were proper benchmark. It sustained one minor Canadian claim that Commerce should consider whether subsidy was passed through to independent lumber producers if tenured producer sold government-origin logs to these producers. *August 2005*: WTO Subsidy Compliance Panel found Commerce failed to conduct required pass-through analysis in its Section 129 determination and in its first administrative review. United States appealed in September 2005. *December 2005*: WTO Subsidy Compliance Appellate Panel rejected U.S. appeal. Canada secured retaliatory right of C$200 million against United States.
	Commerce	*December 2004*: Commerce completed its first final administrative review of countervailing duty order, establishing subsidy rate of 16.4 percent as of February 2005. *December 2005*: Commerce completed its second final administrative review of countervailing duty order, establishing new subsidy rate of 8.7 percent. *June 2006*: Commerce completed its third preliminary administrative review of countervailing duty order, establishing new subsidy rate of 11.23 percent.

TABLE 8-7 (continued). Results of the Litigation Track: What Has Been Decided and What Has Not?

Subject	Avenue	Results and further actions
Countervailing duty (subsidy)	NAFTA	*January 2005*: Canadian parties initiated NAFTA panel review of Commerce's first administrative review of countervailing duty order and later requested NAFTA panel review of Commerce's second administrative review. Both cases were withdrawn based on Softwood Lumber Agreement of 2006.
Antidumping duty	NAFTA	*July 2003*: NAFTA Dumping Panel affirmed Commerce's usage of "zeroing" in calculating dumping margins and remanded some general issues and many company-specific issues to Commerce.
	Commerce	*April 2004*: Commerce refused to revoke antidumping duty order on West Fraser, whose dumping margin was found to be *de minimis*, and to refund cash deposits collected from West Fraser. Commerce stated that NAFTA panels lacked equity power of U.S. court and could not order Commerce to refund cash duty deposits retroactively.
	NAFTA	*June 2005*: NAFTA panel reversed its position and ruled that zeroing was unlawful. It also ruled that ITC should revoke antidumping duty order on West Fraser.
	Commerce	*July 2005*: Commerce developed transaction-to-transaction comparison method and continued to use zeroing. It found that West Fraser's dumping margin was above *de minimis* and thus did not revoke antidumping order on West Fraser. NAFTA panel had yet to rule on Commerce's third antidumping remand determination when case was withdrawn based on Softwood Lumber Agreement of 2006.
	Commerce	*December 2004*: Commerce completed its first administrative review of antidumping duty order, establishing rate of 3.8 percent for "all other" Canadian producers as of January 2005. *December 2005*: Commerce completed its second administrative review of antidumping duty order, setting rate of 2.1 percent for "all other" Canadian producers as of January 2006.

TABLE 8-7 (continued). Results of the Litigation Track: What Has Been Decided and What Has Not?

Subject	Avenue	Results and further actions
Antidumping duty	Commerce	*June 2006*: Commerce completed third preliminary administrative review of antidumping order, finding 3.47 percent rate for most Canadian producers.
	U.S. Court of International Trade	*January 2005*: Canadian firms initiated court review of first antidumping administrative review results. Case was withdrawn based on Softwood Lumber Agreement of 2006.
	WTO	*April 2004*: WTO Dumping Panel ruled that Commerce had improperly used zeroing in calculating dumping rates and rejected most claims by Canada. *August 2004*: WTO Dumping Appellate Panel sustained ruling of WTO Dumping Panel.
	Commerce	*April 2005*: Commerce issued Section 129 antidumping determination based on transaction-to-transaction comparison method that resulted in 11.54 percent dumping margins for "all other" Canadian producers. Commerce stated that United States had implemented recommendations and ruling of WTO Dumping Appellate Panel in April 2004. Canada appealed to WTO.
	WTO	*April 2006*: WTO Dumping Compliance Panel ruled that Commerce's Section 129 antidumping determination was not inconsistent with WTO rules, affirming Commerce's zeroing method in transaction-to-transaction calculation of antidumping duties. *August 2006*: WTO Dumping Compliance Appellate Panel reversed WTO Dumping Compliance Panel ruling of April 2006. Commerce's zeroing method in transaction-to-transaction calculation of antidumping duties was ruled WTO-inconsistent.
	NAFTA	*March 2006*: Canadian firms requested NAFTA panel review of Commerce's Section 129 antidumping determination. Case was withdrawn based on Softwood Lumber Agreement of 2006.
Constitutional challenge		
NAFTA dispute settlement system	U.S. Court of Appeals, D.C.	*September 2005*: Coalition for Fair Lumber Imports filed lawsuit to challenge constitutionality of NAFTA binational dispute system. *December 2006*: Court dismissed lawsuit.

TABLE 8-7 (continued). Results of the Litigation Track: What Has Been Decided and What Has Not?

Subject	Avenue	Results and further actions
	Challenge to Byrd Amendment	
Byrd Amendment	U.S. Court of International Trade	*May 2005*: Canada sought permanent injunction from court preventing U.S. Customs from distributing cash duty deposits collected from Canadian lumber producers based on Byrd Amendment. *April 2006*: Court ruled that U.S. law implementing NAFTA forbids Byrd Amendment from being applied to imports from Canada and Mexico. *July 2006*: Court issued permanent injunction preventing duty deposits collected on Canadian softwood lumber from being distributed to U.S. producers.
	WTO	*September 2002*: WTO panel determined that Byrd Amendment was not consistent with WTO rules. *January 2003*: WTO appellate panel upheld key panel findings against Byrd Amendment. WTO arbitrator subsequently gave United States 11 months (until December 27, 2003) to bring its measure into compliance. United States failed to meet deadline. *January 2004*: Dispute settlement body considered requests for retaliation authorization made by Canada and European Union, Brazil, Chile, India, Japan, Mexico, and South Korea. *August 2004*: WTO arbitrator ruled that Canada and 10 other countries could retaliate against United States on up to 72% of annual level of U.S. antidumping and countervailing duties collected with their respective exports and disbursed under Byrd Amendment. *March 2005*: Canada announced it would retaliate by applying 15 percent surtax on imports of live swine, cigarettes, oysters, and certain specialty fish (live ornamental fish and certain frozen fish) from United States. Implementation of duties began May 1, 2005.
	Congress	*December 2005*: Congress repealed Byrd Amendment, effective October 2007.

9

Lumber IV

The Negotiation Track, 2001–2006

Although expecting a fight, Canadian interests were shocked by the intensity of the first salvo by the Coalition for Fair Lumber Imports when on April 2, 2001, it charged Canada with "predatory" trade practices and alleged a subsidy and dumping rate of 68 to 78 percent, which amounted to almost the value of Canada's softwood lumber exports. One trade official compared it to a nuclear first strike (*Vancouver Sun* 2001e).

Initial Engagements

The calls for negotiation resurfaced soon after the Department of Commerce made its preliminary affirmative countervailing duty determination in August 2001. In the ensuing years, both the Coalition for Fair Lumber Imports and Canadian producers tried to take advantage of the most recent rulings in litigation to leverage their negotiating positions.

Canadian Prime Minister Jean Chrétien and President George W. Bush met on April 20, 2001, in Québec City, and they spoke again a few days after Commerce's preliminary countervailing duty determination. On both occasions, the lumber issue was raised. Chrétien stated that Bush understood Canada's position that the latest punitive duties on lumber were unfair and knew "that it is not the right thing to do." He said he was convinced the U.S. president would resolve the issue "eventually" but noted that the U.S. government system, with power divided between the White House and Congress, could be unwieldy (*Toronto Star* 2001c). He later said, "Apparently the President does not have the same direct impact on his ministers and departments that fortunately we have in Canada" (*Vancouver Sun* 2001f).

Aside from appealing the preliminary countervailing duty determination to the World Trade Organization, Canada planned a public relations campaign in the United States, but the terrorist attacks on September 11 forced Canada to suspend the campaign. Furthermore, for a few months, producers and government officials on both sides of the border became more conciliatory. It was in this environment that officials from both countries met twice, in Toronto and Washington, D.C., in September and started to negotiate. When President Bush and Prime Minister Chrétien met for the third time in Washington in late September to discuss defense and security issues, they talked briefly on softwood lumber again. On October 16, President Bush named his long-time confidant and former Montana Governor Marc Racicot as special envoy to try to broker a settlement in the lumber dispute with Canada. There was speculation that Bush wanted the softwood dispute off the table so that the two countries could focus on security issues.

On September 27, 2001, Doman Industries Ltd., the second-largest lumber producer in coastal British Columbia, proposed an interim 15 percent export tax on lumber shipped to the United States whenever lumber prices fell below US$250/mbf while both sides tried to work out a permanent deal. The proposal was rejected by Ontario and Québec, and the Canadian government did not take it seriously, citing no consensus in the country.

On October 15, B.C. Forests Minister Mike de Jong delivered a package of forest policy changes to U.S. officials, aimed at putting to rest concerns that the forestry industry in British Columbia was subsidized and helping B.C. companies become "more competitive, more dynamic, and ideally, more profitable." The proposed policy changes were these:

- auctioning off 13 percent of its timber and setting the price for the remaining Crown timber on those auction sales and other factors;
- eliminating cut controls and processing requirements;
- eliminating companies' ability to "blend" stumpage rates for high-value timber with stumpage for low-value timber;
- ending below-cost timber sales, which encourage harvesting of uneconomic timber;
- awarding long-term tenures on the basis of competitive bids;
- permitting long-term tenures to be subdivided and transferred freely, opening up competition for tenures;
- eliminating mill closure regulations; and
- eliminating the forest industry from Job Protection Commission assistance, which has been used to aid companies in gaining financial help and to keep them operating in market downturns.

Although the package did not specify elimination of the provincial log export restrictions, it mentioned that the policy changes would "free up the flow of fiber." Québec made a similar proposal. Ontario informally considered using prices in two U.S. states—Michigan and Minnesota—as the basis for calculating its stumpage but decided not to go that far for fear of adverse consequences for Canada's legal case.

The B.C. package failed to win the coalition's approval. John Ragosta said he was watching closely as the B.C. government prepared to revamp its forest policy and trying to be helpful. He praised British Columbia's planned forest policy changes but cautioned that unless the province abandoned its stumpage system in favor of timber auction, the changes would only make matters worse (*National Post* 2001b).

Some Canadian industry observers believed the real issue was that some U.S. producers, burdened with inefficient mills and dwindling timber supplies, were simply trying to drive up lumber prices by cutting down on supply. Reid Carter of National Bank Financial said that U.S. producers "want to keep us out of the market, not become more competitive." Douglas McArthur, a senior fellow in public policy at the University of British Columbia and a former senior B.C. government official involved in Lumber III, stated that the only reasonable option for Canada was to take the lumber fight to WTO and NAFTA. He said,

> Consistently, for the last 10 years or more, the Americans have been trying to put a cap on our share of the market at around 30 percent. U.S. negotiators insist what they really want is a free market in Canada, but that's the trap ... Now that negotiations are going, the Americans—and they're good at this—will start their threats. We have never won at these negotiations.... British Columbia should not be trying to satisfy the Americans by changing the way it runs its forests. The U.S. lobby will never be satisfied. (*National Post* 2001b)

On November 6, Racicot held talks with Canadian Trade Minister Pierre Pettigrew in Ottawa and indicated that he wanted to resolve the thorny softwood lumber dispute within 45 days. He still had not succeeded when, in January 2002, he assumed the chairmanship of the Republican National Committee. When the news broke on December 5, 2001, that Governor Racicot had been appointed as the party chairman, there was a sense of urgency and desire to get a deal done before he left for his new post. For its part, Commerce released a six-page U.S. position paper, which listed what the U.S. lumber industry wanted:

- competitive, open markets in timber sales;
- B.C. logs open to export;
- the end to long-term tenures that lock up timber supply;
- elimination of cut controls that force companies to harvest irrespective of market conditions; and
- elimination of requirements that companies process the timber they harvest.

The main differences between the U.S. position paper and the B.C. package were items 1 (open markets in timber sales) and 3 (end to long-term tenures). There was speculation that the B.C. government might be able to ease log export restrictions gradually (item 2), and the other two items were included in the B.C. package.

The B.C. forest industry would object to dismantling the long-term tenures and would likely ask for compensation if the government did so. Would the compensation be seen as a subsidy, and would B.C. taxpayers agree to foot the bill? Furthermore, many industry observers, including the president of U.S.-based Louisiana-Pacific Corporation, Mark Suwyn, suggested that a free bidding process would lead stumpage prices down rather than up, since the vast majority of Canadian wood—particularly in regions of British Columbia where considerable excess costs were being levied—would only have one freight bidder (*The Free Trader* 2001). Third, one or a few bidders would hardly constitute a competitive market. Finally, auctions have resulted in huge losses from timber sales for the U.S. Forest Service, and neither the public nor the coalition would tolerate such a result in Canada.

Most importantly, even if Canadian provinces made necessary forest policy reforms under some kind of agreement made by the two governments, Canadian producers could still face complaints from U.S. producers and possibly punitive trade actions, and the U.S. government could not do much about them, because under U.S. law, American producers are guaranteed the right to file countervailing and antidumping complaints. The U.S. position paper did not raise the possibility of legislated changes exempting softwood lumber from complaints. Instead, it listed only three possible remedies:

- The U.S. industry signs letters stating that the proposed Canadian policy changes remove any injury to them.
- The U.S. industry waives its statutory rights to file complaints, an option that would be hard to enforce.
- Both countries establish a bilateral panel that would review Canada's reforms and issue opinions on whether a countervailable subsidy still exists. However, industry in both countries would have to waive its rights as well.

Given their experience with a no-injury-letter under the Softwood Lumber Agreement, some Canadian producers did not see how such a letter would prevent the coalition from possibly launching another countervailing duty petition in the future. The other two options were impractical as well. Referring to the U.S. position paper, David Gray, cochair of the Free Trade Lumber Council, said,

> The U.S. government is finally saying what we have been observing for a while: The U.S. Commerce Department isn't really driving the bus. Any deal is not going to be between the Canadian and American governments. The U.S. lumber industry is going to have their pound of flesh anyway you put it.... The power the U.S. industry exerts over any long-term solution is reason enough for Canada to seek a World Trade Organization ruling, rather than negotiating with the U.S. government. (*Vancouver Sun* 2001g)

The four major timber-producing provinces soon made their position public: They could make a symmetrical deal with the United States that involved policy changes for unfettered access to the U.S. market, with each country making changes backed by legislation (*Vancouver Sun* 2001g). However, the word "legislation" was absent from the U.S. position paper.

The U.S. position paper also offered the same commitments to refrain from imposing restraints under Section 301 and 201 cases it offered Canada as part of the 1996 Softwood Lumber Agreement. It further stated that the United States could terminate the current countervailing and antidumping duty investigations only if the domestic industry agreed to withdraw the petition. The coalition opposed terminating the current investigations and favored suspending them, which would allow the U.S. government to reapply the duties at current levels if a deal could not be reached.

On January 22, 2002, the coalition submitted to the U.S. Trade Representative several combinations of potential forest policy reforms by Canadian provinces in three areas—timber pricing systems, tenure policies governing which companies could purchase provincial timber rights, and laws mandating minimum cuts or requiring that mills remain open. The coalition stated that its preferred option for British Columbia was setting two-thirds of its timber up for auction and lifting its log export ban, even though it was not countervailable under WTO rules (*Inside US Trade* 2002a).

Canadians, on the other hand, waited for an official response and counterproposal from the United States. When none was forthcoming, B.C. Forests Minister Mike de Jong said the United States had treated Canada "despicably." On February 13, the coalition formally rejected the province's offer to settle, saying the proposal "does not address substantive issues of timber subsidy and dumping" and nothing short of "a large majority" of provincial timber put up for auction would end the dispute. In the end, it offered Canada three options:

- eliminating policies that the coalition said protected the Canadian lumber industry;
- imposing an interim agreement—a border tax and export-volume restrictions were two possibilities—to eliminate U.S. concerns while reforms were negotiated; or
- facing the "full vigor" of U.S. trade law (*Gazette* 2002a).

The official U.S. position was to do a suspension agreement before February 19, 2002, 30 days prior to its final countervailing and antidumping duty determinations in order to make it legal. At a February 19 meeting between officials from the two countries, the United States proposed to use a cross-reference system that compared prices between the countries, between provinces, or between different parts of a single province. The Canadian industry did not agree to a cross-reference system that would use U.S. prices. Interestingly, the coalition was also skeptical of the cross-reference proposal, since it was uncomfortable with cross-province and in-province price comparisons (*Inside US Trade* 2002a).

When the February 19 deadline expired, U.S. officials reinterpreted that the deadline should be March 21. On February 25, Prime Minister Chrétien told Parliament that President Bush was extremely aware of the lumber problem and that they both hoped to find a solution. In the following weeks, negotiations intensified.

On March 9, the United States offered an agreement framework that would suspend the imposition of countervailing and antidumping duties on Canadian exports by having the Canadian government impose an export tax. The framework also called for a binational lumber working group to monitor the implementation of both countries' commitments under the agreement. Canada, on the other hand, was more interested in a short-term agreement that would allow further negotiations toward a durable solution to end the softwood dispute. Canada objected to the U.S. proposal partly because under the U.S. antidumping statute, "substantially all" (85 percent) of the exporters had to agree to such a deal for it to take effect, and at least two large lumber exporters in Canada had vowed to reject it. The two sides also disagreed over the size of the export tax (the coalition was pushing for 50 percent), how long it would be in place, what the effect would be to Canada's legal challenge to the U.S. duties in WTO and NAFTA, and what role the binational lumber working group would play (*Inside US Trade* 2002c).

A new element in the March 9 document was that the United States offered to issue a policy bulletin through Commerce within one year of signing the agreement that would outline its methodology for calculating stumpage subsidies and dumping margins in future trade cases. This would provide guidelines for Canadian exporters on how to avoid dumping allegations and for provinces on how to structure their stumpage policies to avoid subsidy allegations.

Canadian industry groups were reluctant to sign on to the policy bulletin without seeing it. Furthermore, they doubted it provided the necessary assurances, since the U.S. proposal offered a commitment only to consult with Canada in the context of the proposed binational working group before issuing, rescinding, or modifying the policy bulletin; it did not promise the bulletin would be binding. Finally, there was no guarantee that Commerce would calculate antidumping or countervailing duty the same way the next time, since it could say that the circumstances were different and that the guidelines it used previously no longer applied (*Inside US Trade* 2002c).

On March 21, 2002, U.S. officials proposed an export tax on a sliding scale ranging from 19.3 to 32.9 percent, and Canada proposed an export tax that ranged from 0 to 15 percent. The coalition rejected Canada's offer of an interim agreement that included a variable export tax, forest policy reform, and the coalition's withdrawal of legal challenge. Canada rejected a last-minute U.S. offer that Canada self-impose a 19.3 percent export duty for five years and drop its complaints to WTO.

Thus, discussion of a suspension agreement broke off March 22. In a follow-up news conference, Senator Baucus said, "The message for our good friends in

Canada is clear: The U.S. will not tolerate Canadian lumber protectionism." Rusty Wood, chairman of the Coalition for Fair Lumber Imports, said, "Truth is on our side. That's why this battle is so easy for us" (CBC News 2002).

More Proposals to Settle

Commerce made its final affirmative determination of subsidy and dumping at a combined rate of 29 percent (which was later reduced to 27.22 percent in May 2002) on Canadian softwood lumber imports on March 21, 2002. Soon there-after, the Coalition for Fair Lumber Imports approached the U.S. government about restarting negotiations with Canada. Its draft proposal, dated April 18, 2002, called for a withdrawal of the antidumping duties against Canadian pro-ducers and substituting a variable tax mechanism based on lumber price. Under this proposal, the base lumber price would be set at US$327/mbf; no taxes would be paid if the actual price was equal to or greater than the base price; if the actual price was $20 below the base, a 5 percent tax would apply; if the actual price was $30 below it, a 10 percent tax would apply; if the actual price was $40 below it, a 14 percent tax would apply (*The Free Trader* 2002a).

In addition, the proposal would require Canada to collect a 19.34 percent export tax on all Canadian lumber exports to the United States. To suspend the export tax, Canadian provinces would have to either auction more than 65 percent of their timber annually or increase their stumpage by the amount determined by Commerce.

The coalition's offer was seen as more regressive than the U.S. position of March 21. For one thing, it would force Canadian exporters to pay fees that would, based on 2001 price data, average 28 percent. In addition, it appeared to be designed to ensure that decisions reached by Commerce would become per-manent, beyond both appeal and dispute settlement. Not surprisingly, there was little interest in Canada to start the negotiation on these terms.

On May 1, 2002, the B.C. Lumber Trade Council proposed a three-tier export tax system (20 percent if lumber price index was equal or less than US$290/mbf, 15 percent when it was between $290 and $380/mbf, and 0 per-cent when it was equal to or greater than 380/mbf) with some exemptions on most of the valuable lumber products and remanufactured lumber. The Free Trade Lumber Council called the B.C. council's proposal a nonstarter (*The Free Trader* 2002b).

All eyes turned to the U.S. International Trade Commission, which was expected to rule whether U.S. producers were injured by Canadian lumber imports. On March 22, 2002, 51 U.S. senators wrote a letter to ITC Chairman Stephen Koplan "to express the need for action by the ITC regarding Canadian softwood lumber." The senators "expect a strict application of the law in those instances where a specific Canadian province is found to have subsidized lum-ber or dumped lumber on the U.S. market" (Baucus 2002). On May 2, 2002, by a vote of four to zero, ITC ruled that Canadian lumber imports threatened to injure the U.S. lumber industry. A 27.22 percent tariff was applied on Canadian lumber after May 22, 2002.

On August 2, 2002, Québec Premier Bernard Landry joined B.C. Premier Gordon Campbell in calling on the Canadian government to "reinitiate" negotiations with the United States. Some Canadian producers were unsure whether reinitiation of negotiations would have any positive results because of the way negotiations had fallen apart in March. American Consumers for Affordable Homes was also suspicious of new talks, for a different reason. It feared the Canadian government, bowing to pressure from British Columbia, would agree to include an export tax. The consumer group was backing a resolution sponsored by 10 U.S. senators that called for Commerce and the U.S. Trade Representative to ensure that the WTO and NAFTA panels reviewing the lumber duties were not delayed. It also called on President Bush to continue discussions with Canada to "promote open trade between the United States and Canada on softwood lumber free of trade restraints that harm consumers" (*Inside US Trade* 2002d).

With the support of the coalition, Commerce proposed, on August 23, a new approach to defuse the softwood lumber fight with Canada that involved reducing existing countervailing duties on Canadian lumber from individual provinces as they made changes to timber policies that the United States considered illegal subsidies. This approach entailed unilateral actions by the United States under existing law that could be done on a province-by-province basis (*Inside US Trade* 2002e).

The centerpiece of this new approach was a to-be-developed policy bulletin, originally proposed on March 9. The bulletin would provide a "road map" for provinces to reform their forest policy in return for a changed-circumstances review by Commerce, with the possibility that they would get a lower or zero countervailing duty rate.

British Columbia was again most receptive to the new approach. Other Canadian provinces were doubtful and feared that it could be used as a strategy to initiate a backroom deal with British Columbia in order to put pressure on other provinces to change their timber policies. They also feared that the new approach could be used to develop a fallback mechanism for calculating the countervailing duty margin apart from comparing provincial prices to prices in the States, and the United States would use it to buttress its legal arguments in WTO and NAFTA. The coalition dismissed as ridiculous the notion that the new approach was aimed only at bolstering its legal case by pointing out the longtime U.S. position—that reforms in the areas of tenure, stumpage, and mandates would lead to fair-market prices in Canada (*Inside US Trade* 2002f).

On November 20, 2002, Steven Rogel, CEO and president of Weyerhaeuser Company, which was the largest softwood lumber producer in North America and had operations in both countries, offered a Weyerhaeuser Company (2002) proposal. First, immediately establish a sliding border tax on softwood lumber exports, starting at 25 percent and dropping to zero as the price rises, end countervailing and antidumping duties, and halt all petition, litigation, and appeals. Second, negotiate changes in Canada's log-pricing practices to more closely mirror those in the United States. Rogel also called for an "equitable distribution of Canadian funds already deposited" since May 2002 and an exemption of the export tax for some products, such as western red cedar, of which Weyerhaeuser was a major producer.

In responding to a question from a reporter in the news conference announcing the proposal, Rogel stated that he had talked to coalition members but declined to say what they thought about his proposals. Soon, Ragosta stated that he liked the proposal. Susan Casey-Lefkowitz, a senior lawyer for the Natural Resources Defense Council, also liked it (*National Post* 2002).

The Weyerhaeuser proposal failed to win support from the Canadian government, however. Minister Pettigrew said, "It goes against everything that has been part of the consensus that we have built for almost three years now. We shouldn't impose on ourselves border measures that would actually legitimize what the Americans have been doing, which we've been saying for a long time is unfair" (*Gazette* 2002b).

The proposal did not win much support in British Columbia, either. While agreeing with Rogel that "a hell of a lot of people are going to pay a hell of a price" if Canada chooses to rely on legal remedies to fight its case and thus "it is preferable to try to negotiate a mutually agreeable long-term deal," B.C. Forests Minister Mike de Jong was opposed "to unreasonable U.S. demands." John Allan, president of the B.C. Lumber Trade Council, said the border tax was too high (*National Post* 2002).

In early December 2002, British Columbia floated yet another proposal of its own, calling for a variable export tax system topping out at 17.5 percent (17.5, 12.5, 7.5, 2.5, and 0 percent when monthly lumber prices were below US$290/mbf, between $290 and $320/mbf, between $320 and $350/mbf, between $350 and $380/mbf, and above $380/mbf, respectively), a withdrawal of the antidumping duty order, and the refund of all duty deposits. The proposal did not call for a U.S. withdrawal of the countervailing duty order or a termination of Canada's legal challenge. Although the coalition did not endorse the B.C. proposal, as lumber prices continued to fall despite U.S. duties reaching 27.2 percent on Canadian lumber, it renewed its call for a negotiated interim settlement in a December 12, 2002, letter to Commerce Under Secretary Grant Aldonas (*Inside US Trade* 2003a).

Nearly a Deal

After initial engagements, various parties nearly came up with an agreement in 2003, ending or more likely suspending the two-decade-long lumber dispute. An impetus for resolution was that producers on both sides of the border were hurt by a continued slump in lumber prices (*The Economist* 2003). In addition, the intention of the U.S. Customs and Border Protection to distribute a small portion of the duties collected, and the lack of prospects for a quick and clear victory to either side in litigation provided incentive to negotiate. Finally, Canadian politics played a role in the 2003 negotiations.

On January 6, 2003, Commerce published the first draft of a policy bulletin. Under Secretary of Commerce Aldonas spearheaded the efforts. Aldonas, a lawyer representing British Columbia in Lumber III, had been one of the most involved U.S. government officials in Lumber IV before he left the U.S. government in early 2005. He understood the industry positions in both countries and had an interest in finding a long-term, durable solution to the dispute.

In February 2003, he tried to explore the possibility of "marrying" the reform proposal with an interim agreement that would substitute a sliding scale export tax for U.S. duties. To this end, he organized a summit of CEOs from both sides of the border in Washington, D.C. The summit, in Weyerhaeuser Company CEO Rogel's words, was "candid and constructive." No numbers (on the level of export tax) were raised in the discussion, and government officials were present, although American Consumers for Affordable Homes charged that the meeting would be a price-fixing game by industry representatives.

On January 28, days before the summit, Senator Craig, along with 10 other senators, introduced a bill (S. 219) in Congress that would, in effect, double the combined antidumping and countervailing duty rate to 45 percent. Craig and others acknowledged that this action was a pressure tactic aimed at getting Canada back to the negotiating table (*Congressional Record* 2003).

On February 5, Commerce issued a second draft of its policy bulletin. Like the first draft, it retained an "effects test" stating that "changes in policies and practice per se will not be the basis for the department findings; rather, that the changes result in the increased operation of market forces." Commerce would examine whether individual provinces had eliminated policies and practices as part of a changed-circumstances review. The bulletin envisioned different reference pricing schemes for the three largest timber-producing provinces (British Columbia, Québec, and Ontario), the first based on auction sales, the second on private sales in the province or in other jurisdictions, and the third on use of a cross-border comparison methodology in which the reference price would be based on prices in the United States. The policy bulletin indicated that a 270-day period for the changed-circumstances review would not begin until all provinces had made necessary reforms.

Canadian industry and governments, on the other hand, wanted a binational panel of experts to determine whether provinces had implemented policy reforms as stated in the bulletin. Canadian interests feared that the Coalition for Fair Lumber Imports would make the changed-circumstances review (*Inside US Trade* 2003b). They also disagreed that all provinces had to make reforms before the review could start.

Initially, the interim solutions and long-term solutions were tied together. In late March, Aldonas indicated that Commerce might publish the policy bulletin without an interim agreement, which boiled down to numbers (tax rates) that the industry on both sides of the border could not agree on. The coalition assumed that the Canadian provinces were unlikely to agree to a deal once the policy bulletin was published. Later, it floated a more nuanced argument, that the policy bulletin should not be final until an interim agreement was reached. Publishing the policy bulletin would not make it final, since its publication would trigger a 30-day period for public comments. These comments could be used to change the policy bulletin. Once that 30-day period was up, Commerce faced no statutory requirements to finalize the bulletin (*Inside US Trade* 2003c).

Commerce published the policy bulletin in the *Federal Register* on June 24, 2003. It did not include a model for Québec. The bulletin stated that provinces must auction a "substantial portion" of their timber and use the resulting prices as a basis for pricing the remainder of the timber. However, it did not specify an amount of timber that must be auctioned. Although some Canadian industry representatives argued that auctioning 20 percent of timber should suffice, Aldonas indicated that this might not be enough. The coalition proposed that two-thirds be auctioned (*Inside US Trade* 2003e). Interestingly, the amount of timber being auctioned in U.S. markets did not even approach this threshold.

* * *

In early 2003, a new U.S. industry group, the Value Added Wood Products Alliance, which represented lumber remanufacturers, including makers of mobile homes, wood trusses, and others, changed its position in the dispute. Many of the same firms represented by the alliance had backed duties on Canadian lumber in 2001. But in February 2003, the alliance asked the coalition to soften its position and accept a quick end to the softwood battle. The reason was that the duties created an incentive for Canadian producers to get into the remanufacturing business and ship to the U.S. duty-free, and U.S. remanufacturers now had Canadian competition (*National Post* 2003a).

Canadian and U.S. officials held talks in February 2003, but they quickly broke off. The negotiations were unable to crack two critical issues: the level of an interim export tax pending longer term measures, and the return of any of the US\$1 billion in duties collected so far to Canadian companies.

The coalition sought a rate as high as 25 percent to replace the then-current 27 percent U.S. duties. The Canadian side was based on the B.C. proposal and pushed for a cap at 18 percent. Canadian producers wanted the United States to return all duties it collected, while American producers wanted the money to go to them. The U.S. government proposed using part of the duties to fund a new council that would monitor future trade (*Toronto Star* 2003).

U.S. and Canadian officials met again on May 15, 2003, when another U.S. proposal that would link an export tax on Canadian imports to Canada's share of the U.S. lumber market surfaced. The proposal had two options. The first option specified a 25 percent export tax if Canada's share of the U.S. market was 29 percent or more in the previous two quarters and a 15 percent export tax otherwise (*Inside US Trade* 2003d).

Under the second option, Canadian lumber would be hit with an 18 percent export tax if Canada's market share reached 29 percent. For every point Canada's market share increased, its export tax would increase 3 percent, and for every percentage point below 29 percent that Canada's market share fell, the export tax would be reduced by 4 percent. This meant that if Canada's market share were 34 or 35 percent, where it had hovered for a decade, the export tax would be 33 or 36 percent, respectively, and there would be no export tax on Canadian imports if Canada's share was 24 percent (*Inside US Trade* 2003d). In addition, the coalition wanted to keep the duties collected so far. This proposal was immediately rejected by Minister Pettigrew, who called it "laughable" (*Ottawa Citizen* 2003).

In response, Canada proposed, on May 22, that if the Canadian share of the U.S. market fell below 30.8 percent (or about 91 percent of the actual Canadian share in 2002, 34 percent, which was roughly 17.1 bbf/year), Canadian producers would not face any export tax. For the next 2.1 percent of U.S. market share, exports would be assessed a US$25/mbf tax, which would increase to $50/mbf for the next 2.1 percent of U.S. market share. Once Canadian lumber accounted for 35 percent of U.S. market share, the export tax would be prohibitively high, at $100/mbf. Finally, Canada wanted the United States to refund all the duties collected and drop its trade cases once the interim agreement took effect. In return, Canada would end its legal challenges in WTO and NAFTA.

The proposal would cover the Maritime Provinces. In late May 2003, producers from these provinces, along with Canada's independent lumber producers from Québec, Ontario, Manitoba, and Alberta (under the name of Canadian Lumber Remanufacturers' Alliance), called on Minister Pettigrew to withdraw this offer. Traditionally, independent producers accounted for some 5 to 10 percent of Canada's softwood lumber trade with the United States (*Canada Newswire* 2003).

The coalition, through Commerce, countered the Canadian offer in June 2003 with a 13 percent tax on all lumber exports to the United States until those exports equaled 29.7 percent of the U.S. market. After that, Canadian exports would be assessed an export tax of US$175/mbf. This would amount to a 50 percent tax if lumber prices were about $350/mbf, and 70 percent if lumber prices were $250/mbf. Such a tax would practically lock Canada's share at about 30 percent. The U.S. proposal was to keep two-thirds of the duty deposits and return the rest to Canadian exporters (*Inside US Trade* 2003e).

As noted in the previous chapter, in July 2003 U.S. Customs (CBP 2003) indicated that it intended to distribute duties received for fiscal year 2003 in connection with antidumping and countervailing duty orders and findings. The notice applied to several million dollars (of C$1.6 billion collected by then) of antidumping duties that some small companies had neglected to protect

(*National Post* 2003b). This notice might have instilled in some Canadians a sense of urgency for a negotiated settlement. At the end of July 2003, Aldonas and the Canadian lumber negotiator, Doug Waddell, agreed to make an interim agreement, subject to the approval of their respective domestic industry and governments. The agreement was on these terms:

- a fee-free base (of Canadian lumber, about 16.8 bbf) up to 30 percent of U.S. share;
- a US$50/mbf fee between 30 and 30.99 percent, a $75/mbf fee between 31 and 32.5 percent, and a $125/mbf fee above 32.5 percent;
- a five-year term;
- a policy bulletin with exit ramps for each province (provinces exit when they complete a changed-circumstance review);
- revocation of the antidumping duty order upon entry into the interim agreement;
- $150 of the million antidumping duty deposits going to a trust fund that promotes North American lumber, and the rest split between the two countries;
- no disbursements of countervailing duty deposits until revocation, then split evenly between the two countries (*The Free Trader* 2003).

The coalition immediately came back with a new demand that would put a US$50/mbf export tax on Canadian lumber shipments once they rose to 28 percent of the U.S. market and a prohibitive export tax of $125/mbf once they rose to 30.5 percent. It also demanded an antisurge mechanism, which would put a cap on the amount of export allowed for a province if it completed changes to its timber pricing system but one or more other provinces did not do so.

The new demand was "totally unacceptable" to Canada, whose lumber producers had already had serious issues with the proposal agreed upon by the two negotiators (*Inside US Trade* 2003f). On July 31, Aldonas stated in a news release, "Unfortunately discussions on an interim agreement for the softwood lumber dispute ended without resolution ... we were unable to come to a meeting of the minds" (Aldonas 2003).

As noted in the previous chapter, the NAFTA Injury Panel gave Canada a resounding victory on September 5, 2003. Undaunted, the coalition continued to complain about the July joint government proposal. In a letter sent to Aldonas on September 26, 2003, Rusty Wood insisted on limiting Canadian access to the U.S. market to 30.5 percent. On October 29, the coalition made a "retrograde" proposal that would put a US$225/mbf tax on all Canadian imports above 30.5 percent of the U.S. market. The proposal also called for an "antisurge" measure, an even split of cash deposits, and a termination of Canada's legal challenge in WTO and NAFTA. The only concession the coalition made was to agree to an immediate return of almost half of the more than

US$1.5 billion duty deposits instead of making Canadian producers wait until provinces completed reforms of their timber policies (*Inside US Trade* 2003g).

The very first items in the proposal stated that the proposal was about "substantial reduction of imports" and that the $225/mbf tax was necessary "to achieve a significant reduction in Canadian imports." More than half of the Canadian industry called on their government to reject the proposal. In a November 3, 2003, letter to Minister Pettigrew, Free Trade Lumber Council cochair Frank Dottori, presidents of two Ontario industry associations, the chair of Alberta Lumber Trade Council, and the presidents of two large B.C. lumber producers (West Fraser Timber Ltd. and Tolko Industries Ltd.) stated,

> In summary, this proposal picks up on the July approach and imposes even more stringent conditions on Canadian exporters of softwood lumber and Canadian governments, and it is *not* a basis that we, the undersigned, would find acceptable as a way of settling the dispute.
>
> More specifically, the very high wall of US$225 per thousand board feet, above the very low market share of 30.5 percent, would not only prove an impassable barrier for Canadian exporters, it would gravely affect the Canadian market itself and most likely negate any attempt of reforming provincial forest policies.
>
> This latest proposal also makes it abundantly clear that the U.S. Coalition's main goal is reducing our market share irrespective of policy reform in Canada. Their secondary goal is to acquire half the cash deposits and do it quickly, before the Canadian legal victory with NAFTA is confirmed on appeal, and they lose all possibility of ever getting *any* of those monies. (Dottori 2003, emphasis original)

Canada subsequently rejected the coalition's proposal. But in a tit-for-tat fashion, Canada came up with its own "retrograde" proposal, which was contained in correspondence from Doug Waddell to Aldonas on November 14. The proposal called for duty-free imports of Canadian lumber at 32 percent of U.S. consumption (or 17.624 bbf), and anything above that would be taxed at US$200/mbf. The duty deposits, with interest, would be split 75–25 between importers of record and the U.S. Treasury after $25 million had been set aside for a North American industry fund. The antidumping duty order would be revoked, and the countervailing duty order would remain in place. The countervailing duty deposit rate could be reduced to zero upon (1) a final settlement in NAFTA and (2) the application of statutory offset provisions. The WTO countervailing duty appellate body report would be adopted. The WTO and NAFTA injury litigation would stay, which allowed the possibility of revoking the countervailing and antidumping duty orders if no threat of injury was found (Waddell 2003).

This proposal upset some Canadian producers, who said they had not been informed before it was made to the United States. One Canadian government official subsequently labeled it not a proposal but a mere follow-up to a phone conversation between Waddell and Aldonas. The coalition did not accept the Waddell proposal either, because it did not include all the details needed to reach a solution and the proposed 75–25 split of cash deposits was a step back from the July joint government proposal of a 50–50 split. American Consumers for Affordable Homes was puzzled by the Waddell proposal, given the Canadian legal victories in WTO and NAFTA. It urged Canada to reject quotas and fight for free market access to the United States through WTO and NAFTA. At the end of November, it seemed the Waddell proposal would not be accepted as a basis for an interim agreement.

* * *

Things took a turn in early December 2003 when the two countries appeared to move even closer (than in July) to making a deal. This was motivated by a leadership change in Ottawa. Prime Minister Jean Chrétien retired and was replaced by Paul Martin on December 12. Martin reportedly wanted to improve Canada's relations with the Bush administration, which were damaged in part by Canada's refusal to go into the Iraq war in 2003 and by trade disputes. He perhaps wanted to see the lumber dispute solved before taking office as prime minister. Furthermore, several sources noted the friendship between Chrétien's chief of staff, Eddie Goldenberg, and Keith Mitchell, a managing partner in a British Columbia law firm representing the B.C. lumber industry, and suggested Mitchell could lose influence in Martin's government. These factors led Canadian government officials to make a series of concessions (*Inside US Trade* 2003h).

Thus, instead of pulling back from the Waddell proposal, the Canadian government made another offer on December 2 that was very close to the coalition's position. Under this new proposal, the cash deposits would be split 52–48, and the tax-free imports would be 31.5 percent (or about 92.5 percent of Canada's then-current market share) after which a US$200/mbf export tax would apply. The proposal had language similar to the Waddell proposal on the antidumping duty order. On the other hand, the United States would not have to revoke its countervailing duty order, and Canada would only suspend its countervailing duty case in WTO and terminate the NAFTA cases (thus forgoing all the legal victories Canada had had in NAFTA) (*Inside US Trade* 2003h).

The lifespan of the proposed agreement would be five years, and it included an "exit ramp" for provinces to get the export tax eliminated if they were found by Commerce to have sufficiently changed their timber policies. But this mechanism could not be used for the first three years of the agreement, and to have the export tax lifted, at least three provinces making up at least 75 percent of Canadian exports to the United States would have to pass a changed-circumstances review. Short of having the export tax completely eliminated under these circumstances, individual provinces that successfully completed a changed circumstance could get a 7.5 percent increase in their exports to the

U.S. market before having to pay the export tax. Further, this bonus could not be achieved until three years into the agreement. This would function as an antisurge mechanism. Finally, the Maritime Provinces would not be excluded (*Inside US Trade* 2003h).

Supporters and opponents of the proposal in the Canadian lumber industry voiced their opinions to Minister Pettigrew at a conference call on December 10. Supporters of the deal included Weldwood Canada, which was then owned by U.S.-based International Paper, U.S.-based Weyerhaeuser Company, International Forest Products Ltd., Slocan, and Abitibi-Consolidated. Opponents included Québec-based Tembec and Domtar, British Columbia–based Canfor, Doman Industries, West Fraser Timber Co. Ltd., TimberWest Forest, and Tolko Industries, and industry associations in Québec, Ontario, and Alberta (*Wall Street Journal* 2003).

Tembec's December 10 statement opposing the deal accused the Canadian government of surrendering to the United States even as it continued to win legal victories in WTO and NAFTA. Tembec President and CEO Frank Dottori said, "It is amazing that our own government is about to give away control of its forest policy and is even paying for it with industry money." He threatened to sue the federal government to block the deal. Producers from the Maritime Provinces stated they would support the deal only if they could secure a quota of 2 bbf. American Consumers for Affordable Homes and the National Lumber and Building Material Dealers Association urged USTR to reject the proposal (*Inside US Trade* 2003i).

In the end, there was not much time for Pettigrew to build better support for the deal before he was reshuffled to another position in the Martin cabinet. On January 12, 2004, the new trade minister, Jim Peterson, told Trade Representative Robert Zoellick and Commerce Secretary Evans that there was no support from the provinces, even though he personally wanted to see the deal succeed.

Since Canadian producers could receive quota rents and thus might be harmed to a lesser extent by a quota arrangement than the duties, their rejection of the December proposal was due to two particularly sticky issues—quota allocation and the split of duties collected (which was close to US$2 billion by the end of 2003) with the United States. They feared that the latter would allow U.S. producers, as the Byrd Amendment permitted, to keep about US$1 billion of the duties, which would almost guarantee that the coalition would be around to launch another attack, just when it looked like the coalition might be under serious stress from dissension within as a result of Georgia-Pacific's withdrawal from it.

Quota allocation pitted Canadian companies against each other. Companies supported the proposal if they thought they could get a sufficiently high quota. Interestingly, the Canadian government proposed to use lumber export volume between April 1 and September 30, 2001, as the basis for quota allocation. The stated reason for choosing this period was that it coincided with the operations of the national export monitoring program. Presumably, it was also mostly under "free trade." However, it was in this period that some industry leaders had openly called on Canadian producers to refrain from exporting too much, for fear that the United States would make countervailing duties retroactive. Some companies did cut back their exports. Others did not. Now those that did would be penalized if a quota-based deal was signed.

Among firms that did cut back their exports to the United States during the period were Canfor and West Fraser Timber. Slocan Forest Products, one of the more vocal supporters, increased sales and would be rewarded by receiving more quota. Yet it was the behavior by Slocan, not Canfor and West Fraser, that infuriated the Americans and harmed the Canadian defense in the first place (*Vancouver Sun* 2003).

In addition, provinces were worried that there was no clear road map leading them to free trade and that giving up Canada's challenge in NAFTA was too much, after the NAFTA Injury Panel had just ruled in Canada's favor. As in the past, it proved too difficult for the Canadian government to build consensus among the major lumber-producing provinces and competing companies.

The Aftermath

In the ensuing two years, as more NAFTA and WTO rulings emerged, the parties would not be able to get as close as in July and December 2003 in negotiating for a settlement. Even though proponents for a negotiated settlement in Canada argued that U.S. intransigence and the Byrd Amendment would show the folly of Canada's relying on international trade rulings to sway the United States to abandon duties on Canadian lumber and governments in both countries pushed for a negotiated settlement, the majority of Canadian lumber producers opposed negotiations on the terms set in 2003. Nonetheless, negotiations occurred periodically against the background of legal and administrative actions.

In April 2004, Aldonas went to British Columbia to see the forest policy reforms the province had implemented. He recommended that the Coalition for Fair Lumber Imports go and take a look itself. (The coalition did take a tour but did not comment on whether the reforms were sufficient.) Aldonas stated that he still preferred a comprehensive agreement with Canada, but if that was not possible and British Columbia was ready to make a deal, the United States ought to be ready as well (*Vancouver Sun* 2004).

On May 17, Minister Peterson expressed a desire to reengage with the United States to find a durable, policy-based solution. Canadian industry objected to having Commerce be the sole arbiter of whether provinces changed their forestry policies sufficiently to gain unrestricted access to the U.S. market; it demanded that a binational panel of judges (whose decision would be binding) be part of a negotiated settlement (*Inside US Trade* 2004a).

In early October, following a conversation with Commerce Secretary Evans, Minister Peterson asked Canadian producers to return to the negotiating table. Secretary Evans told Peterson that there existed a small window of opportunity for the two countries to reach a negotiated settlement between the U.S. presidential election on November 2 and mid-December, when Commerce was to unveil the results of its first final administrative review.

On November 17, Senator Baucus introduced a bill in Congress (S. 2992) that called for speedy liquidation of the US$3 billion duty deposits (*Congressional Record* 2004b).

On November 23, 14 U.S. senators wrote a letter (Craig 2004) to Secretary Evans, asking him to pressure Canada into a negotiated settlement by taking two steps. First, Commerce should account for the full value of subsidies and dumping when it issued its first final administrative review of the antidumping and countervailing duty orders on Canadian imports. The letter stated, "Commerce found 18.8 percent subsidies in 2002. There have been no relevant factual developments since then; the subsidies are as high or higher than they were in 2002." How could this be, given that Commerce had found a subsidy rate of 9.24 percent and a dumping rate of 3.98 percent in its June 2004 preliminary administrative review? The senators' letter stated,

> Commerce should, as in 2002, measure the value of Canadian lumber against prices for comparable wood fiber in the open and competitive timber or log markets immediately on the U.S. side of the border ... It is crucial that Commerce not measure the value of the Canadian timber against any prices from transactions wholly within Canada, including prices from timber in the eastern-Canada Maritimes provinces....
>
> We strongly urge the Commerce Department to convey to Canada that U.S. law would forbid return of any duty deposits should a dispute panel force the U.S. government to revoke the Canadian lumber countervailing duty or anti-dumping duty order. Commerce should stress that the only legal basis for return of any deposits would be a negotiated settlement.

Between November 30 and December 2, 2004, during his first official visit to Canada after being reelected, President Bush again called for a negotiated settlement. He also agreed that the NAFTA system needed a fix. Prime Minister Martin was reported to have told him, "How come the Americans can't accept the results of five or six panels?" Martin said, "We not only raised the lumber issue, but also said that there is something with a dispute settlement mechanism that simply allows these kinds of things to go on and on" (*Ottawa Citizen* 2004).

Commerce released the final results of its first administrative review of the antidumping duty and countervailing duty orders on December 14, 2004. It indeed changed its benchmark from the first preliminary administrative review and used log prices in Washington State as a benchmark for alleged subsidy in

British Columbia (a cross-border comparison method) and timber prices in the Maritime Provinces as a benchmark for other provinces. Canadian interests accused Commerce of bowing to political pressure, as evidenced by the letter from 14 U.S. senators (Craig 2004) that called on the department to use the cross-border comparison method that would give President Bush much needed "negotiating leverage." Since this was the fourth benchmark Commerce had used since 2001, John Allan, president of the B.C. Lumber Trade Council stated in a news release, "It's difficult to imagine a more arbitrary process than the one in which Commerce is constantly changing the rules of the game to reach predetermined results." Outraged, Canadian industry representatives cancelled a meeting with their U.S. counterparts scheduled for December 16, 2004.

In January 2005, the coalition asked the U.S. government to launch a new WTO challenge over Canadian log export restrictions. As of this writing, the U.S. government had not yet taken action on this request.

On January 24, 2005, Aldonas said that the United States would not return lumber duty deposits without a negotiated settlement. Two days later, Minister Peterson rejected the possibility of further negotiations with the United States as long as it refused to return the deposits even if the underlying orders were revoked (*Gazette* 2005).

On March 8, the Canadian government sent an initial proposal for a solution of the lumber dispute to provincial ministers and U.S. Commerce Secretary Carlos M. Gutierrez. The proposal called for Canadian provinces to collect an unspecified amount of export tax, which could be withdrawn as provinces instituted forest policy reforms. The new proposal differed from previous settlements considered over the previous three years in at least two critical ways. First, it called on the United States to return all duty deposits plus interest. Second, it called on the parties to establish an independent panel that would determine when provinces have conducted the necessary reforms to remove themselves from the export tax. Those reforms would be spelled out in province-specific annexes to the agreement. Although Gutierrez and the coalition welcomed it as a good first step to restart negotiations, the coalition indicated that there were aspects that it "could not support as presented" (*National Post* 2005).

On March 23–24, government officials from the two countries met in Toronto. The level of tax was not discussed because Canadian government officials did not have a mandate to do so. Aldonas suggested that the United States could accept returning a larger portion of the collected duties if Canada agreed to a higher export tax, or vice versa. He also said it would be difficult for the coalition to accept a binational panel to determine whether provinces had made the necessary reforms to have the export tax eliminated for their lumber (*Inside US Trade* 2005b).

On April 4, a meeting of industry and government officials from both countries was held in Chicago, following a meeting of government officials the previous week. The structure of an export tax and the coalition's demand for an "effects test" once Canadian provinces made policy changes were at the center of the discussion. The coalition favored a tiered tax that would rise as prices fell, while Canada supported a fixed *ad valorem* tax capped at a certain amount when prices were high (*Inside US Trade* 2005c).

On April 19, 2005, 47 members of the U.S. House of Representatives, including Majority Whip Roy Blunt (R-Missouri), Minority Whip Steny Hoyer (D-Maryland), Appropriations Subcommittee Chairman Jim Kolbe (R-Arizona), and Ways and Means Committee Member Richard Neal (D-Massachusetts), wrote a letter to President Bush, urging him to comply with the international agreements that the United States had signed, including prompt compliance with panel rulings rather than repeated delays, and the refund, with interest, of antidumping and countervailing duty deposits as soon as the NAFTA Extraordinary Challenge Committee upheld the NAFTA Injury Panel (Blunt 2005).

In early May 2005, the United States sent two lumber proposals to Canada. One originated from the coalition, and the other was from the U.S. government and was based on the coalition's proposal. Both proposals called for a province-specific export tax of 25 percent when the lumber price was below US$325/mbf, sliding to 15 percent when the lumber price was $325–$400/mbf and to 5 percent when the price exceeded $400/mbf. The proposals made the export tax more prominent by stating that once it was established, negotiators could continue to work out the "exit ramp." The proposals also mentioned the use of an effects test but did not raise the issue of how to divide the more than US$3 billion duty deposits (*Inside US Trade* 2005d).

Commenting on the May 2005 U.S. offer before the next lumber meeting in July 2005, John Allan of the B.C. Lumber Trade Council stated, "It's fair to say the policy agenda paradigm is off the table now. The American lumber industry is reverting back to the position that it's not about policy, it's about restraints at the border. At the end of the day, that's what they want—it's the volume" (*Vancouver Sun* 2005a).

Between July 18 and 20, talks between U.S. and Canadian government officials and industry leaders in Washington, D.C., failed to make progress. The talk was partly driven by a pending NAFTA Extraordinary Challenge Committee decision. The coalition proposed a 25 percent export tax on all softwood lumber exports sold at less than US$325/mbf, 15 percent for products sold between $325 and $380/mbf, and no tax when the price was above $380/mbf. The coalition's tax level was higher than what Canadian firms paid (about 20 percent) at the time and deemed unacceptable. Interestingly, the coalition proposed a new exit ramp: Provinces had to institute market-based changes to forest policies that would raise stumpage fees anywhere from 100 to 230 percent, with no provision for future reductions in the Crown timber-cutting payment. The coalition did not budge on a previous demand to keep about half the US$4 billion in lumber duties already paid by Canadian producers. Canadian government and industry rejected the proposal but agreed to attend another meeting scheduled for August 22 (*Inside US Trade* 2005e).

On July 22, U.S. Commerce Secretary Gutierrez stated that Canada could forget about getting any duty deposits back and that he was not interested in a Canadian export tax as a way of replacing the duties currently in place. The two countries were as far apart as ever in the lumber dispute (*Vancouver Sun* 2005b). On August 16, Minister Peterson announced that Canada was pulling out of negotiations with the United States following the NAFTA Extraordinary Challenge Committee decision on August 10 (*Seattle Times* 2005).

Reengagement

The minority government led by Prime Minister Martin collapsed in November 2005. As a result, Canada held its federal election on January 23, 2006, and the Conservative Party, led by Stephen Harper, won more seats than any other party. In early February, Harper formed a new minority government and named David Emerson, a former industry minister in the Martin government, as the minister of international trade. Emerson was the former CEO and president of Canfor Corporation, the largest softwood lumber producer in Canada and a former deputy minister in British Columbia. The forest industry, especially in British Columbia, supported Emerson's new position.

The call for reengagement in negotiation renewed soon after the Canadian election. In mid-February, several newspapers in Canada reported that there had been a negotiated deal on the table back in early November 2005, shortly before the Martin government collapsed. The Canadian industry, particularly the lumber industry in interior British Columbia, had killed it. The deal, put together by Frank McKenna, then Canadian ambassador to the United States, called for a 15 percent export tax on companies in the B.C. interior on top of a nationwide quota of 34 percent of the U.S. market share. As part of the deal, Canadian producers would get back 70 percent of the C$5 billion duty deposits, and the U.S. government would not disburse the remaining 30 percent to its industry under the Byrd Amendment.

The Canadian industry saw three major problems with the deal. First, it involved the return of only 70 percent of the duty deposits to Canadian lumber producers, as opposed to the 100 percent they felt entitled to. Given that the Byrd Amendment would not expire until late 2007, the U.S. government could still give in under congressional pressure and distribute the 30 percent to U.S. companies even if it signed an agreement not to do so.

Second, the deal involved a Canadian quota, limiting shipments to 34 percent of the U.S. market. But B.C. interior producers, in addition to that, would have to pay an extra 15 percent export tax. They could not agree to a high duty *and* a quota.

Finally, the proposed deal had a term of seven years, with no palatable escape clause. When the whole concept of negotiating an end to this dispute got off the ground, Canada's goal was to find an enduring settlement that would change forest management policies and establish completely free trade—the clearly defined exit ramp. Policy reforms made in British Columbia would not be recognized as part of the deal (*Vancouver Sun* 2006).

The Harper government was keen to have a better relationship with the United States. In early February 2006, former federal Finance and Trade Minister David Wilson was named Canada's new ambassador to the United States. Wilson oversaw Canada's withdrawal from the Memorandum of Understanding in 1991, and he stated that the first item on his agenda in Washington, D.C., was trying to solve the lumber dispute. He would present his credentials to the president on the same day he arrived in Washington (March 13)—an unusual move viewed as a sign of getting down to business in an urgent fashion (*National Post* 2006).

The Bush administration also wanted to have a better relationship with Canada. But by not honoring the NAFTA panel ruling, it alienated its allies in Canada, where mistrust of the United States was high. President Bush echoed Harper's "pushiness" in trying to solve the softwood lumber dispute when they met in Cancun, Mexico, at the end of March. The Cancun summit shifted the softwood talks into high gear as it became clear that both Bush and Harper wanted to get this dispute settled (*National Post* 2006). Deputy Trade Representative Susan Schwab became the chief U.S. negotiator on softwood lumber.

In January 2006, Commerce cut the countervailing duty rate in half (to 8.7 percent) and the antidumping duty rate to 2.1 percent (barely above the *de minimis* level of 2 percent) in its annual administrative reviews. The action was seen in Canada as a sign that the United States wanted to settle on these terms (a tax level of roughly 10 percent).

Meanwhile, on the legal front, the NAFTA Subsidy Panel upheld, on March 17, Commerce's determination that Canadian subsidy was *de minimis*. The panel's decision was published on March 23. The U.S. government had until April 27 to decide whether to file a NAFTA extraordinary challenge.

Although few expected that another NAFTA extraordinary challenge committee would reverse the NAFTA Subsidy Panel's unanimous decision, the Canadian government wanted to avoid "encouraging" the United States to file a challenge, which would make it more difficult to negotiate a settlement. More importantly, if the second NAFTA extraordinary challenge committee ruled against the United States and the U.S. government ignored the ruling again, as the first had done, what would the Canadian government do? Canadians who had felt cheated after the first ruling was ignored would lose a great deal of confidence in dealing with the United States and could blame their own government. Yet the United States was an important trading partner for Canada. At this juncture, some politicians in Ottawa thought that it was in Canada's (and their own) interests to give the United States a chance for a deal before it had an opportunity to reject the second NAFTA extraordinary challenge committee ruling. Subsequently, the softwood lumber talks intensified, aiming for a resolution by April 27.

In the meantime, three of the largest Canadian lumber producers, Canfor Corp., Abitibi-Consolidated Inc., and Weyerhaeuser Canada, began to lay the groundwork for a deal. They formed a loose pan-Canadian coalition and pushed for a negotiated settlement to the dispute—even if it meant leaving some money on the table. They tried to allay the Canadian government's fears about a possible political backlash to a negotiated deal (*National Post* 2006).

On April 22, President Bush and Prime Minister Harper spoke on softwood lumber again, which gave their negotiators additional signals that they wanted to see a deal soon. Despite some last-minute struggles, including public opposition from Ontario and Québec to details leaked out on April 25, the Canadian government secured support from major provinces, and the negotiators signed off on a four-page Framework Agreement on April 27.

The Framework Agreement would run more than 70 pages when it was initialed by government representatives from the two countries on July 1. In Canada, opposition to it mounted in the summer as legal developments favorable to its producers came out, and provinces demanded modifications, threatening to derail the whole agreement. In late August, major timber-producing provinces and lumber producers offered support to the agreement, and with the support of Bloc Québécois, the Harper government got it approved by Parliament.

The two countries then signed the Softwood Lumber Agreement of 2006 on September 12. In the ensuing month, the text of the agreement would be modified twice before it was implemented, on October 12. One critical issue was that the September 12 version of the agreement was conditioned on the withdrawal of all pending lawsuits. It became clear later that neither certain Canadian producers nor the Coalition for Fair Lumber Imports was willing to do that. Consequently, the October 12 version merely specified what the Canadian and the U.S. government should do (such as "shall seek to dismiss" or "shall fill joint motion to dismiss" or "shall continue to seek modification") with respect to certain lawsuits.

The main terms of the Softwood Lumber Agreement of 2006 are as follows:

Orders and deposits. The United States revokes the countervailing and antidumping duty orders on Canadian softwood lumber imports and stops collecting duty deposits. It keeps US$1 billion of the estimated US$5.4 billion in deposits, and the remainder goes to Canadian companies. The amount going to the United States is divided: $500 million to members of the coalition, $50 million for joint initiatives benefiting the North American lumber industry; and the remainder ($450 million) to meritorious initiatives in the United States as identified by the U.S. government in consultation with Canada.

No new case. The United States will not self-initiate and will dismiss any petition for antidumping and countervailing duties on Canadian softwood

TABLE 9-1. Export Measures under the Softwood Lumber Agreement of 2006

Random Lengths framing lumber composite prices	Option A: Export charge (%)	Option B: Export charge plus volume restraint[a]
More than US$355	0	0
US$336–355	5	2.5% + regional share of 34% of U.S. consumption
US$316–335	10	3% + regional share of 32% of U.S. consumption
US$315 or less	15	5% + regional share of 30% of U.S. consumption

a. A region's market share is based on its average share of Canadian exports to the United States during calendar years 2001–2005.

lumber. Further, it will not take any other trade actions or initiate investigations with respect to Canadian softwood lumber. U.S. producers accounting for more than 60 percent of U.S. production provide irrevocable "no injury" letters.

Border measures. The border measures include export measures, a third-country trigger, and an antisurge mechanism. Table 9-1 shows the export measures for the regions (defined as B.C. interior, B.C. coast, and each of the provinces east of British Columbia), which choose either an export charge, varying on the monthly Random Lengths Framing Lumber Composite Prices, or an export charge plus volume constraint. The third-country trigger of refunding export charges takes effect during any two consecutive quarters if (1) the third-country share of U.S. lumber consumption increases by 20 percent, (2) Canadian share is decreasing, and (3) the U.S. share is increasing in each such quarter when compared with the same two consecutive quarters in the preceding year. Finally, the antisurge mechanism is triggered if a region's shipments exceed 110 percent of its allocated share in a month, in which case the export charge on shipments from that region will be increased by 50 percent.

Exceptions and exclusions. The export charge on products valued at more than US$500/mbf will be charged as if their value were at US$500/mbf. Canada will limit the export charge on remanufactured lumber products from companies operating independently of tenure holders to the first mill price. The border measures do not apply to at least 32 companies and products made from logs harvested in Atlantic provinces and in the Yukon, Northwest Territories, or Nunavut.

Policy exits. Canada, with full participation of the provinces, and the United States will make best efforts to define criteria for determining whether a region's timber pricing and forest management systems could qualify for exemption from border measures within 18 months after the agreement takes effect.

B.C. stumpage. British Columbia is allowed to keep its new market pricing system, in which the provincial government uses stumpage received from competitive bidding to set the stumpage prices for standing timber under other tenure arrangements.

Dispute settlement. Disputes over the application or interpretation of the agreement or the implementation of mutually agreed policy exits will be resolved through a binding dispute settlement process. A tribunal of three commercial arbitrators from the London Court of International Arbitration will serve as the final dispute settlement body.

Duration. The agreement will be for a term of seven years and may be renewed for two additional years.

Termination. Either party may, at any time after the agreement has been in effect for 23 months, terminate it by providing one month's notice. Should the United States terminate it, a 12-month standstill on trade remedy action is observed, in addition to the 12-month standstill on U.S. trade remedy action upon the expiry of the agreement.

Legal actions. The parties agree to terminate some legal cases.

Anticircumvention measures. Neither party will take action to circumvent commitments set out in the agreement or to offset the export measure. If exports from the Atlantic provinces to the United States exceed 100 percent of softwood lumber production in these provinces in any quarter, then exports to the United States from the Atlantic provinces in the following quarter will be subject to a penalty of C$200/mbf on the excess.

An Assessment: Who Wins and Who Loses?

The Softwood Lumber Agreement of 2006 was a victory for the Harper government and the Bush administration, since both had called for a settlement for securing a better bilateral relation. On the surface, it seemed to be at least as favorable to the Canadian industry as most other proposed settlements in the previous five years, including the two that were close to being signed in July and December 2003. The US$1 billion duty deposits to be kept in the United States would represent only some 4 to 5 percent duty on Canadian lumber imports since May 2002. The export charge (or export charge plus volume constraint) is on a sliding scale (starting at 0 percent when lumber price reaches US$355/mbf and rising to 15 percent when lumber price is under $315/mbf) and seems reasonable, given that the average monthly lumber price from May 2002 to April 2006 was $355.6/mbf (Random Lengths, various years). That means that Canadian producers will not pay much export tax if lumber prices stay at this level during the term of the agreement. However, this price level is achieved, in part, by the 27.2 to 10.8 percent duties (and a very high level of lumber demand), and is thus not the price expected for the next seven to nine years without restrictive measures on Canadian lumber imports.

The tax level—specified for the periods both before and after the 2006 agreement entered into force—is not much different than what Zhang (2003) called for—a 5 percent export tax as the basis for a negotiated settlement. It is far below what the Coalition for Fair Lumber Imports has demanded and slightly below what Commerce found in its second (last) final administrative review, 10.8 percent. Had such a deal been available three or four years earlier, the vast majority of Canadian producers would have taken it. It would have been acceptable for them, given that most litigation had yet to produce meaningful results.

However, the agreement of 2006 might be a few years too late for some Canadian producers, since they (and their governments) gave up most of their legal victories and dropped some pending litigation—strategies that might prove costly in the long run.

On the other hand, the coalition got US$500 million that it arguably was not entitled to receive, based on the U.S. Court of International Trade ruling on April 7, 2006, before the Framework Agreement was signed. It also secured midterm trade restrictions on Canadian lumber and gave up virtually nothing legally or administratively (such as policy exits and the constitutional challenge). The coalition is a winner.

The losers are U.S. lumber consumers. They pay higher prices for lumber and face a more volatile lumber market. The National Association of Home Builders urged the U.S. and Canadian governments to reject the agreement and even threatened to aggressively look for lumber from Russia and other countries. But in the end, the call from consumer groups did not have much impact for the agreement to enter into force, even though they could disrupt the agreement later by importing more lumber from other countries.

A close look at the Softwood Lumber Agreement of 2006 reveals that, in the long run, Canadian industry and governments may lose more than giving up the US$1 billion duties and accepting a managed trade regime in softwood lumber. These additional losses include the following:

- Canadian firms surrendered US$500 million to their competitors only 20 days after the Court of International Trade decided that the U.S. competitors could not legally receive any of the Canadian deposits.
- The NAFTA panel system is being tested, not only because the agreement does not honor any of the NAFTA panel rulings, but also because the United States continues to treat NAFTA panel decisions as prospective, preventing the return of cash deposits when Commerce or ITC final determination is overturned. Few, if any, Canadian firms would accept going before a NAFTA panel knowing that, even were they to win, they would not get their duty deposits back. The court rulings (CIT 2006a, 2006b) have brought some legitimacy to the NAFTA panel system. But the agreement did not specify that the United States would stand by the court rulings.
- It is questionable whether there will be a true exit ramp from managed trade after 18 months, since it must be "mutually agreed."
- The border measures could impose rates of tax that exceed any duty rates that might have survived litigation.
- The duration of the agreement is likely to be longer than the time (one to two years) needed to complete all remaining litigation in Lumber IV, which

could result in a revocation of countervailing and antidumping duty orders as well as a full refund.

- Canadian federal and provincial governments will not be permitted to change forestry policies in any manner that could be interpreted as assisting forest industry because of the anticircumvention measures, nor can any new assistance be provided, even though what are included in the measures are debatable.

Thus, given the results of the litigation in the previous five years, the coalition seems to have gotten the most from the Softwood Lumber Agreement of 2006. So pleased are they that the coalition's congressional supporters urged the Bush administration to stick with the Framework Agreement reached in April 2006 when the Canadian government had some difficulty securing support from its industry and wanted to modify it in the summer of 2006.

By giving up US$1 billion and accepting a managed trade arrangement, Canadian industry might hope to have peace in the lumber trade with the United States. But if the recent history of the lumber dispute tells us anything, it is that there might not be any lasting peace: Economic and natural conditions change, firms' competitive positions change, new politicians emerge, and those who suffer under the agreement will protest and try to circumvent it. The 2006 Softwood Lumber Agreement itself is so complex that some parts may conflict, and some provisions are subject to interpretation. Most importantly, with little downside to taking any complaint to the dispute resolution process, and given the high returns from past softwood lumber dispute resolution processes, the coalition, with the support of its allies in Congress and the Bush administration, will no doubt launch many disputes over the life of the agreement.

If the long-term costs are considered, the Canadian government and industry may have secured only a short-term peace deal. On the other hand, there is much uncertainty about what the coalition and U.S. government will do and what the results of litigation will be. It is also true that U.S.–Canada relations are negatively affected by the softwood lumber dispute, and neither government wants the dispute to continue to poison the relationship. So the Canadian government has argued that it is taking a reasonable approach in the face of never-ending aggression on the part of the United States.

Interestingly, it was the Conservative Party that opted for the Free Trade Agreement, including in particular a dispute resolution mechanism, because it had reached two conclusions: (1) Canada had to have guaranteed, unfettered access to the U.S. market as long as it was obeying trade rules, and (2) such guaranteed access had to be protected by the rule of law because Canada would not normally get the better of political bargains. The Softwood Lumber Agreement of 2006 betrays both those propositions. It does not deliver free trade, and it is a political bargain forsaking entirely the rule of law enshrined in FTA (Feldman 2006).

If the Coalition for Fair Lumber Imports could win in Lumber II, Lumber III, and Lumber IV, why has it not gone after producers in other Canadian forest sectors, such as pulp and paper? After all, Canadian pulp and paper is made of wood. Is the political economy in the pulp and paper sector somehow different?

10

Comparative Political Economy

The Softwood Lumber War and the Newsprint Tariff Battle

Historically, the United States had tariffs on many forest products imports from Canada and elsewhere, including pulp, newsprint, other paper, and paperboard. After three decades of tariff battle on newsprint imports around the turn of the 20th century, the United States enacted the Reciprocity Act of 1911, which effectively free-listed newsprint and wood pulp from Canada, and the Underwood Tariff Act of 1913, which "admitted free of duty newsprint and wood pulp from all parts of the world and without qualification of any sort" (Ellis 1948, *88*). In the 1980s, the value of Canadian newsprint exports to the United States was similar to that of softwood lumber.

This chapter presents the political economy of the newsprint tariff battle and of the softwood lumber war. Even though the disputes are some 70 years apart and the newsprint tariff battle was more of a struggle between two main U.S. domestic factions, they illustrate the political, economic, and institutional factors that have influenced trade conflict between the two countries.

First, the two disputes are the largest and longest-lasting trade conflicts between the two countries, and wood is a major component of the disputed products. Indeed, these are the largest forest products trade disputes in the world. The newsprint battle lasted for nearly 30 years, and the modern version of the softwood lumber dispute has run nearly as long.

Second, the direct causes of the disputes are similar (cheaper Canadian timber resources and a gradual loss of U.S. industry competitiveness). The primary timber resource for making newsprint in the 1910s was spruce, and it was not until the 1960s that the development of a new, more affordable technology made production of newsprint from other species an economic reality. The United States was running out of spruce around 1910, which was abundant in Canada. High newsprint prices in the United States, made possible in part because of a protective tariff, forced newspaper publishers to lobby for tariff reduction and elimination. Similarly, environmental regulations have removed millions of acres of forests from logging in the United States since the 1970s (Cashore 1998). Since 1977, timber scarcity has forced U.S. softwood lumber producers to pay as much as a 2 percent annual increase in real stumpage prices (Zhang and Bliss 1998), while Canadian imports increased.

Third, the issues ("cheap imports") and tactics (mobilizing political forces and utilizing legal means such as antitrust law and countervailing duty law) used by U.S. producers and consumers in both disputes are similar, although the circumstances and market structure differ. Yet the results of the disputes are different—U.S. consumers won the newsprint battle, and U.S. producers won the softwood lumber war, at least for now.

The Newsprint Tariff Battle[1]

Newsprint is a wood pulp paper that came into general use in the United States in the 1870s. It is a mix of mechanical (80–85 percent) and chemical (15–20 percent) wood pulp, which is made from pulpwood (small logs, since large logs, the so-called sawlogs, are used for making lumber or plywood). In the early days of newsprint manufacturing the primary raw material was spruce. The papermaking process also depends on the availability of large amounts of pure water for the production of power and for carrying cellulose. The very first newsprint mills were established in New England, where spruce, water, and financial capital were relatively abundant in the 19th century. When spruce resources dwindled there, newsprint production moved to the Midwest.

Before 1910, the United States had largely been self-sufficient in newsprint (to be exact, newsprint imports accounted for a mere 1.5 percent of domestic production in 1909), and there were no newsprint mills in Canada even though a few mills started to make pulp and other paper products in the early 1900s. However, by 1920, the Canadian newsprint industry had nearly caught up with the U.S. newsprint industry in production, and the share of Canadian newsprint was 43 percent of all Canadian pulp and paper production (Table 10-1). In 1925, Canadian newsprint took about 50 percent of the U.S. market.

The two major players in the newsprint tariff battle were U.S. newsprint makers and U.S. newspaper publishers (newsprint consumers). The newspaper publishers naturally sought cheap raw material. The newsprint manufacturers, often conglomerates, wanted to pay dividends to their investors and therefore desired high prices for their outputs. The inevitable frictions arrayed the two interests on opposite sides of a long series of controversies (Ellis 1948). Canadian pulp manufacturers who pressured their federal and provincial governments to adopt a log (sawlogs and pulpwood) export restriction policy provided indirect support and credence to the U.S. publishers.

U.S. newsprint producers had enjoyed tariff protection for a long time before 1911 (import tariffs were a major source of revenue for the U.S. government in the 19th century). As early as 1878 the newspaper publishers asked, unsuccess-

TABLE 10-1. Summary Statistics of the Canadian Pulp and Paper Industry, 1900 and 1920

	1900		1920	
Type of product	*Quantity (1,000 tons)*	*Percentage*	*Quantity (1,000 tons)*	*Percentage*
Newsprint	n.a.	n.a.	876	43
Market pulps	75	38	820	40
Other papers and paperboard	125	62	339	17
Total	200	100	2,035	100

Source: Davis et al. (1957).

fully, the U.S. government to lower the import tariff on newsprint and pulp. As of 1897, the tariff on newsprint and wood pulp was around 15 percent (Table 10-2).

Gradually, however, a combination of increasing demand and declining supply—primarily because of the shortage of spruce in the United States and an embargo of pulpwood export from Crown lands in Canada—generated economic and political pressures that resulted in the removal of the tariff on newsprint imports between 1911 and 1913.

A turning point for the international fight over the newsprint tariff was 1897. After a spike in newsprint prices that year, U.S. newspaper publishers, under the umbrella of the American Newspaper Publishers Association (now the Newspaper Association of America), started to fight with the newsprint producers on two fronts: antitrust litigation and tariff reduction legislation. The fight on antitrust led to the dissolution of the General Paper Company, a combination of 26 mills in the Midwest in 1906, but the largest papermaker—International Paper Company—survived with no apparent injury. International Paper would become the third largest newsprint producer in Canada in the 1930s (Roach 1994). As noted earlier, it divested its Canadian pulp and paper operations in the late 1970s and became a founding member and strong supporter of the Coalition for Fair Lumber Imports.

A return of high prices in 1907 motivated the publishers to step up their pressure and to demand both tariff reduction and observance of the antitrust law. Their pressure was sufficient to induce President Theodore Roosevelt to recommend removal of the duty on wood pulp (but not newsprint) on December 3, 1907. In the following years, it became evident that of the two vehicles of attack—tariff reduction and antitrust prosecution—the former was the more promising, though the latter was by no means abandoned.

In the meantime, the specter of ultimate shortage of raw materials was beginning to rise in the United States, and more Canadians, realizing that their forests held a treasure essential to satisfying the United States' appetite for news, were beginning to feel that at least the first step of paper manufacture, the making of wood pulp, should be performed north of the border. Although at least

TABLE 10-2. U.S. Tariffs on Newsprint and Wood Pulp, 1846–1913

Law	Duty
All goods, 1846	Pulpwood, 20% Wood pulp, 20%[a] Newsprint, 20%
Mongrel Tariff Act, 1883	Pulpwood, free Wood pulp, 10% Newsprint, 15%
1888	Pulpwood, free Wood pulp, $2.50/ton (slightly less than 10%) Newsprint, 15%
McKinley Tariff Act, 1890	Pulpwood, free Mechanical pulp, $2.50/ton (slightly higher than 10%) Chemical pulp, $6/ton (slightly higher than 10%) Newsprint, 15%
Wilson-Gorman Act, 1894	Pulpwood, free Wood pulp, 10% Newsprint, 15%
Dingley Tariff Act, 1897	Pulpwood, free Wood pulp, $1.67/ton Newsprint, $6/ton for newsprint valued at less than or equal to $40/ton; $10/ton for newsprint valued at $40–$50/ton (15%–19% based on newsprint price of $33–$40/ton), plus a retaliatory measure ($2/ton newsprint × the amount export duty on pulpwood in $/cord)[b]
Payne-Aldrich Tariff Act, 1909	Pulpwood, free Wood pulp, $1.67/ton for pulp originated from any area not limiting the exportation of printing paper, pulp, or wood Newsprint, $3.75/ton, with a surcharge of $2/ton if Canada did not remove its restrictions on pulpwood export, plus a retaliatory measure (an additional maximum of 25% *ad valorem* duty might be charged if Canada discriminated against the United States)
Reciprocity Agreement, 1911	Wood pulp, newsprint, other paper from Canada valued at no more than $80/ton, free if no export duty, export license fee or other export charge, or any prohibition or restriction in any way of the exportation of such paper, board, wood pulp or the wood, effective immediately after the American Congress acted and regardless of Canadian acceptance or rejection of the agreement as a whole
Underwood Tariff Act, 1913	Pulpwood, free Wood pulp, free Newsprint, free if valued at no more than $50/ton

a. Wood pulp did not exist in 1846. However, on March 13, 1872, Secretary of the Treasury George S. Boutwell of Massachusetts (in which state the paper industry was then concentrated) ruled that wood chip was dutiable under the "dried pulp" provision of the Tariff Act of March 2, 1861. Obviously, Boutwell interpreted the law broadly in favor of his compatriots (Ellis 1948, *12*).
b. See text in this chapter.
Source: Ellis (1948, 1960, 1968).

as early as 1893, some Canadians were urging their government to place an export tax on logs with the objective of forcing American capital to move into Canadian pulp manufacture, the Canadian government did not act.

In 1897, the Canadian government considered imposition of an export duty on pulpwood and sawlogs, hoping to induce the United States to enter reciprocity negotiations on trade issues. As the Dingley tariff bill progressed in the U.S. Congress and it became increasingly likely that it might contain provisions inimical to Canadian interests, the pressure increased in the summer of 1897. As a result, the Canadian government requested and received authority from Parliament to impose an export levy on sawlogs and pulpwood if it deemed such to be necessary. Although the Canadian government insisted that it had no intention of applying the export duty immediately, the arrangement itself was an element of potential threat to the United States.

On the U.S. side, the Dingley Tariff Act of 1897 contained a threat to Canada:

> That if any country or dependency shall impose an export duty upon pulpwood exported to the United States, there shall be imposed upon printing paper when imported from such country or dependency, an additional duty of one-tenth of 1 cent per pound for each dollar of export duty per cord so imposed, and proportionately for fractions of a dollar of such export duty. (Ellis 1968, 32)

Thus, the U.S. Congress warned Canada against interfering with free passage of pulpwood and sawlogs across the border. The Dingley Act also raised the tariff rate on wood pulp and newsprint and put publishers on notice. The American Newspaper Publishers Association soon started to charge the formation of a trust of papermakers that monopolized the business, raised the price of paper by US$8/ton, and "taxed" them more than US$4 million a year. This, in the minds of some members, was a conspiracy to tax knowledge, to levy tribute on education, and to blackmail intelligence itself. Pressure from the association stimulated numerous legislative proposals in 1899, which slumbered in committee pigeonholes because of a desire in Congress to avoid the general tariff discussion.

As the Canadian government did not exercise the power to levy an export tax on pulpwood and sawlogs, timber-producing provinces started considering provincial restrictions. In 1898, the Canadian Lumbermen's Association and some Canadian pulp manufacturers called for free importation in return for free exportation—that is, the United States should freely admit pulp and manufactured lumber if Canada allowed logs to leave the country without restriction. They demanded an immediate export tax on sawlogs and pulpwood equal to the American duty on pulp imports unless the United States removed its levies on both mechanical and chemical pulp. Another suggestion was to increase sharply stumpage dues but rebate most of these in the case of wood pulped in Canada.

The first fruits of restrictive sentiment were found in 1899 in Ontario's regulation forbidding the exportation of pulpwood cut from Crown lands (effective in 1900). Ontario's log export restriction policy was considered a move brought about by the failure of the federal government to take action. It was dictated by a sense of grievance against the retaliatory provisions of the Dingley Act and by a desire to stimulate the growth of a Canadian wood pulp industry. Other provinces followed and enacted their own log export restriction laws in the next few years. Québec, for example, first levied an export tax on pulpwood cut from Crown lands and later (in 1910) banned log exports from Crown lands. British Columbia and New Brunswick implemented their log export bans in 1906 and 1911, respectively.

Thus it was evident that by around 1900, Canadians were becoming conscious of the power of resource possession. They were aided in their propaganda by a gloomy U.S. Forest Service report that Americans were consuming between three to four times the annual growth of domestic pulpwood. Resource conservation soon became President Roosevelt's justification for his proposal in 1907 to remove the tariff on imports of Canadian wood pulp, if, as a quid pro quo, Canada agreed not to levy duties on the export of wood and remove its log export bans. Canadians, on the other hand, were furious that the United States wanted to grab their resources after it had nearly depleted its own. Resource conservation thus became another justification for provincial governments to implement their log export restriction policy.

In 1908 and 1909, the newsprint tariff battle intensified. The American Newspaper Publishers Association lobbied for the removal of pulp and paper duties with retaliatory levies in case export duties were imposed. When this measure failed to pass in Congress, it lobbied for free pulp, free paper, and reciprocity with Canada for free pulpwood.

The newspaper publishers would be disappointed initially. In the ensuing Payne–Aldrich Act of 1909 (signed into law on August 5, 1909), the tariff on pulp stayed the same, and that on paper was reduced by a meager US$0.25/ton (from $6/ton to $5.75/ton or $3.75/ton plus a $2/ton surcharge if Canada did not lift its export restrictions on pulpwood) (Table 10-2). Moreover, a new, broad retaliatory measure, which could be used against Canada beginning March 31, 1910, *if it discriminated against the United States*, would bring an additional, maximum rate of tariff of about 25 percent. The newsprint manufacturers won this round of the tariff fight in 1909.

Canada, the essential source of raw material for newsprint manufacturing, was antagonized, and an international problem was created. It was against this background that Québec announced on September 6, 1909, the prospective prohibition of exportation of Crown-land wood (to be implemented in 1910). Since Ontario and Québec refused to lift their export restrictions on pulpwood, the United States imposed the retaliatory duty of an additional US$2/ton on newsprint imports on August 26, 1909, raising the total duty to $5.75/ton.

This left the impending possibility of the imposition, after March 31, 1910, under maximum provisions of the Payne–Aldrich Act, of an additional 25 percent levy on Canadian newsprint, estimated at about US$8.75/ton, bringing the total possible duties to a prohibitive figure of US$14.50/ton, or approximately 42 percent. The likelihood that Canada might be subjected to the maximum rate was enhanced by the fact that it had just negotiated a treaty whereby France received preferential rates that might be interpreted as discrimination against the United States, thereby subjecting not only newsprint but all Canadian goods imported into the United States to the 25 percent additional levy. Thus, a long-standing controversy over newsprint and the control of market and resources insinuated itself first into the enactment of tariff legislation in the United States, then into log export restriction legislation in Canada, and finally into general trade relations between the two countries.

The potential trade war in the spring of 1910 resulting from the maximum provisions of the Payne–Aldrich Act of 1909 was averted by a timely personal intervention in diplomacy by President William Taft and Canadian cooperation. In essence, Canada extended to the United States a largely formal concession similar to the one it gave to France, which made it possible for President Taft to announce that there was no discrimination against the United States. During the discussion, President Taft proposed, and the Canadians agreed, to pursue the question of trade relations on a broader scale, looking for reciprocity.

The Reciprocity Agreement announced on January 26, 1911, took the form of legislative enactments in each country. As embodied in the legislation, the United States free-listed newsprint and wood pulp produced in Canada other than from Crown-land wood, which was not subject to export restrictions. Interestingly, this provision became effective immediately upon congressional acceptance of the Reciprocity Agreement, and regardless of whether Canada ratified it. The rejection of the Reciprocity Agreement by Canada following a hectic political campaign meant that the only positive outcome of the 1910–1911 U.S.–Canada reciprocity negotiations was free-listing of pulp and paper (as well as lumber) from Canada. Newspaper publishers finally prevailed.

At the beginning of the reciprocity negotiations, the United States was demanding the removal of restrictions on the exportation of pulpwood and sawlogs by Canadian provinces in return for free pulp and newsprint into the United States. The Canadian negotiators pointed out that the Canadian government could not apply pressure to the provinces because export restrictions on resources were a provincial matter. The Reciprocity Agreement adroitly avoided disturbing Canadian provincial autonomy by following the wood, not the provinces—that is, if wood were free from restriction, such as wood from private lands, the products of that wood would come into the United States free of duty. In this way, it won over the American publishers by giving them access to newsprint free of duty as long as the newsprint was produced from pulpwood that was not restricted to export.

On the other hand, the Reciprocity Agreement did not alienate too much those American newsprint producers who had secured access to private wood-lots in Canada, hoping to export pulpwood into the United States. In fact, most pulpwood exports to the United States were from private woodlots when the Reciprocity Agreement was negotiated.

Originally, a bill introduced in Congress to effectuate the agreement proposed to admit Canadian pulp and paper (the latter not valued at more than US$80/ton) free of duty when no export tax or prohibition was levied upon exports, as part of the general agreement, and dependent upon its adoption by both countries. The newspaper publishers' supporters in Congress later added a new Section 2 that carried the pulp and paper (and lumber) provisions into operation immediately after Congress acted, regardless of Canadian acceptance or rejection of the Reciprocity Agreement as a whole.

Two other developments that occurred during the congressional debate of the Reciprocity Agreement merit brief mention. One was the turn of discussion in the event of a report of production cost advantage to Canada. On May 17, 1911, the U.S. Tariff Board (the predecessor of the U.S. International Trade Commission) presented a report of its investigation into the pulp and paper situation, indicating that newsprint cost US$32.88/ton in the United States compared with $27.53/ton in Canada, a differential of $5.35 (of which the cost of wood accounted for $4.71), or 19.5 percent in favor of Canada (Table 10-3). (Here is a situation similar to that of the softwood lumber dispute.) Although at that time, this would normally have been considered a good Republican argument for protection against a cheaper foreign commodity, the exigencies of the situation transformed it into a plea for reciprocity as a means of cheapening costs to American consumers. The political support for the newspaper publishers in Congress was enormous.

The other development was the defeat of an amendment proposed by representatives and senators from paper-producing states, who argued that no pulp and paper should enter the United States from Canada until all provincial restrictions had been removed. The newspaper publishers' fight was victorious, and efforts by paper manufacturers in 1912 and afterward to repeal the Reciprocity Agreement were unsuccessful.

The Reciprocity Agreement marked a step in what was doubtless an inevitable northward progress of newsprint manufacturing. In mid-December 1911, it was reported that within the six months since the passage of the Reciprocity Agreement, 81 new ventures capitalized at more than $83 million had been incorporated in the Canadian pulp and paper industry.

The newspaper publishers' victory would be further solidified in the Underwood Tariff Act of 1913, whose practical effects were to permit free entry of newsprint (valued at less than $50/ton) and mechanical pulp from any part of the world. Adoption of the Underwood Act's top limit of US$50/ton left paper valued between $50/ton and $80/ton (specified in the Reciprocity Agreement)

TABLE 10-3. Average Cost of Newsprint Manufacturing in the United States and Canada, 1910–1916 (US$)

	1910		1913		1916	
	U.S.	Canada	U.S.	Canada	U.S.	Canada
Ground wood	13.27	8.49	12.07	8.54	11.33	8.47
Sulfite	8.63	7.41	0.82	7.97	7.33	6.74
Other materials	0.84	0.99	1.26	1.17	1.09	1.13
Total materials	22.74	16.89	21.35	17.68	19.75	16.34
Labor	3.27	3.19	3.49	2.75	3.34	2.36
Other costs	6.87	7.45	6.89	8.20	7.24	7.01
Total costs[a]	32.88	27.53	31.73	28.63	30.23	25.71

a. Not including depreciation.
Source: Southworth (1922).

from a third country subject to duty. However, Canadian newsprint exports to the United States would be below either limit for many years.

The effect of the Reciprocity Agreement on newsprint prices was apparent in 1913, when largely increased Canadian production came on line. A drop of about US$3/ton was registered, and prices continued to decline until 1916, when wartime controls on production by the Canadian government, labor shortages, increasing demand from American purchasers, and the U.S. entry into the World War I all contributed to a reversal of the trend.

Canadian imagination was equal to the task of evading the Payne–Aldrich restrictions on Crown-land products. Québec producers, emulating an earlier example in British Columbia, prevailed upon the provincial government to remove its restrictions on exportation of logs cut from the tracts of four leading paper producers. These producers had no intention of exporting logs, but removal of the restrictions permitted them to claim free entry for their paper to the United States. Faced with the prospect of an influx of Canadian paper produced at cheaper prices, American paper producers began moving some of their capital to Canada and shifting their U.S. production to other grades of paper on which the margin of profit was greater (Roach 1994).

The elimination of the U.S. tariff and other factors contributed to a rapid expansion of the Canadian paper industry. In 1925, Canadian newsprint production capacity surpassed U.S. production capacity, and the United States imported more newsprint from Canada than it manufactured itself. Since then, the Canadian share of U.S. newsprint consumption has exceeded 50 percent for many years.

After the removal of the import tariff, the growth of the Canadian newsprint industry was largely due to its low average cost of production. The estimated costs of production in favor of Canada were about 10 to 20 percent between 1910 and 1916 (Table 10-3). The difference in wood cost contributed to the lion's share (some 80 percent) of the difference in average variable costs. Canada had an immense advantage in spruce and other pulpwood from the extensive stands on Crown lands, the export of which to the United States was forbidden. The comparative and competitive advantage of Canadian newsprint production was obvious. Canadian dominance in newsprint manufacture would happen eventually, but the removal of the tariff hastened the northward movement of the newsprint industry.

The Political Economy: A Comparison

So how did U.S. newsprint consumers, coming from a disadvantaged position and facing an import tariff on their raw materials and strong opposition from U.S. newsprint producers, eventually win the newsprint tariff battle in 1911 and 1913? How have they managed to preserve their victory for so long? Conversely, why were U.S. lumber producers able to secure restrictive measures on Canadian lumber imports, which had been free of duty before 1987?

At the onset, we notice that the general political and economic environment in which these two trade conflicts took place is similar to or has even moved toward free trade. Trade laws in the United States have changed toward free trade in the last century (Gilligan 1997). The overall tariff rate on U.S. imports has declined significantly. International trade agreements, developed at multilateral or binational levels, have made international trade of goods and services freer than ever.

Second, the political system and trade politics have changed little in the United States and Canada. An industry in a real or perceived disadvantage position—whether because of an import tariff or competition from foreign producers that might be subsidized by their governments—still appeal to their elected representatives and bureaucratic officials. Appeals and pressure from various industries—those in favor of certain trade remedies and those opposed to them—have often made politicians and bureaucrats take action. Lobbying goes on, and politicians continue to respond to constituent demand when political and economic rents are available.

Third, the behavior of consumers and producers is the same now as a century ago. Consumers want cheap materials—no matter where they come from and whether or not they are subsidized. Producers prefer to have high prices, which bring more profits to them and their shareholders.

The different outcomes in these two conflicts can only be explained by the difference of strengths in, and interplay of, U.S. consumers, Canadian producers, and Canadian federal and provincial governments versus U.S. producers and their allies in Congress. The inability of the former to offer Congress something significant enough to counterbalance the Coalition for Fair Lumber Imports in the softwood lumber dispute has directly resulted in restrictive measures on Canadian lumber imports in the past 20 plus years. Other factors, such as conservation and environmentalism, have contributed indirectly, and to a much lesser extent, to the different outcomes of these two trade disputes.

Specifically, the differences lie in these factors:

First, the newsprint tariff battle started as a fight between two powerful domestic industries—the U.S. newspaper industry and the U.S. newsprint manufacturing industry. It was only when Canadians realized the power of their forest resource possession and desired to develop their own pulp and paper industry that they became a player. Without doubt, a shrewdly designed export restriction policy in Canada played a significant role in making the United States abandon its newsprint tariff and in facilitating the newsprint industry move northward. But still, the repeal of the newsprint tariff was primarily due to lobbying by the U.S. newsprint consumers. This was largely a domestic fight, and U.S. newsprint consumers were an initiator and participant in the battle.

In contrast, the softwood lumber dispute began as a dispute between a domestic industry and a foreign (Canadian) industry, and U.S. lumber consumers have had only an advisory or amicus status. Lumber consumers were hardly in the game in Lumber I and were poorly organized in Lumber II. It was not until the final episode in Lumber III, after the Softwood Lumber Agreement had inflicted much pain that they started to lobby strongly against the 1996 Softwood Lumber Agreement. In recent years, they were able to neutralize somewhat the influence of the lumber industry in the U.S. Congress, but the coalition still has the upper hand.

Although U.S. newsprint consumers must have preferred to have free trade in pulpwood, their immediate and most important goals were free trade in newsprint and pulp. Therefore, the primary goals of U.S. newsprint consumers and Canadian newsprint producers were similar. In the lumber dispute, the cooperation between some Canadian lumber producers and U.S. lumber consumers sometimes broke down when their interests diverged. In 1995, when certain Canadian lumber producers thought they could get quota rents and a five-year peace, they bought into the idea of a tariff-rate quota and signed the 1996 Softwood Lumber Agreement against the wishes of U.S. lumber consumer groups. In 2006, Canadian producers and governments signed a new agreement, again against the wishes of U.S. lumber consumers.

Second, the media industry (the newsprint consumers) was a more concentrated and powerful interest group than U.S. homebuilders. Less concentration means less coherent political lobbying and power for U.S. lumber consumers. Further, U.S. lumber consumers might have other policy agendas, such as a tax credit for mortgage investment and labor safety. The Coalition for Fair Lumber Imports had a powerful weapon in this regard, since it correctly pointed out again and again that the cost of lumber is only a small fraction (about 3 to 11 percent) of housing costs on average—and that a 0.25 percent reduction in a 30-year mortgage rate would neutralize the impact of a 10 percent hike in lumber prices that resulted in a US$1,000 increase in housing costs. A rational calculus would imply that millions of lumber consumers, each with a small tariff-induced loss, would not organize to counterbalance the influence of geographically, financially, and product-concentrated lumber producers.

In contrast, the U.S. media industry was much more effective than U.S. homebuilders in drawing the attention of public officials. Having a large number of readers (especially in cities) and being the only mass media outlet at the time—there was, of course, no television or radio or Internet available in 1910—the American Newspaper Publishers Association could shape public opinion. Ellis (1960, 233) noted, "The power of the press in a democracy is enormous, and any alleged threat to its 'freedom,' be it failure to maintain adequate supply of its raw material, brings the Congressional representatives of several thousand publishers to instant and respectful attention." The politically powerful newsprint consumers could afford to wage a political war against the newsprint producers for several decades until the tariff on newsprint imports was repealed. On the other hand, U.S. lumber consumers have had to put up with tariffs or other trade restriction measures for most of the past 20 plus years.

Third, American ownership of Canadian newsprint production capacity has been much higher than that of Canadian softwood lumber production capacity in the past few decades. Zhang (1997) and Pearse et al. (1995) find that U.S. investors invest more in the Canadian paper industry than in the Canadian wood products industry. After losing the tariff battle in 1911, quite a few U.S. paper producers established mills in Canada and integrated backward (upstream) to forest resources. Since a large number of U.S. producers now own paper mills in Canada, they would oppose any restrictive measures against Canadian newsprint imports. Therefore, it is not surprising that few tariff proposals on newsprint imports have been made even though the Canadian share of U.S. newsprint consumption has often been more than 50 percent in the past 80 years and newsprint and softwood lumber production use similar raw materials. It is also interesting to note that a few lumber-producing firms with undertakings in Canada, including Weyerhaeuser Company and Pope & Talbot, Inc., are not members of the coalition and do not support trade restriction measures against Canadian lumber.

Fourth, the Canadian industry and governments were united and played hardball with the United States all the way in the newsprint tariff battle but have been, at times, divided and willing to negotiate and compromise in the lumber trade dispute. The Canadian pulp and paper industry was in its infancy around 1900, and Canada had little or nothing to lose by playing hardball with the United States. Ontario did not back down and repeal its log export restrictions when the United States put retaliatory measures in the 1897 Dingley Tariff Act. Québec followed Ontario by prohibiting pulpwood exports from Crown lands immediately after the United States adopted a more threatening provision in the 1909 Payne–Aldrich Tariff Act.

Perhaps the fact that only two major provinces—Ontario and Québec—were practically involved in the newsprint tariff battle made coordination between federal and provincial governments easier. On the other hand, Canada had at least five distinguishable industry groups in the softwood lumber dispute—the Maritime Provinces, Québec, Ontario, coastal British Columbia, and interior British Columbia. Coordination among these groups and between federal and provincial governments was difficult, and at times, there were suspicion and even mistrust among producer groups in different regions and provinces.

The willingness of Canadian federal and provincial governments to negotiate in the lumber dispute perhaps could be explained by the fact that the lumber industry was mature and Canadian sawmills alone directly employed some 150,000 workers in the late 1980s, and the economic and political stakes were high. Fearing that they could lose more by being dragged into a long dispute, Canadian provincial and federal governments periodically accepted a series of short-term deals, which had the effect of prolonging the dispute. The Canadian governments acceptance of short-term deals might also be related to other objectives, such as keeping the free trade negotiation on track in 1986 and improving broad U.S.–Canada relations in 2006. The frictions between Canadian firms—those who have and those who have not (quality wood, quota)—in various parts of the country were evident in Lumber III and Lumber IV and contributed to the lack of a unified and consistent Canadian position. The coalition could thus divide and conquer the Canadian lumber industry and use various tactics to get what it wanted.

This infant industry versus mature industry argument probably carries less weight, considering that in 1920–1922, Canada continued to play hardball with the United States over its log export restrictions even after it had established a strong newsprint industry. Some large American interests held leases on Crown lands in Canada before the adoption of log export bans. They requested (and were subsequently denied) compensation from provincial governments. Around 1920, they exerted pressure to secure the lifting of the embargoes. This pressure had concrete results in two pieces of federal legislation in the United States.

One was the joint congressional Underwood Resolution endorsed by President Warren G. Harding, which called for a five-person commission to present to the Canadian federal and provincial governments the claims of Americans holding leases on Crown lands, acquired prior to the restrictive policy and to negotiate for the cancellation of such policy as it applied to the Americans. If the commission failed to secure this end by negotiation, it was to "investigate, consider, and report to Congress, what action should be taken to secure the cancellation of the restrictive orders so that they should not continue to militate against the interests of the people of the United States affected by them" (Ellis 1948, *121–24*). However, President Harding did not appoint this commission, perhaps after receiving the message that the Canadian provinces would stand firm because pulpwood embargoes were absolutely necessary for their economic welfare, and the mere fact that certain American interests were adversely affected by these restrictions was insufficient ground for altering them.[2] Privately threatened embargoes on shipments to Canada of coal and sulfur, two necessary materials in pulp manufacture for which Canada was largely dependent on the United States, did not materialize, either. The Canadians were indeed uncompromising.

The desire for retaliation expressed itself in U.S. legislation that would place a duty on imports from Canada of finished products that used Canadian pulpwood as an input. The U.S. House of Representatives in 1922 passed a tariff bill that provided for a 10 percent retaliatory duty on newsprint from Canada. This retaliatory duty, however, was to take effect only if the president chose to do so. No presidents have invoked such power, considering the vast political clout wielded by the media industry.

The Canadian pulp and paper industry was focused on gaining free access to the U.S. market around 1900. Free access to the U.S. market meant profit maximization. Therefore, the Canadian pulp and paper industry was single-minded in demanding the removal of U.S. tariffs on newsprint and pulp. In the lumber dispute, however, market access and profit maximization for producers might not necessarily mean the same thing. Some Canadian producers with sufficient quota could accumulate quota rents and thus preferred the tariff-rate quota system, while other producers that did not have significant quota allotments were hurt.

Finally, environmentalists in both countries indirectly helped the U.S. lumber producers win the recent softwood lumber trade dispute. After successfully lobbying for a reduction in timber harvests from public lands in the United States (which contributed to the closing down of sawmills and an increase in the Canadian share of U.S. lumber consumption), some environmentalists wanted to find a way to protect Canadian forests. Writer and film director Oliver Stone (1996) voiced his opinion that Americans had a duty to stop British Columbia from repeating the mistake made by the Americans who had "killed the soul of our land" by harvesting old-growth forests. Although Stone did not directly call for a tariff, some environmentalists in both countries did (Hamilton 1994), and several environmental groups in British Columbia had an unusual alliance with the Coalition for Fair Lumber Imports in the softwood lumber trade dispute (Cashore 1998).

Certainly, sawlogs cost more in lumber production than does pulpwood in newsprint production. However, the 1913 battle over newsprint tariffs demonstrates that cost differences between the two countries were not the primary reason that the United States levied and then lifted a tariff on newsprint imports in the first place. It also demonstrated that international trade settlement mechanisms, though potentially helpful, are not essential to settling a trade dispute.

Notes

1. Most of the material in this section is drawn from Ellis (1948, 1960, 1968) and Southworth (1922).

2. President Harding's untimely death in 1923 might have contributed to inaction as well.

11

An End to the War?

Lessons Learned and the Prospects for the 2006 Agreement

At the beginning of this book, I introduced six puzzles surrounding the U.S.–Canada forest products trade. First, why is there free trade for most goods and services between the two countries but not for softwood lumber? Second, why are the results of the newsprint tariff battle and the softwood lumber dispute so different, even though both products are made of wood? Third, why in the past 20-plus years has each country at times given up trade arrangements that were beneficial to the country as a whole? Fourth, why have politicians and leaders of an industry that is somewhat integrated across the border been unable to break the deadlock for so long? Fifth, why does the U.S. lumber industry continue to seek administrative trade protection in countervailing duties while the total number of countervailing duty cases has declined? Finally, why have the NAFTA and WTO trade dispute settlement mechanisms not worked for softwood lumber?

The short answer to those questions is interest group politics and institutional arrangements. In both countries, special interest politics has dominated the political discussion related to the lumber and newsprint trade disputes. In the newsprint case, powerful U.S. newsprint consumers eventually won the tariff war of 1897–1913 and have held onto their victory since 1911, despite having come from a disadvantaged position (with an existing import tariff on newsprint) and facing strong opposition from the U.S. newsprint producers.

In the lumber trade dispute, the main interest groups in the United States are domestic lumber producers that want to profit more by curtailing foreign competition and thereby raising lumber prices and domestic production, and to a much lesser extent, domestic lumber consumers that prefer free trade and lower lumber prices. In Canada, the main interest group is the somewhat regionally fragmented lumber industry. These interest groups have often been able to get their respective governments to go along with their demands. When one of these groups sees an opportunity to advance its interest, it urges its government to act in a way that inflicts wounds to the other groups. This tactic, however, often serves as an invitation for the other groups to fight back and thus prolongs the dispute. Since their interests differ among and within these major groups, a compromise is often hard to achieve, especially when the U.S. lumber producers have strong support from their representatives in Congress and Canadian producers have the sympathy of their provincial governments.

This dynamic is further aggravated by some institutional arrangements: the relative strength of Canadian provincial governments compared with the federal government in forest resource management, which explains Canada's inability to identify and maintain a united and consistent position; the leverage that Congress has on the executive branch in trade matters; and U.S. trade laws that do not give consumers a legal standing in trade disputes. Other factors, such as economics, legal frameworks (U.S. trade law, the bilateral Free Trade Agreement, the North American Free Trade Agreement, the World Trade Organization), and the apparent willingness of the two governments to cut a deal on softwood lumber as a way of advancing other national (and the politicians' own) interests, have contributed to the longevity of the lumber dispute and the ultimate victory for the U.S. lumber industry.

The Underlying Causes of the Lumber Dispute

As noted earlier, certain U.S. lumber producers have alleged that the Canadian lumber industry is subsidized by its provincial governments through below-market stumpage fees. This is the apparent, rhetorical cause of the modern softwood lumber dispute.

In the eyes of these U.S. producers, the Canadian subsidy is motivated by Canadian provinces' pursuit of social objectives rather than a fair market value for standing timber. They also reason that powerful Canadian producers would not hesitate to ask the provincial governments for subsidies. Finally, the provincial governments have the policy means—including administratively set stumpage fees, manufacturing requirements, appurtenant clauses, minimum cut requirements, lax annual allowable cuts, and prohibition of log exports—to subsidize their industry.

In theory, administratively set stumpage fees could be lower or higher than market-driven stumpage prices, or about equal. Was Canadian lumber industry subsidized? Is it subsidized? The Department of Commerce reached three negative determinations in 1983, 1994, and 2006, once on its own and twice under the direction of FTA or NAFTA binational panels. There was also an uncontested preliminary affirmative determination in 1986 when the two countries settled under the Memorandum of Understanding. These are about all of the legal conclusions on the subsidy allegation.

The truckloads of legal briefing and background papers by parties involved in the dispute notwithstanding, there has been no independent, refereed study on the subsidy issue during the course of the lumber dispute, partly because it

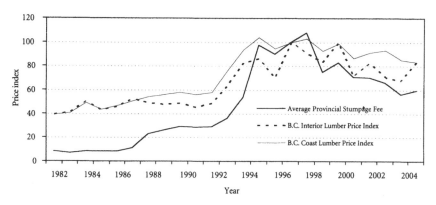

FIGURE 11-1. Average Provincial Stumpage Fees and Lumber Price Index in British Columbia, 1982–2005

Note: Fiscal year ending March 31, 1997 = 100.
Sources: Statistics Canada (http://www.statcan.ca/start.html) (series P4798 and P4799 for lumber price index) and British Columbia Ministry of Forests (various years) (for original stumpage fees in C\$/m³).

is political, but mostly because it is difficult to study. Empirically, stumpage prices vary significantly in different regions within a state, across states, and among different ownerships in the United States, not to mention between the United States and Canada. Thus, although one could conduct a hedonic study on the determinants of stumpage fees in Canada, with the nature of the stumpage sale (competitive versus administratively determined) as one of many variables, and avoid using the cross-country comparison method that was rejected by the NAFTA Subsidy Panel and called into question by the WTO Subsidy Appellate Panel in Lumber IV, it is difficult practically to measure and control for everything else. Thus, such a study likely would be subject to legitimate criticism. Further, the study needs to be conducted in a region that is substantially smaller than a province, and in order to make an inference to the province, there need to be several studies.

The next best approach may be to find out whether Canadian stumpage fees vary with the market conditions for the product (lumber, pulp, and paper). This would require an examination of the correlation between lumber prices and stumpage fees over a period of time.

Figure 11-1 shows annual softwood lumber price indexes for interior and coastal British Columbia and the annual average stumpage fees in the province. Although the average stumpage fees cover both sawtimber and pulpwood, it is clear from Figure 11-1 that the average stumpage fees in British Columbia are highly correlated with the lumber price indexes in that province. Further, the stumpage fees have risen faster than the lumber price indexes in the past 20 years.

All else being equal, to the extent that stumpage fees increased faster than lumber prices in Canada, the Canadian lumber industry would lose its compet-

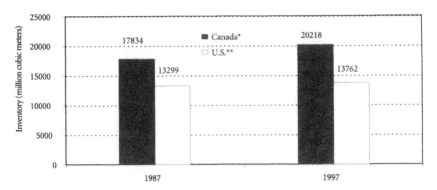

FIGURE 11-2. Total Softwood Timber Growing Stock in the United States and Canada, 1987 and 1997

*Defined as gross merchantable wood on stocked, timber-productive, no-reserve forests. Source: Canadian Forest Service (2004).
**Defined as growing stock on timberland.
Source: Smith et al. (2004).

itive advantage and market share against the U.S. lumber industry. The Coalition for Fair Lumber Imports has succeeded not only in getting stumpage prices in British Columbia (and other provinces) to rise faster than lumber prices, but also in putting various trade restriction measures on Canadian lumber imports in the past 20 years. As a result, the coalition's actions have enhanced the competitiveness of the U.S. industry (Nagubadi and Zhang 2006).

The real underlying cause of the lumber dispute is the difference in softwood timber resource endowments between the two countries. With the exception of Reed (1986, 2001), not many studies have looked at this difference. Resource endowment, as international economics textbooks routinely teach—is the foundation of comparative advantage, and comparative advantage leads to specialization in production and trade.

Canada has more softwood growing stock than the United States by a ratio of 3 to 2 (Figure 11-2). This fact—Canada has an absolute advantage in softwood timber resources—often surprises many forestry students and professionals in the United States.

If one considers only the difference in absolute softwood timber resource endowment and assumes everything else is equal, Canada could, hypothetically, have about 59.5 percent of the softwood lumber production in North America (Table 11-1). This translates to a 49.5 percent share of U.S. lumber consumption, since the Canadian softwood lumber industry has a nearly 100 percent share of its own domestic market and exports some 10 percent of its production to other countries. Even if softwood lumber production is equally distributed between the two countries, Canada could theoretically have 38.3 percent of the U.S. market (Table 11-1).

TABLE 11-1. Actual and Hypothetical Share of U.S. and Canadian Softwood Lumber in the North American Market

Sector	Amount (mmbf)	Share (percentage)
Actual, 2001		
Consumption by sources of supply		
Domestic supply	33,845	62.77
Imported from Canada	18,689	34.66
Imported from other countries	1,377	2.55
Total apparent U.S. consumption	53,920	100.00
Production		
United States	34,656	54.30
Canada	29,166	45.70
Total North America production	63,822	100.00
Hypothetical distribution of total North American production		
Scenario I: Production is equal to share of softwood growing stock		
U.S. production (0.405 × total North American production of 63,822)	25,848	40.50
Canadian production (0.595 × total North American production of 63,822)	37,974	59.50
U.S. share of domestic market[a]		47.94
Canadian share of U.S. market (1–0.0255–0.4794)[b]		49.51
Scenario II: Production is equally distributed between the two countries		
U.S. production (0.50 × total North American production of 63,822)	31,911	50.00
Canadian production (0.50 × total North American production of 63,822)	31,911	50.00
U.S. share of domestic market[a]		
Canadian share of U.S. market (1–0.0255–0.592)[b]		38.30

a. Assuming all U.S. domestic production is consumed domestically.
b. Assuming imports from other countries stay at 2.55 percent, as in 2001.
Source for 2001 data: Canadian Forest Service (various issues).

On a per capita basis, Canadians have a much bigger advantage to the Americans, a 13-to-1 ratio in softwood timber resource endowment (Figure 11-3). It is no wonder that a country like Canada, with such an absolute advantage in softwood timber resources, would have lower stumpage prices than the United States and would have taken an increasing share of the U.S. market in the past few decades. This 13-to-1 ratio also implies that administratively set stumpage fees may, in fact, be higher than what would result from market forces in Canada.

I do not suggest that everything else is equal. Timber grows much more slowly in Canada than in most parts of the United States. Also, under current

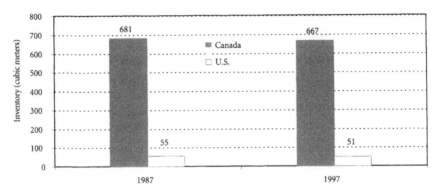

FIGURE 11-3. Per Capita Softwood Timber Growing Stock in the United States and Canada, 1987 and 1997

Note: See Figure 11-2 for data sources.

conditions, some softwood inventory probably is not economically, ecologically, or politically accessible in Canada. Some environmentalists will fight hard to keep timber harvesting from Crown lands at its current level, or lower.

Nor do I suggest that the Canadian share of the U.S. lumber market will or should necessarily rise to 38–49 percent or, conversely, that U.S. production will or should necessarily decline much from the current level any time soon. U.S. producers will fight to keep the Canadian share as low as possible. Plus, it will be politically unacceptable in the United States if the Canadian share of the U.S. market goes up too much and too fast.

Canada's competitive advantage in its lumber industry needs more than trees on the ground. Political stability, sound economic and trade policy, the availability of a competent labor force, secure supplies of energy, and suitable infrastructure are also essential. Under Porter's (1991) five-element competitiveness model, factor endowment is just one element of competitiveness; the others are domestic and external demand, support industries, competition, and government policy. A rich natural resource base is not sufficient to sustain international competitive advantage; that can flow only from continuing improvement and innovation, which depend on dynamic interaction among all the other elements. Moreover, resource abundance tends to weaken incentives to innovate (Pearse et al. 1995).

Nonetheless, the increase in Canadian exports to the United States in the past 40 years was perhaps inevitable—with or without U.S. trade actions. The United States needs lumber that Canada is ready and happy to supply. U.S. consumers want affordable lumber. Trade actions have slowed down the pace of Canadian lumber exports, but Canadian lumber imports have still been rising slowly, in absolute terms. Without such actions, the share of Canadian lumber in the U.S. market certainly would be higher than the current 34 percent.

Explaining the Longevity of the Dispute

Even if the softwood lumber trade dispute was unavoidable, why has it gone on for so long?

McNabb (2004) uses a "circle to hell" model, developed by former B.C. Deputy Minister of Forests Don Wright, to explain the lack of a durable solution for the softwood lumber dispute (Figure 11-4). The model starts with differences in forest landownership and stumpage pricing systems in the two countries. For three reasons—market forces are harder to see and governments might have constrained market forces in Canada, the Canadian share of U.S. consumption is increasing, and the profit margins of U.S. lumber firms are low—certain U.S. lumber producers believe they cannot compete against "subsidized" Canadian producers. The solution for these U.S. producers is to raise Canadian lumber production costs. That in turn leads to a curtailment of Canadian imports and higher lumber prices in the United States. Higher lumber prices lead to higher timber prices and an increase in lumber production capacity in the United States. The end result is that several years after an initial increase in Canadian production costs, the profit margins of U.S. lumber producers fall again. This prompts the U.S. industry to start another round aimed at increasing Canadian production costs. The circle repeats itself every several years.

This model provides a simple economic explanation of the longevity of the lumber dispute. Because of the administrative nature of the Canadian stumpage system, the Coalition for Fair Lumber Imports has succeeded in making some U.S. lawmakers discount the absolute, comparative, and competitive advantage of the Canadian industry in terms of resource endowments and productivities and support restrictive measures on Canadian lumber imports. Attacking the Canadian industry has become a fertile rhetorical ground for

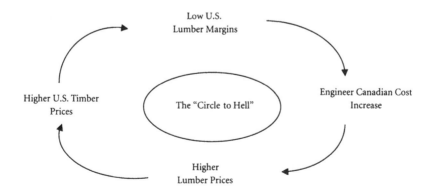

FIGURE 11-4. The "Circle to Hell" Model of the U.S.–Canada Softwood Lumber Dispute

Source: McNabb (2004).

the coalition. Because the difference in stumpage systems is portrayed as Canada's fault, protectionists in the United States demand more, and indeed get more, concessions from Canada even though no subsidy was found when the case was decided in 1983 or went to final appeal in 1994 and 2006.

The most important factor behind this "circle to hell" model is interest politics.

Political factors. The Coalition for Fair Lumber Imports is well organized and plays interest group politics better than U.S. consumer groups. Since inception, it has "owned" some U.S. lawmakers. Usually, at some important juncture of negotiation or litigation, these lawmakers exert pressure on the U.S. administration and Canadians in the form of letters, public hearings, speeches, or legislative actions. A core group of U.S. senators, mostly from the lumber-producing states in the Pacific Northwest and South, plus other senators who exchange political favors with them, have sometimes constituted a voting majority or a significant block that no U.S. president could ignore. These senators help initiate changes in U.S. trade laws that benefit the coalition and block legislation that is detrimental to the U.S. lumber industry. Under political pressure and U.S. trade laws, Commerce and the International Trade Commission have arguably used ever-shifting, result-driven methodologies in their respective subsidy, dumping, and injury investigations. Canadians are simply not able to win the lumber dispute when U.S. administrative and independent authorities actively help domestic producers; recall that both Commerce and ITC were repeatedly found by FTA and NAFTA panels to have failed to apply U.S. laws properly.

The political mobilization of U.S. lumber consumers in recent years has provided some counterweight to the coalition. The lobbying of American Consumers for Affordable Homes in Congress, especially in the House of Representatives, which "overrepresents" urban populations, has neutralized, to a degree, the influence of the coalition. Nonetheless, the coalition has had an upper hand in American politics that consumer groups have not been able to overcome in the past and seem unlikely to surmount in the near future.

The Canadian lumber industry is equally, if not more, political. Like U.S. producers, Canadian lumber producers are rent seeking, and they are one of the largest—if not the largest—clients of certain Canadian forest policy networks on issues related to the lumber dispute. Canada's termination of the MOU, even though it benefited the country as a whole in economic terms and even though signing it was questionable in the first place,[1] demonstrates the level of influence of the Canadian lumber industry in Canadian trade politics. One has to wonder, if Canadian producers have had such influence in Canadian politics (especially at the provincial level) for so long, would they not have used their influence to obtain low stumpage fees—whether such stumpage fees were defined legally as a subsidy or not?

The problem for the Canadian lumber industry is that it is fragmented at both the provincial and the regional levels. On several occasions, the coalition has taken advantage of these divisions to impose its will on the Canadian lumber industry.

Canada's official position on lumber trade has been influenced by its general dependency on trade with the United States. Secure access to U.S. markets is important to the Canadian government. The real or perceived abandonment of its lumber industry by the Canadian government in 1986 in order to secure a broader free trade agreement with the United States exemplifies the Canadian government's objective of secure access to U.S. markets as a top priority. At times, the Canadian government was willing to make peace with the United States and sign a negotiated agreement, more so than certain Canadian lumber producers or provincial governments. In addition, a trade surplus with the United States has made the Canadian government reluctant to use its oil and gas as a weapon and leverage in the softwood lumber dispute.

If the "circle to hell" model provides a "natural," economic explanation for the longevity of the lumber dispute, what is the role of politicians in prolonging it? Lawmakers need interest groups like the coalition. Most politicians want to survive the next election and may be more interested in a short-term fix rather than a truly long-lasting resolution to the dispute. Some U.S. and Canadian politicians may have little political incentive to find a long-lasting resolution, since they want the interest groups to come back to them periodically with more campaign contributions and support and win the next election.

There are other factors prolonging the dispute as well.

Legal factors. Foreigners do not vote in domestic elections, and thus Canadians' voices and concerns typically are ignored by the U.S. political and legal system. More importantly, the economic impact of lumber trade restrictions on U.S. consumers is not considered under U.S. trade laws. American lumber consumers do not have legal standing and are not on equal footing with American producers, even though they eventually pay the costs of all trade restrictions on lumber imports. U.S. producers can see evidence for subsidy in Canada and claim injury to themselves without having to worry about injury to U.S. consumers. Trade restrictions make legal and economic sense to U.S. producers but not to U.S. consumers. Finally, U.S. administrative laws are numerous and imprecise and thus are subject to manipulation and political pressure.

This does not mean that U.S. producers have had legal and economic victories on all issues related to the lumber dispute. Log export restrictions are one of these issues. Log export restrictions in both the United States and Canada reduce domestic log prices and benefit domestic lumber producers. Yet, a WTO panel ruled in 2001 that log export restrictions were not a countervailable subsidy. The coalition has not been able to persuade the U.S. government to challenge Canadian log export restrictions in Lumber IV.

Because the general benefits of free trade far overweigh the costs, international trade has become freer in the world, and protectionism is slowly losing ground. There are multinational institutions (WTO and NAFTA) that deal with trade protectionism. However, some of these institutions have just grown out of infancy, and their effectiveness in dealing with trade disputes is being tested.

With complicated legal issues to resolve, lawyers are in high demand in a case as big and significant as the lumber dispute. When many lawyers are involved and a large amount of money is at stake, it is easy to understand the longevity of the dispute. As Percy (2004) stated, "the lumber dispute is the cash cow for lawyers." It seems possible, if not likely, that just like some politicians, some of these lawyers have been willing to advance their own financial interests at the expense of finding a genuine resolution.

Institutional factors. Provincial ownership of forest resources and provincial stumpage systems in Canada are institutional arrangements that directly contributed to the lumber dispute; the political institution of federalism in both countries make both governments susceptible to special interest politics. The U.S. Senate worked as it was designed—to offer small, less populous states a voice in the national political arena. With Canadian subsidy an article of faith for some U.S. senators from lumber-producing states and other U.S. politicians, their voices and opinions have been reflected in the investigating authorities' decisions in the past 20 years. Protectionism in lumber has prevailed.

Canadian political institutions do not work as well in trade conflicts with the United States. Interprovincial and interregional politics is apparent in the lumber trade dispute. The Canadian government has many constituents to listen to and has been inconsistent in dealing with the lumber dispute. It sought free trade with the United States but agreed to the MOU in Lumber II. It denied the allegation of subsidy and won the FTA panel rulings but turned around and signed the Softwood Lumber Agreement of 1996 in Lumber III. It vowed to fight in NAFTA and WTO in Lumber IV, but at times showed a great willingness to accept a negotiated deal in Lumber IV. Indeed, it signed the Softwood Lumber Agreement of 2006 after winning strongly in NAFTA and U.S. courts and achieving some victory at WTO. By so doing, it not only failed to take full advantage of its legal victories, it gave US$1 billion to the United States, half of which went to its primary adversary, the Coalition for Fair Lumber Imports, and left some critical legal questions to the interpretation of the U.S. industry and government, including the authority of NAFTA, the practice of zeroing, subsidy, and the legal right to the return of duty deposits. These issues will continue to haunt not only the Canadian lumber industry but also other Canadian industries in disputes with the United States. The U.S. trade harassment that the Canadian government vowed to get rid of through the FTA (and NAFTA) will continue.

In short, the softwood lumber dispute involves many issues and many players in complicated political, economic, legal, and institutional settings. Some issues make economic but not legal sense; others make political and legal but not economic sense. The mix of economics, legality, institutional arrangements, and politics has made the dispute long and sometimes bitter and acrimonious.

The political, economic, legal, and institutional settings have produced and nurtured the most critical factor—that there is no down side for the coalition to continue to fight political and legal battles against Canadian lumber imports. Even if it lost after three to five years of litigation, the lumber price increase in these years would have generated increased profits far greater than the costs of litigation. The inability of U.S. consumers—hindered by high transaction costs and U.S. trade laws—to fight the coalition, the division of interests in Canada, and the willingness of the Canadian government to compromise in the lumber dispute give the coalition extra incentives to fight on and take home war prizes in the MOU and the two softwood lumber agreements. A truly long-term and durable solution has not been found, even though all parties say they want one.

Possible Solutions and Potential Routes

What would a durable solution for this lumber dispute look like, and what would it take for both countries to get there?

Here is what the Coalition for Fair Lumber Imports (2005) wants:

> The U.S. lumber industry has consistently made clear that all that is needed to resolve the softwood lumber dispute is for the Canadian provinces to sell their timber in a truly open and competitive market. U.S. sawmills can compete with anyone on a fair and level playing field, but not with foreign treasuries that are in partnership with their industry. "Free trade" is a meaningless term unless trade practices are fair, too. Canada's trade practices in softwood lumber are not fair and won't be until the subsidies end and there is open and free competition for timber as well as lumber.

The coalition also stated that it "vigorously supports the U.S. government's pursuit of free trade principles and a negotiated settlement based on reasonable Canadian commitments to timber policy reform. Until then, we will defend our rights to relief under U.S. law."

U.S.-style timber sale system. Since the public in Canada has not yet shown strong support for privatizing public forest lands, selling provincial timber in an open and competitive market means that Canadian provinces must adopt a stumpage sale system that is similar to the one used by the U.S. Forest Service. It is not at all clear that the coalition truly wants a U.S.-style system, given that the Forest Service is losing money in its national forest timber sales. Perhaps it is banking on the fact that the provincial governments could not and do not want to do so under social, economic, and political pressure, for several reasons.

First, the economic pressure stems from the public treasury and possible demand for compensation if tenure holders lose their timber-harvesting rights. Will such compensation be deemed a subsidy? Provincial governments are unlikely to embark on such a reform, which would have uncertain results.

Second, there is no guarantee that timber prices would go up if Canadian provinces adopted a U.S.-style system, especially in regions with only one or a few possible buyers. It is possible that timber prices would rise in some regions and decline in others, with the results being roughly similar to the current system. It is also possible that timber prices would rise initially and then decline. The coalition, however, will not tolerate the provinces' receiving less revenue under a new system.

Third, the Canadian lumber industry has argued that it is not subsidized, by pointing to the three negative determinations by Commerce in 1983, 1994, and 2005. So why should the provincial governments remove their timber rights and adopt a U.S.-style system?

Finally, politicians in Canadian provinces prefer public ownership of forest lands, which gives them the flexibility in dealing with First Nations land claims and future land-use changes.

Litigation. Litigation assisted the Canadian lumber industry in Lumber III and Lumber IV. Might litigation lead to a durable, long-term solution? Several cases, including the one on Canadian producers' rights to all duty deposits once a NAFTA panel rules against the United States, are ongoing. The constitutionality of the NAFTA panel system has not been ruled on by U.S. courts.

Had the Softwood Lumber Agreement of 2006 not been implemented and should Lumber IV be concluded completely in Canada's favor (all duty deposits are returned to Canada and the antidumping and countervailing duty orders are revoked), the coalition would likely launch another countervailing and antidumping duty case and start Lumber V. Should Canada win Lumber V conclusively, then the interests in continuing the lumber dispute would diminish and there would be a durable solution—that is, free trade of lumber for the foreseeable future.

Based on the experience of the two most recent rounds of the dispute, Lumber V could take another five to seven years beyond the time necessary to conclude Lumber IV. If the Canadians win legally in Lumber IV as well as in Lumber V, free trade for lumber might be realized in 2013–2015, roughly one century after newsprint went on the free list and 30 years after the modern lumber war began officially.

Thus, litigation could lead to a durable solution in the long run. In the near term, a durable solution could be reached only if the coalition loses its political support in Congress and realizes that it cannot win another countervailing duty case. Should the coalition also lose a few major financial backers, such as International Paper, which has sold most of its timberland and lumber mills, it might reconsider its position. Political pressure from U.S. consumers and Canada in a firm and persistent manner could help the two countries reach a durable solution sooner.

Negotiation. Will negotiation lead to a durable solution? A series of short-term, negotiated settlements might constitute a long-term solution, but in reality they are all short-term deals. The MOU and the first Softwood Lumber

Agreement were short-lived. The 2006 agreement is for seven to nine years, and either country can withdraw from it after two years.

The bridge between a short-term and a long-term solution is a clear exit map. That's the role that Commerce's policy bulletin is supposed to play. As of this writing, the policy bulletin is not finalized, and Canada has not agreed to abide by it. Although a policy exit is mentioned in the Softwood Lumber Agreement of 2006, it is unclear whether it will be developed in time and implemented smoothly. Two critical questions remain: What are the exit criteria and who serves as the arbitrator of whether Canadian provinces have met the criteria?

With Commerce's impartiality being called into question,[2] Canada has pushed for a binding binational panel of experts to adjudicate whether individual provinces have made sufficient forest policy reforms and can export lumber to the United States free of any trade restrictions. In addition, Canadian provinces would like to have a hard and fast rule and threshold (percentage of timber that is auctioned) built in the policy exit, and the coalition would like to set the threshold high. Aside from the serious differences on these thorny issues, the policy exit remains a viable long-term solution, at least theoretically. In reality, a policy exit may not be sufficient, since it requires a degree of trust that does not exist and tolerance for a government-controlled system.

Moderate and voluntary constraints. Another durable solution is that Canada agrees to some kind of simple, voluntary, moderate, midterm or long-term restriction on its softwood lumber exports to the United States. In spite of being too complicated and neither voluntary nor simple, the level of restriction contained in the agreement of 2006 is moderate. In a sense, the Softwood Lumber Agreement of 2006 could have been one mechanism for achieving this result.

* * *

In 2003, before any significant results from the litigation track in Lumber IV had come out, Zhang (2003) proposed a simple negotiated long-term settlement that would put a 5 percent export tax on Canadian lumber exports to the United States and earmark the tax revenue to be used in advertisements promoting North America softwood lumber and in forestry-related research and development. Further, he proposed that Canada continue to reform its forest policy to make stumpage fees reflective of market conditions, rather than basing them on arbitrary, administrative targets. The United States was advised to get rid of its countervailing and antidumping duty orders and refund Canadian producers all the duty deposits it had collected since May 2002. Both sides would withdraw their petitions in WTO and NAFTA. Most importantly, the term of this settlement should be long—a minimum of 10 years.

If this proposal is accepted, legal uncertainty, fees and expenses, and market uncertainty will evaporate, and that would benefit all parties involved. In addition, each major player in the dispute will get some extra benefit.

The U.S. producers receive a long-term export tax on Canadian lumber imports, giving them some protection and enhancement in profitability. The tax rate is lower than the then-current rate but is not much lower than the 6.51 percent determined by Commerce in Lumber III. In addition, when the promotion campaign and research financed by the tax revenues promotes North American softwood lumber and advances its production technology, U.S. producers will benefit from an increase in consumer demand and help their products compete better against such substitutes as steel and non-North American lumber.

U.S. consumers are better off than with the 27.2 percent duty (which was lowered through administrative reviews later). Removing uncertainty would also reduce lumber price volatility.

Canadian producers benefit from lumber promotion, which increases lumber demand, and from research and development which would help reduce production costs over time. They would not have to give any legal ground on the matter of subsidy. Their contribution of a 5 percent export tax would be considered as goodwill to the development and further integration of the North American lumber industry.

For the U.S. and Canadian governments, a major block in improving their bilateral relationship would be removed. Since whether and which country gets the tax revenue have never been a major issue in this dispute, replacing the U.S. duties with a Canadian export tax should be acceptable to both governments.

John Ragosta of the Coalition for Fair Lumber Imports stated in the summer of 2003 that this proposal was ludicrous. Now, the coalition has accepted the Softwood Lumber Agreement of 2006, which contains an effective 4–5 percent U.S. duty on Canadian lumber imports from 2002 to 2006. On the other hand, as suggested in Chapter 9, the Canadian government's acceptance of an agreement similar to the one proposed in Zhang (2003), after all of its legal victories, might not be wise in the long run.

* * *

A natural ending for the dispute. Two circumstances might contribute to development of long-term and durable solutions: an increase in American ownership of the Canadian lumber mills (and vice versa), and a significant decline in Canada's comparative and competitive advantage with respect to softwood resource endowments. If either of these two conditions occurs, the lumber dispute could slowly dissipate.

U.S. lumber producers might want to consider buying more Canadian lumber mills, just as they acquired Canadian pulp and paper mills in the 20th century. If Canadian lumber producers are indeed subsidized and keep some kind of windfall profits or economic rents, American producers could improve their profitability by purchasing some Canadian lumber firms. Similarly, Canadian lumber producers could consider increasing their investment in the United States.

Enhanced integration of the North American lumber industry would diminish the chance for prolonging the trade dispute. Pearse et al. (1995) find that Americans own some 45 percent of pulp and paper manufacturing facilities in British Columbia. The American ownership of pulp and paper manufacturing facilities in Québec and Ontario could be higher. If Americans own a similar or a larger share of Canadian sawmills, the lumber dispute likely will subside.

On the other hand, Canada's vast natural softwood resources have been under stress because of the mountain pine beetle and forest fires as well as timber harvesting and conservation uses. It is conceivable that after 20 to 30 years, once its natural forests are depleted by human or natural forces, Canada's comparative and competitive advantage in resources and productivity over the United States will decline significantly. Already, the National Association of Home Builders (2006) reports that other countries' share of the U.S. lumber market rose from 0.8 percent in 1996 to 4.9 percent in 2005, and Haynes (2003) predicts that in 2050, Canada's share of the U.S. lumber market will decline to 25 percent, while other countries' share will increase to about 15 percent and the share for domestic producers will stay at 60 percent. If the projection by Haynes (2003) proves true, and especially when lumber imports from other countries to the United States rise quickly, the softwood lumber trade dispute could also become history in coming decades, if not sooner.

* * *

In sum, a long-term, durable solution might involve one of the following options:

- Canadian provinces sell most or a significant portion of timber on the open market, as the Coalition for Fair Lumber Imports demands.
- Litigation leads to free trade of lumber after the conclusion of Lumber IV and possibly Lumber V.
- A series of short-term deals are negotiated, in combination with a mutually recognized long-term agreement on an exit ramp leading to free trade and a binding dispute resolution system.
- A long-term settlement is negotiated, based on moderate, reasonable, and hopefully voluntary Canadian trade restrictions that are simple to implement.
- American ownership of Canadian sawmill facilities increases, and vice versa, making the trade dispute slowly disappear on its own.
- Canada's comparative and competitive advantage over the United States in softwood resource endowment declines, and with it, the Canadian share of the U.S. lumber market.

The first two options are somewhat extreme. The final two are for the long run. Most likely, a long-term, durable solution would involve the other two options. In fact, with some exceptions, the Softwood Lumber Agreement of 2006 is a combination of these two options.

Where to Go from Here?

Interestingly, even before the Framework Agreement was reached on April 27, 2006, the lumber market had pointed to a conclusion in Lumber IV since August 10, 2005, when the NAFTA Extraordinary Challenge Committee affirmed that there was no threat of injury to the U.S. lumber industry. Specifically, the price spread between lumber delivered to Boston and Toronto, which increases under trade restrictions and decreases under free trade, nearly disappeared from August 2005 to March 2006 (Figure 11-5). That is, the lumber market expected that the United States would revoke the current countervailing and antidumping duty orders, at least prospectively, as of August 10, 2005. Whether the United States returns the duties collected before August 2005 is another matter.

Now that the Softwood Lumber Agreement of 2006 is implemented, what can we expect for softwood lumber trade between the two countries in the next seven to nine years and beyond, assuming either country will not scrap it in two years?

If history provides a guide, there will still be trade frictions in softwood lumber during the term of the 2006 agreement. British Columbia wanted to terminate the MOU after four years even though it had been excluded from its effects; industry groups in both countries and U.S. consumers were unhappy with the 1996 agreement after two years. In both cases, trade frictions, negotiations, and arbitrations ensued.

An agreement to manage trade flows cannot incorporate all future changes in market conditions, natural events, and other factors, whether foreseen or unforeseen, and thus it will be resisted by one or more segments of the industry in both countries when they find themselves hampered by it. General economic conditions and lumber markets change; new competitors, interest groups, and politicians emerge; and the relative competitiveness of the softwood lumber industry in the United States and Canada as well as within Canada evolves over time. As these changes occur, adversely affected Canadian producers will voice their concerns and demand additional quotas or assistance from the provincial and federal governments.

On the other hand, the Coalition for Fair Lumber Imports will, no doubt, try to enforce the 2006 agreement to the extent possible. With the 2006 agreement as complex as it is, little disincentive for the coalition to bring forward cases, the high return it received in previous softwood lumber dispute settlement panels, and the support it has had in the U.S. Congress and administrations, it is possible that the coalition will launch many disputes over the life of the 2006 agreement.

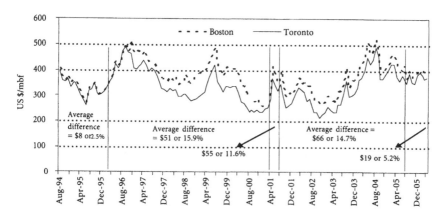

FIGURE 11-5. Spruce–Pine–Fir Lumber Prices in Toronto and Boston Markets, August 1994–April 2006

Note: For eastern spruce–pine–fire, kiln-dried, 2x4, standard and better.
Source: Random Lengths, Inc. (various years).

For example, the 2006 agreement does not incorporate exchange rate fluctuations. What happens if, as has happened in the past 10 years, the Canadian dollar goes down or up 30 percent against the U.S. dollar? If the Canadian dollar depreciates 30 percent against the U.S. dollar and everything else is equal, based on the elasticity estimate of 0.4 by Adams et al. (1986), the Canadian share of the U.S. lumber market should theoretically go up 12 percent from the current level, to 38 percent. If so, certain Canadian producers will not be happy with the agreement that puts a cap of 30 to 34 percent, beyond which they have to pay export taxes. On the other hand, if the Canadian dollar appreciates 30 percent against the U.S. dollar and Canada still takes 34 percent or more of the U.S. market share, the coalition will not be pleased.

Further, the 2006 agreement does not consider changes in inflation, interest rates, housing starts, technical advance, production capacity, and natural events such as bug infestation and fire threats. Any of these factors could affect U.S. demand and supply for lumber. Over time, the defined threshold could prove too high or too low for some producers.

As in previous agreements, the 2006 agreement will undoubtedly have unintended consequences. The anticircumvention clause in the agreement is a virtual guarantee of arbitration. The yet-to-be defined policy exit is a source of dispute. The termination clause after two years of implementation creates uncertainty. Thus, there may be many disputes over the life of the 2006 agreement, and when the time comes—that is, when the majority of producers in either country feel the marginal benefits of the agreement do not cover the marginal costs—they will lobby their governments to terminate it.

On the other hand, there is growing fatigue among the players in both countries, and the 2006 agreement could run its course for the next seven to nine years. After it expires in 2013–2015, a Lumber V is likely unless (1) the lumber industry in North America becomes much more integrated; (2) the comparative and competitive advantage of Canadian lumber producers over U.S. producers in resource endowment and productivity declines significantly; and (3) the authority and constitutionality of NAFTA and especially the rights to return of all duty deposits are established. Both countries would then either negotiate for a settlement or go through litigation again—or do both, as long as litigation does not go too far in Lumber V.

The chance of further trade frictions in softwood lumber will be enhanced if the constitutionality and authority of NAFTA are not settled before the agreement expires or is terminated. Although some major legal issues are unresolved or left in the coalition's favor, the 2006 agreement will depress lumber prices in Canada and increase lumber prices in the United States, making another antidumping duty case unlikely after its expiration. Nonetheless, the 1996 agreement did not prevent the coalition from filing an antidumping duty case in Lumber IV because Commerce disregarded the so-called below-cost sales in Canada. The coalition's reward for litigation makes Lumber V more likely.

The coalition would likely be discouraged from pursuing another case if Lumber IV had been expensive, there was no dividend from the duties, and most of the legal results had gone against them. With the departure of International Paper from the timber and lumber business and of Georgia-Pacific from the coalition, Lumber V could become improbable, even moreso if all the duty deposits were returned to Canadian producers, giving them an opportunity to buy assets in the U.S. market. The 2006 agreement reverses all those developments and demonstrates that bringing cases against Canada is rewarding (Feldman 2006).

What Has Been Learned?

The softwood lumber dispute is an education in American and Canadian politics, law, and institutions, particularly as to the U.S. legislature's role in shaping trade policy and the influence that industry lobbies in both countries have on government decisionmaking in trade and resource management. It has demonstrated the values and limitations of the NAFTA and WTO dispute settlement mechanisms and highlighted the need to strengthen these mechanisms. It has also illustrated the difficulty of solving a highly politicized trade case in a system that is tilted against foreigners and ignores the welfare of domestic consumers, and the process and uncertain outcomes when the free trade ideal collides with interest group politics in a powerful country.

The primary conclusions of this book are six.

1. The United States lost its comparative and competitive advantage over Canada in softwood lumber production because of deteriorating resource endow-

ments, partly caused by public policy that limits timber supply, and an increase in demand for lumber, which is largely driven by population increase.

2. Forest landownership and timber price policy are based on historical events; there is no evidence that either the U.S. or Canadian provincial governments do not want to maximize their respective economic rents from timber— although the resulting ownership patterns are different in the two countries and the Canadian stumpage system is administrative.

3. Politics has overridden economics in the lumber dispute.

4. Legal and institutional factors (domestic institutional arrangements, FTA, NAFTA, and WTO) have contributed to the prolonging of the dispute.

5. A long-term solution could be based, as before, more on political terms and less on economic rationale.

6. Long-term solutions can be simple but may not be reached for some time, since many players with different interests are involved, information is imperfect, the market is evolving, and more importantly, the U.S. lumber and timber industries now have vested interests in opposing a return toward free trade or a more reasonable level of managed trade.

Bilateral lessons. There are at least four lessons and implications of the dispute for future softwood lumber trade between the two countries. First, the lumber dispute is about rent seeking, interest group politics is the dominant factor, and politics often overrides economics. Both U.S. and Canadian lumber producers, wanting to maintain and enhance their profitability, have lobbied their governments to act on their behalf. Economics (resource endowment and comparative and competitive advantage) was the real cause of the dispute; the alleged subsidy is the apparent cause. Legal frameworks (U.S. laws, FTA, NAFTA, WTO) and institutional frameworks (public ownership of resources, federalism) have contributed to the longevity of the dispute. The dispute has been a headache for some politicians and many industry leaders on both sides of the border even though the two countries have generally good diplomatic and economic relationships and the forest industry is somewhat integrated across the border.

Second, notwithstanding rhetoric from the Coalition for Fair Lumber Imports about "market-based" changes to provincial stumpage, the lumber dispute is all about limiting Canada's market share and raising prices in the U.S. market. It is rational for the coalition to demand trade restrictions against Canadian lumber imports. It is another matter if the U.S. government ignores the welfare of domestic lumber consumers.

In recent years, the coalition has sought to restrict the Canadian share of the U.S. market to 30–34 percent. The dispute has hurt the Canadian lumber industry, slowed its exports to the United States, and thus enhanced the competitiveness and profitability of the U.S. industry. Yet victory for the U.S. lumber industry is periodic and uncertain because the Canadian lumber industry has fought back and won the legal battles in Lumber I, Lumber III, and most of the skirmishes in Lumber IV. The U.S. lumber industry's victory is limited because the absolute and comparative advantage of the Canadian lumber industry in resource endowment and productivity is large, U.S. consumers want affordable lumber or lumber substitutes, and non-Canadian lumber is coming to the U.S. fast, all of which makes sustained, high lumber prices in the U.S. markets unobtainable.

Third, the lumber dispute shows that the coalition's allegations (of level of Canadian subsidy) have been overblown and that Commerce's and ITC's analyses and determinations are vulnerable and can be overturned in the NAFTA binational review. This, combined with significant increases in stumpage fees in the major lumber-producing provinces, WTO's blessing of log-export controls (which violate principles in economics), and NAFTA's and WTO's rejection or questioning of the cross-border comparison method, will make it harder for the coalition to substantiate its contention that Canadian lumber production is subsidized. In the meantime, the continual litigation is causing fatigue, and some U.S. lumber producers are recognizing that Canada's market share in the United States may be contained but cannot be reduced much and that they have to worry about lumber imports from other countries.

Fourth, despite the agreement of 2006, the softwood lumber dispute is likely to continue for a while. Although some convergence of Canadian and U.S. forest policy (and this means forest policy reform in Canada) is inevitable, Canada is unlikely to adopt the same timber sale system used by the U.S. Forest Service. It is equally unlikely that U.S. consumers and Canadian governments will gain more political power than the U.S. lumber industry or that the incentives for the coalition to continue to fight legal and political battles will disappear. Thus, the dispute could easily go on for decades unless the lumber industry is further integrated across the two countries and Canada's comparative and competitive advantage in lumber declines significantly.

After a few decades, some natural forests in Canada could be locked up for conservation purposes, and the remainder could be largely depleted by natural (for example, insect outbreaks) and human forces and replaced with second growth. Then the comparative and competitive advantage of the Canadian lumber industry would decline or disappear. Furthermore, the U.S. industry could then face challenges from other countries, especially those in the Southern Hemisphere, where timber grows much faster. At that time, the lumber trade dispute could finally become history.

Wider lessons. As for trade in other goods and services between the two countries and with other countries, several lessons can be learned from the softwood lumber dispute.

First, interest group politics is expected to continue driving most trade conflicts among the United States, Canada, and other countries. Even though international trade enhances global economic welfare, producers that have lost their comparative and competitive advantages will lobby their respective governments to restrict trade. Should these governments cave in to that pressure, trade disputes and frictions will occur and even intensify when a lot of money and a large market share are at stake.

At the least, interest group politics will continue to dominate trade policy in the United States, where political, legal, and institutional arrangements have provided incentives and rewards for U.S. domestic producers to lobby for restrictions on foreign goods. Although the United States is a country of law, trade laws can be changed and reversed by legislative amendments and administrative guidelines. Sometimes, a small but vocal minority can succeed if it is as tenacious and aggressive as the coalition. All a U.S. industry or a segment of an industry (it need not be a majority) has to do is orchestrate political pressure. In a political system in which lawmakers' political lives depend on financial contributions, political pressure is not difficult to generate. If a trade dispute can be escalated high enough in the U.S. political system, the U.S. industry can gain a great tactical advantage over the foreign industry.

Second, because the U.S. position on trade conflicts is sometimes based on political calculation and its superior power (large market) and because U.S. law is malleable, countries with relatively small economic power may not expect to win a large and politicized trade dispute with the United States, especially when the disputed products are taking a large share of the U.S. market. Consequently, these countries may want to have a better dispute settlement mechanism than the current NAFTA and WTO systems, one that can settle a trade dispute faster and in a predictable way.

The NAFTA Chapter 19 dispute settlement mechanism has its value. But its authority and constitutionality have not been firmly upheld, and it has not worked well in a large trade dispute like softwood lumber. Indeed, it will be dead internationally if the current U.S. interpretation—that NAFTA panel decisions have only prospective effect—is not overturned, since few Canadian or Mexican firms are likely to bring a case before a NAFTA panel knowing that the best possible result, even if they win, is to get duty refunds prospectively. U.S. firms, on the other hand, could still use the NAFTA Chapter 19 dispute settlement mechanism in Canada and Mexico. But these two countries could alter their laws in conformity with U.S. laws, which would make the NAFTA dispute settlement mechanism useless and irrelevant in these two countries as well.

In other bilateral free trade agreements (such as those with Singapore and Chile), the United States has done away with the binational panel system. The WTO dispute settlement mechanism provides the right to retaliate only if a country wins a trade case. However, retaliation will not work well if a country has a trade surplus or is smaller than the country it wants to retaliate against.

The NAFTA and WTO trade dispute mechanisms need to be strengthened. One way to strengthen them is to incorporate into the dispute mechanisms the interest of domestic consumers as well as that of domestic producers. In this way, consumers could provide some counterbalance to domestic producers so that future trade disputes could be avoided or settled quickly. It would also be helpful if the authority and constitutionality of NAFTA were firmly established and the right to full refunds were protected in case of an adverse NAFTA panel ruling against the initial petitioner. The WTO trade dispute mechanism could be more effective if a WTO panel ruling not only gives the winning country the right to retaliate after appeal, but also requires the losing country to bring its trade measures immediately into compliance or to provide a full refund of duty deposits retroactively to the date when the WTO panel ruling is published.

Third, free market access to the United States could be hard for other countries to get if Canada cannot reach it in softwood lumber. The softwood lumber dispute has demonstrated that despite the extent of trade between the United States and Canada and despite their good political and diplomatic relationships, they have their own parochial economic interests, and domestic politics can and often does dominate international politics. Canadians hurt their chance to secure free trade in lumber when their united front among producers, provincial governments, and the federal government was broken. As the U.S. government has used Section 129 of the Uruguay Round Agreement Act to block the implementation of NAFTA panel decisions, non-North American countries should not be surprised if the U.S. government uses it in a WTO appeal process or U.S. domestic judicial review process to frustrate the implementation of WTO panel decisions that are against the United States.

Fourth, incentives built into institutional and legal frameworks matter. As we noted earlier, there is no downside for the coalition to continue litigation in the lumber dispute. If this filing incentive is not removed under U.S. trade laws or diluted by NAFTA and WTO panel rulings, the lumber dispute (and other large disputes) will be long lasting. On the other hand, if stumpage prices are determined arbitrarily irrespective of product (lumber, pulp, and paper) market conditions, Canadian lumber producers will have incentives to lobby their provincial governments for low stumpage and benefit at the expense of Canadian provincial treasuries.

Fifth, there is a law of unintended consequences. The lumber dispute has benefited non-North American lumber producers and the producers of substitutes for lumber, limiting the level of lumber price increase in the United States. The initial, short-term price jump induced by the 1996 Softwood Lumber Agreement gave U.S. and Canadian producers signal to increase their production capacity, which hurt them later when lumber demand was down. The antidumping order in Lumber IV might have backfired. Similarly, it might not be wise for an industry to put too much of its fate in the hands of trade lawyers. A better way might be to use market mechanisms, such as mergers and acquisitions, to enhance its own efficiency and profitability.

Finally, resource subsidy is an actionable item under international trade laws. Many countries have public ownership of forests, and some have used systems similar to Canadian forest tenures to manage their forest land. If an industry in such a country started to export large quantities of its products to the United States, Canada, the European Union, or other countries, and if it were indeed subsidized or perceived to be subsidized, a trade dispute could develop. For these countries, pricing their publicly owned timber resources based on market conditions may ensure that they get a fair return from these resources and minimize the chance of international trade conflict.

Notes

1. The termination of the MOU was also seen as regaining Canada's sovereign rights to resource management. The experience of Lumber III and Lumber IV shows that, at best, Canada is only partially successful on this front.

2. As an example, *Inside US Trade* (2005f) reported that Commerce Undersecretary nominee, Franklin Lavin, told the Senate Finance Committee that trade experts at Commerce had assured him that there were ways to recalculate the countervailing duties on Canadian lumber that would keep the rate above the *de minimis* level despite a NAFTA panel remand order. He stated that Commerce would "turn over every single stone we can" to keep the countervailing duty order in place and ensure that "American workers are not undermined by unfair trade practices."

References

Adams, D.A., and R.W. Haynes. 1980. The 1980 Softwood Timber Assessment Market Model: The Structure, Projections and Policy Simulations. *Forest Science* Monograph 22.

Adams, D.M., B.A. McCarl, and L. Homayounfarrokh. 1986. The Role of Exchange Rates in Canadian-United States Lumber Trade. *Forest Science* 32: 973–88.

AF&PA (American Forest and Paper Association). 2006. 2006 Statistics: Paper, Paperboard & Wood Pulp. 1111 19th Street, N.W., Suite 800, Washington, DC.

Aldonas, G. 2003. Statement by Under Secretary Grant Aldonas on Softwood Lumber Discussions. U.S. Department of Commerce. News Release. July 31.

Anderson, F.J., and R.D. Cairns. 1988. The Softwood Lumber Agreement and Resource Politics. *Canadian Public Policy* 14: 186–96.

Apsey, T.M. 2006. *What's All This Got To Do with the Price of 2x4's?* Calgary, AB: University of Calgary Press.

Apsey, T.M., and J.C. Thomas. 1997. *The Lessons of the Softwood Lumber Disputes: Politics, Protectionism, and the Panel Process.* Council of Forest Industries, Vancouver, BC.

Asian Wall Street Journal. 1992. U.S. Ruling on Canadian Exports of Lumber Threatens Trade Pact. March 9, 20.

Atiyeh, V. 1981. Statement of the Honorable Victor Atiyeh, Governor of the State of Oregon. In *Forest Products Industry Issues: Joint Hearing before the Subcommittee on International Trade and Subcommittee on Taxation and Debt Management of the Committee on Finance, United States Senate, Ninety-Seventh Congress, First Session, November 24, 1981.* Washington, DC: U.S. GPO, 1982; 53–64.

Bangor Daily News. 1995. Kantor Says Lumber Dispute a Top Priority: Trade Representative Warns of Tariff on Softwood Coming from Canada. December 21, 1.

Baucus, M. 2002. Letter to ITC Chairman Stephen Koplan. Signed by 50 Other Senators. March 22.

———. 2005. Letter to Commerce Secretary Carlos M. Gutierrez. Signed by 20 Other Senators. October 20.

Becker, G.S. 1983. A Theory of Competition among Pressure Groups for Political Influence. *Quarterly Journal of Economics* 98: 371–400.

Binkley, C.S., and D. Zhang. 1998. The Impact of Timber-Fee Increases on B.C. Forest

Products Companies: An Economic and Policy Analysis. *Canadian Journal of Forest Research* 28(4): 617–35.

Blunt, R. 2005. Letter to the President. Signed by 46 Other Congressmen. April 19.

Boyd, R.G., and W.F. Hyde. 1989. *Forest Sector Intervention: The Impacts of Regulation on Social Welfare.* Ames: Iowa State University Press.

British Columbia Ministry of Forests. 1987. Province of British Columbia Presentation to the U.S. Government. Prepared by Ben Marr, Tom Lee, and Hartley Lewis. Victoria, BC. November.

——. 1994. *British Columbia Stumpage and Royalty Changes on May 1, 1994.* Valuation Branch. Victoria, BC.

——. Various years. *Annual Report.* Victoria, BC.

Buffalo News. 1994. Canada Wins Softwood Lumber Dispute. August 4, A14.

Bullock, D.S. 1992. Objectives and Constraints of Government Policy: The Countercyclicity of Transfers to Agriculture. *American Journal of Agricultural Economics* 74: 618–29.

Canada Newswire. 2001. Forest Industry Chief Executives Identify Major Drivers of Change. March 8.

——. 2003. Independent Lumber Producers Join Maritimes for Withdrawal of Latest Federal Proposal on Softwood Lumber. May 30.

Canadian Embassy to the U.S. 1991. Letter to U.S. State Department. September 3.

Canadian Foreign Affairs and International Trade. 1994. *News Release No. 248.* December 15.

Canadian Forest Service. 2004. *Selected Forest Statistics in Canada.* Forest Information Management Division, Natural Resources Canada. 580 Booth Street, Ottawa, ON.

——. Various issues. *Canada–United States Softwood Lumber Agreement Quarterly Statistical Monitor.* 580 Booth Street, Ottawa, ON.

Carliner, M. 1996. Personal communication. October 28.

Cashore, B. 1998. *Flights of the Phoenix: Explaining the Durability of the Canada-U.S. Softwood Lumber Dispute.* Canadian-American Public Policy No. 32. The Canadian-American Center, University of Maine, Orono.

Cashore, B., and G. Auld. 2003. British Columbia's Environmental Forest Policy in Perspective. *Journal of Forestry* 101(8): 42–47.

CBC News. 1986. The Journal: American Tariff Threatens Free Trade Talks. October 16. http://archives.cbc.ca/500f.asp?id=1-73-787-4781 (accessed July 20, 2006).

——. 2002. The National: Negotiations End in Failure; Canada Admits Defeat. March 22. http://archives.cbc.ca/500f.asp?id=1-73-787-4781 (accessed July 20, 2006).

CBP (U.S. Bureau of Customs and Border Protection). 2003. Distribution of Continued Dumping and Subsidy Offset to Affected Domestic Producers. *Federal Register* 68(134): 41597–654. July 14.

CIT (U.S. Court of International Trade). 1986. *Cabot Corp. v. United States,* 620, F. Supp. 722.

——. 2006a. Slip Op. 06-48: *Canadian Lumber Trade Alliance et al. v. United States et al.* Consol. Court No. 05-00324. April 7.

——. 2006b. Slip Op. 06-104: *Canadian Lumber Trade Alliance et al. v. United States et al.* Consol. Court No. 05-00324. July 14.

——. 2006c. Slip Op. 06-109: *Tembec Inc. et al. v. United States.* Consol. Court No. 05-00028. July 21.

——. 2006d. Slip Op. 06-152: *Tembec Inc. et al. v. United States.* Consol. Court No. 05-00028. October 13.

Coalition for Fair Lumber Imports. 2005. http://www.fairlumbercoalition.org/ (accessed March 25, 2005).

Congressional Record. 1985a. 99th Cong. 1st sess., vol. 131(60), H 355. February 7.

———. 1985b. 99th Cong. 1st sess., vol. 131(60), H 3085. May 9.

———. 1985c. 99th Cong. 1st sess., vol .131(79), S 8068. June 13.

———. 1985d. 99th Cong. 1st sess., vol. 131(70), S 7214. May 24.

———. 1985e. 99th Cong. 1st sess., vol. 131(33), H 1358. March 21.

———. 1985f. 99th Cong. 1st sess., vol. 131(48), S 4635. April 23.

———. 1995a. 104th Cong. 1st sess., vol. 141(132), S 11810. August 8.

———. 1995b. 104th Cong. 1st sess., vol. 141(173), S 16663. November 3.

———. 1997. 105th Cong. 1st sess., vol. 143(55), H 2156. May 1.

———. 2003. 108th Cong. 1st sess., vol. 149(15), S 1671. January 28.

———. 2004a. 108th Cong. 2nd sess., vol. 150(125), S 10420. October 5.

———. 2004b. 108th Cong. 2nd sess., vol. 150(132), S 11431. November 17.

Craig, L. 1985. Letter to the President. Signed by 37 Other Congressmen. October 29.

———. 2004. Letter to Secretary of Commerce Donald Evans. Signed by 13 Other Senators. November 23.

Crane, D. 1988. So Much for the Dispute Settlement Mechanism. *Toronto Star,* A23.

Dana, S.T. 1956. *Forest and Range Policy: Its Development in the United States.* New York: McGraw-Hill Book Company.

Davis, J., A.L. Best, J.M. Smith, D.A. Wilson, P.E. Lachance, and S.L. Pringle. 1957. *The Outlook for the Canadian Forest Industry.* Hull, QB: Queen's Printer and Controller of Stationery.

Devadoss, S., A.H. Aguiar, S.R. Shook, and J. Araji. 2005. A Spatial Equilibrium Analysis of US–Canadian Disputes on the World Softwood Lumber Market. *Canadian Journal of Agricultural Economics* 53(2-3): 177–92.

Dewey Ballantine. 1986. Overview of U.S. Softwood Lumber Industry. U.S. Lumber Briefing to a Group of U.S. Officials. Dewey, Ballantine, Bushby, Palmer & Wood. January 14.

Dezell, M. 1992. Being a Political History of Softwood Lumber Dispute. Presented to Hartley Lewis, Legislative Assembly of British Columbia, Victoria, Canada.

DOC (U.S. Department of Commerce). 1983. Final Negative Countervailing Duty Determination: Certain Softwood Lumber Products from Canada. *Federal Register* 48: 24159–24183. May 31.

———. 1986a. Carbon Black from Mexico: Preliminary Results of Administrative Review. *Federal Register* 51: 13269–13273. April 18.

———. 1986b. Preliminary Countervailing Duty Determination: Certain Softwood Lumber Products from Canada. *Federal Register* 51: 37453–37469. October 22.

———. 1991. Self-Initiation of Countervailing Duty Investigation: Certain Softwood Lumber Products from Canada. *Federal Register* 56: 56055–56057. October 31.

———. 1992a. Preliminary Affirmative Countervailing Duty Determination: Certain Softwood Lumber Products from Canada. *Federal Register* 57: 8800–8817. March 12.

———. 1992b. Final Affirmative Countervailing Duty Determination: Certain Softwood Lumber Products from Canada. *Federal Register* 57: 22570–22624. May 28.

———. 1993. *In the Matter of Certain Softwood Lumber Products from Canada: Redetermination Pursuant to Binational Panel Remand.* USA-92-1904-01. September 17.

———. 1994. United States–Canada Free-Trade Agreement, Article 1904 Binational Panel

Reviews: Request for an Extraordinary Challenge Committee. *Federal Register* 59: 21754–21755. April 26.

———. 2001a. Notice of Preliminary Affirmative Countervailing Duty Determination, Preliminary Affirmative Critical Circumstances Determination, and Alignment of Final Countervailing Duty Determination with Final Antidumping Duty Determination: Certain Softwood Lumber Products from Canada. *Federal Register* 66: 43186–43216. August 17.

———. 2001b. Notice of Preliminary Determination of Sales at Less Than Fair Value and Postponement of Final Determination: Certain Softwood Lumber Products from Canada. *Federal Register* 66: 56062–56078. November 6.

———. 2005a. Notice of Determination under Section 129 of the Uruguay Round Agreements Act: Antidumping Measures on Certain Softwood Lumber Products from Canada. *Federal Register* 70: 22636–22646. May 2.

———. 2005b. *Remand Determination in the Matter of Sales at Less Than Fair Value of Certain Softwood Lumber from Canada.* Secretariat File No. USA-CDA-2002-1904-02. NAFTA Binational Panel Review. July 13.

———. 2005c. *Fifth Remand Determination in the Matter of Certain Softwood Lumber from Canada.* Secretariat File No. USA-CDA-2002-1904-03. NAFTA Binational Panel Review. November 22.

———. 2005d. NAFTA Panel Decision: Fifth Remand Determination Countervailing Duty Investigation on Softwood Lumber from Canada. News Release. November 22.

Dottori, F. 2003. Letter to Pierre S. Pettigrew in Reference of U.S. Coalition's Proposal of October 29, 2003. November 3.

Driggs, M.A. 1985. Memorandum for John A. Svahn (Assistant to the President for Policy Development) (Subject: EPC Meeting, EC Steel Negotiations and Canadian Lumber). October 23.

Economic Policy Council. 1985a. Minutes of Economic Policy Council Meeting, October 24.

———. 1985b. Minutes of Economic Policy Council Meeting. November 26.

The Economist. 2003. A Simple Lesson in Economics: The Softwood Lumber Dispute. February 1, 366(8309): 49.

Ellis, L.E. 1948. *Print Paper Pendulum: Group Pressures and the Price of Newsprint.* Piscataway, NJ: Rutgers University Press.

———. 1960. *Newsprint: Producers, Publishers, Political Pressures.* Piscataway, NJ: Rutgers University Press.

———. 1968. *Reciprocity 1911: A Study of Canadian–American Relations.* New York: Greenwood Press.

Feldman, E.J. 2006. *The Deal.* Baker & Hostetler LLP. Washington Square, Suite 1100, 1050 Connecticut Avenue, N.W., Washington, DC 20036-5304.

Financial Post. 1987. B.C. Hikes for Tax Bite. September 21, 6.

———. 2001. Secret Talks on Softwood: Canada and U.S. Scramble: Attempt to Avoid Embarrassing Trade War over Imports. March 24, 1.

Foreign Affairs and International Trade Canada. 1999. Developing a Canadian Position on Possible WTO Industrial Goods Tariff and NTMs Negotiations. Discussion Paper. http://www.international.gc.ca/tna-nac/discussion/wto_tar-en.asp? (accessed January 17, 2007).

Fox, I.K. 1991. The Politics of Canada–U.S. Trade in Forest Products. In *Canada–United*

States Trade in Forest Products, edited by R.S. Uhler. Vancouver: University of British Columbia Press, 15–56.

The Free Trader. 2001. Louisiana-Pacific President Makes Major Speech on SLA. Free Trade Lumber Council. 1 Place Ville-Marie, Suite 2821. Montreal. January 11, 8.

———. 2002a. Analysis of the Coalition's Proposal. Free Trade Lumber Council. Montreal. May 15, 2–20.

———. 2002b.Comments on BCLTC Counter-Proposal.

———. 2003. Lumber IV: Interim Measures Proposal.

FTA Extraordinary Challenge Committee (FTA ECC). 1994. *Memorandum Opinions and Order in the Matter of Certain Softwood Lumber Products from Canada.* United States–Canada Free Trade Agreement Article 1904.13 Extraordinary Challenge Committee. ECC-94-1904-01USA. August 3.

FTA Injury Panel. 1993. *Decision of the Panel Reviewing the Final Determination of the U.S. International Trade Commission in the Matter of Softwood Lumber from Canada.* United States–Canada Free Trade Agreement Article 1904 Binational Panel Review. USA-92-1904-02. July 26.

———. 1994a. *Decision of the Panel on Review of the U.S. International Trade Commission's Second Remand Determination in the Matter of Softwood Lumber from Canada.* United States–Canada Free Trade Agreement Article 1904 Binational Panel Review. USA-92-1904-02. January 28.

———. 1994b. *Decision of the Panel on Review of the Remand Determination of the U.S. International Trade Commission in the Matter of Softwood Lumber from Canada.* United States–Canada Free Trade Agreement Article 1904 Binational Panel Review. USA-92-1904-02. July 6.

FTA Subsidy Panel. 1993a. *Decision of the Panel in the Matter of Softwood Lumber Products from Canada.* United States–Canada Free Trade Agreement Article 1904 Binational Panel Review. USA-92-1904-01. May 6.

———. 1993b. *Decision of the Panel on Remand in the Matter of Softwood Lumber Products from Canada.* United States–Canada Free Trade Agreement Article 1904 Binational Panel Review. USA-92-1904-01. December 17.

Gardner, B.L. 1983. Efficient Redistribution through Commodity Markets. *American Journal of Agricultural Economics* 65: 225–34.

———. 1987. Causes of U.S. Farm Commodity Programs. *Journal of Political Economics* 95: 290–310.

Gazette. 1986a. Carney Sold Out Forest Industry. September 11, B7.

———. 1986b. Still Hope for Lumber Deal. October 4, H3.

———. 1991. U.S. Considers Tariffs on Canadian Lumber. April 20, E2.

———. 1996. Quebec Seen as Key to Softwood Dispute: U.S. Trade Representative Set to Respond to Call for Action. February 2, D3.

———. 2002a. U.S. Lumber Lobby Slams Door Offer. March 14, D2.

———. 2002b. Feds Balk at Firm's Softwood Solution: Forest Giant's Bid to Broker a Settlement Would Legitimize U.S. Stand, Pettigrew Says. November 21, B3.

———. 2005. Minister Slams U.S. Hard Line on Softwood Duties. January 27, B3.

Gilligan, M.J. 1997. *Empowering Exporters: Reciprocity, Delegation, and Collective Action in American Trade Policy.* Ann Arbor: University of Michigan Press.

Globe and Mail. 1986. U.S. Administration Courts Key Senators on Free Trade. April 18, B12.

————. 1987. Industry, Government at New Low at End of Softwood Lumber Affair. January 7, B1.

Gorte, R.W. 2001. *Softwood Lumber Imports from Canada: History and Analysis of the Dispute.* Report RL 30826. Washington, DC: Congressional Research Service.

Haley, D. 1980. A Regional Comparison of Stumpage Values in British Columbia and the U.S. Pacific Northwest. *Forestry Chronicle* 56(10): 225–50.

Hamilton, G. 1994. Environmentalists Side with U.S. Lobby on Subsidies. *Vancouver Sun,* April 8, D1.

Hart, M., B. Dymond, and C. Robertson. 1994. *Decision at Midnight: Inside the Canada–US Free Trade Negotiations.* Vancouver: University of British Columbia Press.

Haynes, R.W. 2003. *An Analysis of the Timber Situation in the United States: 1952–2050.* General Technical Report PNW-GTR-560. Portland, OR: USDA Forest Service, Pacific Northwest Research Station.

Hird, J.E. 1993. Congressional Voting on Superfund: Self-Interest or Ideology? *Public Choice* 77(October): 333–357.

Horlick, G. 1991. United States: Court of Appeals for the Federal Circuit Opinion in PPG Industries, Inc. v. United States. *International Legal Materials* 30: 1179–1196. March 22.

————. 2006. Personal communication. June 16.

Howard, J.L. 2001. *U.S. Timber Production, Trade, Consumption, and Price Statistics 1965–1999.* Research Paper FPL-RP-595. Madison, WI: USDA Forest Service, Forest Products Laboratory.

Howse, R. 1998. *Settling Trade Remedy Disputes: When the WTO Forum Is Better Than the NAFTA.* Commentary 111. Toronto, ON: C.D. Howe Institute.

Inside US Trade. 1986. USTR Gets Tough on Lumber Dispute, Canadians Reported 'Outraged.' April 4.

————. 2002a. U.S. Group Submits Proposed Provincial Reform in Softwood Fight. January 25.

————. 2002b. WTO Declines to Rule on U.S. Law Governing Trade Remedy Decisions. June 7.

————. 2002c. Canada Sees U.S. Plan as Insufficient to Guarantee Lumber Access. March 15.

————. 2002d. Quebec Premier Calls for Canada to Restart Lumber Talks with U.S. August 9.

————. 2002e. Commerce Launches Province-Specific Approach to Softwood Fight. August 30.

————. 2002f. U.S. Reaches Out to More Canadian Provinces on Softwood Lumber. September 20.

————. 2003a. B.C. Lumber Proposal Prompts New U.S. Industry Push for Deal. January 3.

————. 2003b. Commerce Issues Second Draft Lumber Paper as Talks End without Deal. February 7.

————. 2003c. Commerce Poised to Publish Policy Bulletin on Canadian Lumber. May 9.

————. 2003d. U.S. Floats Tax Based on Market Share as Lumber Talks Resume. May 16.

————. 2003e. Canada Studying New U.S. Offer to Strike Interim Lumber Deal. June 20.

————. 2003f. Government Deal Falls Apart after Coalition Counteroffer. August 1.

————. 2003g. U.S. Producers Offer New Deal in Lumber Fight with Canada. November 7.

————. 2003h. Canada Offers New Lumber Proposal as Two Sides Edge Closer to Deal. December 5.

————. 2003i. Canadian Momentum toward Lumber Deal Appears to Be Slowing. December 12.

————. 2004a. Canadian Industry Pressures Government to Change Negotiating Stance. May 7.

————. 2004b. Canada Says U.S. Undermines NAFTA by Keeping Softwood Lumber Duties. July 2.

————. 2005a. Aldonas Says U.S. Will Not Return Lumber Duty Deposits without Deal. January 28.

————. 2005b. U.S., Canada Reengage in Lumber Talks, Industry Meeting Planned. April 1.

————. 2005c. U.S., Canadian Industries Make Little Progress in Lumber Talks. April 8.

————. 2005d. U.S. Sends Two Lumber Proposals to Canada; No New Talks Planned. May 13.

————. 2005e. Softwood Talks End with No Deal, But Possible Signal of Flexibility. July 22.

————. 2005f. Commerce Nominee Pledges to Keep Canada Lumber Duty in Place. October 21.

————. 2006a. Appellate Body Rules against Zeroing in Administrative Review. April 21.

————. 2006b. U.S. Court Dismisses Coalition Challenge of NAFTA Panel System. December 15.

ITC (U.S. International Trade Commission). 1982. *Conditions Relating to the Importation of Softwood Lumber into the United States.* Investigation No. 332–134. Pub. 1241. April.

————. 1985. *Conditions Relating to the Importation of Softwood Lumber into the United States.* Investigation No. 332–210. Pub. 1765. October.

————. 1986. *Refined U.S. and Canadian Softwood Lumber Employment Data.* Office of Industries. January.

————. 1991. *Softwood Lumber from Canada.* Investigation No. 701-TA-312 (Preliminary Affirmative), Pub. 2468. December.

————. 1992. *Softwood Lumber from Canada.* Investigation No. 701-TA-312 (Final Affirmative). Pub. 2530. July.

————. 1993. *Softwood Lumber from Canada.* Inv. No. 701-TA-312 (Remand), Pub. 2689. October.

————. 1998. *Summary of Statutory Provisions Related to Import Relief.* Pub. 3125. August.

————. 2002. *Softwood Lumber from Canada.* Inv. Nos. 701-TA-414 and 731-TA-928, Pub. 3509. May.

————. 2004. *View of the Commission in Response to the Panel Decision and Order of August 31, 2004.* Submitted to NAFTA Secretariat. September 10. http://www.usitc.gov/pub/reports/opinions/fremand3opin.pdf (accessed on October 1, 2004).

————. 2006. *Value of U.S. Imports for Consumption, Duties Collected, and Ratios of Duties to Values 1891–2005.* Statistical and Editorial Services Division, Office of Information Services. February 2004. http://dataweb.usitc.gov/scripts/ave.pdf (accessed June 7, 2006).

Jansen, G.W.V. 1984. *Canada–United States Trade Relationships: The Lessons of the Softwood Lumber Countervail Case.* Executive Bulletin No. 27. The Conference Board of Canada. August 27.

Joskow, P. 1972. Determination of the Allowed Rate of Return in a Formal Regulatory Proceeding. *Bell Journal of Economics and Management Science* 3(2): 632–44.

Kalt, J. 1988. The Political Economy of Protectionism: Tariffs and Retaliation in the Timber

Industry. In *Trade Policy Issues and Empirical Analysis*, edited by R.E. Baldwin. Chicago: University of Chicago Press, 339–68.

Kaplan, G.B. 1986a. Memorandum for DOC Under Secretary Bruce Smart. March 8.

——. 1986b. Memo for Public File. December 5.

Kernell, S., and G.C. Jacobson. 2000. *The Logic of American Politics*. Washington, DC: CQ Press.

Kerr, J.C. 1999. Letter to Tom Stephens. *Vancouver Sun*. October 15, A1.

——. 2006. Personal communication. February 17.

Kinnucan, H., and D. Zhang. 2004. Canadian Impacts of the 1996 Canada–U.S. Softwood Lumber Agreement. *Canadian Journal of Agricultural Economics* 52(1): 110–19.

Kreps, D., and R. Wilson. 1982. Reputation and Imperfect Information. *Journal of Economic Theory* 27: 253–79.

Kreps, D., P. Milgrom, J. Roberts, and R. Wilson. 1982. Rational Cooperation in the Finitely Repeated Prisoners' Dilemma. *Journal of Economic Theory* 27: 245–52.

Kuehne, M.J. 2006. Personal communications between September 1 and September 30.

Lange, W. 1986. Lumber Imports and Fair Trade. In *Proceedings of the 19th Annual Lakehead University Forestry Association Forestry Symposium*. Thunder Bay, ON. January.

——. 2003. Personal communication. February 21.

Li, Y., and D. Zhang. 2006. Incidence of the 1996 U.S.–Canada Softwood Lumber Agreement in the Lumber Industry: The Case of the U.S. South. *Forest Science* 52(4): 422–31.

Lindsey, B., M.A. Groombridge, and P. Loungani. 2000. *Nailing the Homeowner: The Economic Impact of Trade Protection of the Softwood Lumber Industry*. Center for Trade Policy Analysis No. 11. Washington, DC: CATO Institute.

Macrory, P. 2002. NAFTA Chapter 19: A Successful Experiment in International Trade Dispute Resolution. Commentary 168. Toronto: C.D. Howe Institute.

Madison, J. 1787. The Same Subject Continued: The Union as a Safeguard against Domestic Faction and Insurrection. *Federalist No. 10*. In *The Daily Advertiser*, No. 22.

Margolick, M., and R.S. Uhler. 1986. *The Economic Impact of Removing Log Export Restrictions in British Columbia*. Report 86-2. Forest Economics and Policy Analysis Research Unit. Vancouver: University of British Columbia.

Martin, P. 2005. Address to the Economic Club of New York. October 6.

Mattey, J.P. 1990. *The Timber Bubble That Burst: Government Policy and the Bailout of 1984*. New York: Oxford University Press.

McCallum, M. 1997. The Forest Industry in British Columbia, 1996. In *Tenth Annual British Columbia Forest Industry Conference*. Vancouver, BC: Price Waterhouse.

McCarthy, S. 1992. U.S. Offer on Lumber Rejected. *Toronto Star*, April 8, F1.

McClellan, S. (White House Press Secretary). 2005. Press Brief. October 14.

McCloy, B. 1986. Canadian–U.S. Lumber Trade. In *Proceedings of the 19th Annual Lakehead University Forestry Association Forestry Symposium*. Thunder Bay, ON. January.

McNabb, L. 2004. A B.C. Perspective on the Softwood Lumber Dispute. Presented at Canadian Institute of Forestry and Society of American Foresters Joint 2004 General Meeting and Convention. Edmonton, Canada. October 1–5.

Mehmood, S., and D. Zhang. 2001. A Roll Call Analysis of Endangered Species Act Amendments. *American Journal of Agricultural Economics* 83(3): 501–12.

Melrose, M., J. Elliot, and P. Heard. 1986. *Lumber Protectionism Fails to See the Forests from the Trees*. Issue Alert 11. Washington, DC: Citizens for a Sound Economy.

Milgrom, P., and J. Roberts. 1982. Predation, Reputation, and Entry Deterrence. *Journal of Economic Theory* 27: 280–312.

NAFTA Dumping Panel. 2003. *Decision of the Panel, In the Matter of Certain Softwood Lumber Products from Canada: Final Affirmative Antidumping Determination.* Article 1904 Binational Panel Review Pursuant to the North America Free Trade Agreement. Secretariat File No. US-CDA-2002-1904-02. July 17.

———. 2004. *Decision of the Panel Respecting Remand Determination, In the Matter of Certain Softwood Lumber Products from Canada: Final Affirmative Antidumping Determination.* Article 1904 Binational Panel Review Pursuant to the North America Free Trade Agreement. Secretariat File No. US-CDA-2002-1904-02. March 5.

———. 2005. *Decision of the Panel Following Remand, In the Matter of Certain Softwood Lumber Products from Canada: Final Affirmative Antidumping Determination.* Article 1904 Binational Panel Review Pursuant to the North America Free Trade Agreement. Secretariat File No. US-CDA-2002-1904-02. June 9.

NAFTA Extraordinary Challenge Committee (NAFTA ECC). 2005. *Opinion and Order of the Extraordinary Challenge Committee: In the Matter of Certain Softwood Lumber Products from Canada.* Article 1904 Extraordinary Challenge Pursuant to the North America Free Trade Agreement. Secretariat File No. ECC-2004-1904-01USA, August 10.

NAFTA Injury Panel. 2003. *Decision of the Panel, In the Matter of Softwood Lumber from Canada: Final Affirmative Threat of Material Injury Determination.* Article 1904 Binational Panel Review Pursuant to the North America Free Trade Agreement. USA-CDA-202-1904-07. September 5.

———. 2004a. *Remand Decision of the Panel, In the Matter of Softwood Lumber from Canada: Final Affirmative Threat of Injury Determination.* Article 1904 Binational Panel Review Pursuant to the North America Free Trade Agreement. USA-CDA-202-1904-07. April 19.

———. 2004b. *Second Remand Decision of the Panel, In the Matter of Softwood Lumber from Canada: Final Affirmative Threat of Injury Determination.* Article 1904 Binational Panel Review Pursuant to the North America Free Trade Agreement. USA-CDA-202-1904-07. August 31.

NAFTA Subsidy Panel. 2003. *Decision of the Panel in the Matter of Certain Softwood Lumber Products from Canada.* North America Free Trade Agreement Article 1904 Binational Panel Review, USA-CND-2002-1904-03. August 13.

Nagubadi, R., and D. Zhang. 2006. Competitiveness in the Sawmills and Wood Preservation Industry in the United States and Canada. *Forest Science* 52(4): 340–52.

National Association of Home Builders (NAHB). 2006. Sources of Softwood Lumber Consumed in the United States.

National Post. 2000. All-Out War Next Step in Timber Trade Dispute. March 11, D06.

———. 2001a. Lumber Deal with U.S. Dead. February 2, C04.

———. 2001b. B.C. Softwood Changes Could Further Irk U.S. November 19, FP4.

———. 2002. Pettigrew Nixes Idea of Softwood Border Tax. November 21, FP3.

———. 2003a. U.S. Group Switches Sides on Softwood: Opposing Tariffs. February 12, FP7.

———. 2003b. U.S. Softwood Duty Payout Angers Ottawa. July 17, FP3.

———. 2005. New Political Will May Solve Lumber Dispute. March 14, FP3.

———. 2006. How the Softwood Deal Was Done: Framed by Personal Relationship of Harper and Bush. April 29, A1.

Nelson, R.A. 1982. An Empirical Test of the Ramsey Theory and Stegler-Peltzman Theory of Public Utility Pricing. *Economic Inquiry* 20: 227–90.

Noll, R. 1989. Economic Perspectives on the Politics of Regulation. In *Handbook of Industrial Organization*, vol. II, edited by R. Schmalensee and R. Willig. New York: North-Holland.

Nordhaus, W.D., and R. Litan. 1992. *The Impacts of Stumpage Charges on Prices and Trade Flow on Forest Products.* February 18.

Olson, K.S. 1986. Memorandum on Timber Summit on March 20, 1986. Submitted to Canadian Forest Industries Council. March 20.

Olson, M. 1965. *The Logic of Collective Action.* Cambridge, MA: Harvard University Press.

———. 1982. *The Rise and Decline of Nations: Economic Growth Stagflation and Rigidities.* New Haven, CT: Yale University Press.

Oregon Governor's Timber Strategy Panel. 1981. Report by Governor's Timber Strategy Panel. In *Forest Products Industry Issues: Joint Hearing before the Subcommittee on International Trade and Subcommittee on Taxation and Debt Management of the Committee on Finance, United States Senate, Ninety-Seventh Congress, First Session, November 24, 1981.* Washington, DC: U.S. GPO, 1982, 68–78.

Oregonian. 1992a. U.S. Cuts Planned Tariff on Canadian Wood. May 16, D1.

———. 1992b. Bush Gives Pledge to Canada on Disputes. May 21, F1.

———. 1994. High Wood Prices Linked to Tariff. January 26, B1.

———. 1996. U.S., Canada Yet to Reach Timber Pact. January 10, E5.

Ottawa Citizen. 1986a. Tariff Price for Talks: U.S. Advisor. June 9, A1.

———. 1986b. B.C. May Hike Lumber Charge to Avoid Paying Tariffs in U.S. September 8, A11.

———. 1991. Bush Opposes Changes in Canada Lumber Pact, Says U.S. Trade Official. March 22, B5.

———. 1992. Canada–U.S. Trade: Bush Envoy Calls for Cooler Talk. March 13, C5.

———. 1993. Free Trade: U.S. Mounts Challenges to Panel Rulings. November 6, H10.

———. 1994a. Trade Disputes: White House Divided over Tariffs on Canadian Lumber. March 9, C5.

———. 1994b. Americans Seek to Keep $800 Million Lumber Duties. August 6, H2.

———. 2001. Pettigrew Appeals for United Front. March 23, F3.

———. 2003. U.S. Softwood Proposal "Laughable": Pettigrew Spurns Suggestion of 33% Export Tax. May 17, D1.

———. 2004. Bush Agrees NAFTA Needs a Fix. December 1, A5.

Packwood, R. 1985. Letter to Honorable Clayton Yeutter, U.S. Trade Representative. Signed by 9 other U.S. Senators. October 1.

Pareto, V. 1927. *Manual of Political Economy.* New York: A.M. Kelley.

Pearse, P.H., D. Zhang, and J. Leitch. 1995. Trends in Foreign Investment in Canada's Forest Industry. *Canadian Business Economics* 3(3): 54–68.

Peltzman, S. 1976. Toward a More General Theory of Regulation. *Journal of Law and Economics* 19(2): 211–40.

———. 1984. Constituent Interest and Congressional Voting. *Journal of Law and Economics* 27(1): 181–210.

Percy, M.B. 1986. *Forest Management and Economic Growth in British Columbia.* Economic Council of Canada. Supply and Services Canada. Ottawa.

———. 2004. *One Forest under Two Flags: The Context for Sustainable Forests.* A Keynote

Address at the Canadian Institute of Forestry and Society of American Foresters Joint 2004 General Meeting and Convention. Edmonton, AB. October 2–6.

Percy, M.B., and C. Yoder. 1987. *The Softwood Lumber Dispute and Canada–U.S. Trade in Natural Resources.* Halifax, NS: The Institute for Research on Public Policy.

Peterson, J. 2004. Letter to U.S. Commerce Secretary Donald Evans. June 22.

Plecas, R.S. 2006. Personal communication. August 11.

Porter, M.E. 1991. *Canada at Crossroads: The Reality of the New Competitive Environment.* Ottawa: Supply and Services Canada.

Ragosta, J. 2003. Personal communication. July 24.

———. 2006. Personal communication. November 17.

Random Lengths, Inc. 2004. U.S.–Canada Trade Dispute Timeline. http://www.random-lengths.com/base.asp?s1=In_Depth&s2=U.S.–Canada_Trade_Dispute (accessed March 15, 2005).

———. Various years. Yearbook: Forest Products Market, Prices, and Statistics.

Rausser, G.C., and W.E. Foster. 1990. Political Preference Functions and Public Policy Reform. *American Journal of Agricultural Economics* 72: 290–310.

Reagan, R. 1986a. Letter to Senator Steve Symms. April 22.

———. 1986b. Letter to Senator Robert Packwood. May 8.

Reed, F.L.C. 1986. The Timber Supply Context of the Lumber War of 1986. Starker Lecture Series. Oregon State University, Corvallis, OR. November 6.

———. 2001. *Two Centuries of Softwood Lumber War between Canada and the United States: A Chronicle of Trade Barriers Viewed in the Context of Saw Timber Depletion.* Prepared for the Free Trade Lumber Council, Montreal.

Ritchie, G. 1993. U.S. Protectionism Claims Canadian Casualties. *Wall Street Journal.* March 6, A8.

———. 1997. *Wrestling with the Elephant: The Inside Story of the Canada–U.S. Trade Wars.* Toronto: Macfarlane Water & Ross.

Roach, T.R. 1994. *Newsprint: Canadian Supply and American Demand.* Durham, NC: Forest History Society Issue Series.

Rushford, G. 1998. Larry Summers Swats Home Builders with 2x4. *Wall Street Journal.* July 10, A15.

Schattschneider, E.E. 1935. *Politics, Pressure, and the Tariff.* New York: Prentice-Hall.

———. 1960. *The Semi-Sovereign People: A Realist's View of Democracy in America.* Hindsdale, IL: Dryden Press.

Schloss, H. 1998. Letter to the Editor: Lumber Trade Pact Wasn't Circumvented. *Wall Street Journal.* July 17, 1.

Scott, A.D. forthcoming. *Evolution of Property Rights in Natural Resources.* New York: Oxford University Press.

Seattle Post-Intelligencer. 1990. Mosbacher Pledges to Protect U.S. Softwood Lumber Industry. November 16, C1.

———. 1991. Import Duties May Be Used against Canadian Timber Trade Subsidy. February 23, B3.

———. 1993. Canada Wins Round in Softwood Dispute. December 18, B3.

———. 1996. Canada Will Export Less Lumber to U.S.: Tentative Agreement Should Give Relief to Domestic Producers. February 17, B3.

Seattle Times. 1986. Canada Eyes Steps to Avoid Tariff. September 24, B4.

———. 1989. Canada Accused of Smuggling Timber. April 10, D4.

———. 1991. Senate Urges Lumber Retaliation. September 21, A12.

————. 1992. Legislators Urge Cut in Timber Subsidies. April 7, F1.

————. 2005. Canada Cancels Lumber Talks with U.S. August 17, C3.

Shapiro, I. 2006. Personal communication. February 25.

Shinn, D. 1987. *U.S. Response to Canadian Softwood Lumber Imports.* Twenty-Ninth Session of the Senior Seminar. Washington, DC: U.S. Department of State Foreign Service Institute.

Singleton, M. (Chairman of the Coalition for Fair Lumber Imports). 1995. Fundraising letter. 1775 Pennsylvania Ave., NW, Washington, DC 20006. June.

Smith, W.B., P.D. Miles, J.S. Vissage, and S.A. Pugh. 2004. *Forest Resources of the United States, 2002.* General Technical Report NC-241. St. Paul, MN: USDA Forest Service, North Central Research Station.

Southworth, C. 1922. The American–Canadian Newsprint Industry and the Tariff. *Journal of Political Economy* 30: 681–97.

Spelter, H. 2000. Softwood Price Declines. *Wall Street Journal.* August 28, A19.

Stanbury, W.T. 2000. *Environmental Groups and the International Conflict over the Forests of British Columbia, 1990 to 2000.* Vancouver, Canada: SFU-UBC Center for the Study of Government and Business.

Statistics Canada. 2003. *Historical Statistics of Canada.* Catalogue 11-516-XIE. http://www.statcan.ca/english/freepub/11-516-XIE/sectiong/sectiong.htm# Foreign (accessed July 30, 2003).

————. 2007. http://www.statcan.ca/bsolc/english/bsolc?catno=65C0003 (accessed January 17, 2007).

Stennes, B., and B. Wilson. 2005. An Analysis of Lumber Trade Restrictions in North America: Application of a Spatial Equilibrium Model. *Forest Policy and Economics* 7(3): 297–308.

Stephens, T. 1999. Letter to Jake Kerr. *Vancouver Sun.* October 15, A1.

Stigler, G. 1971. The Theory of Economic Regulation. *Bell Journal of Economics and Management Science* 2(1): 3–21.

Stone, O. 1996. Hollywood and Our Wood. *Vancouver Sun.* June 26, A13.

Teske, P., S. Best, and M. Minstrom. 1994. The Economic Theory of Regulation and Trucking Deregulation: Shifting to the State Level. *Public Choice* 79(2): 247–56.

The Economist. 2003. A Simple Lesson in Economics: The Softwood Lumber Dispute. February 1, 366(8309): 49.

Time. 1986. Warning Shot: The White House Gets Tough on Trade. June 2.

Toronto Star. 1986. How Lumber Became Free Trade Obstacle. April 13, A18.

————. 1988a. Canada Sells Its Soul on Softwood Lumber Deal. July 13, A25.

————. 1988b. U.S. Complains Canadian Actions Break Lumber Deal. July 28, E1.

————. 1989a. Key U.S. Senator Charges Violations of Lumber Pact. April 7, C2.

————. 1989b. Crosbie Says U.S. Unyielding on Softwood. April 11, B3.

————. 1991. Soviet Events Change Agenda for Meeting of PM, Bush, August 27, A4.

————. 1992a. Lumber Tax Called Threat to Free Trade. February 14, B1.

————. 1992b. Lumber Duty Just Another Reason Why Canada Should Rely on GATT. March 8, H4.

————. 1994a. Americans Challenge Ruling on Lumber. February 25, E1.

————. 1994b. U.S. Congress's Lumber-Duty Threat 'Debases and Dilutes' Free Trade Deal. August 27, B1.

————. 1994c. Spat Called Threat to Tree Trade; Battle over Softwood Lumber Goes to Court. September 16, B1.

——. 1994d. U.S. Lobby Ends Suit Aimed at Our Lumber. December 16, E1.

——. 1996. Losing on Lumber. February 21, A8.

——. 2001a. Trade Minister Defends Forestry Management. March 20, D1.

——. 2001b. American Lumber Lobby Ready to Ignite Trade War: Threaten to Use 'Dirty Secrets' against Canada. March 8, D12.

——. 2001c. PM Says He Gave Bush "Hell" on Lumber. August 22, A10.

——. 2003. Talks Break Off with U.S. on Softwood Lumber Duties; Demands by U.S. Lumber Industry Called 'Excessive', Pettigrew Says. February 26, E2.

Trudeau, P.E. 1991. *Towards a Just Society.* Montreal: Viking Adult.

Truman, D.B. 1951. *The Government Process.* New York: Knopf.

Uhler, R.S. (ed.) 1991. *Canada–United States Trade in Forest Products.* Vancouver: University of British Columbia Press.

Ulrich, A.H. 1990. *U.S. Timber Production, Trade, Consumption, and Price Statistics 1960–88.* Miscellaneous Publication No. 1486. Madison, WI: USDA Forest Service, Forest Products Laboratory.

U.S. Bureau of Census. 1975. *Historical Statistics of the United States, Colonial Times to 1970.* Bicentennial Edition, Part 1. Washington, DC.

U.S. Bureau of Economic Analysis. 2006. U.S. International Transactions Data. http://www.bea.gov/bea/international/bp_web/simple.cfm?anon=202&table_id =2&area_id=3 (accessed August 1, 2006).

U.S. Embassy to Canada. 1986. Fax to Secretary of State and U.S. Department of Commerce (Subject: Softwood Lumber CVD Case: Canada Will Contest the Decision But Supports Continuing Trade Negotiations). October 17.

USTR (U.S. Trade Representative). 1991. Initiation of Section 302 Investigation and Request for Public Comment on Determinations Involving Expeditious Action: Canadian Exports of Softwood Lumber. *Federal Register* 56: 50738–40.

——. 1994. *News Release.* December 15.

——. 2006. *News Release.* October 13.

van Kooten, G.C. 2002. Economic Analysis of the Canada–United States Softwood Lumber Dispute: Playing the Quota Game. *Forest Science* 48: 712–21.

Vancouver Sun. 1982. Go for Import Restraints, U.S. Mill Urged. April 22, C7.

——. 1983. U.S. No-Subsidy Ruling Gives a Lift in Spirits to B.C.'s Mill Workers. March 9, A2.

——. 1987a. Kempf: From Mavick to Minister. January 15, B4.

——. 1987b. Kempf Spent Years on Socred Backbench. March 7, A13.

——. 1987c. Kempf Reveals Secret U.S. Talks. April 2, A1.

——. 1987d. Did Kempf Trip Tip Faltering Standard? April 28, B4.

——. 1988a. Settling Fights: What Happens When We Disagree. March 15, A7.

——. 1988b. Loophole for a Knotty B.C. Problem. March 16, B3.

——. 1988c. Forest Ministry Agrees to Stumpage Fee Cuts. June 8, A13.

——. 1988d. B.C. Accused of Wood Fee Violations. July 15, D4.

——. 1989. Premier Upset by Allegations That He Lied. November 25, A1.

——. 1991a. Canada Taking Swing at Costly U.S. Softwood Tariff: Trade Minister Marshals Case to Repeal Pact. March 1, C5.

——. 1991b. Softwood Deal Must Be Retained, U.S. Senators Say. March 8, B5.

——. 1991c. Deputy Washington-Bound to Launch Forestry Concerns. August 7, D2.

——. 1991d. Begin Lumber Talks with U.S., Premier Says: Mulroney Asked to Ensure Fast Start to Negotiations. August 15, D2.

———. 1991e. Wilson Says Lumber Issue Still Irritant. August 19, D8.

———. 1991f. U.S. Anger Feared after Lumber Tax Cancelled. September 4, D1.

———. 1992a. U.S. to Face Challenge on Ruling, Wilson Vows. March 7, A1.

———. 1992b. Kempf's New Clothes Cloak of Scorn. March 26, B1.

———. 1993. Canada Hails Major Move towards Axing Lumber Duty. March 7, D1.

———. 1994a. U.S. Consents to Obey Order to Drop Duties: Trade Row over Softwood Lumber Far from Over, Says IWA Economist. January 7, A1.

———. 1994b. Way Cleared for U.S. Softwood Challenge. February 24, D9.

———. 1994c. U.S. Waves Stick on Softwood Lumber-Duty Refund. December 7, D1.

———. 1994d. U.S. Tariff Refunds Gift-Wrapped for Softwood Industry. December 16, E1.

———. 1995a. Canada Keeping Softwood System. July 12, D3.

———. 1995b. Softwood Talk Fraying Nerves of Top U.S. Negotiator. October 13, D3.

———. 1996. B.C. Wants Equity in Softwood Deal: Softwood: Talks Scheduled. January 23, D1.

———. 1998a. Clark Plans to Defend Stumpage Cuts: B.C.'s Premier Is Taking to Washington, D.C. July 7, A1.

———. 1998b. Drilled-Studs Puzzles Canadians. December 18, F4.

———. 1999a. Marchi No Fan of Softwood Deal: Existing Canada–U.S. Softwood Lumber Agreement Expires in 2001 and Could Be Abandoned, Says Concerned Canadian Trade Minister. March 9, D2.

———. 1999b. Forest Firms Split on Trade Deal. April 9, A1.

———. 1999c. B.C. Won't Sign New Softwood Deal with U.S. June 16, D1.

———. 2000. Divided Approach to Softwood Deal Won't Wash, Minister Says. September 13, D2.

———. 2001a. Ambassador Goads U.S. in Softwood Scrap. March 3, F2.

———. 2001b. U.S. Tax Payers' Group Backs Canada in Trade War. March 9, F7.

———. 2001c. Energy Shouldn't Be Part of Lumber Trade War, Minister Says. March 10, C1.

———. 2001d. Quebec Stand in Lumber Dispute 'Is a Threat to B.C.' March 14, A1.

———. 2001e. Put All Trade Issues on the Table. April 3, A1.

———. 2001f. Softwood Is 'Top Priority': PM. November 9, A1.

———. 2001g. Forest Reform No Guarantee U.S. Will Stop Trade Action. December 14, C1.

———. 2003. Despite Rejection, Softwood Deal Still Possible. December 15, D3.

———. 2004. B.C. Seeks Separate Lumber Pact. April 2, F1.

———. 2005a. NAFTA at Stake in the New Round of Lumber Talks. July 13, D3.

———. 2005b. Canada and U.S. as Far Apart as Ever on Softwood. July 27, D4.

———. 2006. Emerson Must Get Debate with U.S. on NAFTA. February 15, D5.

Waddell, D. 2003. Letter to Grant Aldonas. November 14.

Wall Street Journal. 1988. U.S. Group May Seek Duty on Some Lumber Imports. June 28, 1.

———. 1991. Canada Ends Lumber Pact with U.S.; 1980's Trade Dispute May Be Rekindled. September 4, A14.

———. 1992. Mulroney Protests against U.S. Stance on Trade Issues. May 21, A8

———. 1999. U.S. Officials Inform Canada It Intends to Let Lumber-Import Accord Wither. October 1, A4.

———. 2003. Canada–U.S. Lumber Talks Set Back: British Columbia Producer Opposes a Proposed Deal to Settle Trade Dispute. December 12, B7.

Washington Post. 2001. Canada Bristles at U.S. Tariff on Lumber. February 28, E3.

Washington Times. 2003. Eluding Tariffs; Firms Look at Options in Steel, Lumber Trade. January 20, C13.

Wear, D.N., and K.J. Lee. 1993. U.S. Policy and Canadian Lumber: Effects of the 1996 Memorandum of Understanding. *Forest Science* 39:799–815.

Westbrook, T.J. 1981. Statement of Tom Westbrook, Representing Northwest Independent Forest Manufacturers Association. In *Forest Products Industry Issues: Joint Hearing before the Subcommittee on International Trade and Subcommittee on Taxation and Debt Management of the Committee on Finance, United States Senate, Ninety-Seventh Congress, First Session, November 24, 1981.* Washington, DC: U.S. GPO, 1982, 149–162.

Weyerhaeuser Company. 2002. Weyerhaeuser Offers Solution to Bring Down Lumber Trade Wall between U.S and Canada. News Release. November 20.

Whiteley, D. 2006. Personal communication. September 28.

Widman Management. 1982. U.S. Protectionism and the Issue of Countervailing Duties. Executive Summary. Vancouver, BC: Wideman Management Consultant.

Wolff, A.W. 1986. To Mac Baldrige—Today's Oxymoron: Canadian Government Credibility on Lumber. September 12.

WTO Dumping Panel. 2004. *Report of the Panel: United States—Final Dumping Determination on Softwood Lumber from Canada.* WT/DS264/R. April 13.

WTO Injury Compliance Appellate Panel. 2006. *Report of the Appellate Body: United States—Investigation of the International Trade Commission in Softwood Lumber from Canada, Recourse to Article 21.5 of the DSU by Canada.* WT/DS277/AB/RW. April 13.

WTO Injury Compliance Panel. 2005. *Report of the Panel: United States—Investigation of the International Trade Commission in Softwood Lumber from Canada, Recourse to Article 21.5 of the DSU by Canada.* WT/DS277/RW. November 15.

WTO Injury Panel. 2004. *Report of the Panel: United States—Investigation of the International Trade Commission in Softwood Lumber from Canada.* WT/DS277/R. March 22.

WTO Subsidy Panel. 2003. Report of the Panel: United States—Final Countervailing Duty Determination with Respect to Certain Softwood Lumber from Canada. WT/DS257R. August 29.

WTO Subsidy Appellate Panel. 2004. *Report of the Appellate Body: United States—Final Countervailing Duty Determination with Respect to Certain Softwood Lumber from Canada.* AB-2003-6. WTT/DS257/AB/R. January 19.

WTO Subsidy Compliance Appellate Panel. 2005. *Report of the Appellate Body: United States—Final Countervailing Duty Determination with Respect to Certain Softwood Lumber from Canada, Recourse by Canada to Article 21.5 of the DSU.* AB-2005-8. WTT/DS257/AB/RW. December 5.

WTO Subsidy Compliance Panel. 2005. *Report of the Panel: United States—Final Countervailing Duty Determination with Respect to Certain Softwood Lumber from Canada, Recourse by Canada to Article 21.5* (DS257). WT/DS257/RW. August 1.

Yandle, B. 1989. *The Political Limits of Environmental Regulation: Tracking the Unicorn.* New York: Quorum Books.

Yeutter, C. 1985a. Memorandum for the Economic Policy Council (Subject: Canadian Softwood Lumber Imports). October 22.

———. 1985b. Letter to ITC Chairwoman Paula Stern. October 24.

———. 1986. Letter to Senator David H. Pryor. April 17.

Yin, R., and J. Baek. 2004. The US–Canada Softwood Lumber Trade Dispute: What We Know and What We Need to Know. *Forest Policy and Economics* 6: 129–43.

Zhang, D. 1995. An Economic Analysis of Log Export Restrictions in British Columbia. In *Proceedings of the 25th Southern Forest Economics Workshop: A World of Forestry*, edited by J. Caulfield. New Orleans. April 17–19, 168–78.

———. 1997. Inward and Outward Foreign Investment: The Case of U.S. Forest Industry. *Forest Products Journal* 47(5): 29–35.

———. 2001. Welfare Impacts of the 1996 U.S.–Canada Softwood Lumber (Trade) Agreement. *Canadian Journal of Forest Research* 31(11): 1958–67.

———. 2003. A Proposal to End the U.S.–Canada Softwood Lumber Trade Dispute. In *Society of American Foresters 2003 Convention Proceedings*. Buffalo, NY. October 25–30.

———. 2006. Welfare Impacts of the 1996 U.S.–Canada Softwood Lumber Agreement: An Update. *Canadian Journal of Forest Research* 36(1): 255–61.

Zhang, D., and J. Bliss. 1998. Alabama Stumpage Price Trends. *Alabama Treasured Forests* 18(2): 20–22.

Zhang, D., and D. Laband. 2005. From Senators to the President: Solving the Lumber Problem or Else. *Public Choice* 123(3-4): 393–410.

Zhang, D., and P.H. Pearse. 1996. Differences in Silvicultural Investment under Various Types of Forest Tenure in British Columbia. *Forest Science* 44(4): 442–49.

Zhang, D., and C. Sun. 2001. U.S.–Canada Trade Disputes and Softwood Lumber Price Volatility. *Forest Products Journal* 51(4): 21–27.

Zusman, P. 1976. The Incorporation and Measurement of Social Power in Economic Models. *International Economic Review* 17: 447–62.

Index

About the Author

Daowei Zhang is professor of forest economics and policy in the School of Forestry and Wildlife Sciences at Auburn University. He received his master's degree from Beijing Forestry University, and his Ph.D. from the University of British Columbia. His research interests cover the economic and policy aspects of forest resource management-property rights, institutional economics, political economy, forest products trade, land-use modeling, forest finance, industrial and non-industrial private forest ownership and management, forest-based economic development, and international forestry. His scholarly articles have appeared in *Forest Science*, the *Canadian Journal of Forest Research*, the *Canadian Journal of Agricultural Economics*, the *American Journal of Agricultural Economics*, *Land Economics*, *Economic Inquiry*, and *Public Choice*.

Dr. Zhang has been a research contributor and/or consultant to the Food and Agriculture Organization of the United Nations, the Center for International Forestry Research, the U.S. Forest Service, the University of Helsinki, the Chinese State Forestry Administration and provincial government of Sichuan, and several private companies in the United States. He was on the Board of Directors of the Pinchot Institute for Conservation from 2000 to 2006.

For Product Safety Concerns and Information please contact our EU
representative GPSR@taylorandfrancis.com Taylor & Francis Verlag GmbH,
Kaufingerstraße 24, 80331 München, Germany

Printed and bound by CPI Group (UK) Ltd, Croydon, CR0 4YY

08/05/2025

01864355-0005